SIDESHOW U.S.A.

T0373131

SIDESHOW U.S.A.

Freaks and the American Cultural Imagination

Rachel Adams

THE UNIVERSITY OF CHICAGO PRESS

CHICAGO AND LONDON

The University of Chicago Press
The University of Chicago Press, Ltd., London
© 2001 by The University of Chicago
All rights reserved. Published 2001
Printed and bound by CPI Group (UK) Ltd, Croydon, CR0Y4Y
16 15 14 13 12 10 09   3 4 5 6 7 8
ISBN-13: 978-0-226-00539-3
ISBN-10: 0-226-00539-9

Library of Congress Cataloging-in-Publication Data

Adams, Rachel.
    Sideshow U.S.A. : freaks and the American cultural imagination / Rachel Adams.
        p.   cm.
    Includes bibliographical references and index.
    ISBN 978-0-226-00538-6 (cloth)   ISBN 978-0-226-00539-3 (paper)
        1. Sideshows—Social aspects—United States.   2. Circus performers—United States.
    3. Abnormalities, Human.   4. Popular culture—United States.   I. Title: Sideshow U.S.A.
    II. Title.

    GV1835 .A33   2001
    791.3′5′0973—dc21   2001027803

♾ The paper used in this publication meets the minimum requirements of the American National
Standard for Information Sciences—Permanence of Paper for Printed Library Materials,
ANSI Z39.48-1992.

Contents

Contents

Illustrations

Acknowledgments

Freaks represent themselves as radically individuated subjects when in fact they are the products of sustained collaboration. So too, this book could not have been written without the friendship and intellectual generosity of many different people. In its early stages and before, Maurizia Boscagli, Jonathan Freedman, Giles Gunn, Connie Penley, and Julee Raiskin were inspiring teachers and rigorous critics. Carl Gutiérrez-Jones and Chris Newfield continue to provide friendship and advice. Seminars at the School for Criticism and Theory with Dominic LaCapra and Elaine Scarry transformed my thinking at a crucial moment.

For help with archival research, I thank Charles Silver at the Museum of Modern Art's Film Department; Steve Johnson at the New York Zoological Society; Joan Knudsen at the Phoebe Apperson Hearst Museum of Anthropology at the University of California, Berkeley; the staff at the Bancroft Library at the University of California, Berkeley; the American Museum of Natural History; the New-York Historical Society; the City Museum of New York; the theater collections in the Houghton Library at Harvard University and in the Harry Ransom Humanities Center at the University of Texas, Austin; and the Billy Rose Theater Collection at the New York Public Library. Film stills from Tod Browning's *Freaks* are from the collection at the Margaret Herrick Library of the Academy of Motion Picture Arts and Sciences. Particular thanks are due to Phillips Verner Bradford, who kindly shared his grandfather's unpublished writings with me, and Ira Jacknis, who spoke to me as I was beginning my research on Ishi. Personal interviews with Jennifer Miller and Dick Zigun were invaluable sources of knowledge about New York's contemporary sideshow world, as was my chance meeting with Fred Kahl during jury duty in the summer of 1999. Thanks to David Rakoff for suggesting the artwork that decorates the book's cover. I am grateful to David Carbone, Zoe Leonard, and Rosamond Purcell for allowing me to reproduce their magnificent visual work and to Theresa Babineau at the University of California, Berkeley, and Simone Subal at the Paula Cooper Gallery for help with reproductions. Sam Adams generously provided photographs to illustrate the epilogue. At various points during my research on the book, I was fortunate to have the assistance of Heather Angell, Britta Feyerabend, and Marissa Parham. Megan Van Duesen collected film stills from the Margaret Herrick Library. Joy Hayton, Michael Mallick, Isabel Thompson, Yulanda Denoon, Kathleen Savage, and Page Jackson were always there when I needed help. I also thank my graduate students, particularly the participants in my seminar on American studies in spring 2000, for their ongoing interest in the project. I could not be happier with my editor at the University of Chicago Press, Alan Thomas, and the rest of the project staff, particularly Randy Petilos, Mark Heineke, and Jenni Fry.

Funding for research has been generously provided by the Council for Research in the Humanities and a Chamberlain Fellowship, both from Columbia University, and a Mellon Fellowship from the Harry Ransom Humanities Center at the University of Texas, Austin. Preparation of the manuscript was assisted by a grant from the University Seminars program at Columbia University. Portions of this book have appeared elsewhere, and I thank the original publishers for permission to reprint. In a somewhat different form, chapter 4 was published in *American Literature* 71.3 (September 1999). Chapter 7 is included as "Carnival, Community, and 'the spectacle of white folks'" in *The Black Female Body*, edited by Kimberly Wallace Sanders (Ann Arbor: University of Michigan Press, forthcoming). Selected passages from chapter 8 were taken from "An American Tail: Freaks, Gender, and the Incorporation of History in Katherine Dunn's *Geek Love*," in *Freakery: Cultural Spectacles of the Extraordinary Body*, edited by Rosemarie Garland Thomson (New York: New York University Press, 1996).

Almost every chapter of this book has benefited from the opportunity to present it as work in progress. I thank audiences at Trinity College; Dartmouth; New York University; the Visual Culture Seminar coordinated by Nick Mirzoeff and Marin Stange; the Columbia University seminar in American studies; the Americas seminar at Harvard University; the New York Americanist Group; and panels at MLA and ASA annual meetings for lively and challenging discussions of my work.

I have been fortunate to write this book in the company of supportive and inspiring colleagues at Columbia and Barnard. Particular thanks are due to Casey Blake, Marcellus Blount, Nick Dames, Ann Douglas, Kathy Eden, David Eng, Robert Ferguson, Jonathan Gill, Eileen Gillooley, Lisa Gordis, Bob Hanning, Ursula Heise, Jean Howard, Jennie Kassanoff, Christina Kiar, Karl Kroeber, Jonathan Levin, Martin Meisel, Ed Mendelson, Christia Mercer, Roz Morris, Gary Okihiro, Bob O'Meally, Ann Pellegrini, Greg Pflugfelder, Martin Puchner, Maura Spigel, and Deborah White. Above all, the talented women in my writing group—Julie Crawford, Kristina Milnor, and Sandhya Shukla—continue to show me how to balance teaching, research, and life. Among the many others whose friendship and insight made a difference, Joanna Bockman, Lenny Cassuto, Amanda Claybaugh, Jay Cook, Cathy Jurca, Roze Hentschell, Emily Jenkins, Valerie Karno, Amy King, Susan Lepselter, Lisa Makman, Cyrus Patell, Ben Reiss, Shaindy Rudoff, Mark Simpson, and Liza Yukins deserve special mention. I am even more deeply indebted to those who read some or all of the manuscript: J. D. Connor, Lenny Davis, Gina Dent, Maria Farland, Laurel George, Tim Gray, Jon Heggland, Heather Hendershot, Andy Hoberek, Eric Lott, John Lowney, Jean Lutes, Sean McCann, Anna McCarthy, Stephen Paul Miller, Donald Pease, David Savran, Gus Stadler, Michael Szalay, Michael Trask, Rosemarie Thomson, Robyn Wiegman, Mark Williams, Deborah Williams, and Andrew Zimmerman.

I am grateful to my family and extended family—Diane, Ed, Naomi, Sam, Kathy, Olivia, and Michael—who always believed, from the time I was a childhood bookworm, that I would write a book of my own. My greatest debt is to Jon Connolly, who has been my companion at more freak shows than he would like to remember, in addition to living daily with this project for many years. Because his patience, wisdom, and generosity have left their mark on every page, this book is dedicated to him.

OVERTURE
Recovering Otis

Members of New York City's sideshow world like to recall Otis Jordan, a man born with significantly underdeveloped arms and legs who made his career by performing as a human curiosity for over twenty years. Calling himself the Frog Man, Otis drew a crowd by using his mouth to assemble, light, and smoke a cigarette, an act developed a generation earlier by the limbless Prince Randian, also known as the Human Caterpillar. In 1984, Otis's scheduled appearance at the New York State Fair aroused the ire of a concerned citizen, who decried the exhibition of disabled persons as freaks. Annoyed by the negative attention, Otis claimed that he did not perceive his work as degrading and resented the protestor's apparent disregard for his interests. This controversy, which pitted the disabled man's right to earn a living against community standards of taste and decency, provides a framing narrative for the most comprehensive study of American sideshows, Robert Bogdan's *Freak Show: Presenting Human Oddities for Amusement and Profit.* Having begun with an account of the protestor's point of view, Bogdan ends his book with a description of his own meeting with Otis. Observing Otis's dexterity and independence, Bogdan is struck by his surprising ignorance of the freak show's historical legacy. "As I queried [Otis]," he writes, "I discovered that he knew nothing of the rich history of the freak show. He got into the business in 1963, too late to see it in its prime, too late to know of the business greats."[1] Although *Freak Show* concludes by affirming Otis's perspective, Bogdan tells a story of decline that can have only one outcome: "the bannerline, the picture he sold, and other aspects of the show contained some of the elements of the old days, but the extravagantly embellished presentation was gone as was the splendor of the grand days of the freak show."[2] Otis represents the last gasp of the dying tradition chronicled in the pages of Bogdan's work.

Almost ten years after the publication of *Freak Show,* I began my own research on freak shows in the United States. My investigation revealed that what Bogdan had taken to be the death throes of a popular institution was a false alarm, for freak shows have seen a renaissance in the fifteen years since the completion of his

1

study. Despite predictions of their impending demise, freak shows never really vanished. During the period of their decline, they maintained a firm hold on the imaginations of the many Americans who had visited them in better days. This imaginative afterlife gave rise to a certain paradox: as actual freak shows were evicted from popular culture, their representational currency multiplied, granting them symbolic importance in inverse proportion to their declining status as a profitable mode of live entertainment. Those born after the freak show's heyday had passed find its history and iconography preserved in literature, film, and the visual arts. At the dawn of the new millennium, representations of freaks continue to multiply, accompanied by a resurgence of live freak shows in popular culture and performance art.

The writing of this book coincides with, and takes its impetus from, a cultural climate witnessing the proliferation of freaks of all kinds. The freak show's reappearance has been greeted with interest by scholars in the humanities and social sciences. But a more unexpected development is that the new generation of freaks are knowing readers of cultural studies, sell volumes of poststructuralist philosophy at bookstands during performances, and have been known to incorporate critical theory into their acts.[3] The ultimate outcome of this collaboration between scholarship and entertainment remains to be seen, but it makes the freak show one of the most promising sites for a study of the resilience and plasticity of popular culture, for—in the words of Joshua Gamson—freaks are, indeed, talking back.[4]

Understanding the freak show as both a powerful symbol and a mode of popular entertainment, *Sideshow U.S.A.* studies its recurrence in twentieth-century American culture. The story told in this book relies on two interconnected bodies of evidence. First, it makes use of material found in archives, memoirs, and historic sites such as Coney Island to offer a more complex view of the American freak show than those that have been provided before. Although they have often been treated as an ephemeral form of amusement, freak shows performed important cultural work by allowing ordinary people to confront, and master, the most extreme and terrifying forms of Otherness they could imagine, from exotic dark-skinned people, to victims of war and disease, to ambiguously sexed bodies. In a nation that prides itself somewhat contradictorily on its affirmation of individuality *and* its ability to assimilate differences, the freak show has political and social, as well as psychoanalytic significance. With its heterogeneous assemblage of bodies, the sideshow platform is both a source of entertainment and a stage for playing out many of the century's most charged social and political controversies, such as debates about race and empire, immigration, relations among the sexes, taste, and community standards of decency. As it delves into the realm of serious politics and history, the freak show maps the anxieties and fantasies that undergird collective responses to contemporary events. Much of this book is devoted to analyzing the diverse audiences who attended freak shows and the ways in which they understood what they saw; however it also considers the perspectives of those who earned a living by managing, promoting, or exhibiting themselves as human curiosities. Autobiographies, photographs, letters, and anecdotal evidence are particularly important sources for reconstructing the experiences of people who have rarely had a place within official histories of the American century.

These forgotten stories are interwoven with a second, related strand of argument about the rich array of literary and visual representation inspired by the freak show. Far from marginal, freak shows have exerted a strong grip on the form, as well as the content, of American arts and letters throughout the course of the twentieth century. The convergence between literature and mass entertainment is the humorous subject of an 1896 cartoon in *Life* magazine, which depicts the era's most important writers as a collection of human curiosities (figure 1). As literary production becomes increasingly commercialized, the sketch suggests, it is difficult to distinguish author from sideshow sensation. A somewhat different version of this point is made by Joan Schenkar's 1979 *Signs of Life,* a play in which Henry James and P. T. Barnum share the stage.[5] While it is difficult to think of a more unlikely pair, Schenkar implies that the celebrated litterateur and the father

FIGURE 1. "Life's Literary Side Show," 1896. Literature and popular culture converge in this cartoon depicting famous nineteenth-century authors as human curiosities.

3

of show business each benefited from similar forms of gender privilege. She drives this point home by alternating the dialogue between these characters with scenes that draw parallels between the ailing Alice James and the exploitation of a freak called the Elephant Woman. The play's irreverent coupling of James and Barnum is a fitting image for the ways that freak shows provoked an invigorating and contentious exchange between the lowest registers of popular culture and more socially legitimate arts. In addition to the working-class audiences that formed their primary constituency, they were attended by authors, artists, politicians, scientists, and philosophers. Their appropriation within literature, museum arts, and scholarly criticism is a reminder that innovation does not always trickle from top to bottom; popular culture has regularly served as rich inspiration for more elite representational forms. What these representations share is a willingness to grapple with the complex dynamics of identification and disavowal set in motion by confrontations with the extraordinary figures exhibited on the sideshow platform. However, the way they approach this problem varies greatly with the course of history and from one text to another.

This introduction provides an overture to some of the central concerns of *Sideshow U.S.A.*, each of which will be elaborated in subsequent chapters. Making a somewhat artificial distinction, I devote separate sections to actors and venues, freaks and freak shows. Beginning with freaks themselves, the sideshow's most important feature, I consider both their psychoanalytic and social dimensions. A figure par excellence for the complex and shifting dynamics of identification, the problems of self and other that constitute a central preoccupation for the psychoanalyst, *freak* is also a performative identity that varies depending on the particularities of cultural and historical context. That context is the subject of the second section of this chapter, which explores the structure, reception, and circulation of freak shows in the twentieth century. Whereas critics have devoted considerable attention to the freak show's content, I argue that its significance can only really be understood when these insights are supplemented by information about what it meant to audiences and the performers themselves. As the twentieth century progressed, these questions about reception grew more complex as conflicts over taste and morality, exploitation and labor, set the stage for the freak show's appropriation within literary and visual culture.

A Frame of Mind, a Set of Practices
Glancing through an archive of old freak photographs sometimes yields surprising results, such as the portraits of people with extremely long hair or nails, tattoos, and women in pants included alongside more patently unusual figures such as

midgets, fat ladies, and wild men (figure 2). These images attest to the fact that freakishness is a historically variable quality, derived less from particular physical attributes than the spectacle of the extraordinary body swathed in theatrical props, promoted by advertising and performative fanfare. Whereas once human prodigies were treated as the bearers of divine meaning, by the nineteenth century freaks had no inherent significance, although their anomalies seemed to cry out for interpretation. As a result they required narratives about exotic places, miraculous events, or horrifying accidents that might give coherence to bodies that otherwise suggested an intolerable fragmentation and dissolution of meaning.

FIGURE 2. Naomi Sutherland, exhibited as a sideshow attraction because of her extremely long hair. The fact that this otherwise unremarkable woman was represented as a sensation attests to the plasticity of the category of *freak*. Courtesy Theatre Arts Collection, Harry Ransom Humanities Research Center, the University of Texas at Austin.

"Freak," writes Bogdan, "is a frame of mind, a set of practices, a way of thinking about and presenting people. It is the enactment of a tradition, the performance of a stylized presentation."[6] Describing *freak* as a social role, Bogdan
underscores the importance of understanding its formation within a particular
context and set of historical circumstances. Whereas Bogdan employs the term
performance to characterize the freak show as a theatrical mode, I will use the
concept somewhat differently to argue that *freak* is not an inherent quality but an
identity realized through gesture, costume, and staging. Following Judith Butler's
description of gendered performance, *freak* might also be conceived as "an identity instituted through a stylized repetition of acts."[7] Repetition serves both to reinforce that identity and to destabilize it through the introduction of slight, but
potentially consequential, differences. As I will argue in chapter 7, the freak's performative dimensions are nowhere more evident than in the figure of the wild
man, a person of color whose act dramatized the racist equation of dark skin with
savage exoticism. In his 1905 memoir of circus life, W. C. Thompson recalls a wild
man caught shooting craps who "had hastily torn a clay pipe from his mouth and
become again a weird, uncivilized being."[8] While the discrepancy between identities onstage and off is abundantly clear in the case of the wild man, it is equally
true of disabled actors who must also be seen as performing, not embodying the
essential qualities of, freakishness. To conceive of freaks in this way is to defy the
sideshow's own logic, whereby the freak's stasis on the sideshow platform mirrors
the enduring and irreversible quality of her condition. Freak shows are guided by
the assumption that *freak* is an essence, the basis for a comforting fiction that
there is a permanent, qualitative difference between deviance and normality, projected spatially in the distance between the spectator and the body onstage. To
characterize *freak* as a performance restores agency to the actors in the sideshow,
who participate, albeit not always voluntarily, in a dramatic fantasy that the division between freak and normal is obvious, visible, and quantifiable.

To use the rubric of performance is not to dismiss the fact that some bodies are
so visibly different from the norm that their deviance cannot be concealed or ignored. Freaks are creatures who lurk in the unsteady seams where corporeal matter meets with fantasy, drama, and promotional hype. Although the components
of freakishness change with time, the centrality of the body remains a constant
and determining feature of the freak's identity. Indeed, it is the confrontation with
the human form mirrored back in distorted embodiments of excess or lack that
makes the freak show a profoundly visceral experience, a flirtation with the abject
realm where the human and the nonhuman collide. Freak aficionado Mark Twain
evokes this jarring effect in *Those Extraordinary Twins* when he describes how

Rowena and Patsy Cooper are stunned by their initial meeting with the conjoined brothers Luigi and Angelo: "conscious of nothing but that prodigy, that uncanny apparition that had come and gone so suddenly—that weird strange thing that was so soft-spoken and so gentle of manner and yet had shaken them up like an earthquake with the shock of its gruesome aspect."[9] Despite the twins' handsome faces and cultivated demeanor, the first glimpse of their sensational body inevitably produces a wrenching physiological response in each person they encounter.

Any attempt to account for the human prodigy's capacity to produce such moving, gut-level responses calls out for psychoanalytic, as well as social, analysis. The canon of Freudian psychoanalysis, which itself might be described as a freak show of monstrous corporeal distortions, provides a framework for understanding how unconscious disturbances register in our perception of our own and others' bodies. Freaks, according to Elizabeth Grosz, are a limit case for considering "the ways in which the body is lived and represented, the inputs and effects of the subject's corporeality on its identity."[10] Encountering freaks, we contemplate the potential dissolution of our own corporeal and psychic boundaries, the terror and excitement of monstrous fusion with the surrounding world. If identity formation, whether individual or collective, involves a dual gesture of incorporation and repudiation, freaks remind us of the unbearable excess that has been shed to confer entry into the realm of normalcy. The figures of the half man–half woman, the dog-faced boy, or conjoined twins confront us with their refusal of the apparently primal distinctions between man and woman, human and animal, self and other. Psychoanalysis tends to treat that refusal as a horrifying loss, yet at its most optimistic it may inspire a more capacious understanding of the human in which such decisions are no longer foundational, but some among many options.

The assumption of identity always entails the acquisition of desired attributes and the refusal of the intolerable abject. Freaks embody this cast off refuse, reminding the viewer of the costs of normality, but also stirring doubts about whether she really belongs there. The price of admission buys permission to gaze at another's body with the expectation that the look of curiosity will be met by the "blank, unseeing stare" essayist Joseph Mitchell attributes to the seasoned freak performer.[11] But spectators may be disconcerted to find their gazes returned, often laden with resentment or hostility. When Frankie Addams enters the Freak Pavilion in Carson McCullers's *Member of the Wedding*, she is disturbed because it seems that the performers "looked at her in a secret way and tried to connect their eyes with hers, as though to say: *we know you!*"[12] Instead of a reassuring *disidentification*, in which the spectator recognizes her difference from the body

7

onstage, the sideshow is more often a space of *identification,* in which the viewer projects her own most hidden and perverse fantasies onto the freak and discovers them mirrored back in the freak's gaze. Understood psychoanalytically, of course, these processes of identification and repudiation are consonant with one another.[13] "Do you think I will grow into a Freak?" Frankie asks anxiously, articulating precisely the questions about the stability and permanence of identity that are depicted, in exaggerated form, by the sideshow's pageant of marginality.[14]

The unpleasant stirrings of mutual recognition presumed to accompany the exchange of gazes between performer and spectator has given rise to numerous interpretations of freaks as metaphors or doubles for what Leslie Fiedler calls the "secret self."[15] In fact, as Diana Fuss describes it, metaphor—the substitution of one term for another—is the primary logic of psychoanalytic accounts of identification, the complex, ongoing process whereby the subject comes to define itself in relation to others.[16] It is not surprising that the moments of intense identification and disavowal occasioned by the sideshow are so often read as metaphors for self-other relations, as when Fiedler writes, "I feel my spine tingle and my heart leap as I relive the wonder of seeing for the first time my most private nightmares on public display *out there.*"[17] While I am interested in what such an understanding might tell us about the work of identification, this book resists reading representations of freaks as purely metaphorical, an approach that would entail substituting the material history of the sideshow and its performers with speculation about the artist's own interior dramas.

The problem with an exclusively psychoanalytic account of freaks is that it threatens to universalize phenomena that are historically and culturally variable, and to appropriate the details of individual lives as effects of authorial subjectivity. The popularity of Freudian psychoanalysis among influential American critics of the postwar period has had a formative impact on the interpretation of literary and artistic representations of deviant bodies.[18] Because of its interest in the double, the irretrievably divided condition of all human subjectivity, as well as its disdain for popular culture, cultural criticism drew attention away from the freak's historical dimensions and towards the freak as a universal symbol for human alienation and despair. "The final horrors," writes Leslie Fiedler in *Love and Death in the American Novel,* "as modern society has come to realize, are neither gods nor demons, but intimate aspects of our own minds."[19] The consequences of Fiedler's position will be more fully explored in chapter 6. I will simply remark here that while fictional representations of freaks cannot be crudely reduced to simple sociological or historical referents, their meaning is equally diminished by reading them exclusively as archetypes for timeless human preoccupations.

Freaks announce themselves as the antithesis of normality, and part of the sideshow's frisson arises from the audience's recognition of the ease with which freak and normal may slide unsteadily into one another. To study images of the freak as they recur throughout the course of the twentieth century is not only to consider the most extreme forms of deviance. It is also to chart the unsteady contours of normality, a concept whose origins Lennard Davis has convincingly traced to the development of statistical science in the nineteenth century.[20] As the boundaries and definition of normality have changed dramatically over time, the value placed upon being normal has also shifted in response to the cultural climate. For example, whereas in Cold War America nonconformity such as sexual perversion or communist sympathies could have dire consequences, by the late 1960s a youthful counterculture had made freakishness a valued sign of rebellion. To acknowledge that freakishness abides at the heart of the normal is hardly a revelation, but this book will trace the less familiar narrative of how we came to assume the mutual embeddedness of the two concepts. It is an important historical lesson to recognize that freaks were not always understood as the flip side of normality; at one time, their bodies were read as figures of absolute difference who came from elsewhere and bore the portentous imprint of divine or cosmic forces. In the wake of deconstruction and psychoanalysis, we now seem capable of understanding such extreme corporeal alterity *only* as a necessary byproduct of the oppressive and exclusionary operations of the normal. As medical science has eradicated many of the disabilities that once afflicted sideshow freaks, we have become increasingly eager to find those distortions buried within ourselves, to describe them as an effect of subjectivity (the "Other within" of psychoanalysis) or of Western systems of logic (the binary opposition of deconstruction). Situating contemporary perspectives on freakishness historically may encourage us to interrogate our present desire to absorb the category of *freak* within the everyday to the point that it becomes banal. Throughout this book, I will ask whether taking representations of freaks seriously might teach us not just to probe the tortured depths of our own subconscious, but how to coexist with others who are unlike us instead of engulfing or rejecting their differences.[21] We need better ways of accommodating the broad swath of human variability without explaining it away as an effect of our own imagining.

Writing a book about freaks has occasioned an array of responses ranging from bemusement to distaste, which inevitably return to a question of semantics: Why freaks? The task would have been easier if *freak* were more firmly bound to a recognizable political configuration, such as disability, race, or gender. These identitarian categories all played a part in determining the oddities displayed on

sideshow platforms of the past. And as minority groups have organized into political coalitions, the revision of terminology, which involves substituting voluntary
labels for degrading slurs, has been an important strategy in the struggle for self-
definition. However, freaks cannot be neatly aligned with any particular identity
or ideological position. Rather, *freak* is typically used to connote the absence of
any known category of identity. Accordingly, I have decided to use a word that is
faithful to the deliberate imprecision of the original sources. In the context of the
sideshow, labeling a person a *freak* evacuates her humanity, authorizing the paying customer to approach her as an object of curiosity and entertainment. Blunt
and unsparing, *freak* recalls a climate in which the misfortunes of some became
sources of entertainment and profit for others.[22] As I will explain further in chapter 4, this choice of vocabulary is inspired, in part, by the critics and activists who
have wrested the term *queer* from its original pejorative connotations, while insisting on the memory of violence and shame in its past. I am drawn to *freak* because, like *queer,* it is a concept that refuses the logic of identity politics, and the
irreconcilable problems of inclusion and exclusion that necessarily accompany
identitarian categories. Throughout the book, I will persistently interrogate the
meanings that accrue around the use of *freak* in a given context, attempting to
maintain the balance between historical perspective and politically efficacious appropriation.

The Greatest Show on Earth: Exhibiting Freaks in the United States

Because the history of freak shows has been well documented by others, a brief
survey should be sufficient to situate it in the context of the nineteenth- and twentieth-century United States.[23] Evidence of anomalous births, called monsters or
lusus naturae (freaks of nature), is found in the earliest historical records. Considered a sign of past crimes or a harbinger of cataclysmic events, the prodigious
body inspired awe, terror, and, eventually, entrepreneurial activity. The practice
of exhibiting human curiosities for profit extends back at least as far as the Renaissance. In Shakespeare's *Tempest,* for example, Trinculo speculates on the financial
benefits of displaying Caliban as an ethnographic freak, describing him in the hyperbolic terms of the showman as a monster "legged like a man, and his fins like
arms!"[24] This book concentrates on a narrower frame of reference that begins
with the union of commercial and scientific interests, the birth of mass culture,
and the demographic changes that gave rise to freak shows in the nineteenth century. Freak shows were part of a broader development of mass entertainment that
included amusement parks, circuses, dime museums, and vaudeville.[25] The
emergence of an amusement industry in the United States was enabled by an ex-

panding middle class that was increasingly concentrated in urban centers, enjoying shorter work weeks and more disposable income, and by technological innovations such as electricity and the steam engine. These developments were accompanied by an ideological shift in American attitudes towards leisure, which came to be seen as a necessary and salutary counterpart to the work ethic.[26]

At the forefront of a burgeoning culture of entertainment was P. T. Barnum, who realized the commercial potential of the American freak show with the purchase and exhibition of Joice Heth, a black woman claiming to be the 161-year-old nurse of George Washington. While not the first to profit from the display of human oddities, Barnum was responsible for transforming the freak show into a coordinated business venture enhanced by advertising, promotional materials, and celebrity appearances. Founded in 1841 in the heart of New York City, Barnum's American Museum offered multiple attractions that promised to educate and uplift, as well as entertain, its middle- and working-class clientele; one ticket guaranteed admission to lectures, theatrical performances, an animal menagerie, and a glimpse at curiosities both living and dead. After the American Museum burned to the ground for the second time, Barnum joined forces with James Bailey and took his collection of performing humans and animals on the road as part of the largest circus ever to tour the United States. Barnum's lengthy and varied career ensured that the traveling circus, the carnival, and the dime museum would bear his indelible imprimatur.[27]

The Barnumesque promise of more for your money was realized structurally in the freak show, or the ten-in-one, where an entire collection of human oddities could be viewed for one price. On the sideshow platform individuals with mental and physical disabilities were grouped indiscriminately alongside nonwhite or non-Western natives and performers with talents such as snake charming, contortion, and belly dancing. Providing multiple improvisations on its broader theme, the freak show offered a panoramic view of the most sensational forms of alterity at any given historical moment. Its changing cast of characters speaks of a seemingly tireless ability for reinvention in the search for profit and notoriety. Recognizing that publicity was the most valuable commodity of all, more than once Barnum destroyed or undermined his own product in order to reap the financial rewards of the media circus he had created. The plasticity of sideshows is also apparent in their rapid incorporation of current events. "Remember," wrote journalist William Fitzgerald in 1897, "I am speaking of America—the land of real humor, of ingenuity, of resource. When some important political or other event agitates that great country, topical side shows spring up with amazing promptness."[28] In order to preserve their ability to surprise and entertain, freak shows have often been known to manipulate their stock cast of characters in response to immediate social and political preoccupations. For example, an article in a New York daily about a three-headed woman exhibited at a Bowery museum speculates on the problems she would cause should women gain the vote. "The question would at once arise as to whether the now complex woman should be entitled to one vote or three," the male author opines, "and howsoever this question might eventually be decided, there would be years of vexatious litigation filling all of the courts in the meanwhile, and very possibly the country might become involved in the throes of a deadly civil war resulting from it."[29] In a climate of more overt racism, dark skin was enough to secure a position as a wild African savage, a sideshow staple until at least the middle of the twentieth century.[30] However, racial freaks are taboo on the programs of contemporary freak shows such as the Jim Rose Circus, the Bindlestiff Family Cirkus, and the Coney Island Circus Side Show. Drawing connections between the transgendered bodies and queer identities of their performers, these troupes specialize in granting visibility to sexual and gender perversions that would have been unthinkable in the past. The persistence of freak shows, which have seen a subcultural renaissance in the last ten years, attests to their greater flexibility when compared to an equally popular nineteenth-century entertainment like minstrelsy, so heavily reliant on racial humor that it could not survive a growing intolerance to racism.[31] Because it is relatively devoid of any specific meaning, the freak show's content has fluctuated over time while its structure has remained relatively constant.

The freak show's formal composition and spatial layout set the terms for how the prodigious body will be understood. Inside the tent or dime museum, the existential difference between freak and audience is concretized in the physical separation between the onlooker and the living curiosities resting on the elevated platform. A confluence of visual, auditory, and tactile sensations sets the stage for the audience's experience of the prodigious body. Sweltering heat, the smells of popcorn and animal dung, abusive exchanges between carnies, freaks, and customers—these are the freak show's Proustian mnemonics, capable of summoning back powerful recollections in those who once were there. The structure of the freak show has typically been described as a form of spectacle, a term that accurately captures the sensational, formulaic qualities of the exhibition space.[32] Unlike the raucous interactions of carnival, its more unruly festive predecessor, the modern phenomenon of spectacle is premised on the sensory dominance of the visual and the measured distance between the viewer and the choreographed activity of the performers.[33] Contrasting the dynamism of carnival and the stasis of spectacle in her discussion of freak shows, Susan Stewart writes, "[T]he spectacle exists in an outside at both its origin and ending. There is no question that there is a gap between the object and its viewer. The spectacle functions to avoid contamination: 'Stand back ladies and gentlemen, what you are about to see will shock and amaze you.'"[34] This is a convincing description of the sideshow's intended effect: the customer is expected dutifully to absorb the spieler's monologue while gazing at the prodigious body in awestruck wonder, then making a docile exit.

However, historical evidence reveals how rarely this theory was realized in practice, for sideshows are hardly spaces of restraint or decorum, and things seldom go as planned: freaks talk back, the experts lose their authority, the audience refuses to take their seats. Spectacle relies on a degree of submission that has little consonance with the rowdy, undisciplined clientele that most regularly attended freak shows or the behavior of performers enduring uncomfortable and exploitative working conditions. "I don't take no back talk from nobody," asserted Jane Barnell, a bearded lady interviewed by Joseph Mitchell, who remarked on her reputation for telling off persistent interlocutors and once slapping a carnival owner.[35] If freaks could misbehave in unpredictable ways, customers also frequently caused disruption by attempting to unmask the fraudulence of human exhibits. Born in the era of humbug and confidence men, freak shows promised to shock and amaze, but also encouraged their audiences to question what they saw, to remain vigilant about the possibility of deception.[36] As a consequence, the sight of the freak's body seems not to have produced stunned silence, but shouts of laughter or outrage, knowingly incredulous comments, or rude prodding intended to prove its unreality. That the form of the freak show itself was far more interactive than critics have acknowledged makes a difference in how its impact on viewers and performers is to be understood. This book is particularly concerned with ruptures in the anticipated order of things, when freaks and spectators break the rules by making physical or verbal contact across the velvet rope.

Over the past century, the freak show's survival has been threatened by public protest and legal battles commonly articulated in terms of morality, but always undergirded by struggles over economic and cultural capital. As they lost their purchase on respectability, freak shows provided employment and entertainment for America's most marginal populations. Debates over the shows' propriety inevitably bring the benevolence of middle-class citizens into conflict with the rights of a socially and economically underprivileged class to work and amuse itself in ways that may arouse disgust or disapproval from others. This issue is clearly at the heart of the disputes over Otis's appearance, as it was in an October 1972 lawsuit leveled against World Fair Freaks and Attractions, heard by the Supreme Court of Florida.[37] The case overturned a law holding the exhibition of disabled persons as freaks "morally intolerable" by concluding that it put an unfair burden on disabled persons who had no other means of earning a living. *Freaks v. Hodges* reveals the extent to which standards of self-respect and appropriate behavior are entwined with issues of class. The questions it raises are not simply economic, but extend to ongoing tensions between freedom of expression and aesthetic judgment. Protest against the bad taste exhibited by sideshows is not reserved to live performances, but follows freaks as they move into audiovisual media such as film and fine arts. Tod Browning's film *Freaks,* the photography of Diane Arbus and Joel Peter Witkin, and Katherine Dunn's cult novel *Geek Love* have aroused controversy and condemnation because they introduce the most grotesquely sensational aspects of the freak show to art and literature. Framed by a rhetoric of decency and common sense, these scandals cannot be detached from the social and economic circumstances that inform hierarchies of taste, producing distinctions between art and pornography, theater and exploitation show.[38]

Debates over the propriety of human exhibition often bring community standards into conflict with the rights of marginalized constituencies to support themselves financially. The freak show is not only a form of entertainment; it is also a place of employment for those who advertise, manage, and perform in its attractions.[39] Katherine Dunn's *Geek Love,* the subject of chapter 8, introduces the subject of the freak's labor when Lil Binewski—having intentionally birthed a prodigious brood—asks, "What greater gift could you offer your children than an inherent ability to earn a living just by being themselves?"[40] But her question must be read ironically, as the novel is well aware that freaks can never just "be themselves." Freaks are not born; they are made, and their making relies on the collaborative efforts of many hands who work behind the scenes. Although the freak's labor has at times been an explicit topic within her presentation, scholarship on freak shows has largely overlooked this fact. In an era before welfare or worker's compensation, severely disabled persons often claimed that placing themselves on exhibition was their sole means for making a living. Having paid the price of admission, the spectator was invited to see herself as committing a socially responsible act by supporting someone who would otherwise be forced to rely on charity. For example, a paragraph on the back of a souvenir *carte de visite* of a man with enlarged, severely misshapen fingers attributes the cause of his affliction to being struck by lightning at the age of six. "He would gladly undertake any labor that would furnish him a livelihood, but how can he? Yielding, therefore, to the suggestions of friends he offers for sale his photograph, hoping that the small profit derived therefrom will contribute to his maintenance and support."[41] Displaying himself only at the urging of friends, the disabled man underscores his own reticence and the social acceptance of his activities. Excluded from the realm of productive labor, the freak embodies the virtues of hard work and independence by becoming the source of a living wage. Throughout the course of this book we will spend time on both sides of the curtain, considering the freak show's structure and reception, but also its meaning for those who knew it as a profession and a place of work.

Freak shows make visible bodies that would later become wards of state, confined to institutions and absolved from the need to work by social welfare.[42] Telling their stories from variety of angles, *Sideshow U.S.A.* is not a teleological narrative and resists the tendency to oversimplify by condemning past practices from the perspective of a more humane and tolerant present. While the marginalized groups represented at the freak show have made significant social, political, and legal advances, discrimination based on bodily difference once made so visible on the exhibition platform endures in more muted forms. A counterpart to this study is the history of the institutionalization of the mentally and physically disabled. Whereas the freak show paraded the deviant body for all to see, the institution concealed abnormality from view. Ironically, both performed the work of normalization by establishing standards for segregating the deviant from the normal. It would be a mistake to see institutions as the corrective to the freak show, for removing certain kinds of deviance from sight does not necessarily indicate a more humane or progressive attitude towards disability. Whereas the institution's more explicit purpose is to shelter those who cannot care for themselves, it also cleanses public space of the indigent, the insane, and the disabled. As Henri-Jacques Stiker writes in his history of disability, "[S]ocieties have never succeeded in integrating difference *as such*. Either the social group integrates difference in order to make it disappear or integrates partially while excluding certain forms even more, or it excludes radically while paying lip service to the concept of integration. We cannot take any one of the formulas that history has chosen at a given moment and erect it into an ideal."[43] A more egalitarian social order would not hide people with disabilities from sight, but grant them visibility without perceiving them as freaks. In a culture so reliant on appearance as a gauge of personal value, this is no mean task. But it is one that the authors and artists represented in this study take very seriously, committing their work to imagining social formations that could accommodate, without eliminating, the great range of human variability. One goal of *Sideshow U.S.A.* is to understand how and why certain bodies have been designated as objects of visual curiosity, and how some have managed to transform that situation into a source of profit, creativity, and social critique.

The image of the freak show has resonated in especially powerful ways for authors and artists who perceive themselves as marginalized on the basis of physical appearance. Race, gender, and disability are three of the marked categories that emerge repeatedly from one chapter to the next, for these are the primary terms used to discriminate among individuals in American culture. "I am invisible," writes the narrator of Ralph Ellison's *Invisible Man*, "simply because people refuse to see me. *Like the bodiless heads you see sometimes in circus sideshows*, it is as though I have been surrounded by mirrors of hard, distorting glass."[44] In the freak show of mid-century U.S. race relations, the Invisible Man implies, it is easier to be deceived by illusions than to attempt the difficult work of seeing the inequalities they obscure. Likewise, describing her internment during World War II, Monica Sone recalls, "I felt like a despised, pathetic two-headed freak, a Japanese and American, neither of which seemed to be doing me any good."[45] But the literature of marginalized groups has also transformed this disempowering play of social visibility and invisibility into an oppositional resource. The protagonist of Maxine Hong Kingston's *Tripmaster Monkey*, Wittman Ah Sing, parodically incorporates the orientalist figures of conjoined twins Chang and Eng into his one-man show. They shout at the crowd, "You want to know if we feel jointly. You want to look at the hyphen. You want to look at it bare."[46] In Wittman's monologue, the original Siamese twins embody the complexities of Asian American assimilation and cultural difference, their band of skin an emblem for the immigrant's hyphenated identity. As the freak show is taken up by authors such as Sone, Ellison, Kingston, E. L. Doctorow, James Baldwin, and Toni Morrison, we are reminded that it may serve as a powerful symbol for social criticism but also a painful reminder of the injustices once made visible on the sideshow platform, many of which persist in more veiled forms into the present day.

Step Right Up!

The movement of *Sideshow U.S.A.* is roughly chronological and its trajectory is designed to illuminate a chain of influence in which references to earlier representations are incorporated into and transformed by subsequent literary and artistic expressions. At the same time, this progression is regularly interrupted to explore the way that representations delve into, recall, and refract the past. The history of the freak show will not unfold as an unbroken narrative, but will surface in fragments, as it illuminates textual analysis. The book is divided into three independent but interrelated sections called acts, a label that pays tribute to the original form. Each act is unified by its treatment of pivotal questions about the relationship between self and other, normalcy and deviance. Unlike a play, the variety shows where freaks would have performed presented acts as an ensemble in which each part could stand independently, but also contributed to the development of the whole. Because visitors came and went at different points during the cycle, their experiences varied depending on the moment of entry and departure. So too, the individual acts in *Sideshow U.S.A.* may be read asequentially or in isolation, choices that will produce a somewhat different impression than if the reader proceeds in the order provided.

Act 1 is set in the first third of the twentieth century, when the freak's absolute Otherness is widely taken for granted. During a period when race, gender, and physical ability constitute barriers to complete social and political participation, the freak's body is an exaggerated instance of a more general tendency to see physiological differences as definitive measures of personhood. In chapters 2 and 3, the freak is a figure who brings charged questions about the boundaries and definition of the human to a boiling point. Once safely contained on the sideshow platform, freaks ignite controversy when they appear in other venues, threatening to contaminate more respectable cultural institutions with the stain of sensationalism and excess. Chapter 2, "Freaks of Culture: Institutions, Publics, and the Subjects of Ethnographic Knowledge," is about conflicts over the treatment and public presentation of human specimens in the first decades of the twentieth century. In an era of burgeoning professionalism, men of science seek to establish the scholarly authority of their work, and the purity of the institutions that employ them, by defining it against the debased form of the freak show. At the same time, aspiring showmen borrow the mantle of professional dignity and academic credentials to grant legitimacy to the exhibition of human curiosities. While ordinarily these constituencies would have little to do with one another, their interests collide around two of the era's most controversial ethnographic exhibits: Ota Benga, an African pygmy displayed in the Monkey House at the Bronx Zoo in 1906, and Ishi, a Yahi Indian who lived at the University of California Museum of Anthropology from 1911 to 1915. During a period that saw the expansion and reorganization of cultural institutions, experts and their publics are pitted against one another in a struggle to determine the nature and extent of the racial freak's humanity. These prodigies bring the fraught relationship between the life sciences and popular entertainment to a head.

Whereas chapter 2 charts the seepage of the freak show's personalities and theatrical strategies into institutions of scientific research and education, chapter 3, "Sideshow Cinema," is about the translation of the freak show from live performance to film as it is dramatized by Tod Browning's *Freaks* (1932). Browning's contradictory film celebrates the freak show as a vibrant, antihierarchical arena of sexual and social multiplicity, while condemning its potential for exploitation. The cinematic apparatus in *Freaks* assumes a didactic function by training the viewer to recognize the humanity of the disabled body, then violating its own assumptions by showing the freaks' capacity for murderous violence. Because of its enduring influence on subsequent representations, Browning's film is a pivotal text for understanding the varied meanings accorded to the freak as exhibits of human curiosity become increasingly rare within popular culture. As actual freak shows decline, their afterlife is kindled with the screening of Browning's *Freaks* to a new generation of filmgoers. The history of its reception—its widespread denunciation in depression-era America and critical acclaim on its rerelease in 1962—shows how attitudes towards freaks do not always move towards condemnation, but may vacillate unevenly between acceptance and repudiation.

As the sideshow is expelled from American popular culture in the first half of the twentieth century, it is taken up by the more elite forms of literature, art photography, and scholarly inquiry. The post–World War II period is the context for act 2, which documents how identification with the freak's extreme marginality enables authors and artists to describe various forms of personal alienation. Once a figure of absolute difference, the freak becomes an aspect of self; facilitated by the growing popularity of Freudian psychoanalysis, the deviant Other is taken up as the embodiment of the awkward and fragmentary experience of subjectiity. Reconceiving the freak as the byproduct of a repressive cultural environment (rather than an alien outsider) opens up the possibilities of social criticism. Contemporary events such as the civil rights movement, the sexual revolution, and counterculture bring injustices once displaced onto the sideshow platform into the domain of public debate and political activism. Each chapter in this act explores representations of the freak show in the mid-twentieth century that negotiate the relationship of individual nonconformity to a social context intent on discriminating between normality and deviance. Chapter 4, "'A mixture of delicious and freak': The Queer Fiction of Carson McCullers," analyzes the intersection between the freak, queer sexuality, and racial hybridity. Queer theory offers a useful paradigm for understanding how McCullers's fiction recuperates the term *queer* to escape the limitations of binary oppositions between homo- and heterosexuality, male and female, black and white. Anticipating the performance art that will end this study, McCullers aligns *queer* and *freak*. Because they are not beholden to traditional categories of identity, these concepts are both dangerous and promising, indicating the threat of visible nonconformity and holding out the promise of social formations more accommodating to human variety. Chapter 5 focuses on Diane Arbus's images of freaks and misfits, which have been described more than once as the visual counterpart to the fiction of Carson McCullers. Too often, Arbus's attraction to freaks has been understood exclusively in terms of her unhappy life and suicide. But her well-known portraits look different when seen as an attempt to revise the impersonal gaze of turn-of-the-century commercial freak photographers such as Matthew Brady and Charles Eisenmann. At once a technology of realism and illusory artifice, photography has been interested in depicting the deviant body since its inception. Familiar with this historical legacy and a fan of freak shows, Arbus borrows from earlier visual genres, replacing distance with intimacy, composure with uncomfortable, transitory gestures. As a result, she forms a bridge between an earlier generation of professionals who participated in the profitable business of freak exhibition and contemporary art photographers who take physical deviance as their subject.

Unlike the work of McCullers and Arbus, Leslie Fiedler's *Freaks: Myths and Images of the Secret Self* has never been read biographically. Chapter 6, "From Sideshow to the Streets: Performing the 'Secret Self,'" argues that Fiedler's study of human prodigies is an outgrowth of the author's attempt to manage his own ambivalence about the tumultuous events of the 1960s, the decade when the meanings and visibility of freaks explodes exponentially. An aging writer who has always spoken on behalf of the outcast, Fiedler recoils at the prospect of oppressed groups coming together to demand parity in the public realm. In *Freaks,* he deflates the significance of recent political and cultural dissidence by situating the sixties as a disappointing conclusion to a lengthy history of freaks in which monsters and human prodigies evolve into hippies and rock stars. My reading juxtaposes Fiedler's vision of the freak with freaks in the writing of countercultural radicals (or *freaks*) such as Abbie Hoffman and Jerry Rubin to demonstrate unexpected continuities: each author's identification with freaks lays claim to the marginality of a white masculine self as his authority is threatened by the rising voices of disenfranchised coalitions. Taken together, these authors represent the expanded significance of the term *freak* that, since the 1960s, has had a resounding impact on subsequent understandings of the sideshow's history and culture.

If embodied deviance in the work of McCullers, Arbus, and Fiedler is easily interpreted as the dark underside of normalcy, authors in the final act return to the sideshow's original conviction that there is an absolute difference between freak and normal. At the same moment when critical theory turns to antiessentialist accounts of the body and self, the fiction of Toni Morrison and Katherine Dunn insists that identity, both individual and collective, is rooted firmly in the physical body. Denying that corporeal differences can be transcended in the interest of a common humanity, they recycle the freak show to describe contexts in which the

19

body is a marker for determining the politics of community, the grounds for excluding some and granting entry to others. Toni Morrison's *Beloved* is the subject of chapter 7, "The Black Look and the 'spectacle of whitefolks,'" which takes a visit to the freak show as the novel's paradigmatic scene. When former slaves become the audience for a troupe of freaks, the two marginalized groups confront one another with suspicion and hostility. This moment of failed communication sets the stage for the appearance of the ghostly Beloved, who shares many of the freaks' characteristics yet helps the damaged community to work towards a more affirming collectivity formed on the basis of embodied suffering. Chapter 8, "Maternal Impressions," approaches Katherine Dunn's novel *Geek Love* as a commentary on gender, biotechnology, and contemporary reproductive politics conveyed through the story of a family of carnival freaks. As in the classic sideshow, Dunn describes the freak's identity in biological terms. Along with family history, freakishness can be passed from one generation to the next, much as characters in *Beloved* transmit the trauma of slavery from mother to child. Mothers are at the heart of *Geek Love*, for they are storytellers whose bodies hold the terrible and fantastic power of reproduction, the only source of authentic, "born freaks."

The epilogue, "Live from New York," turns from literature to performance art as freak shows are revived in the late 1980s and 1990s. The neighborhoods of Coney Island, Manhattan's Lower East Side, and Williamsburg, Brooklyn, are the settings for artists who are self-consciously refashioning different aspects of the sideshow's past. These spirited and politically savvy variety shows belie the conclusion that the freak show is a dying medium, or one that it is inherently and irredeemably exploitative. They pay tribute to the centrality of the freak show within the history of American popular culture by keeping it alive for a new generation. And at their best, these performances seek to redress the nativism, racism, and sexism that fueled sideshows in the past. However, there is also a less optimistic side to this story. Whereas the sideshow revival makes inspired connections with a vibrant gay, lesbian, and queer subculture, its resurrection relies on a certain degree of forgetting. Not all groups that have a historical association with the freak show are so eager to reappropriate it for their own ends. The ongoing social and legal struggles of people with disabilities and racial minorities attest to the fact that, although they are no longer exhibited as freaks, the realities of appearance-based discrimination persist in American culture.

A form of popular amusement and a recurrent symbolic figure, the freak show has left an enduring imprint on American culture. The pages that follow illuminate unrecognized aspects of its history by studying its appropriation in literature, film, theater, and fine arts. Likewise, well-known texts will read differently when considered in the context of the popular culture of freak shows. When T. S. Eliot introduced Djuna Barnes's *Nightwood* by cautioning readers against seeing its bizarre cast of queers, misfits, and circus folk as "a horrid sideshow of freaks,"[47] his point was to cordon off the novelist's artistry from the degraded terrain of mass entertainment. If I manage to prove, on the contrary, that our understanding of American literary and visual culture of the past century is enriched and deepened by recognizing, rather than denying, the centrality of the freak show, this book will have accomplished its purpose.

As in the sideshow talker's spiel, much has been said, all of it inadequate to describe the encounters that will unfold over the course of this book. They represent the product of my own odyssey through the rich, appalling, exciting, and terrible tapestry woven by the American freak show. In the pages that follow, my own critical voice, like that of a carnival barker, will dominate, but I have tried, wherever possible, to leave a space where freaks can talk back. Sideshows typically end with a gaff, a hidden attraction that can only be viewed for an extra price. Those gullible enough to pay are almost always disappointed by what they find when the final curtain is parted. There is no gaff here, for my goal is not to have the last laugh by proving that you, reader, are a sucker, but to become one participant in an ongoing, garrulous, and often irreverent dialogue, involving many voices that, I hope, may resound well into the new century.

> *Don't go yet!*
> *You're just inside the door, and wonders,*
> *each more sensational than the last, await you within!*
> *What follows is not for the faint of heart!*
> *But if you proceed, brave reader,*
> *you will not be disappointed . . .*

☞ *ACT ONE*

ACT ONE

FREAKS OF CULTURE
Institutions, Publics, and the Subjects
of Ethnographic Knowledge

Few visitors to the Bronx Zoo stop to look at the old Monkey House, which now stands dark and empty off to the side of the park's main thoroughfare. A sign attached to the cages announces that their simian occupants have been moved to more contemporary, naturalistic habitats. It does not mention that perhaps the most disturbing chapter in the zoo's history took place on that very spot, an episode the New York Zoological Society would very much like to erase from memory. In September 1906, Ota Benga, a Batwa Pygmy from Central Africa, became the Bronx Zoo's most sensational attraction when he was displayed in the Monkey House with an orangutan named Dohong.

In contrast to the zoo's dusty cages, so unrevealing about their unsavory history, the Hearst Museum of Anthropology at the University of California, Berkeley, has been unable to repress the traces of similar events in its own past. A Yahi Indian from Northern California, known as Ishi, or "the last Stone Age man," brought unprecedented crowds when he was exhibited there from 1911–1915. The current museum staff hopes to put their limited space to other uses, but the Ishi exhibit remains so popular that they have been unable to retire it.

The zoo and the anthropology museum—the former mute about its transgressions, the latter openly self-critical—are unlikely spaces to begin a book about freak shows, which we tend to associate with the most degraded zones of popular culture. Nonetheless, each briefly presented a living human specimen who, like the freaks found at sideshows, carnivals, and dime museums, drew crowds simply because he was the only one of his kind. Thus, for a short time the nation's grand civilizing institutions unwittingly engaged with the sensational, profit-driven mode of the freak show. This chapter looks at the debates over racial classification, institutional authority, and the politics of class resentment that converged around the African and the Native American when they were represented as ethnographic freaks. The controversies they aroused concerned not only questions of racial definition, but also the relationship of scientists, intellectuals, and showmen to the institutions and publics they claimed to serve. Two men who could hardly have been more culturally or geographically remote, their lives took strikingly parallel courses because each was the last known survivor of his people, brought into sudden contact with Western civilization through the violent consequences of progress.

The great public institutions erected in America during the nineteenth century were conceived as monuments to the accomplishments and potential of a nation poised to become a global power. Defining themselves against the disorderly clutter of popular entertainment, institutions such as museums, parks, and zoos sought to enlighten their visitors through the strict organization of space and regulation of behavior. How the rise of these institutions, and the epistemological and disciplinary changes they introduced, impacted the exhibition of human specimens is a significant and largely unexamined episode in the history of the freak show. Cultural institutions are an important, if counterintuitive, place to inaugurate this study because the distinctions they encouraged set the stage for ongoing antagonisms between the professional and the amateur, education and amusement, high and low aesthetic forms that figured prominently in the representation of freaks throughout the twentieth century.

Freak shows of the nineteenth century brought together a hybrid cast of performers that included the physically or mentally disabled, natives from non-Western countries, and persons with unusual talents. Knowledge about these varied curiosities, once indiscriminately categorized as freaks, would eventually condense into the fields of anthropology, medicine, and human biology. But the first freak shows, visited by patrons from across the class spectrum, benefited from an atmosphere in which elite and popular culture were less segregated, and academic knowledge less clearly partitioned into discrete disciplines. The subsequent emergence of an institutional culture in the United States had particularly wide-ranging consequences for the common practice of displaying people of color as freaks. The racial economy of these exhibitions, premised on the interchangeability of dark bodies, is aptly summarized in the 1936 memoir of press agent Dexter Fellows: "The Borneo aborigines, the head-hunters, the Ubangis, and the Somalis were all classified as freaks. From the standpoint of the showman the fact that they were different put them in the category of human oddities."[1] While this statement attests to a colonial mentality that assumes the inferiority of all nonwhite people, it also bespeaks the showman's disregard for the categorical subtleties so important to the sciences of racial measurement and classification.[2] As the scientific professional and the entertainer sought authority over the exhibition of ethnographic freaks, their divergent styles would increasingly come into conflict.

The community leaders, scientists, and entertainers who claimed to speak on behalf of Ota Benga and Ishi clashed over who was best qualified to represent each stranger to the audiences clamoring to see him. The convergences in these stories remind us that they flow from similar national fantasies. National fantasies, as Lauren Berlant describes them, are the imaginative counterparts to the juridical identity of the nation-state; varied and particular, they are the symbolic narrative framework that invests official fictions of social and political unity with meaning.[3] Ishi and Ota Benga are the products of such fantasies about "America" and its expanding global presence at century's turn. Exhibited in New York and San Francisco, these men were viewed by spectators whose heterogeneity reflected the growing ethic and class diversity of urban populations in the United States. Not only did crowds react to the visible spectacle of curious bodies on display, but to the largely invisible presence of professional experts who managed those encounters. As stranded survivors were transformed into freaks, experts and audiences alike were forced to confront the institutional processes that made such transformations possible.

Science and Spectacle

While individuals have been exhibited as freaks for hundreds of years, the orchestrated spectacle of the freak show was born in the mid-nineteenth century of a conjunction between scientific investigation and mass entertainment. This period saw the development of a widespread institutional culture, which required the more exacting management of space and time, and division and specialization of professional expertise.[4] Growing cities, shrinking work weeks, and new technologies driven by steam and electric power provided ideal conditions for the rise of commercialized forms of entertainment such as the circus, the amusement park, and the dance hall.[5] While the goal of the cultural institution was to enlighten, civilize, and discipline its beneficiaries, entertainers sought to thrill and amuse in order to turn a profit. While the former aimed to improve its audiences by offering instruction and moral guidance free of the marketplace, a consumer-oriented popular culture catered to their desires and pleasures.[6] Yet education and entertainment often merged in tense, if profitable, collaboration around the display of freaks. The history of the freak show's efflorescence in the second half of the nineteenth century is thus punctuated by a contentious dialogue between the lofty discourses of the museum and the university and the promotional hype of the commercial entrepreneur. Accredited scholars attempted to distance themselves from the entertainment industry as they were pushed into competition for its audiences, while showmen ridiculed the experts' knowledge, yet sought legitimacy by appropriating the conventions and rhetoric of the life sciences.

The heightened emphasis on professionalism changed what had been a long-standing collaboration between scientists and entertainers in the exhibition of freaks. Freak shows had always drawn on ethnographic and medical discourses to grant legitimacy to the fantastic narratives they wove around the bodies on display.[7] The signatures and commentary of doctors, explorers, politicians, and royalty appended to promotional pamphlets provided confirmation of the freak's authenticity. Likewise, physicians and natural scientists benefited from their affiliation with sideshows, which provided them with a reliable supply of rare corporeal anomalies for examination. Always on the lookout for new sensations, entertainment entrepreneurs capitalized on the public's growing interest in exotic cultures by employing more nonwhite performers as savages, cannibals, and missing links, whom they added to the established menu of freaks with curious talents, physical and developmental disabilities (figures 3 and 4). As freak show scouts traveled to remote areas of the globe in search of unique curiosities, their efforts overlapped with those of natural scientists, explorers, and missionaries. Framed in a pseudoethnographic language by showmen who called themselves "doctors" and "professors," anthropological exhibits at the freak show often provided American audiences with their primary source of information about the non-Western world.

The widening divergence of the scientific professions and the entertainment industry is related to the increasing size and influence of the middle class in America. At one end of the spectrum, the professional exerted authority over the domain of the university and the arts, of disinterested social privilege and cultural authority; at the other, the entertainer dominated the realm of commerce and popular amusement. Yet the middle class, to which most Americans belonged, possessed of leisure time and discretionary income, relied simultaneously on the professional's specialized knowledge and respectability and the pleasure and diversion of the amusement industry. Indeed, despite the apparently antithetical qualities of showman and scientist, numerous venues required the interaction of erudition and commercial savvy. The importance of this niche was recognized by P. T. Barnum, the father of commercialized mass entertainment, who persistently straddled the divide between high and low culture by promoting his American museum and traveling shows as respectable venues for women, children, and families.[8] The spaces traversed by Ota Benga and Ishi—the museum, the theater, the world's fair, the zoo—were also the lumpy terrain of the middle class, heterogeneous sites where the showman and the professional engaged in an ongoing and unresolved conflict for legitimacy and audience.

As each of these spaces facilitates an encounter that authorizes one person to gaze at another, it borrows the formal features of the sideshow, and the body on

FIGURE 3. An ethnographic freak advertised as a "South Sea Islander." The man's wide-eyed expression, tribal costume, and abundant props create an impression of primitive exoticism. The painted studio backdrop enhances his association with the wildness of nature. Courtesy Theatre Arts Collection, Harry Ransom Humanities Research Center, the University of Texas at Austin.

display, transformed into a unique and curious object, becomes a freak. Freak shows combine the drama and costuming of the theater with the more sober conventions of the scientific exhibit. Freaks may pose in passive acknowledgment that the body itself is an object of sufficient interest or perform a sequence of activities designed to showcase their unique abilities. Despite the repetitive quality invited by this structure, the sideshow requires a direct confrontation between audience and performer, ensuring that each cycle involves slight but potentially consequential differences. Unlike media transmitted through mechanical reproduction, human exhibits provide opportunities for unanticipated exchanges between customers and freaks. Ota Benga and Ishi were displayed within institutional settings that promised to make racial, national, and species differences culturally intelligible. Instead they produced confusion and doubt. At a moment when Americans expressed a particular interest in the exotic and foreign, the prospect of contem-

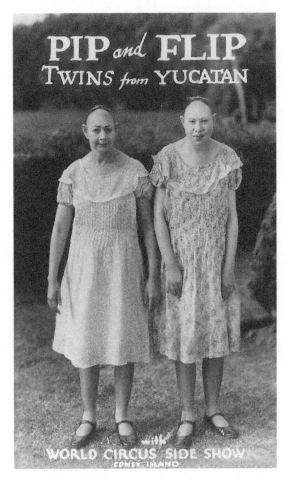

FIGURE 4. Souvenir photograph of Pip and Flip. These microcephalic twin sisters, who were actually born in Georgia and named Elvira and Jenny Snow, also appear in Tod Browning's *Freaks*. Claiming that they come from Yucatan, this publicity image illustrates the common strategy of attributing non-Western origins to people with developmental disabilities. Courtesy Theatre Arts Collection, Harry Ransom Humanities Research Center, the University of Texas at Austin.

plating the representative of a remote culture at close range had widespread appeal. But as they did so, the spectators came to question their own place within the hierarchy of human races and the narratives of progress on which that hierarchy relied.

This chapter is particularly concerned with the presentation of human freaks in sites intended for animals or inanimate artifacts, a practice that confuses the established relationships among audiences, performers, and professionals, as well as the function of newly established institutional spaces. When the public could see a "genuine Wild Indian" at the University of California's Hearst Museum of Anthropology, how could it be distinguished from Barnum's American Museum, famed for the exhibition of such oddities as the Feegee Mermaid, Tom Thumb, and William Henry Johnson, the "What Is It?" When an African man was locked in the Monkey House at the Bronx Zoo, what made this spectacle different from the savages, cannibals, and missing links that frequented the sideshow platform? The unexpected placement of a human being in a university museum or a zoo necessarily shaped the meeting between specimen and spectator in particular ways, but also called into question the purpose of the institution and the professional men who orchestrated the encounter. Significantly, the exhibition of Ota Benga and Ishi provided occasions for viewers not only to consider their superiority to representatives of primitive cultures but to express resentment against the guardians of cultural authority who directed encounters between the races from offstage.

These encounters assume an opposition between the whiteness (normality) of the audience and the deviance of the racial freak. In contrast to both the freak's unique abnormality and the professional's rarified expertise, "the public" is conceived as a featureless, uniform mass. Rosemarie Thomson has argued that part of the cultural work of the freak show was to reassure diverse audiences of their claim to citizenship: "[T]he figure of the freak is . . . the necessary cultural complement to the acquisitive and capable American who claims the normate position of masculine, white, nondisabled, sexually unambiguous, and middle class."[9] As Thomson explains, freak shows were often frequented by the populations that would be most likely to feel disenfranchised from the imagined community of U.S. citizenship and therefore comforted by the sight of bodies more radically Other than their own. But the gesture of repudiation enscripted in the act of paying to look is often coupled with an equally intense identification, a dynamic magnified in the case of those spectators who are already aware of their own marginality. To be a member of the audience could also serve as a reminder of the injustices that turn some people into curious objects for the entertainment of others. The African and the Native American each produced strong responses of recognition: Ota Benga caused anguish in the African Americans who saw the monstrosity of U.S. racism embodied in the spectacle of a black man in a cage, whereas Ishi inspired the guilty regret of white men who viewed the Indian as a more noble survivor of their own imagined past. But as the following discussion will show, each recognition is in fact a misrecognition, in which the sympathetic onlooker reads himself into the body on display, obliterating its personhood as completely as the most exploitative exhibit.

Exhibit A: The African Savage

In September 1906, New York newspapers carried the story of a human exhibited in the Monkey House at the Bronx Zoo. The person was Ota Benga, a Central

African Batwa who had been brought to the United States by explorer and some-time Presbyterian missionary Samuel Verner to be part of the Pygmy village at the 1904 Saint Louis World's Fair.[10] Ota Benga chose to remain when the other par-ticipants returned to Africa, in part because he no longer had a home there. A vic-tim of Belgian colonialism, he had returned from a hunt to find that his tribe (including his wife and children) had been slaughtered by tax collectors of King Leopold's Force Publique, who sold him into the tribal slave market where he was purchased by Verner. After the Fair ended, Verner traveled the United States with his African companion until the impoverished explorer left him at the Bronx Zoo under the care of its director, William Hornaday. For a few weeks Ota Benga wandered freely around the zoo in relative anonymity. Zookeepers encouraged him to spend more time in the Monkey House, where he had been sleeping since his arrival, until one day they locked him inside.

Conflicts over the African's place—literally where and how to house him, for the idea of his freedom seemed intolerable to all—immediately arose among the representatives of scientific and religious institutions, as well as the audiences who clamored to see him. These struggles over cultural authority were amplified by their inseparability from questions about race. For African American commu-nity leaders, Ota Benga represented, on the one hand, the tragedies of Western imperialism and the intolerable persistence of domestic racism; on the other, he provided them with clear evidence that Africans were inferior to American blacks. If freak show representations of Africans as savage wild men were unacceptable, so too was the equation of primitive African tribes with respectable black Ameri-can citizens.

The outrage of prominent African Americans is not surprising, for zoo visitors found Ota Benga sharing a cage with Dohong, an orangutan trained to wear clothes, ride a bicycle, and eat at a table. In an era when Darwinian theory regu-larly provided scientific justification for racial prejudice, the exhibit suggested an evolutionary proximity between Africans and apes. Moreover, a conjunction of props and performance associated Ota Benga with the primitive savagery of the freak show wild man: bones were scattered around the floor of the cage, and he was encouraged to charge at the crowds while baring his teeth, which were filed to sharp points as is customary for the Batwa.[11] As a finishing touch, a sign attached to the cage explained its contents: "The African Pygmy, 'Ota Benga,' Age, 28 years. Height, 4 feet 11 inches. Weight 103 pounds. Brought from the Kasai River, Congo Free State, South Central Africa, by Dr. Samuel P. Verner, Exhibited each afternoon during September."[12] This sign establishes the relationship of the sci-entific professional to his object of study. Using the definite article, it proclaims

Ota Benga a unique, rather than representative, specimen. His passivity contrasts with the purposive activity of the explorers and zoologists. Verner, hardly a "Dr." of any kind, is depicted as a disembodied abstraction, absent the fleshly details of age, height, weight, and region that describe his charge.

Although there are no photographs of Ota Benga in the Monkey House, several images taken during the world's fair attest to his visual status as a racial freak, a stranded anomaly caught between two worlds. A photograph reproduced in the Bradford and Blume biography, *Ota Benga: The Pygmy in the Zoo,* shows him playing the molimo, a traditional, horn-shaped instrument. The authors note that it was originally captioned by anthropologists, "A Savage's Idea of Music." However, they do not mention that their copy is cropped from an original panorama in which Ota Benga is surrounded by a group of male spectators (figures 5 and 6).[13] Together, the original and cropped versions illustrate the construction of the ethnographic subject by a team of experts who choreograph his movements then step back to watch the show, erasing all signs of the intervention. Up close, Ota Benga appears to stand alone in an open field, whereas the expanded perspective shows the context for such a "natural" setting, a semicircle of observers dressed in Western suits and hats, with the architecture of the world's fair faintly visible on the horizon.

Photographs were popular souvenirs at sideshows, world's fairs, and dime museums, where they were available for visitors to purchase after seeing an attraction. Often appropriating the conventions of middle-class portraiture, *cartes de visite* of freak performers emphasized the subjects' peculiarities by contrast with their ordinary posture and dress. A souvenir photograph of Ota Benga frames him in the frontal, three-quarter-length shot typical of contemporary portraiture. The exoticism of his dark skin, bare chest, and broad grin is all the more striking because of the banality of his pose (figure 7). Whereas the average sitter was supposed to wear a look of disinterested composure, we must assume that Ota Benga's smile was demanded by the photographer to show off his sharply pointed teeth, the attribute that most distinguished him from an ordinary black person. According to the pseudoethnographic logic of the world's fair, Ota Benga's teeth were indisputable evidence of his cannibalism, a practice that located him halfway between animal and human. Their importance in the sensationalism surrounding the Saint Louis Pygmy exhibit is evident in an article written by Verner himself, in which he proclaims, "[H]ave you seen otabenga's [*sic*] teeth! They're worth the 5 cents he charges for showing them to visitors on anthropology hill out at the World's Fair. Otabenga is a cannibal, the only genuine African cannibal in America today. He's also the only human chattel. He belongs to the Exposition

FIGURES 5 AND 6. Ota Benga
playing the molimo at the
Saint Louis Exposition, 1904.
In the cropped version of
the photograph, Ota Benga
appears to be standing alone
against a natural expanse of
grassland. Uncropped, the
photograph reveals clusters
of white male spectators
with the fair's architecture
faintly visible on the horizon.
Together these images
illustrate the use of photography to create anthropological subjects. Negative
336071, courtesy Depart-
ment of Library Services,
American Museum of
Natural History.

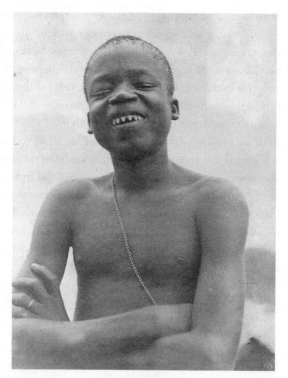

FIGURE 7. Souvenir portrait of Ota Benga at the Saint Louis Exposition. While Ota Benga's pose borrows some of the conventions of portraiture, his bare chest, wide grin, and sharp teeth attest to his difference from an ordinary sitter. His expression, more a grimace than a smile, was demanded by the photographer in order to show off his pointed teeth. Negative 299134, courtesy Department of Library Services, American Museum of Natural History.

company. Step right up."[14] Adopting the tone and posture of a sideshow spieler, Verner provides the written complement to the photographs of Ota Benga, exaggerating the oddity of his freakish human specimen through the use of exclamation points and hyperbolic description.

If Ota Benga is turned into a freak by a convergence of science and entertainment, these were irreconcilable pursuits for Samuel Verner, who desired the excitement and financial rewards of a successful career in show business, as well as the social and educational legitimacy of the professional. Posing his questions in the name of science in his 1903 memoir, *Pioneering in Central Africa,* Verner asked of the Pygmies, "Who and what are they? Are they men, or the highest apes? Who and what were their ancestors? What are their ethnic relations to the other races of men? Have they degenerated from larger men, or are the larger men a development of Pygmy forefathers? These questions arise naturally, and plunge the inquirer at once into the depths of the most heated scientific discussions of this generation."[15] Verner's attempt to insert himself into the era's "most heated scientific discussions" bespeaks his own anxious relationship to the accredited experts who passed judgment about the value of the artifacts he brought back from his African travels.[16] Alternately obsequious and resentful, Verner's writings reveal a man who longed for acceptance within elite social and professional circles, yet remained perpetually on the margins, lacking the proper institutional or familial connections.[17] As an explorer, he experienced the subordination of the collector to the scholar that was characteristic of the scientific community at the turn of the century, which was divided between what Curtis Hinsley calls "gatherers on the one hand, theorizers on the other."[18]

If Verner's queries are evidence of his effort to insinuate himself within an academy that was closing ranks around an elite cadre of trained specialists, they also propel him into the popular domain of the freak show. His questions echo nearly verbatim those raised by P. T. Barnum's famous exhibit, the What Is It?—a black man advertised as a hybrid of human and animal species (figure 8).[19] In fact, publicity materials for the What Is It? describe the creature as a fusion of African and orangutan, exactly the same mixture implied by the cohabitation of Ota Benga and Dohong:

FIGURE 8. Publicity poster for P. T. Barnum's What Is It? Advertised as a missing link between primitive humanity and the orangutan, this sensation was exhibited in New York during the period of Ota Benga's confinement in the Bronx Zoo. It is likely that many viewers equated the two human curiosities, much to the dismay of African American community leaders. © Shelburne Museum, Shelburne, Vermont.

Is it a lower order of MAN? Or is it a higher order of MONKEY? None can tell! Perhaps it is a combination of both. It is beyond dispute THE MOST MARVELOUS CREATURE LIVING, it was captured in a savage state in Central Africa, is probably about 20 years old, 2 feet high, intelligent, docile, active, sportive, and PLAYFUL AS A KITTEN. It has a skull, limbs, and general anatomy of an ORANG OUTANG and the COUNTENANCE of a HUMAN BEING.

Exhibited from the 1860s to 1924 in New York City and elsewhere, the What Is It? may have been viewed by the same people who visited Ota Benga at the zoo, where they would have been provided with a strikingly similar account of what they saw. From his reference to Central Africa to his invocation of a species hierarchy in which some human races were indistinguishable from their simian ancestors, Verner's account replicates the details of the Barnum poster.

That Ota Benga's confinement turned the Bronx Zoo into a freak show was an opinion voiced by more than one newspaper report. As the *New York Tribune* editorialized, "The exhibition of a little wild man from Africa in a cage by the side of apes and other beasts in not an altogether agreeable episode, although doubtless no offense is meant by it, and it must be recalled that for many years it has been a common practice for 'Circassian girls,' 'fat women,' 'living skeletons,' and other eccentric human beings voluntarily to make 'museum freaks' of themselves, on exhibition by the side of baby elephants and educated pigs."[20] Any doubts about Ota Benga's cooperation were dispelled by comparing him with other human curiosities who were understood to be voluntary participants in their own commodification. The article's implicit alignment of anomalous people with animals—a common strategy in the stage personae of sideshow performers—made the zoo the symbolic equivalent of the freak show (figure 9). The more conventional distinction between humans and animals firmly established by the bars of a cage was reconfigured in terms of differences among humans based on race and national affiliation.

Ota Benga's presence in the Monkey House presented a generic confusion as the respectable space of the zoo, informed by the organizational principles and educational goals of science, merged with the sensationalistic format of the sideshow. Responding to accusations that confining a man in a cage was degrading and inhumane, zoo director William Hornaday hotly countered that the Monkey House was the most comfortable and convenient place for Ota Benga to meet the large crowds who wanted to see him. Unlike a circus or sideshow, the zoo had no space reserved for the exhibition of human subjects, he claimed. Hornaday's assertion that the zoo was merely responding to public desires obscured the fact that

FIGURE 9. This wild man poses with a monkey to suggest an evolutionary proximity to his simian ancestors. The fact that the monkey is wearing clothes and the man is dressed in fur further confuses the distinction between the two. Courtesy Theatre Arts Collection, Harry Ransom Humanities Research Center, the University of Texas at Austin.

those desires were produced by the advertisement of Ota Benga as a curiosity. For some time he had wandered the zoo's grounds unnoticed, and it was only his incarceration in the Monkey House that turned him into a sensation. In answer to the protests of African American community leaders, Hornaday denied that he had placed Ota Benga alongside the monkeys to suggest an evolutionary link: "I am a believer in Darwinian theory . . . but I hope my colored brethren will not take the absurd position that I am giving the exhibition to show the close analogy of the African savage to the apes."[21] Moreover, he announced the exhibit as a part of his larger mission to use pleasure and entertainment to encourage a wholesome public interest in scientific matters.

This statement coincides with Hornaday's more general goals as director of the zoo, a position that required him to remain solicitous of public desires despite his admitted disdain for many of his customers, whom he described as "low lived beasts who appreciate nothing and love filth and disorder."[22] The construction of the New York Zoological Park was one instance of a broader development of managed public spaces, such as museums, concert halls, and playgrounds, which aimed to provide both recreation and instruction in civic virtue.[23] The park's civilizing mission was echoed in its spatial layout and architectural design. A microcosm of America's imperial aspirations, the zoo boasted the biggest and most inclusive animal collection in the world.[24] Inspired by the architecture of the world's fairs, its model was not the hybrid clutter of the midway but the austere Halls of Science. Helen Horowitz explains, "[T]he park was committed to exhibiting typical members of each species, rather than some of the rarities of nature. *It was to be no sideshow.* Nor was it to encourage the breaking of natural laws by the development of new hybrids among its specimens. Each species was to be kept separate in its own enclosure, a marked contrast to the city outside the park where such control could not be exercised over human beings."[25] Its administrators insisted that the zoo's combination of amusement and education was superior to the tawdry spectacles of sideshows, circuses, and dime museums. According to Bradford and Blume, "Director Hornaday liked to draw a sharp distinction between his institution and Coney Island, his highbrow elephants and the carny animals that belonged to circuses or amusement parks."[26] The orderly display of animals, each representative of its kind, was one strategy for differentiating the zoo's scientific mode of classification from the messy hybridity of the freak show or the midway.

The impulse towards hierarchy and discrimination carried over in Hornaday's ideas about the zoo's occupants. Although some zoo animals were taught to wear costumes and perform tricks, Hornaday relied on a discourse of class to distinguish his select group from their counterparts in circuses and carnivals. Describing his favorite animal species as morally and intellectually superior to many of the human races, Hornaday's writings are the dark counterpoint to his public justification of Ota Benga's confinement for reasons of convenience alone. They demonstrate that the allegations of African American community leaders were well justified, for according to Hornaday's personal hierarchy, "[i]t is a far cry from the highest to the lowest of the human race; and we hold the highest animals intellectually are higher than the lowest man."[27]

Dohong, Ota Benga's companion in the Monkey House, proved that he was a fine specimen of the better animal species by learning to perform everyday human activities for the entertainment of zoo visitors. But if Hornaday claimed that his trained monkeys were one step from being citizens, he had a far different attitude towards the most degraded representatives of the human race. "Some sensitive minds shrink from the idea that man has 'descended' from the apes. I never for a moment shared that feeling. I would rather descend from a clean, capable and bright-minded genus of apes than from any unclean, ignorant, and repulsive race of the genus *Homo.*"[28] This claim locked the perverse logic of the Ota Benga exhibit into place, for it implied that the Pygmy was not only the lowest of human species, but beneath many animal species in intellect and cultural development. Even worse than the ministers' complaint that the exhibit equated black men with apes, Hornaday's reasoning suggested that the Pygmy was in fact inferior to his simian counterpart.

African American community leaders were at the forefront of the protest against Ota Benga's confinement. Their comments emphasize the importance of their own social and professional respectability while revealing a deep ambivalence about the role of scientific knowledge in contemporary debates about race. Despite Verner's conclusion that "my experience and observation completely convince me . . . that these Pygmies are human beings in every sense of the word," African Americans were not so sanguine about the effects of the exhibition on the eager crowds of zoo visitors.[29] All too aware that they were confronting the same public who would have been drawn to the What Is It? their responses betray a frustration that in the struggle for racial uplift, the African American intellectual constantly had to prove his distance from demeaning popular representations of blackness.[30] They were attuned to the frequency with which such representations were legitimated in the name of science.[31]

Registering their protest in New York newspapers, African American religious leaders argued that the exhibit was an insult to their race, which already lacked the social and political opportunities available to other citizens. Although they did not identify with the Pygmy themselves, they felt sure that zoo visitors would equate the caged African with American blacks. As Reverend Gordon, superintendent of the Howard Colored Orphan Asylum, put the matter, "[Y]ou people . . . are on top. We've got to rise. Why not let us, and not impede us? Why shut a boy up in a cage with chimpanzees to show that Negroes are akin to apes? Give us opportunities."[32] To display a black man at the zoo linked black men and apes, suggesting biological as well as a social obstacles to racial betterment. "We are frank enough to say we do not like this exhibition of one of us with the apes. We think we are worthy of being considered human beings with souls," a second minister commented to reporters.[33] While subsequent events illustrated the limits of the minister's identification with Ota Benga, his use of the inclusive pronoun here acknowledges his awareness that African and black American would be aligned in the imagination of the zoo visitor.

Not only was the exhibit an affront to African Americans, but to humanity as a whole, an accusation the clergymen connected to the nation's own shameful history of race relations. "Only prejudice against the negro race made such a thing possible in this country," wrote Dr. Gilbert, pastor of the Mount Olivet Baptist Church. "I have had occasion to travel abroad, and am confident that such a thing would not have been tolerated a day in any other civilized country."[34] In their condemnation of American racism, the ministers' identification with the African transcended national borders; he was "one of us" by virtue of a skin color that made both African and black American the objects of discrimination.[35] Ota Benga's mistreatment at the hands of zoo authorities forced Gilbert to look abroad, and to conclude that far from being the most enlightened democracy, the United States was among the most retrograde in terms of its racial attitudes. This argument posed the greatest challenge to the freak-making aspects of the exhibit, as I have described them above, for it found savagery at the heart of the very institutions that claimed to uphold civilization itself. If the freak show relied on the divide between the aberrant body on display and smug normality of the spectator, the ministers claimed that the practice itself threatened the humanity of all involved: confining an African visitor in a monkey's cage made those responsible as uncivilized as any wild man. Science, rather than confirming the humanity of some against the freakishness of others, dehumanized the scientist and his audience, as well as his specimen. Instead of inspiring moral uplift, the nation's great institutions were the stage for the most barbaric consequences of modernity.

But the ministers' argument did not end on that powerful note. Ironically, as they spoke on behalf of the black race, they revealed their own prejudices against Africans, and Pygmies in particular.[36] Although the sign clearly indicated that he was nearly thirty, they called Ota Benga a "boy," a patently insulting term in the mouths of African American men who could easily have experienced a similar offense themselves. On the matter of Ota Benga's feeble mental abilities and moral sensibility, they urged that his scant resources should be nurtured rather than neglected, and they advocated civilizing him by introducing him to Christian virtues and teachings. Ota Benga became for them a microcosm of the American exceptionalism that undergirded contemporary missionary efforts in Africa, which sought to instill Western values through religious evangelism.[37]

These class and nativist biases became more pronounced following Ota Benga's release into the care of African American clergy. Newspaper accounts of his stay at the Howard Colored Orphan Asylum describe Ota Benga's intractable mixture of a childlike intellect and mature vices, such as smoking and the incurable longing for human flesh. According to one article, the staff faced the difficult task of turning the Pygmy into a "gentleman." With predictable regularity, references to cannibalism crept into reports on his progress, for although "he [went] to Sunday school with the other inmates of the institution," the heathen Ota Benga would "sing at the top of his voice in his own tongue the song which his people sang while gathered around some nicely cooked missionary who had been sizzling on the fire for several hours, and who was all ready to be eaten."[38] Efforts to imbue the "inmate" with Christian virtues were overshadowed by the allure of jungle savagery, which endured like an indelible stain. In the end, religious authority proved no more capable of affirming the humanity of the visitor than the cold reason of science or the explosive fictions of the popular press.

Ultimately, this living specimen, having passed through numerous identities from explorer's faithful native informant to colorful midway inhabitant to ape-like savage to heathen cannibal, could no longer tolerate his sojourn among the civilized. In March 1916, Ota Benga, apparently distraught at the difficulties of returning to Africa, took his own life by shooting himself with a stolen revolver. The exact motive for his suicide remains veiled in the editorials that followed, which are far more revealing about the ongoing conflicts among the forces of scientific, religious, and popular authority that sought to determine the fate of ethnographic freaks. Hornaday, who proclaimed in his "Wild Animals Bill of Rights" the obligation of zoo animals to labor in exchange for care and feeding, commented dismissively on Ota Benga's death: "[E]vidently . . . he felt that he would rather die than work for a living."[39] A more sympathetic reporter wrote that the episode at the zoo "contained the story of civilization in microcosm [for] . . . it was always so. For ages man has acted in just this way. We entice the backward race into our well secured back yard and tease it with straws or knives or laws. We become a nation of sociologists, look at the curious object's teeth, feel his muscle, prick his skin. . . . And if he is peevish or irritable—if he is so lost to virtue as to show signs of anger—our indignation begins to move us, and belike is soon lashed into a fury. And if he lets fly an arrow, there's an end of it. We say he has committed suicide, for we like euphemisms."[40] Resentful at the creeping influence of professionalization, the author accused the United States of becoming "a nation of sociologists," guided by unfeeling intellectual principles. He charged the experts with recycling the mistakes of the past, granted new legitimacy because they were couched within an inscrutable, specialized terminology. In this reporter's eyes, the methods and procedures of science, which transformed the inhabitant of another country into a "curious object," differed from the freak show only insofar as they wore the mantle of accredited professionalism.

In some cases, to live as a freak means to be accepted into a community unified on the basis of shared marginality. To be another kind of freak, particularly a savage cannibal, however, means, by definition, exclusion from the community of civilized persons. Although his voice remains silent, Ota Benga's final gesture speaks in a language that defies the hyperbole of the showman, the pieties of the minister, and the jargon of the scientist. His death tells us that to be a freak is to inhabit an intolerable space, regardless of whether one is literally confined in a cage, or in the imagined cages erected to barricade savagery from civilization, the impurity of popular culture from the enlightened pursuits of the mind.

And what of Samuel Verner, the man responsible for bringing Ota Benga out of Africa, delivering him up to the world's fair anthropologists, abandoning him at the Bronx Zoo and the Orphans' Asylum? Having alternately exploited the Pygmies' freak potential and vigorously defended their humanity, Verner lamented shortly after Ota Benga's removal from the zoo, "We were simply two friends, travelling together, until, for some inexplicable reason, New York's scientists and preachers began wrangling over him, and the peaceful tenor of our way was so ruthlessly disturbed. . . . If he survives scientific investigation, reportorial examination and eleemosynary education, perhaps he may rejoin me on our further travels, and be happy in the sunshine of the Kasailand."[41] The same man who, a few months earlier, urged the world's fair visitor to step right up to observe the savage human chattel subsequently expressed longing for the company of his dark friend. In this, Verner is guilty of what Renato Rosaldo calls the "imperialist nostalgia" that strikes when "someone deliberately alters a form of life, and then regrets that things have not remained as they were prior to the intervention."[42] Dreaming of a classless, biracial, masculine intimacy as old as the nation's literary origins, Verner anticipated a time when he could travel unimpeded with his nonwhite brother. Like the black ministers, his identification slipped back and forth opportunistically, at one moment branding Ota Benga as a barbarian Other, acknowledging him as a peer and companion at another. His fantasy illustrates the extreme malleability of the freak's identity, which bears, at best, only a tenuous attachment to the subject's personal history or physical body.

As we have seen, much of the meaning accorded to ethnographic freaks derives from prevailing stereotypes, which are disseminated as much by those who claim the status of experts as by the producers and consumers of popular culture. In the next section, the story of Ishi—also understood to be the last of his kind— will demonstrate how a different set of stereotypes than those used to describe the African governed understandings of the Native American. Any comparison of the two must be sensitive to the distinctive histories of these groups within the United States, their very different significance to American anthropologists, and the various ways in which they were exploited by interested parties, from scientists to showmen and mass media. All told, these portraits of racial freaks may provide little information about the subjects themselves, but they are revealing documents of the struggles over profit, authority, and professional turf that occurred behind the scenes of the institutions that took as their mission the production and dissemination of culture.

Exhibit B: The Last Wild Indian

The passing of Ishi, whom I will describe as Ota Benga's Native American counterpart, encouraged in his white male companions lyric passions akin to those expressed by Samuel Verner. Saxton Pope, Ishi's doctor and friend at the University of California, wrote regretfully, "and so departed the last wild Indian of America. With him the neolithic period terminates. He closes a chapter in history."[43] In elegizing his patient, Pope articulates the many contradictions that characterized Ishi's reception in modern San Francisco. For the crowds who greeted him with curiosity and affection he was the last survivor of a dying culture, an anachronistic relic of prehistoric times, and a representative of a more natural and wild America.[44] For the anthropologists he was both a figure of inassimilable difference in need of protection from the contaminating influence of civilization and a brother welcomed into their intimate circle of men.

As was the case with his African contemporary, the fragments of Ishi's story provide less satisfying evidence about an individual life than about how racial freaks are made at the seams where institutions, professionals, and their publics inevitably meet. Ishi, like Ota Benga, was "the last of his tribe," a Yahi Indian in his mid-fifties who was discovered in the corral of a slaughterhouse in Oroville, California, in September 1911. Dazed and emaciated from months of starvation, he was turned over to the sheriff, who for lack of a better solution, took him to the county jail. Soon the jail was besieged by reporters and citizens eager to catch a glimpse of the stranger they described as a genuine wild man. His story soon captured the interest of University of California anthropologist Alfred Kroeber, who dispatched his colleague T. T. Waterman to investigate. Waterman determined that the stranger was the sole surviving member of the Yahi, a Native American tribe believed to be extinct. Stilted attempts at communication between the two men revealed that he had spent the last three years hiding in complete isolation after witnessing the murders of his friends and family. Despite living in proximity to miners and homesteaders, he had absolutely no knowledge of or contact with their culture. Kroeber enthusiastically declared the man to be the find of a lifetime, "the most uncivilized and uncontaminated man in the world today,"[45] and named him "Ishi," a generic word for *man* in Yana, his native language. Until his death of tuberculosis four years later, Ishi lived at the university's Hearst Museum of Anthropology, where he educated audiences in the skill of arrowhead making, helped anthropologists to study his language and culture, and worked as a janitor (figure 10).[46]

As news of the wild man at the university museum spread, the anthropologists entrusted with his care were bombarded with requests from enterprising show-men eager to get their hands on a real-life "wild Indian." The sensationalism surrounding Ishi's initial "discovery" posed a problem for the anthropologists who sought to protect him against exploitation by reporters, theatrical managers, and sideshow scouts. As Theodora Kroeber writes, Ishi struck a chord with a public seeking the "illusion and fantasy" promised by "the voice of the barker, falsetto and arresting, which entices the listeners to pay to see what waits behind drawn curtains—be it freak, belly dancer, hypnotist, or wild man from Borneo, or better yet, from Mount Lassen."[47] Many were eager to exploit public desires for novelty and amusement. There was, for example, the vaudeville impresario who proposed that Ishi *and* Kroeber appear onstage at San Francisco's Orpheum Theater. As we

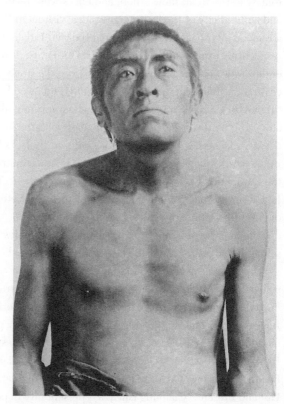

FIGURE 10. A portrait of Ishi taken just after he revealed himself to slaughter-house workers in Oroville, California. Although similar in composition to Ota Benga's portrait, this image of Ishi's gaunt, haunted countenance bespeaks the tragedy of the Vanishing Indian. Courtesy Phoebe Apperson Hearst Museum of Anthropology and the Regents of the University of California.

have seen, it was not uncommon for exotic human curiosities to be represented by men who called themselves "professors" and remarked with apparent erudition on the homeland, culture, and life history of the specimen on display. But Kroeber was not that kind of professor and Ishi, he believed, not that kind of curiosity.[48]

Crowds of visitors flocked to the university museum to shake hands and converse with the wild man from Oroville. Their responses bespeak the perplexity of a public seeking to reconcile the Indians they knew from freak shows, dime museums, Wild West pageants, and popular novels with the stranger they met, who did not fit easily into any of these prefabricated identities. Moreover, their reactions betray a certain confusion about the function of anthropologists and anthropology museums. This uncertainty is apparent in letters sent to the museum intended to assist the anthropologists in deciphering Ishi's language and culture. These helpful hints are evidence that their authors did not understand or respect the firm boundary between their own speculation and the ethnographer's specialized knowledge, acquired through years of training and scholarship. As was customary at the freak show, where audiences were invited to question the nature and authenticity of the human curiosities, visitors to the anthropology museum advanced their own hypotheses about the wild Indian. For example, one missive respectfully expressed doubts about Ishi's identity: "I understand very well how enthusiastic you can be if you have discovered a stone age man in the middle of civilization. But is he such?" The question is followed by the writer's own theory: "To me he looks like a Jewish student who wants to make a hit as [an] impersonator—the most striking point is his likeness with the notorious Dr. Cook the discoverer of Poles."[49] Another visitor confused by Ishi's ethnicity drew upon her rudimentary knowledge of Japanese: "[I] am much interested in the aborigines of the continents. I believe in heredity and environment. Therefor [sic] I think the Japanese and Indian are the same. Many words alike etc."[50] Such were the voices of museum visitors who, having seen Ishi described by one reporter as "a human document, with the key to most of the hieroglyphics lost," believed they had something to contribute to the task of interpretation.[51]

The still permeable boundaries between professional life scientist, amateur collector, and showman generated a war of words, a struggle over who would define the nature and status of the last wild man in America. As in the case of Ota Benga, a rich fantasy life proliferated in the newspaper coverage during the months following Ishi's emergence, topped by headlines such as "Primordial Man Blinks at Civilization's Glare" and "Stone Age Indian Hauled from Forests' Depths by Savants: Creature Found in the Wilds of Feather River a Link between Past and Present." Claiming Ishi as a representative of populations frozen in time since the prehistoric era, one article extols his usefulness to the present: "And this man who epitomizes all these ages of primitive strife for life is now the chiefest treasure in the anthropological department of the university. His stone arrow heads, buckskin thongs, fire sticks, and quaint traps for catching game are more precious to the scientists than their weight in gold."[52] Quite predictably, the author voices the ethnocentric perception that primitive cultures stand outside of history, frozen in place while civilization marches inexorably forward. Many popular accounts refer to Ishi as a less-evolved ancestor, speculating that, like the missing link exhibited at the freak show, he could provide evidence about the common origins of all humanity. However, this article also draws attention to the museum's role in creating value by acknowledging the scientist's ability to transform quaint artifacts into precious objects whose worth is determined outside the realm of the marketplace. With typical ambivalence, the reporter cited above simultaneously mystifies and denigrates the anthropologist's expertise.

The conflict of interest between popular and scientific modes of knowledge is best illustrated in an article by Grant Wallace, a journalist who invited Ishi to a vaudeville show in the hope of generating a good story. In October 1911, anthropologists and reporters took the wild Indian to the Orpheum theater.[53] Filling the front page of the *San Francisco Sunday Call*, Wallace's elaborate account ran alongside Kroeber's more subdued explanation of the evening's events. Their juxtaposition shows how efforts to explain the stranger's responses to the new culture became entangled with the interests of their authors. According to Wallace,

> The university professors, who have added Ishi to their museum of antiquities and curiosities and who are conducting this series of scientific experiments on him, justly regard him as a unique specimen of the genus homo, the like of which does not exist in all the world. They call him the "uncontaminated man," the one man who (possibly from lack of opportunity to talk) has never told a lie; the one man with no redeeming vices and no upsetting sins. This conclusion was decided doubtless from the fact that Ishi had never been brought into contact with the contaminating influences of civilization; therefore to permit the barbarian to mingle with our unsettled civilization is to expose him to contamination.[54]

Classifying the museum's contents as "antiquities and curiosities," Wallace equates the work of university anthropologists with mass entertainment. He suggests the hypocrisy of the scientists' desire to preserve Ishi as an untainted man of nature by sealing him away in a museum. The reporter's scornful tone, use of the

Latin phrase "genus homo," and dubious references to the pedants' disdain for "civilization" and its pleasures reveals his resentment towards the intellectual establishment the professors represent. Wallace conceives of his own social "experiment" as a counter to the experts' scientific methods, a way of demystifying the aura conferred on their objects and methods of study.

It soon becomes apparent that exposing the allegedly untainted Ishi to "the contaminating influences of civilization" was the reporter's express intention. He gleefully takes responsibility for having blemished the innocence of "the primordial savage of the stone age" by "inveigling him into the tinseled ambush of the temple of music and folly," where he deliberately staged Ishi's first encounter with "the silvery voiced and fascinating Orpheum headliner, Lily Lena of the London music halls." As Lena sang directly to Ishi, Wallace observed: "[T]he cold sweat was standing out on Ishi's forehead. His face was drawn. His fingers, grasping the crimson hangings, trembled visibly and his first cigar, which he had been puffing with pretended sangfroid, now slowly grew cold and dropped from his teeth." Making a crude and obvious equation of Ishi's virility with the suddenly extinguished cigar, Wallace enjoys the wild man's discomfort at the sight of a white woman and explains that Ishi thought he was in heaven: "Poor, simple-minded wild man! He could not know that the heaven of white people is never likely to be so crowded as their vaudeville houses, nor that so far there never has been half the scramble to get through the pearly gates that there is every night to get a front seat at the Orpheum's top gallery." The wild man's potentially threatening sexual desire is contained by his complete captivity to Lena's charms. His awestruck ignorance becomes an occasion to celebrate the sophistication and urbanity of the modern audience and to insult the professional anthropologists' stodgy intellectualism.

The importance of this meeting is illustrated by a large graphic that dominates the page, accompanied by a caption that reads: "Sketch of the Meeting of Ishi and Lily Lena. He is Shown in the Costume He Likes Best and She in the Costume the Audience Likes Best" (figure 11). The man in the sketch looks nothing like Ishi but fits perfectly the stereotype of the freakish wild man of sideshows and dime museums. The contrast between the two figures borrows one of the freak show's favorite visual strategies, the juxtaposition of opposites. Their meeting mobilizes a predictable fantasy about the dark-skinned savage's innate attraction to white women. Similar fantasies appeared in the stories of Ota Benga, who aroused concerns about his potential for sexual aggression. But in place of the African man's irrepressible lust, the Indian wild man grows weak and docile when confronted by the white woman's charms.[55] Under the illustrator's pen, the evening's events are

FIGURE 11. This sketch accompanied stories by Grant Wallace and Alfred Kroeber about Ishi's evening at the Orpheum Theater. The caption reads, "Sketch of the Meeting of Ishi and Lily Lena. He is Shown in the Costume He Likes Best and She in the Costume the Audience Likes Best." The image and caption emphasize the disparity between the untutored savage and the white woman, whose entire being is given over to pleasing her civilized audience. Courtesy Phoebe Apperson Hearst Museum of Anthropology and the Regents of the University of California.

transformed into an allegory in which the man of the wilderness is enthralled by the powerful, decadent allure of civilization, embodied in the figure of a woman who is white in both name and appearance.

Reporters and anthropologists alike adopted the position of ethnographic observers to watch Ishi's reception of the show and debate its significance. While Wallace emphasizes Ishi's freakishness through a series of predictable binaries—savage/civilized, dark/light, childlike/complex, innocent/corrupt, natural/urbane—Kroeber's response, printed on the same page, underscores the utter difference of Ishi's cultural orientation. Merging his own distaste for Wallace's scheme with a genuine effort to imagine the effects of the vaudeville spectacle on someone who had never before seen more than fifty people together in one place, the anthropologist insists that while Ishi was indeed awed by the size of the crowd, "the performance itself I am sure he did not appreciate." Kroeber's intention is not to criticize Ishi's taste, but the newsman's inaccurate assessment of Ishi's experience of the evening. "The reporter got his story," Kroeber wrote acerbically in a subsequent account, "but he got it out of his imagination."[56] What Wallace took to be delighted laughter at the antics onstage was, according to Kroeber, "simply the physiological effect of the crowd upon him. His high unnatural giggle is like that of a young girl and does not necessarily signify that any appeal is made to his sense of humor." If Wallace saw the rapidly extinguished cigar as a weak phallic symbol, Kroeber explains that Ishi's laugh is like "a young girl" and not a full-grown man because it is the expression of hysterical symptoms resulting from exposure to the crowd. With the demeanor of a savage and the giggle of a young girl, Ishi is a freak indeed. However a few lines later Kroeber reconfirms Ishi's manhood by asserting that "there is nothing undeveloped about him; he has the mind of a man and is a man in every sense. With the exception of the habits which he has acquired by his manner of living he is thoroughly normal."[57] Deviating significantly from Wallace's description of Ishi's effeminacy, these comments about the Indian's manhood reinforce, by association, the manhood of the anthropologist who accompanied him in the face of stories that depicted the scientists as fussy, overcivilized pedants.

Kroeber's defensiveness must be understood as the byproduct of his efforts to separate the goals and methods of anthropological study from popular forms of ethnographic inquiry. If the difference between the two was clear to the first generation of professional academics and curators, it was less so to the nonspecialized public confronted by many different sources of information about Native Americans, each represented as true and accurate. In his history of the Smithsonian, where ethnography first received institutional status, Curtis Hinsley observes that "anthropology presented an unusual opportunity for making a science, for drawing a clear line between speculative popularization or commercial humbuggery, and the sober search for truth."[58] The establishment of American anthropology in museums and universities necessitated a break with earlier modes of presenting primitive people and artifacts as freakish curiosities. Anthropology museums sought to distinguish themselves from the Barnumesque mode by emphasizing didacticism over entertainment, replacing the jumble of the private collection with organizational logic, and demanding new standards of decorum and seriousness from the visitor. Ishi appeared at a moment when the function and organization of the anthropology museum was in flux. The University of California had determined the need for both a museum and department of anthropology less than a decade before his arrival. Conceived under the auspices of wealthy regent Phoebe Apperson Hearst, the museum was intended to house the vast personal collection of antiquities that she planned to donate to the university. The new museum, established in Parnassus Heights, San Francisco, opened to the public two months after Ishi took up his residence there in 1911.[59] His presence at the opening reception, where he mingled shyly among benefactors, university regents, scientists, and academics, attested to a unique and contradictory relationship between the anthropology museum and the human subjects of ethnographic inquiry. Was he a guest or an artifact? Would he assimilate to the new environment or remain a freakish outsider?

In the face of sensationalistic newspaper accounts, eager crowds, and a deluge of requests from showmen and entrepreneurs who wanted to exhibit Ishi as a human prodigy, anthropologists encouraged him to assimilate by learning English and working for a living. While popular interest in Ishi stemmed from his status as a "curiosity" on the order of a sideshow freak, anthropologists understood him as a unique source of knowledge about a dying culture. In keeping with the almost exclusive emphasis of U.S. anthropology on Native American cultures, Ishi was of far greater ethnographic interest than Ota Benga, whose treatment by scientists seemed only to confirm previously held racial biases about the Pygmies' intractable savagery. The men charged with Ishi's care belonged to a generation that represented significant new developments within the discipline of American anthropology.[60] Kroeber was a student of Franz Boas, an advocate of racial equality who was responsible for bringing the concept of cultural relativism to ethnographic inquiry. As Carl Degler explains, Boas overturned the reigning belief in social evolution, which "held that human groups, or races, passed through a series of stages: from savagery to barbarism and culminating in civilization."[61] Like his mentor, Kroeber rejected the distinctions between savagery and civilization made by European colonial anthropology and echoed in American popular culture, insisting instead that Ishi was the mental and physical peer of his white counterparts.

However, far from overturning popular fantasies with empirical fact, anthropologists created another version of Ishi that corresponded to their own desire for an "authentic" precontact native specimen and turned him into a freak of a different nature.[62] If the popular belief in the Indian's absolute Otherness is encapsulated in the sketch of Ishi and Lena, the anthropologist's intense identification with his subject is captured in a photograph of Ishi and Kroeber (figure 12). A visual representation of the intimacy between the two, this image also illustrates Kroeber's attempt to prove Ishi's "normality" through sartorial means. But the differences between these men belie the more immediate parallelism, for the pale, bearded anthropologist who stands tall with his suit and tie neatly in place clearly is not a double for the shorter, broader, barefoot Ishi, who appears disheveled and uncomfortable in his civilized garb. Ishi is no more "normal" dressed in a suit and

FIGURE 12. Unlike the dramatic opposition between Ishi and the white woman, this photograph of Ishi and Alfred Kroeber indicates the intense identification of the anthropologist with his subject. But superficial similarities only amplify the obvious differences between the younger white man and the aging Yahi. Courtesy Phoebe Apperson Hearst Museum of Anthropology and the Regents of the University of California.

tie than he is swathed in a caveman's furs. Efforts to assimilate him often only further emphasized how alien he was in the modern environment. Instead of showing his equivalence with American men, the photograph suggests the limits of his adaptability to the new culture. The image thus inadvertently mirrors a convention of freak photography in which the pairing of showman and native highlights the contrast between savagery and civilization. Its contradictions are evidence of

Ishi's freakish, indeterminate status as both friend and informant, visitor and captive of a world that had unwittingly cut him off from his own past.

Anthropologists played an important role in shaping popular understandings of Ishi as a perfect, but untutored natural man. Rather than dispelling the myth that Ishi was a "Stone Age" relic, Kroeber's writing for mainstream publications grants it legitimacy with the objective language of science. Claiming that "in short [Ishi] has really lived in the stone age, as has so often been said," Kroeber seems to associate cultural difference with temporal distance, positioning the native as a stranded outcast from history. Read in context, "stone age" refers to the Yahis' rudimentary tools; however, Kroeber's choice of words lends expert authority to the impression created by the newspaper coverage, which depicts Ishi as a relic of an earlier stage of human evolution. The anthropologist quickly warns against such popular misunderstanding by writing sternly, "Ishi himself is no nearer the 'missing link' or any antecedent form of human life than we are; but in what his environment, his associates, and his puny native civilization have made him, he represents a stage through which our ancestors passed thousands of years ago."[63] Disputing the misguided equation between Ishi and the fictitious missing links of freak shows and dime museums, Kroeber asserts Ishi's fundamental equality with his Anglo-American contemporaries. This point reflects the evolution of Kroeber's thinking during this time. Extending the work of Boas, Kroeber was just beginning to formulate one of his most important contributions to the field of anthropology, the decoupling of culture from biology. By insisting that Ishi's differences were social and historical, not physiological, he illustrates his conviction that human physiology was not the proper subject of anthropology.[64] But by enforcing Ishi's biological equality, Kroeber appears to dismiss his culture as a "puny native civilization," giving voice to the same theory of cultural evolution as the newspapers by confirming that the Yahi represented a more primitive version of Western civilization.

In a case that involved the complexities and idiosyncrasies of a living person, the anthropologist's methods proved little better equipped than the showman's to script the encounter between primitivism and modernity. Indeed, one of the consistent features of the varied instances of freak making traced out in this book are the unexpected and often productive ways in which the relationship between the anomalous and the normal may break down. For example, Kroeber was dismayed when Ishi discovered that glue was an indispensable tool in making arrows, for the anthropologist believed that the authenticity of Yahi artifacts would be contaminated by the introduction of new resources. He was uncomfortable displaying Ishi's work in the museum because the purpose of museums, as he saw it, was to preserve artifacts of historically and geographically remote cultures. The modern could not, by definition, be eligible for inclusion within the museum's collections, and, in turn, the subjects of ethnography had to remain permanently excluded from modernity. But in fact, the wild Indian knew nothing of authenticity. An alleged man of nature, Ishi loved doughnuts and flushing toilets. He was more impressed by a retractable window shade than skyscrapers and airplanes. Many Yahi artifacts reflect a creative melding of traditional methods to include materials discarded by settlers such as string, cloth, glass, and even a denim hat. The objects made by Ishi reveal the innovation and adaptability of a culture that was not trapped in the Stone Age, but living alongside that of the anthropologists. In the fragments of his life that survive, Ishi is less a freakish relic to be deciphered by a scientist's knowing gaze or the speechless primordial savage of popular accounts, than an active participant in the recreation of his own past.

If Ishi seemed to provide anthropologists with a unique opportunity to study a vanishing culture, he represented an untainted physical specimen to a man devoted to the science of human biology. The writings of his doctor and friend Saxton Pope often seem inspired as much by his romantic views of the Indian as any empirical evidence, for Ishi was expected to embody a physical perfection unavailable to his more civilized male counterparts.[65] Pope's medical records enthuse, "[Ishi's] stature is magnificent. Although he has lost the typical Indian litheness, there is grace and strength in every contour. For a year he was absolutely perfect."[66] Pope describes Ishi's foot as "a beautiful example of what the human foot should be" and his fingers as "gracefully tapered, pleasing in shape, with fingernails olivoid [sic] in outline, perfect in texture."[67] Echoing Pope's praise, Waterman adds that Ishi's feet "were modeled in plaster by the Department of Pediatrics of the Medical School as examples of perfect and undeformed feet."[68] A dentist who studied at the university during Ishi's stay there recalls that dental students "paid Ishi 50 cents to allow [them] to make a plaster cast of his mouth. In over 60 years of dental practice Ishi's was the most perfect mouth I ever saw."[69] The word *perfect* appears in each of these descriptions of Ishi's physique, lending weight to the idea that he was not a normal man but a freak, a rare, untarnished human specimen whose body became a cipher for contradictory beliefs about the Indian. Although more often negative than positive, the meaning of freaks is always in excess of the body itself, which is treated as a sign requiring reading and interpretation. In this case, Ishi's perfection hearkened back to a time when human society had a more harmonious connection to nature; his fatal illness spoke of the costs of progress.

In the same way that Verner longed to embark on further travels with his African friend, Saxton Pope would later recall his relationship with Ishi using the romanticized terms of the male bonding narrative: "I learned to love Ishi as a brother, and he looked upon me as one of his people. He called me Ku Wi, or Medicine Man, more, perhaps, because I could perform little sleight of hand tricks, than because of my profession."[70] In this nostalgic memory of masculine intimacy, social and racial differences vanish in the mutual love of the Indian and the white doctor.[71] As Robyn Wiegman has argued, the idealistic interracial male bonding scenario erases racial difference, and the inequalities that accompany it, in favor of "the masculine same, a sameness unrelenting in its extrapolation of the white man's heroic alienation, compassion, and guilt."[72] Despite the scientist's claim to objectivity, literary convention shaped the contours of the interaction with his informant. As I have argued, this fantasy of sameness coexisted alongside the fiction of the wild Indian's irreconcilable difference. In the stories of both Ishi and Ota Benga, personal friendship was the palliative to the white man's guilt and the native's tragic encounter with civilization was met by regret and longing for a lost intimacy. But Pope points to the limits of this idealized brotherhood when he proposes that Ishi recognized his curative powers on the basis of magic tricks rather than academic credentials. Whereas the doctor believed Ishi had accepted him as one of his own, he also considered his friend incapable of understanding the nature of modern scientific training. In other words, Pope could become an Indian but Ishi, a primitive trapped in the past, could never grasp the sophisticated nuances of the doctor's professional identity or specialized knowledge.

Ishi confirmed his status as a vanishing Indian by his inability to withstand the debilitating effects of the modern city. Once held up as the embodiment of physical perfection, within four years he was dead of tuberculosis. The anthropologists themselves believed they had hastened his death by working him long hours in their eagerness to extract information before he reached this inevitable end. Popular accounts of his demise, like those of Ota Benga's suicide, concurred, holding the cold, inhumane methods of science responsible for killing off its objects of study. The scant newspaper coverage of Ishi's death, subdued in comparison to the explosion of stories surrounding his appearance, reveals a persistent resentment towards the university faculty.[73] Rekindling the animosity between scientists and popular culture of previous accounts, the journalists charge the professors with sensationalism, while downplaying their own initial interest in the story. Science was to blame for turning the Indian into a curious object and then examining him to death. "He furnished amusement and study to the savants at the University of California for a number of years, and doubtless much of Indian lore was learned from him," one reporter reflects dubiously, "but we do not believe he was the marvel that the professors would have the public believe. He was just a starved-out Indian from the wilds of Deer Creek who, by hiding in its fastness, was able to long escape the white man's pursuit."[74] Exaggerating the significance of their find, the anthropologists were little more than mountebanks who used their status as experts to swindle a gullible public and exploit their object of study. A second article reports suspiciously, "an alleged Stone Age man said to have been adopted by the University of California as a valuable acquisition has just died. To be used by a high-brow institution as an anthropological acquisition is enough to kill any man."[75] Casting a dubious eye on Ishi's status as a survivor of the Stone Age, this piece accuses the museum of hastening his death. No person could withstand the misery of being turned into a "valuable acquisition." Ishi's demise was a consequence not of the innate frailty of his race, but his treatment as a scientific specimen, an abuse to which anyone might succumb. In its antagonism towards professional elites and the institutions that promoted their activities, the popular press reconfigures Ishi from a freakish relic to a person with common human desires and weaknesses.

In Ishi's transformation from Stone Age wild man to anthropologists' victim the process of making freaks is revealed. Freaks are produced not by their inherent differences from us, but by the way their particularities are figured as narratives of unique and intractable alterity. These fictions are not simply the sensationalistic products of exploitative showmen or crude public taste; they are equally the province of the erudite man of science. In the struggle to gain cultural authority and influence, newspapers, showmen, anthropologists, and doctors each sought to prove their ability to shape collective belief, confirming their own importance as the arbiters of public knowledge. What remains of Ishi is the result of these discursive conflicts, words that reveal more about the men who wrote them than about the man who could write only the name he was given by his white benefactors.[76]

The Experts Lose Their Mind

The public never knew of the final indignity Ishi endured. Against his express wishes, the doctors at the university performed an autopsy, making a customary Yahi burial impossible. Despite the professed intimacy between scientist and Indian, the interests of medical curiosity prevailed over the subject's own dying request that his body remain intact.[77] The powerful allure of the freak's body is capable of obliterating all claims to humanity, even in death. As Rosemarie Thomson writes, "extraordinary bodies have been so compelling—so valuable—as bodies throughout human history that whether they were alive or dead had little consequence."[78] Often, the freak's skeleton or corpse was preserved for exhibitions that attracted as many crowds as the living person.[79] To escape the clutches of enterprising grave robbers, the families of freaks such as Chang and Eng and the giant Robert Wadlow took elaborate measures to protect their bodies after burial. Ishi's body was cremated, but his brain was stored for further scientific examination in the Smithsonian archives, where it was lost among other Indian remains. It is an appropriately gruesome modern detail that scientists, disregarding Native American tradition, separated mind and body, relinquishing the corpse to its earthly origins while preserving the organ of intellect and subjectivity.

In February 1999, yet another chapter of Ishi's afterlife unfolded when the brain was found by a new generation of scientists. The misplacement of Ishi's remains provides further evidence of the scientists' professional fallibility. Claiming mastery through the organization and storage of knowledge, the experts' authority is unsettled when the object of study becomes lost in the archive. Newspaper coverage of the brain's reappearance reflects both dramatic changes in our understanding of the history of Native Americans and a continued desire to preserve Ishi as a unique survivor, the last of his tribe. "To put Ishi back together, to get his remains back will be something that people will feel good about. . . . It will give us a sense of healing, a sense of control," commented Larry Meyer, director of the California Native American Heritage Commission. At the same time, it is doubtful that this perceived wholeness of the body can bring closure to Ishi's story, which fits too perfectly the dense mythology of the Vanishing Indian so important to national self-understanding.

In the decades that followed the deaths of Ishi and Ota Benga, freak shows would disperse to the cultural margins, becoming a disreputable but stubbornly persistent form of entertainment. Reliant on a steady flow of ever more extraordinary bodies, sideshow managers found it increasingly difficult to procure new and sensational aberrations as the twentieth century wore on. But more importantly, the expert won out over the showman in gaining the authority to determine the future of the sideshow's former occupants. As physical disability became the province of medical pathology, bodies once described as wonders of nature were reconceived in terms of disease. As anthropologists developed more specialized methods and the notion of cultural relativism became more pervasive, the exhibition of non-Western people as ethnographic freaks was less tolerable. Freak shows were sleazy arenas of exploitation and bad taste, relegated to small towns and bad neighborhoods where they would be patronized by audiences only slightly less marginal than the carnies themselves.

This chapter has revisited a moment when the life sciences, entertainment, and educational enterprises conspired to turn two visitors from other cultures into freaks. Understanding these men as rare objects, sole survivors, the last of their race, gave legitimacy to their placement in the museum, the world's fair, a cage at the zoo. Anxieties about the changing complexion of U.S. citizens and the professional's growing distance from the layperson were reconfigured as debates over the proper treatment and exhibition of these uncommon specimens. Under the penetrating gaze of audiences, scientists, and showmen, their histories and customs were interpreted according to narratives already formed in large part by prevalent beliefs about the African and the Indian. As those beliefs were recycled, they helped transform a diverse public into Americans who defined their incorporation into the national body against the isolate figure of the racial freak. Freaks are rarely allowed to speak for themselves; when they do it is best to listen. We may learn something, since those who pass as freaks inevitably tell us more about ourselves than about that which is radically Other to us. Ota Benga and Ishi both spoke in a language of words and gestures that was often reincorporated into racial stereotypes, but that sometimes consisted of rare, unpredictable responses to the new world that surrounded them. We should not be overly romantic about these gestures, but neither should we see these strangers only as passive victims, abused and then killed off by the world they voluntarily chose to enter. The widely divergent modes of reception and description that accompanied the arrival of these uncommonly brave travelers, whose journeys briefly intersected with the stirrings of modernity in the United States, tell us about the limits of our own understanding, and the conflicts engendered by the awareness of those limitations.

This chapter closes not only with the departure of these visitors, but with an increasing divergence in the paths of the professional life sciences, the entertainment industry, and the sources of educational and moral instruction. Rather than the conclusion, this is only the beginning of our story. Abandoned by anthropologists, doctors, and proprietors of respectable theatrical establishments, human curiosities increasingly populate the imaginative productions of authors and visual artists in the United States. Their recollections of the thrill and terror of the freak show endure in the canon of American arts and letters, as well as less reputable forms of representation. For those who aspire to intellectual and aesthetic activity, the charge seems to come as much from tarrying in the lowest, most abject zones of popular culture as it does from the alterity of the body exhibited as a freak. Ishi's own favored mode of departure is fitting here, for his good-byes were often accompanied by the statement, "You stay, I go."[80] Freaks are inherently mutable and slippery creatures who make our profoundest fears and desires legible on the surfaces of their bodies. They do come and go, their arrival typically greeted with far more sensationalistic fanfare than their departure. When they go, we are left with the capacities of imagination and memory to conjure up new freaks to replace those who have left us behind. It is hoped that we also learn something of the terrible weight of such fantasy projections on those who unwittingly come to bear them. The representations considered in subsequent chapters suggest the power and limitations of that learning process.

FIGURE 13. Tod Browning, director of *Freaks* (1932). *Freaks* © 1932 Turner Entertainment Co. A Time Warner Company. All rights reserved.

During the shooting of Tod Browning's *Freaks,* a drunken F. Scott Fitzgerald, working at the time as a screenwriter for MGM, found himself sharing a table in the commissary with two of its featured actors, the conjoined twins Daisy and Violet Hilton. Just as he sat down to order lunch, "one of them picked up the menu, and, without even looking at the other, asked, 'What are you going to have?'"[1] This banal question, turned extraordinary by the fact that the interlocutor shared a body with the recipient, proved too much for the author, who immediately rushed outside to vomit.[2] It is not surprising that Fitzgerald, a writer whose life and fiction were marked by persistent class anxiety, would object to the intrusion of an el-

60

ement associated with the lowest forms of popular entertainment, the carnival freak show, into his personal space.[3] In contrast to the confusions described in the previous chapter, where visitors applied the freak show's interpretive modes to human exhibits in the zoo and museum, in this case the freak show imposed itself on unwitting bystanders. Fitzgerald's visceral reaction to the twins was echoed by others on the MGM lot, who shared his disgust at the presence of freaks in the commissary of a studio known for its slick, glamorous productions. Indeed, given the entire cast, which included midgets, pinheads, two women without arms, a man without legs, a man with neither arms nor legs, and a bearded lady, the petite and fetching Hilton sisters may have been among its less shocking luncheon companions. So disturbing was the prospect of sharing a meal with the freaks that they had to be assigned to a special table outside (figure 14). The response of the MGM staff prefigured the reception of *Freaks* by American audiences, whose outrage was captured by one reviewer's description of the film as "a catalogue of horrors,

FIGURE 14. The cast of Tod Browning's *Freaks* eating outside at a table on the MGM lot following their expulsion from the studio commissary. Compare this relatively peaceful gathering with figure 17, the still of the raucous wedding banquet scene that takes place in the film. *Freaks* © 1932 Turner Entertainment Co. A Time Warner Company. All rights reserved.

ticketed and labeled, dragged out into the sunlight before the camera to be photographed against whatever background happens to be handy."[4] Public outcry
against the film was so vehement that it had to be pulled from circulation at considerable financial cost to MGM.[5] Stunned by the negative reaction to *Freaks,*
Browning never recovered from his failure and, after making several less controversial films, became a recluse and renounced the career that had made him a fortune, declaring to a friend, "I wouldn't walk across the street now to see a movie."[6]

Freaks, loosely based on the short story "Spurs" by Tod Robbins, takes place
behind the scenes at a low-budget traveling circus, where Hans (Harry Earles), a
midget, falls in love with a big woman, a trapeze artist named Cleopatra (Olga Baclanova). Initially amused by the midget's interest, Cleo begins to take him seriously once she learns that Hans has come into a large inheritance, with which he
intends to finance his retirement from circus life and marriage to his fiancée,
Frieda (Daisy Earles). With Hercules (Henry Victor), the circus strongman, Cleo
plots to wed Hans, poison him, and inherit his money. In response to her advances, the lovestruck Hans breaks off the engagement with Frieda and proposes
to Cleo, who eagerly accepts. Their union is celebrated at a carnivalesque wedding feast that turns ugly when the freaks chant their acceptance of the new bride
as "one of us." She reacts by turning on them in horror, calling them "filthy, slimy
FREAKS."[7] When Hans falls ill after the wedding, the freaks, who are already sus-
picious of Cleo's intentions, learn of her scheme. Following their own code of justice—"offend one and you offend them all"—they plot their revenge against the
two big people. The film ends after the freaks have enacted a grisly retribution by
murdering Hercules and transforming Cleo into a pathetic, feathered creature
who is half chicken, half woman. Frieda is reunited with Hans when, in the company of their sympathetic friends, Venus (Leila Hyams) and Phroso (Wallace
Ford), she visits the mansion where he has retired to nurse his broken heart.

Reactions to the film must be understood historically, as its reception
changed dramatically between the moment of its initial release in 1932 and its revival thirty years later. Browning had made his career in the 1920s by producing
films about characters who, through theft, deception, and murder, seek illegiti-
mate wealth while expressing deep-seated resentment against a moneyed elite.
As a result, he would seem an ideal spokesperson for the anxieties and desires of
Depression-era audiences. And *Freaks,* with its story of a midget punished for
his unearned riches and aristocratic pretensions, would appear to convey popular animosity towards class privilege during this time of economic deprivation.[8]
Yet the film was also made in the context of the sideshow's growing obsolescence,
in the face of the medicalization of disability and changing notions about re-

spectable entertainment. *Freaks'* dramatization of contemporary class antagonisms could not counteract the shocking effects of its severely disabled actors on
viewers who had recently witnessed the wounded veterans of the First World
War and were in the midst of financial collapse.[9] Moreover, at a moment when
extravagant musicals were among the most popular of film genres, the carnival
setting and characters of *Freaks* recalled too vividly the low origins of cinema in
storefront theaters and on the vaudeville circuit. Not only did it reanimate the
conventions of a mode of live entertainment many Americans were eager to
erase from cultural memory, it also explored the way that cinema could intensify
and prolong the experience of a live sideshow by bringing the freak off of the display platform and onto the screen.

Ironically, Browning's death in 1962 coincided with a revival of *Freaks,* which
screened at the Venice Film Festival and has attracted a devoted fandom ever
since. As a consequence of its re-release, almost all of the authors and artists who
appear in later chapters of this study cite Browning's film as the inspiration for
their own thinking about freaks. Leslie Fiedler described his scholarly work
Freaks: Myths and Images of the Secret Self as "a belated tribute to that great director and his truly astonishing film."[10] Diane Arbus was transfixed by the experience of watching an art house revival of *Freaks* and returned to view the film again
and again during the same period that she began her haunting photographic documentation of social marginality. Katherine Dunn's *Geek Love,* which Skal and
Savada describe as "a knowingly postmodern homage to Tod Browning's America," reanimates many of the film's most provocative questions about agency, sexuality, and collective identity.[11] Given this considerable chain of influences, the
film functions in this book not simply as another representation of freaks—for
there is indeed a growing cinematic tradition[12]—but as the foundational text
through which authors and artists in the twentieth century came to understand
the freak show. *Freaks* is not a documentary about sideshow culture, but it became a point of reference for all subsequent representations of that culture, ensuring that the freak show, as Browning envisioned it, remained a vivid aspect of
popular cultural memory. In other words, it is impossible to chart the course of
representations of the freak show in the twentieth century without considering
the enduring significance of Tod Browning, for better or for worse, the auteur par
excellence of freak cinema.

The following analysis of *Freaks* echoes many of the concerns introduced in
chapter 2, which explores what happens to freaks when they move outside the traditional confines of the sideshow, particularly the disturbances they cause in locations that would otherwise shun any association with carnival life. While movies

do not share the cultural prestige of an anthropology museum or even a zoological park, MGM was distinguished by the high quality of its cinematic product. The reaction of employees on the lot suggests how dramatically Browning's film departed from the studio's usual fare. This chapter will argue that *Freaks* makes an explicit formal and thematic link between the medium of film and the freak show. Although both movies and freak shows are forms of popular culture, by 1932 one was an ascendant medium with aspirations to aesthetic value, whereas the other was a residual form that threatened to drag film back to its unglamorous beginnings.[13]

Freaks is significant because, in looking back at modes of popular entertainment on the decline by the 1930s, it reanimates the figure of the freak and the culture of the freak show for a new generation of American audiences. Grappling with the transition from live entertainment to screen, *Freaks* probes the capacity of film to alter perception. Whereas the classic freak show could exploit and dehumanize, the film guides its viewers towards a more sympathetic approach to the disabled body. In contrast to the chaste figures of Ishi and Ota Benga, Browning's cinematic sideshow provides an environment rich with polymorphously perverse sexuality, where a proliferation of erotic proclivities coexist, partners are exchanged, and heterosexuality is one among many options. Ultimately, though, this explosion of sexualities is countered by the sexual propriety of the midget couple, Hans and Frieda, whose perspective increasingly dominates the narrative. It is no accident that the position of moral authority is upheld by a pair of little people, who are the literal embodiment of petite bourgeois conservatism. Although *Freaks* closes by endorsing the more normative perspective of Hans and Frieda, it cannot allow them a happy conclusion. The pair may be reconciled and Hans's fortune restored, but he seems incapable of recovering his vanquished masculinity. In the end, it is hard to say which of the film's wounded characters are the victims, which the antagonists. A multivalent and contradictory narrative, *Freaks*' protean qualities offered varied points of identification to the authors, artists, and critics who would take it as inspiration.

Freaks and the "Cinema of Attractions"
Although it has often screened on the art house circuit, *Freaks* is commonly dismissed as formally uninventive by critics who describe the unusual bodies of the actors as its only real claim to distinction. What they fail to recognize is that the film also pays knowing homage to a medley of historical genres, skillfully putting a variety of formal and narrative conventions to different effects.[14] Structurally, it is a hybrid monster that yokes together elements of the live performance of circus

and carnival, early cinema, as well as later innovations in editing and camera work. As such, *Freaks* seems to be seeking a structure appropriate for showcasing the talents of its freak stars. Formally, it recalls film's origins in earlier modes of entertainment such as the sideshow and vaudeville. Yet at the same time, it makes problematic the kind of looking that such spectacles encouraged by experimenting with the camera's ability to manipulate perspective.

That a circus is the mise-en-scène for Browning's most memorable work is unsurprising, since he often recalled his youthful experiences as a carnival performer as a source of inspiration for his films. As a boy, he ran away from home to join a traveling show, inaugurating a varied career that included work as a spieler for a "Wild Man of Borneo" act, an escape artist, a clown, a contortionist, a blackface comedian, a ringmaster, as well as a live burial in a stunt called the Hypnotic Living Corpse.[15] If Browning himself claimed the influence of show business on the *content* of his films, it also had a *formal* impact, for *Freaks* retains the fragmented structure and playful reversals of illusion and reality of the ten-in-one.

The first half of *Freaks* resists many of the conventions that bring continuity to narrative film, evoking instead the episodic feeling of the circus sideshow. The freaks, as well as many of the nondisabled performers, are introduced by a series of vignettes, which demonstrate their talents and personalities but make little effort to unify the characters through a common storyline. "Circus Slang Gives Picture Local Color" proclaims one of the film's pressbook articles, making reference to the use of authentic sideshow jargon, as well as the fact that "freaks from sideshows all over America played principle roles, and the setting and 'props,' actual circus material, were handled by circus people." Many of the initial appearances take place within a circle of carnival wagons, which is a backstage version of the circus ring. One by one, characters such as Josephine-Joseph, the Half Man–Half Woman, the conjoined twins Daisy and Violet (figure 15), and the Half-Boy Johnny Eck emerge into this space, in a manner more reminiscent of a variety show than a narrative film. Stage and screen identities are blurred as each character goes by the same name they use in their live performances. Many of the early scenes were added to the original script as Browning became fascinated with the performers' remarkable abilities and sought excuses for working them into the diegesis. These seemingly incidental episodes alternate with the more conventional romantic plot involving two couples, Venus and Phroso and the midgets, Hans and Frieda.

The film's fragmented structure not only replicates the conventions of the live entertainment it depicts, but recalls the "primitive" films produced before 1906–1907 that Tom Gunning has called "the cinema of attractions." Direct

FIGURE 15. Publicity still of the conjoined twins Daisy and Violet Hilton (who play themselves in Browning's film) standing inside the circle of carnival wagons. This space backstage is a counterpart to the ring where the circus folk conduct their public performances. *Freaks* © 1932 Turner Entertainment Co. A Time Warner Company. All rights reserved.

descendants of the circus and the carnival, these early films, Gunning writes, "related more to the attractions of the fairground than to the traditions of legitimate theater. The relation between films and the emergence of the great amusement parks, such as Coney Island, at the turn of the century provides a rich ground for rethinking the roots of early cinema."[16] Gunning's insight is significant because it locates the origins of the film industry in precisely the venues that provide the setting for *Freaks*. Many of the initial sequences are short, nonnarrative episodes shot with a relatively static camera that seem to gesture back to the film's cinematic precursors. Form follows content as *Freaks* recalls the cinema's emergence in amusement parks, fairgrounds, and vaudeville.

According to Gunning, the first films screened during variety shows composed primarily of live performances. Borrowing material from circus and stage, early cinema frequently portrayed acrobatic acts, contortionists and exotic dancers, trained elephants, and clowns. As Gunning explains, the short films were introduced with speeches much like the spiel of a sideshow barker, who "builds an atmosphere of expectation, a pronounced curiosity leavened with anxiety as he stresses the novelty and astonishing properties which the attraction about to be revealed will posses."[17] Aesthetically, these shorts tended towards the grotesque or sensationalistic, consciously resisting the "orthodox identification of viewing pleasure with the contemplation of beauty" of a more traditional mode of spectatorship.[18] Relying on surprise and amazement, the cinema of attractions used spectacle to stimulate the viewer instead of attempting to draw her in through identification with the characters, as would become typical of classic narrative film.[19]

Like the cinema of attractions, early portions of *Freaks* are characterized by an aesthetic of spectacle that is only heightened by the stiff, self-conscious performances of many of the disabled actors. These performers do not "act" in traditional ways; their wooden delivery subverts the conventions of classic Hollywood cinema by preventing the spectator from becoming absorbed in the drama. There is hardly a moment in *Freaks* when we can forget that we are watching actors speak their lines, for we are all too conscious of the awkward gap between person and screen persona. Moreover, the narrative itself seems contrived, even by its own terms: the bodies of the actors engaged in the motions of daily life are more fascinating than the thin story of love and vengeance that makes a flimsy pretext for gathering them together. Rather than a driving force, plot becomes incidental to the talents of the film's stars. Yet there is a certain poignancy in their limited thespian abilities. According to Skal, many of the disabled actors shared mainstream America's admiration for the glamorous world of Hollywood.[20] They aspired to be professional actors, not professional freaks.[21] Insofar as most of them are playing themselves in the film—or at least performing the same roles they played in the freak show—*Freaks* is structured to reproduce, not counteract, the sideshow's transformation of bodily difference into freakish spectacle.

The live freak show, like primitive cinema, relies on curiosity to thrill and entertain its audience, discouraging any substantive interaction between viewer and performer. Curious looking enables the paying customer to see the freak as an object on display for the sole purpose of her amusement or education. As I argue throughout this study, the spectacular structure of live performance is often ruptured by the unexpected behavior of audience members or performers. But these interruptions are unintended and the sideshow's format—orchestrated by the spieler's authoritative monologue and the freak's silence—is designed to impede such contact. Despite his borrowing of the freak show's form and his unapologetic depiction of the film's characters as freaks, Browning makes an effort to transform the more negative aspects of looking at the disabled body that the spectacle invites. *Freaks* employs the structure of the freak show and the cinema of attractions, but works to dispel the initial shock that the unusual bodies of its protagonists might evoke, decoupling disability from freakishness by demanding a more engaged—and potentially sensitive—mode of viewing in the audience.

To this end, the film invokes and revises an even earlier cinematic precursor, the stop-motion photography of Eadweard Muybridge, in which multiple shots of the moving bodies of animals and humans reveal details imperceptible to the naked eye. Whereas most of Muybridge's subjects exhibit the dynamics of normative movement, one memorable sequence pictures a legless man propelling himself from a chair onto the floor.[22] This series suggests that curiosity about the disabled body in motion is encoded within the earliest attempts to capture the human form on film. The desire to stare, which is the primary impulse behind the freak show, is addressed by these images. But Muybridge's disabled man is hardly a freak, for his minimal surroundings lack the sensational context that would define him as such. By showing the disabled body engaged in the activities of daily life, Browning hearkens back to the Muybridge photographs. However, his purpose is somewhat different, for he is less interested in movement itself than in experimenting with the cinema's power to alter viewers' understanding of the human body. Rather than using the camera to further degrade the disabled actor, as some negative reviews suggested, *Freaks* proves that film may be instrumental in creating greater tolerance to various kinds of difference.

For example, *Freaks* manipulates scale to demonstrate that size is relative rather than absolute. In the original script, a note that accompanies a scene of the midget couple in Hans's wagon attests to the screenwriters' concern with the relativity of scale: "[I]n these surroundings we become less conscious of them as midgets, because everything about them is in proportion to their size."[23] Similarly, Hans's first impression of Cleopatra is that "she is the most beautiful *big* woman I have ever seen." From his perspective, Cleo is not a "normal" woman but a big one, and the camera aligns the spectator's gaze with his point of view. As Susan Stewart has argued of the social construction of scale, "the miniature is a cultural product, the product of an eye performing certain operations, manipulating, and attending in certain ways to, the physical world."[24] *Freaks* calls attention to the power of the camera to alter the viewer's visual orientation by making size and proportion unfamiliar. Although others have argued that these machinations reverse the categories of freak and normal, the disruption is in fact more subtle, as it unmoors the possibility of such absolute categorical distinctions altogether: the "normal" is an elusive fiction, as is its abject byproduct, the "freak."[25]

Of course traditional freak shows also played with scale, but always in refer-

ence to the normality of the spectator. The viewer's assessment of the freaks onstage must be a comparative one in which she measures the prodigious body
against her own. Live freak shows enhance the bodily extremes of the performers
through contrasts of size (midget and giant), shape (skeleton and fat lady), and
skin color (black and white) that implicitly locate the audience as the standard
against which the abnormal is defined. By contrast, identification with moving images projected into a darkened theater is so intense that it is possible for the
viewer to forget about her own body. *Freaks* makes adjustments in scale to meet
the needs of its diminutive characters without providing a normative point of reference. By creating a context in which Hans and Frieda are not too small, the film
exploits the camera's exceptional ability to destabilize the notion of a proportional
norm, implying instead that bodies should be measured in relation to their environment. When this scale is disrupted by Cleo's presence in Hans's home, she appears to be a giant, her body too large to fit the space best suited to his needs.[26]

In addition to manipulations of scale, *Freaks* blurs the distinctions between
disabled and able-bodied performers in other ways, particularly through its depiction of everyday life. For example, an exchange that, in the film, takes place between Phroso, Venus, and Johnny Eck was originally scripted for the limbless
Randian, who was supposed to crawl towards the couple according to the following instructions: "Phroso and Venus are not startled. They treat Randian like a
normal human being throughout."[27] At another point, Frieda hangs her laundry
out to dry while Venus sews on the steps of her wagon. Although Frieda's wet
clothes appear tiny, they are not the focus of attention, which centers around a discussion of Hans's vulnerability to Cleo's seductions. In two scenes, the armless
ladies, Frances and Martha, eat and drink with their feet. Each is accompanied by
a companion who does not seem to notice this accommodation, as they converse
about some other topic. To treat one another like "normal human beings" is not
the same as to insist on a single standard of normalcy, as the screenwriters' direction might imply. As the film continues, a more normative perspective will pre-
dominate, subordinating the particularities of the body to a conventional system
of activities and social relations. But in the early scenes, "a normal human being"
is one who deserves friendship and respect for the very differences that could not
be tolerated outside of the circus community. These episodes aim to acclimate the
viewer to seeing the freaks as multidimensional, as individuals who have accom-
modated their disabilities by developing other ways of performing everyday activities. Their interests extend beyond the contours of their own extraordinary
bodies, and they require neither pity nor assistance from their more conventionally formed peers.

In this respect, the film's content differs dramatically from the short story on which it is based. "Spurs" represents freakishness as an absolute condition; even when offstage the characters continue to perform in ways that reduce their personhood to their dramatic personae. At the wedding feast, the snake charmer brings her animal charges to the table, and the juggler, M. Jejongle, tosses food, utensils, and dinnerware "although the whole company was heartily sick of his tricks."[28] In contrast to the film's version of the banquet, in which the freaks declare their solidarity and accept Cleo as "one of us," "Spurs" portrays them as "great egotists," so convinced of the superiority of their own talents that there is no possibility of community within the group, for "each one of these human oddities thought that he or she alone was responsible for the crowds that daily gathered at Copo's circus. . . . Their separate egos rattled angrily together, like so many pebbles in a bag. Here was gunpowder which needed only a spark."[29] The inebriated wedding guests begin to fight with each other, quickly descending into physical combat that is more animal than human until "every freak's hands, teeth, feet, were turned against the others. Above the shouts, screams, growls, and hisses of combat, Papa Copo's voice could be heard bellowing for peace."[30] "Spurs" thus reinforces the dominant logic of the freak show, which implies that the performers are less decent, well mannered, and sympathetic than the audience, and therefore deserving of their fate. Monstrous bodily surfaces correspond with monstrous interiority. Extreme corporeal difference is indicative of an egotistical individualism that makes community impossible. Although the action of "Spurs" takes place backstage, focusing on circus life beyond the display platform, it insists that the freak's character and motivations are delimited by the extraordinary contours of her body, whether she is onstage or off.

Browning and his scriptwriters rewrote Robbins's story to invest the freaks with an emotional complexity in excess of their onstage personae. Instead of a group of isolated egotists, backstage the carnies form a sympathetic and fiercely protective community. An early sequence of scenes in the first draft of the screenplay contains a key to understanding Browning's approach. The action begins in the French countryside, where a groundskeeper excitedly tells his master, Monsieur Duval, that he has just witnessed the horrifying sight of "monsters" trespassing on his land. Initially disgusted and outraged to find the freaks cavorting in a sunlit clearing, Duval changes his mind after conversation with Madame Tetrallini, the freaks' friend and caretaker:

MADAME TETRALLINI: Always in hot, stuffy tents—strange eyes always staring at them—never allowed to forget what they are. So you see, M'sieu, when I get a chance, I like to take them into the sunshine—and let them play like children. That is what most of them are—children.

DUVAL: Children—when I go to the circus again, I shall understand.

MT: I know M'sieu—you will remember seeing them playing—playing like children.

D: I shall always remember.

MT: Among all the thousands who come to stare—to laugh—to shudder— you will be one who understands.[31]

Positioned at the beginning of the film, this dialogue is clearly intended to instruct the viewer, as well as Monsieur Duval and his groundskeeper, about how to interpret the events that follow. While the notion that the freaks are innocent as "children" will be called into question as the narrative continues, the initial effect of this description is to dispel the stereotypical association of the disabled body with evil and monstrosity. Set in a pastoral environment away from the fairgrounds, this sequence aligns the freaks with a benevolent and peaceful landscape that contrasts markedly with the depiction of their corrupt "nature" in "Spurs." Moreover, their placement in that setting implicitly challenges the typical understanding of the freak's body as a mistake of "nature."

Several changes to this draft of the script work to undermine its original intentions. Because this scene occurs later in the final version of the film, its pedagogical function is diminished. It comes *after* the opening shot of an audience gazing in horror at something we cannot see, a revision that allows the spieler's voice-over to provoke a more sensationalistic initial reaction to the freak's body. The dialogue is also edited, maintaining the troubling references to the freaks as children, while eliminating the lesson about returning to the freak show with a more sympathetic understanding of the performers. The film's epigraph, added when distribution rights were sold to exploitation impresario Dwain Esper in the 1940s, only increases the confusion by describing the freaks as "mistakes of nature." Although the frame-up praises the accomplishments of "modern science" for "eliminating such blunders from the world," this was never a position endorsed by Browning's version of the story, which is uninterested in pathologizing the freaks by describing their conditions in medical terms. Instead, its critique is directed at the social context that discriminates against the disabled, turning them into targets of laughter or abuse.

Surveying the many mutations of this film gives a better sense of why the surviving version is so confusing and why it often seems to adopt contradictory positions towards its characters. In its extant form, we can see how the first half of

71

Freaks employs the formal structure of the freak show to exploit the talents of its performers, while at the same time attempting to alter the conventional association of disability with freakish monstrosity. Browning accomplishes this goal by using dialogue and mise-en-scène to take the film's characters literally and figuratively off of the freak show display platform, building a paradigm of reception into the narrative itself; by manipulating scale, proportion, and perspective to unsettle normative hierarchies of scale; and by showing the characters backstage engaged in the activities of daily life. The vibrancy of this life, and the uncommon intimacies it encourages, are most pronounced in the treatment of sexuality during the first half of the film.

Carnivalesque Sexualities

As I have argued, *Freaks* is less concerned with establishing the normality of its disabled characters than with subverting the notion of normative standards altogether, a commitment that is most apparent in the film's representation of sexual fantasies and acts. In the same way that its formal hybridity gives way to a more predictable narrative structure, *Freaks* begins by exploring a proliferation of sexual proclivities and ultimately closes down that multiplicity in favor of more standard heterosexual relations. Despite the fact that *Freaks* was released before the tightening of Production Code Administration regulations, changes from the original script chart the sanitization of the story in response to the demands of studio executives and conservative social groups. Nonetheless, the version that made it to the screen preserves a striking number of sexual innuendos, which link the extraordinary body to an array of erotic possibilities inconceivable for more typical cinematic characters. This linkage has the potential to become mere voyeuristic exploitation, but also can be seen as a recognition of the diverse range of erotic activities that step in when conventional sexual arrangements cease to be an option. Within the community of freaks, the heterosexual couple is not the dominant social configuration, but one of many varied expressions of desire and intimacy.

The first draft of the screenplay contains some surprisingly racy scenes that have no counterpart in Robbins's narrative. These perverse and sexually explicit descriptions are the inventions of screenwriters who would necessarily have had to imagine them not only as words on a page but realized in the flesh onscreen. For instance, in the original script the conflict between Venus and Hercules, which appears to have little motivation in the film, starts when the impoverished Hercules encourages Venus to become a prostitute to supplement the income from her legitimate job performing with trained seals. In this early version, the woman occupies a position akin to the freak in that her body functions as a commodity, desirable as much for its exchange value as any of the pleasures inherent in its possession. Venus's refusal aligns her with the disabled performers, who seek meaningful relationships to counteract the objectification they experience on the display platform.

Another instance of how more overt sexual references were muted in the transition from script to screen is a dialogue between Phroso the clown and the conjoined twins. In the film, this playful conversation reveals that when Phroso pinches Daisy, Violet can feel it. While the erotic resonances remain, Phroso's explicit curiosity about each twin's ability to experience the other's sexual pleasure is excised. (Before the film was cast, the twins in the script were named Rosie and Mamie.):

PHROSO: You know, there's one thing about your marriage that's got me puzzled. (Pinches Mamie.) Do you feel that, Rosie?
ROSIE: Yeah.
Phroso pats Mamie on the cheek and asks Rosie
P: Feel that?
R: Sure.
Phroso gets a kick out of this. The girls are still puzzled. Phroso becomes serious and asks Rosie
P: Rosie, what are you going to do tomorrow night after the wedding?
R: Why?
P: Oh, I thought we might step out—if you could get away.[32]

This dialogue derives its humor from the contrast between the twins' innocence and Phroso's knowing jokes about Mamie's impending marriage and, specifically, her wedding night. The conversation is overheard by Mamie's jealous fiancé, Roscoe, who plays a Roman lady during the evening show and is still wearing his feminine costume. Playfully amplifying the scene's sexual confusion, the scriptwriters added the stage direction—"Roscoe is standing indignantly twirling his false breasts." Roscoe's prosthetic bosom is suggestively linked to the inescapable presence of his sister-in-law's body, a feminine excess that may multiply and complicate the pleasures of marital sex. The image of a frustrated man in women's clothing watching the conjoined twins flirt with a clown is toned down in the film, as Roscoe has changed back into his more conventionally masculine dress by the time this exchange takes place.

The most salaciously voyeuristic moment in the script occurs soon after Mamie's marriage as the twins are making the bed which, presumably, they share with Roscoe. Their dress, which has not yet been fastened in the back, hangs open, and the direction to the camera reads, "as Roscoe goes on talking off-scene, we get a flash of where the Twins are joined together."[33] Shot in the bedroom, this scene draws attention to the erotic possibilities of the doubled female body by directing the camera's gaze at the physical site where one body merges with and separates from the other. The band of connective tissue is enticing because it is the specific source of the twins' exoticism, as well as a more general metonym for the many forbidden sites of erotic interest on the surface of the female body that cannot be shown on film. The conjoined female form here does not simply double the erotic possibilities, but multiplies them by providing previously unimaginable points of voyeuristic interest. In the Freudian terms so attractive to Browning, the forbidden peep at the point of connection might stand in for the taboo glimpse of the female genitalia, the site of lack that raises the specter of castration within the male viewer. This brief shot thus seems calculated to arouse intensely ambivalent feelings of sexual desire and anxiety. By the time it appears in the film, the twins' dress is demurely unbuttoned only at the neck, leaving the chance of glimpsing the most exotic and private of corporeal surfaces entirely to the imagination.

That sex is one of the primary ways freaks relate to one another in this narrative is emphasized in the climax of the script (and a lost, uncut version of the film), which implies that Hercules' punishment by the freaks was not death but castration. In the film, Hercules, who has been figuratively castrated by a knife wound to the thigh, crawls through the mud pursued by the vengeful freaks. Next, the film cuts to a terrified Cleo running through the darkened forest. The very literal significance of that editorial cut for events within the diegesis becomes clear in the script and the longer version of *Freaks* when Hercules reappears as a performer at Tetrallini's Freaks and Music Hall. Observing that Hercules is no longer a strong man, Madame Tetrallini remarks that he "has changed a lot": he has grown fat, wears the tuxedo of a dandy, and is singing "in a beautiful tenor voice."[34] Editing demanded by MGM executives required the replacement of castration with death, a conclusion inconsistent with Browning's usual themes. In particular, the films he directed with celebrated actor Lon Chaney repeatedly equate the loss of masculine power and potency with the loss of limbs (*The Black Bird,* 1926; *The Unknown,* 1927; *West of Zanzibar,* 1928) or voice (*The Unholy Three,* 1925).[35] It is more typical of Browning to revel in protracted experiences of male suffering, mutilation, and sexual rejection than to kill off his antagonists.

Despite the revisions demanded by Browning's superiors, the first half of *Freaks* retains numerous sexual innuendoes that imply a rich and varied erotic life among the circus performers. The initial appearance of the half man–half

woman, Josephine-Joseph, is hailed by the Rollo brothers, who usher the hermaphrodite in with a mocking parody of the spieler's banter: "Ah, ha! Just as they
are upon the banner you will see them inside! Living, breathing monstrosities,
Josephine-Joseph, Half-Woman–Half-Man." "Have a cigar, Joseph," one brother
quips with mock courtliness; "You dropped your lipstick, Josephine," says the
other. "Don't get *her* sore or *he'll* pop you in the nose," his brother responds.
Later, the hermaphrodite's physical ambiguity is connected to a multiple and potentially contradictory capacity for desire when Roscoe jokes to Hercules that
Josephine is attracted to him, while Joseph isn't.[36] The extreme anxiety this remark provokes in the hypermasculine Hercules is demonstrated when he punches
Josephine-Joseph in the face for spying on his amorous embrace with Cleo. The
hermaphrodite, who has no lines and no apparent narrative function, serves
throughout the early portions of the film as a figure of sexual indeterminacy who
lurks at the edges of the screen, deriving pleasure from watching the sexual exploits of others. In this, Josephine-Joseph is the character most closely aligned
with the film viewer's own perspective. If a certain kind of feminist film theory
argues that classic Hollywood cinema is dominated by a male gaze, *Freaks* subverts that convention by granting the hermaphrodite the position of voyeuristic
spectator.

   Freaks repeatedly flirts with representations of female desire and sexual pleasure. Having excised much of the suggestive dialogue between Phroso and the
conjoined twins, the film returns to the question of their shared sexual arousal
when Violet passionately kisses her new fiancé, Mr. Vadja, while Daisy stares off
into space with an ecstatic expression on her face. Although they have already said
as much, this scene provides visual confirmation that one twin is able to experience the other's erotic sensations. The most sexually aggressive character in the
film is Cleo, identified early on with the chicken woman she will eventually become. When Hercules visits her after breaking up with Venus, she offers him
some eggs and asks "How do you like them?" while pushing her bosom prominently into his line of sight. Understanding this question as an erotic double en-
tendre, Hercules gazes amorously at Cleo's breasts and grasps her in a passionate
embrace while the eggs sizzle on the stove.[37]

   Even the stilted relationship between Hans and Cleo recalls the perverse
eroticism that is frequently associated with the original freak medium. Often
freak show promoters concocted fantastic marriages between unlikely couples
such as fat ladies and skeletal men, dwarves and giants, or bearded women and
men.[38] Although couched in the chaste language of romantic love, these publicity
stunts implicitly raised questions about the sexual practices of the unusual pair.[39]

It is clear that, from Cleo's point of view, her relationship with Hans is a means to fame and profit: not only does she want his inheritance, but the enhanced career opportunities of such an uncommon partnership (figure 16). Cleo's aspirations are understandable within the logic of the sideshow, where the conventions of bourgeois romance are exploited for commercial value. But Hans, who vehemently resists the economy of the freak show, sees Cleo as "the most beautiful big woman in the world." With the greatest sincerity (which is hard not to read as comedy), he behaves as if he were in a different film altogether, a romance in which he plays a chivalric hero who defends her virginal beauty. This quaint and outdated understanding of love has no place in the bawdy culture of the circus. The dignified and deeply unironic Hans stands out because he endorses a normative heterosexuality that is at odds with the multiplicity of sexual options available inside the carnival gates.

Little Hans and His Big Woman

Freaks diverges both structurally and thematically from the exploration of carnivalesque sexualities when it turns to the story of Hans, who is torn between

FIGURE 16. This publicity photograph of Olga Baclanova (Cleo) and Harry Earles (Hans) exploits the extreme contrast between big woman and little man. Sitting stiffly with his tiny feet dangling in the air, Hans appears more child than romantic suitor. *Freaks* © 1932 Turner Entertainment Co. A Time Warner Company. All rights reserved.

Frieda's devotion and Cleo's sexual allure. In a sense, *Freaks* is two films that co-exist in uneasy juxtaposition: one, a racy, cinematic sideshow, the other, a straight-forward story of romance and vengeance that happens to be set at the circus. This duality explains the considerable critical disagreement over the film's generic classification.[40] According to one 1932 reviewer, "as a horror story, [*Freaks* is] either too horrible or not horrible enough, according to the viewpoint."[41] A more contemporary assessment concurs: "[I]f *Freaks* is not totally satisfying to audiences of today, that is perhaps due, for the most part, to the fundamental conflicts inherent in merging horror and social criticism."[42] These conflicts are built into the film's narrative, which, as I have argued, spends the first hour disabusing the spectator of the traditional association between disability and monstrosity, then climaxes by demonstrating the freaks' extreme capacity for violence. After establishing Hans as a sympathetic character who suffers unwarranted abuse, the spectacle of Cleo's body, mutilated at the hands of the freaks, leaves the viewer unsure about who is the victim and who the aggressor. *Freaks* is never decisive about whether it really wants to humanize its disabled protagonists or to tell a story of love and revenge with unconventional actors as its horrifying antagonists. If the love plot is one of many narrative possibilities during the first half of the film, it moves to the fore-ground in the second half. Moreover, the two parts of *Freaks* are characterized by the distinctive affective resonances of comic laughter and horror. Hysterical emotions that initially seem opposed, ultimately they are part of the same crucible of anxious responses to the freaks' incomplete or excessive corporeality.

What Hans fears most is becoming the object of hysterical laughter derived not from shared humor, but the terrible anxiety evoked by the presence of an accumulation of severely disabled bodies.[43] The nondisabled characters who exhibit such anxious outbursts anticipate the viewer's own response to the sight of the anomalous performers. Indeed, Olga Baclanova, who played Cleo, the character most closely associated with excessive, raucous laughter, recalled the mixed emotions she experienced when Browning first introduced her to her disabled costars: "[H]e shows me a girl that's like an orangutan; then a man who has a head but no legs, no nothing, just a head and body like an egg. . . . He shows me little by little and I could not look, I wanted to faint. I wanted to cry."[44] The actress's hysterical reaction to bodies that appear fragmented or inhuman is translated within the film narrative into her character's neurotic laughter—too loud, too long, and too tinged with fear and anxiety to have any association with humor—which is an auditory leitmotiv that resonates throughout the film.[45] According to Mikita Brottman, in *Freaks* "a horror of undifferentiated, disorganized, uncontrolled relations is echoed in the pathological laughter inspired by visions of human bodies that

77

are mutilated, truncated, interwoven, crossed over, etiolated, doubled, incomplete."[46] Laughter in the film is rarely associated with humor, as the sanctioned jokes of clowns and other circus performers fail to provoke a desired levity. Instead, scenes of humiliation and rejection, usually at the midgets' expense, are accompanied by neurotic convulsions that divide characters from one another. Such laughter is a way of asserting distance from the object of derision, a warding-off gesture that disavows connections between persons and fractures community. Following the Freudian recognition that jokes perform serious cultural work, humor operates as a defensive process in the film by displacing sources of unpleasure into the realm of the comic, which is not really very funny after all.[47] If *Freaks* manipulates narrative and camera to confuse the boundaries between freak and normal, laughter, as the privileged domain of "normal" characters, reestablishes those categories. The film does not encourage the viewer to participate in the forced mirth of its characters: because their laughter is so often of a hysterical rather than a humorous nature, it is not infectious. Rather than enticing us to share the emotions expressed onscreen, it effectively separates us from them.

Freaks neither invites the viewer to participate in the repeated ridicule of Hans by other characters, nor endorses his position, for it consistently refuses to grant his most profound desire, to be "a man like other men." This clichéd phrase becomes ridiculous when it is incorporated into Harry Earles's high-pitched, wooden delivery. Given the psychoanalytic slant of Browning's films, many of which overtly thematize castration anxiety, male impotence, and fetishization, it is impossible not to equate the male protagonist of *Freaks* with Freud's Little Hans, the source of the castration complex. Freud linked Hans's phobic behavior to the traumatic experience of realizing that his mother (a big woman) had no penis, thus generating anxiety about the loss of his own member.[48] In *Freaks*, form and content conspire in the project of unmanning the film's own version of little Hans. The same camera that made scale relative by bringing the concerns of the midget couple into the foreground also frequently undercuts Hans's aspirations by dwarfing him in relation to his surroundings. This is particularly true of his encounters with Hercules and the tall, statuesque Cleo, who make him appear a tiny boy by comparison. By impeding spectatorial identification with his character, the film works visually to make Hans's desires for wealth and romance appear foolish. Early on, Hans has a single opportunity to wield the masculine gaze of power and desire. In this utterly conventional romantic shot, the viewer shares Hans's admiring look as the camera tilts upward towards the beautiful Cleo, perched alluringly on her trapeze. After this initial moment, all subsequent attempts at mastery are consistently undermined by narrative and camera alike. In one scene with obvious

Freudian undertones, Frieda scolds Hans for smoking a large cigar. Attempting to reassert his manly authority, he rebukes her sharply by registering his distaste for women who give orders. But the implication—that he is too small to enjoy the phallic symbol of a more conventionally sized man—is too powerful to be reversed. For the rest of the film, Cleo proceeds to cut Hans's cigar down to size by laughing at him, pinching his cheeks, and telling him that he is "cute." Hans's greatest humiliation occurs at the wedding banquet, where he watches jealously as Cleo and Hercules engage in a passionate kiss.

The wedding feast is a transitional sequence that inaugurates the film's shift into horror mode and the narrative dominance of Hans's story (figure 17). The mood darkens when the freaks attempt to initiate the beautiful bride as "one of us." The tolerant, generous atmosphere of their community suddenly appears ominous. Threatened, Cleo turns on the raucous crowd, silencing them with her cry: "Freaks! Freaks! Filthy, slimy FREAKS!" Significantly, this moment, when the performers are hailed as freaks by an apparent outsider, is also the first time that her laughter is silenced, as the film shifts into horror mode and Hans's story gains

FIGURE 17. The wedding banquet where Cleo responds in horror when the freaks welcome her as "one of us." *Freaks* © 1932 Turner Entertainment Co. A Time Warner Company. All rights reserved.

narrative primacy. Her shocking utterance collapses the distinction that has been established between the disabled actors and their performances as "freaks." Unlike the other circus folk, Cleo cannot see the group as anything other than the freakish personae that they enact onstage. Appalled at the freaks' ritualistic chanting, she turns on her tiny husband, asking aggressively, "What are you going to do? Are you a man or a baby?" Her aggressive questions demand that Hans prove his manhood by defending his beloved. Drunk and poisoned, he is unable to walk home, let alone come to the rescue of his new bride. His infantilization is linked to effeminacy as Cleo, inverting the marital homecoming ritual, carries his limp body across the threshold into his wagon and puts him to bed.

Emasculation is also intimately bound to issues of class, as one of Browning's recurrent cinematic themes is the struggle between members of a criminal underworld (whose lawlessness is often projected physically by bodies that are monstrous or disabled) and an elite upper class. Impotence in a Browning film is not simply a loss of sexual function, but an inability to generate income thorough legitimate means. Although the denigration of the wealthy is a recurrent theme in Browning's work, one that has a particularly timely resonance in his Depression-era films, it is also a longstanding characteristic of sideshow culture. As I argued in the previous chapter, the sideshow, always at the margins of respectability, made light of but also jealously appropriated the conventions of the aristocrat and the professional. Robert Bogdan has termed the freak show's version of gentility, as exemplified by figures such as Tom Thumb, the "aggrandized mode" of presentation. Freak performers who worked in this vein dressed in fine clothes, assumed titles such as "general," "colonel," or "countess," traveled the world to meet with royalty, and were received as respectable members of high society.[49] It is no accident that the wealthiest character in *Freaks* is a tiny man with a German accent, the literal embodiment of a myopic, small-minded European aristocracy. Long before we learn that he is to inherit a fortune from a wealthy relation, Hans is shown to be a ridiculously pretentious figure: he wears a suit and tie even when not in costume, speaks with exaggerated chivalry to both Frieda and Cleo, and woos Cleo by buying her flowers, jewelry, and fine wine. Hans's riches, inherited rather than earned through his own labor, are inconsistent with the tawdry atmosphere of the traveling circus. Aspiring to social and economic respectability, he rejects the working-class members of the carnival community, despite their uncommon tolerance for physical difference of all kinds. Hans's class pretensions, coupled with his implausible assertion of masculine authority, prevent the viewer from identifying with his aspirations or his suffering. His humiliation is in keeping with the film's carnivalesque rejection of class distinctions and social mores, and the plot seems motivated as much by a desire to ensure his degradation as to avenge the wrongs committed against him.

Hans's economic privilege insulates him from the violent revenge enacted by the community of freaks on his behalf. After the discovery of Cleo's treachery, he helps to plot her punishment, but serves more as a mastermind than an actor at the site of brutality. On the night of the crime, we glimpse him chasing Cleo through the darkened forest, distinguished from the rest of the freaks by his white shirt. But Hans is absent from the more disturbing scenes in which the freaks crawl and slither through the mud beneath the carnival wagons, holding guns, knives, and other implements of destruction. Mary Russo argues that this sequence depicts the freaks as "a revolutionary underclass" dressed in caps and dark clothing that bespeak their proletarian status.[50] If this is the case, then Hans, in the stereotypical garb of an aristocrat, provides the rationale for, but cannot be directly implicated in, that revolution.

The film's epilogue proves that without his manhood, Hans's inherited riches can have little value. By refusing to valorize his manly aspirations, the film deviates markedly from the original short story, which concludes with the dwarf's sadistic mastery over the greedy trapeze artist. Whereas in "Spurs," the dwarf Jacques punishes his new wife Jeanne Marie by forcing her to carry him across France, in *Freaks*, Cleo humiliates the drunken Hans on his wedding night by carrying him home on her shoulders. Tod Robbins's big woman is subdued by the phallic sword Jacques brandishes, its power enforced by his vicious dog, St. Eustace. Tod Browning's big woman is punished not by the man she has humiliated, but by the community of freaks who consider the insult to Hans as an insult to them all. The effect of this shift is to highlight the fearful collective power of the freaks, but also to diminish Hans's capacity for avenging his own wounded pride.

Despite the brief shot of Hans pursuing Cleo through the forest during the revenge sequence, his manhood is never recuperated. The film's epilogue finds him living alone in a lavish mansion. When his butler tells him that he has visitors, he requests that they go away. Ignoring his wishes, the guests—who turn out to be his old circus friends Venus, Phroso, and Frieda—insist on seeing him. They find him ensconced in an enormous chair that makes him look all the more tiny. In contrast to Hans's carnival wagon, where alterations in scale brought the space into proportion with his body, the large parlor emphasizes his diminutive stature, a signal that in the world outside of the circus he will be judged in accordance with normative standards of shape and size. Although the scene holds the potential for the estranged couple to renew their relationship, Hans mourns his own humiliation, as well as the loss of Cleo. Rather than declaring his love, recuperating a more conventional masculine authority by becoming the dominant partner, he weeps in Frieda's lap while she comforts him. This ending deviates from the original script, in which Venus and Phroso return to Madame Tetrallini's Freak and Music Hall with a photo of the happily married couple holding their new baby. In that version, the midgets replicate the rendition of bourgeois domesticity enacted in miniature by the famous wedding of Tom Thumb to Lavinia Warren. Although the real couple never bore children of their own, publicity photos picture them holding a baby as a sign of marital bliss and reproductive success. These images turn the couple into a tiny replica of the social norms upheld by big people. However, *Freaks* cannot allow Hans this satisfaction: in an ending that is neither happy nor particularly conclusive, he returns to the same position of childlike feminization that he occupied in his relationship with Cleo. In place of the photograph, a visual representation that can be adjusted to the couple's own proportions, the camerawork of the epilogue reemphasizes Hans and Frieda's deviation from the norm.[51]

In conclusion we must return to one of the most haunting images in the film, the spectacle of Cleo's mutilated body, which hangs ominously over the reunion of Hans and Frieda (figure 18). This is a moment of shocking misogyny on a formal as well as a thematic register, for the camera lingers on the woman's scarred and bruised face, her drooping mouth and vacant eyes, and the incomprehensible layer of feathers that covers her chest. A feeble pair of squawks takes the place of her excessive, raucous laughter. The most obvious interpretation of this ending is to take it seriously, to believe that the freaks are capable of extreme, sadistic violence. Although it is unclear how they have accomplished the metamorphosis of a tall, statuesque woman into a feathered, legless creature, the horrified response of the freak show spectators attests to the credibility of the spectacle. As Russo writes, the transformation is "hard to believe, but, in the realist terms of the film, it is impossible for her to be read as a carnivalesque or cinematic hoax. This residual piece of flesh is insisted upon *as a real woman.*"[52] Within the film's patriarchal logic, Cleo must be punished for her greed and sexual aggression while Frieda, the patient, long-suffering little woman, is rewarded with the comforts of marriage and domesticity. This reasoning also implicates the viewer in the final acts of violence, for our desire to look at the freaks onscreen is revealed to be the same desire that propelled the narrative forward towards the shocking revelation of Cleo's body. The customers gathered eagerly around the exhibit at the beginning of the film launch the spieler into the story of Hans and Cleo; presumably we follow that story in the hope of catching a glimpse of what they have seen. In keeping

FIGURE 18. As punishment for her cruelty and greed, Cleo is transformed into a hideous chicken woman. Are we meant to believe in the reality of her metamorphosis, or see it as one more carnivalesque hoax? *Freaks* © 1932 Turner Entertainment Co. A Time Warner Company. All rights reserved.

with the conventions of the horror film, violence is linked to the gaze.[53] Looking is the primal activity that produces freaks in the first place. As one critic put it, after seeing the last scene, "we are horrified, but we are simultaneously ashamed of our horror; for we remember that these are not monsters at all but people like us, and we know that we have again been betrayed by our own primal fears. Had the picture ended on a more idyllic note we might have been self-satisfied, stuffed with our own tolerant virtue. Instead, we are plunged back into the abyss of our own sick selves, to recall once again that the most fearful inhumanity we can know is our own. With this final scene, then, the double image is complete."[54] This reading assumes that the identification between the viewer and the freaks persists in spite of the monstrosity of their actions. It is an identification that extends beyond tolerance for bodily difference to a sense that freakishness is a quality contained within us all; the surfaces of the disabled body are not radically Other, but reflect back the convolutions of our own tortured interiority. The horrors enacted onscreen are frightening precisely because they incite the viewer to recognize a similar capacity for violence within herself, to see her own sadistic impulses projected in the contours of the freak's body. Hans's participation in the scene of violence, and his subsequent regret, mirror the viewer's own soiled feeling of complicity as the film closes.

However, there is a second possibility that does not see the freak as the audience's monstrous double but as a figure possessed of a distinct, and not necessarily benevolent, agency. Despite Russo's insistence that "it is impossible for her to be read as a carnivalesque or cinematic hoax," Cleo's fate has been read in this way by more than one film critic, an alternative that has enduring implications. According to this interpretation, the story of Cleopatra is a trick that plays on the spectator's willingness to associate the freaks with deviant behavior. Since the film viewer (unlike the sideshow audience) knows that the chicken woman differs from the other freaks because she is played by an able-bodied actress, it is reasonable to doubt her reality. In the spirit of the many gaffs that we have seen the circus folk perform throughout, the chicken-woman is a fabrication; in believing that this is a horror film, and that the freaks are monsters, the audience has been taken for the biggest ride of all. This perspective is more consistent with the first half of the film, in which we see the freaks delighting in jokes, pranks, and magic tricks, wearing different costumes, and playing a variety of roles both onstage and off. If Roscoe performs as a Roman Lady, or Phroso runs around in a suit that makes him look as if his head has been knocked off, it is not inconceivable that Cleo's battered face, feathers, and webbed limbs are also an elaborate ruse.[55] Credulous looking does not produce violence, but it can make the viewer a victim of the humbug on which the freak show is based.

Ultimately, my point is not to determine which of these possibilities is more accurate, as the film itself seems more invested in making a space to display the freaks' remarkable bodies than in weaving a plausible and unified narrative around them. What these varied interpretations suggest, however, are two ways in which the freak show would continue to have meaning as the twentieth century progressed and sideshows became increasingly unavailable to consumers of popular culture. In keeping with the first reading, the freak became a figure akin to the monster of horror or the alien of science fiction. Often displaced in time and space, such monsters are understood to embody contemporary problems or more universal aspects of human nature. From this perspective, the sideshow has little relevance as a historical entity, for the freak's significance is found in her connection with the deviance that is an integral part of subjectivity itself. Freaks are powerful symbols of a common anxiety that underneath the apparent normality of our bodies we are as divided as the conjoined twins, as fragmented as the human torso, as excessive as the fat person. When freaks disappear from popular culture, other monsters will come to replace them. This model is most extensively developed by Leslie Fiedler's *Freaks,* in which the extraordinary body becomes a signifier for the author's "secret self." It is also a key feature of psychoanalytic readings in which the disabled body stirs unconscious responses in the viewer based on her fears about her own bodily integrity.

The second interpretation, in which the chicken-woman is a hoax, recognizes the freak show as a subculture with its own set of beliefs and conventions. Freakishness, from this viewpoint, is a performance that plays on the spectator's assumptions about those who look different. We believe the story of the chicken-woman because we already associate disability with freakish aberrance and monstrous sadism. But in fact, these freaks are not a vengeful community that responds with violence to any perceived insult but a group of actors, savvy about how they are looked at and how to manipulate that look for maximum profitability. The joke is on us, the spectators, and the fact that we are fooled is evidence of our exclusion from the sideshow's insular collectivity. This interpretation does not excuse the freaks for the story they have woven around the chicken-woman, which remains a cautionary tale about excessive female desire and greed. But it is a lesson taught through representation rather than literal violence. And it is one that requires a more complex sense of how freak shows, like film, are an expressive form that thrives on the ability to manipulate illusion and reality.

The contradictions within Browning's film are precisely the quality that opens it to ongoing reinterpretations, which have changed over time and across different viewing communities. A film of little technical sophistication, contrived narrative, and poor acting, *Freaks* continues to provoke and inspire its viewers almost seventy years after its initial release. Its durability is explained by the fact that Browning's daring effort to assemble the most talented and strange collection of living freak performers has never again been replicated. There is no other widely available motion picture that preserves so many of the great sideshow personalities in such unsparing detail. As a result, those who wish to experience the ambivalent pleasures of the freak show must revisit *Freaks.* Whether the spectators who were most profoundly touched by this experience perceived themselves as freaks, believed that those freaks are "one of us," or insisted on the freak's radical Otherness, the imprint of Browning's film will resonate in the representations discussed in subsequent chapters.

☞ *ACT TWO*

ACT TWO

In April 1963 an aging Carson McCullers made a final visit to the deep South, where she met twenty-six-year-old author Gordon Langley Hall at a party in Charleston. At the end of the evening, as the other guests began to go home, she pulled him aside and studied him intently for a moment before remarking gently, "You're really a little girl."[1] Years later, physicians concurred that Hall, who had been sexed male at birth, was biologically female and capable of bearing children. Classified as a transsexual, Gordon Langley Hall underwent gender reassignment surgery and became Dawn Langley Hall. She subsequently married her black butler John-Paul Simmons and gave birth to a daughter.[2] In a 1971 interview, Dawn Langley Simmons credited McCullers with giving her the courage to acknowledge what were at that time highly unconventional desires: "Carson, her senses sharpened by her own affliction, saw me for what I was in a moment of truth and her heart went out to me. I was a freak, yes, a freak, like one of her own characters."[3] The unspecified "affliction" Simmons mentions could refer to McCullers's debilitating chronic illness (which would take her life only four years later), but also to her erotic interest in women as well as men and her preference for triangulated rather than coupled love affairs.[4] However, it was not only McCullers's experiences but the fact that she was a writer, a creator of freaks, that enabled her to detect Simmons's closeted secret. For Simmons, McCullers's proclivity for authoring fictional deviant bodies made her especially sensitive to the pain experienced by real persons designated as "freaks." Likewise, Simmons's own alienation became meaningful when she could understand it through the suffering of McCullers's freak characters.

Taking its cue from Simmons, this chapter will argue that McCullers's fiction is populated by freaks, characters defined by corporeal anomalies that defy the imposition of normative categories of identity. Whether on the sideshow platform or set loose in the world, these freaks are estranged from their own bodies and the society of others. I call them freaks to ground them in a history that has too often been overlooked in readings of McCullers's fiction, which typically describe her characters as universal types whose loneliness and marginality is endemic to the human condition. This interpretive paradigm has dogged Mc-Cullers's work into the 1990s, when even those critics who recognize her concern with particular forms of race- or gender-based oppression continue to connect it to "the variety and complexity of human isolation and . . . the destructive repercussions of that alienation."[5] On the contrary, I will argue that her fiction documents a very specific context in which the boundaries of racial and sexual normalcy were policed with particular rigidity. The tensions between the deviant body and the imperative conformity of the dominant culture are granted visibility at the freak show, an institution outmoded in many parts of the country, but still a thriving business in the small southern towns that are the setting for much of McCullers's fiction.

This chapter recontextualizes two of McCullers's post–World War II novels—*Member of the Wedding* (1946) and *Clock without Hands* (1961)—by exploring the significance of interlocking terms that occupy a privileged position in her writing, *freak* and *queer*. As McCullers uses them, these words do not connote any fixed identity, but a broad opposition to normative behaviors and social distinctions. Put very simply, *queer* refers loosely to acts and desires that cannot be described as heterosexual, whereas freaks, who appear first at the sideshow and then wander at large through her fiction, are beings who make all kinds of queer tendencies visible on the body's surfaces. Freaks and queers suffer because they cannot be recognized by the dominant social order, yet their presence highlights contradictions at the very heart of that order. Sometimes, as in the case of Gordon Langley Hall, they move undetected through its most intimate and selective social circles. Far from the apolitical portrait of human alienation that so many have detected in her work, McCullers situates this interplay of personal suffering and social critique in relation to current events: the end of World War II, the paranoia and conformity that characterized the onset of the Cold War, and the brewing dissatisfaction of racial and sexual minorities that would erupt in the civil rights movement of the late 1950s and the 1960s.[6] As the mainstream culture of postwar America celebrates the return to normality, the freak show surfaces as a reminder of those who live in fear because they cannot fit in.[7] Although McCullers wrote her most important fiction in the cosmopolitan urban centers of Paris and New York City, almost all of it takes place within southern towns where freak shows remained popular, and where those who transgressed racial and gender norms often encountered discrimination and violence if they were found outside of the sideshow tent. In this environment, the deviant body is both the cause of anguish and self-loathing and the inspiration for her characters' struggles to imagine other possibilities whereby queer configurations of sex, gender, and race might be tolerated and even welcomed.

McCullers's fiction occupies a crucial place in this study, for it inaugurates a period when freaks would be seen not as absolute Others, but as aspects of the self and, by extension, of a broader social order intent on securing the boundary between deviance and normality. Whereas the disabled and racial freaks in act 1 are believed to come from outside of and to embody essential differences from the spectator's own world, act 2 charts an increasing tendency to locate the freak within. Freaks do not occur in nature; they are produced by communities that use the physical body as the primary basis for judgments about inclusion and exclusion. Recognizing how often one form of bigotry feeds into another, McCullers summons her own haunting memories of the freak show to condemn the oppression of sexual and racial minorities. But freaks are not simply victims: like Tod Browning, McCullers saw them as the embodiment of an inspiring nonconformity that could not be fully realized within a stifling social atmosphere. Where McCullers differs from Browning is that the filmmaker could locate these alternatives only within the confines of the circus, while she explores the danger and promise of their seepage into the surrounding world, anticipating the forceful alignment between *freak* and *queer* that will resurface in subsequent chapters of this book.

In *Member of the Wedding* and *Clock without Hands*, the freak and the queer are often victims and outcasts, but are also the source for fantasies of remaking the world. Their dreams are woven not in the centers of cultural and political authority, but in bedrooms and kitchens, where the disenfranchised often produce alternatives to official versions of history. These fantasies involve not the erasure of individual particularities, but renewed tolerance of differences that too often become the grounds for divisive antagonism. Mirroring the liberal civil rights movement that inspired McCullers's political vision, her fiction advocates collaboration rather than conflict, coalition rather than separatism. The target of her condemnation is a culture that makes freakishness a source of terror rather than recognizing in each individual what her character John Henry West describes approvingly as "a mixture of delicious and freak."

Freaks, Queers, and Racial Difference

Before turning to the role of the freak show in McCullers's fiction, it is necessary to situate her insistent repetition of the word *queer* in a historical context that links it both to freaks and freak shows and to current redeployments of the term within queer theory. The freak earns her title by a visible inability to fit into recognizable social categories. But like other authors in this book, McCullers does not treat freaks simply as metaphorical figures for alienation or loneliness, but as key players in the sideshows that continued to flourish in the American South, where she was raised, and in New York City, where she worked on much of her important writing. As a girl named Lula Carson Smith, she was a regular visitor to the ten-in-one that was part of the annual Chattahoochee Valley Fair. Years later, living among an eclectic group of authors and artists in Brooklyn, she joined her landlord George Davis to pore over his album of freak photos.[8]

As I have argued, freak shows were designed to reassure the onlooker of her own normality by confirming her difference from the unfortunate beings who posed in front of her. However, in McCullers's fiction such spectacles fail to cement the distinction between deviance and normalcy because her characters identify with the figures onstage, which remind them of their own lonely and uncomfortable experiences of embodiment. Rather than depicting the sideshow as the exclusive domain of freaks, McCullers suggests that each of her characters is, in some sense, a freak who cannot conform to normative standards of comportment and physical appearance.[9] A freak becomes queer when her deviance (often of a sexual nature) is partially hidden, allowing her to assimilate into the dominant culture, but with a constant sense that she does not belong. These characters' recurrent complaint that they feel "caught" comes not from their status as outsiders, but from their enclosure within repressive communities unable to recognize or appreciate the queerness that is an inevitable element of their constitution.

McCullers's interest in unconventional sex and gender identities anticipates many of the insights provided by recent work on queer theory. My point is not that McCullers, writing during an era when the dominant culture was intensely homophobic, could have predicted the present radical politics of queer theory and activism (indeed her own rather imprecise political goal was always tolerance, not revolution), but rather that contemporary articulations of the *queer* offer an ideal vocabulary for revealing previously closeted aspects of her fiction and connecting them to the freak show's experimentation with sex and gender. Likewise, her understanding of the conjoined histories of race and sexuality prefigures queer theory's investment in exploring interlocking forms of difference. In both *Member of the Wedding* and *Clock without Hands,* sexual nonconformity always bears a constitutive relation to the racial hierarchies that structure southern culture.

The *queer* of queer theory and social activism attempts to summon up and transform the violent, pejorative connotations that accompanied the term during McCullers's lifetime.[10] Rejecting the notion that human desire can be contained by identitarian categories like gay and straight, queer theory advocates a more supple understanding of intimacy. Writing of queer activism in the 1990s, Michael Warner has argued that "the insistence on 'queer'—a term initially generated in the context of terror—has the effect of pointing out a wide field of normalization, rather than simple intolerance, as the site of violence."[11] In other words, the *queer* of contemporary queer politics is conceived not in opposition to heterosexuality per se, but in defiance of all kinds of proscriptive social norms. If *homosexuality* and corresponding terms such as *gay* and *lesbian* describe a same-sex desire grounded in identity, *queer* counters a range of normalizing regimes while refusing identity politics altogether. *Queer,* in McCullers's writing, is part of the historical legacy invoked by queer theory, for she uses it to pose persistently messy obstacles to any systematic codification of behavior or desire.

As the story told by Dawn Langley Simmons implies, during McCullers's lifetime *freak* could be used as a synonym for homosexuality or other forms of sexual nonconformity. For example, in a 1937 review of Djuna Barnes's lesbian novel *Nightwood,* Alfred Kazin writes, "[S]ooner or later the thought must occur to any reader of the novel that its characters are freaks."[12] The interchangeability of terms is confirmed in a 1941 glossary to Dr. George Henry's *Sex Variants* in which the word *freak* is followed by the simple explanation, "a homosexual."[13] In a 1947 gay advocacy publication called *Vice Versa,* author Lisa Ben acknowledged the pejorative connotations of these synonyms when she pleaded the case for lesbians by asking the public to "cease to condemn them as freaks, as weaklings, tragedies of nature."[14] Lest these uses of *freak* seem unconnected to the sideshow, the association is all too clear in a 1936 article published in *Current Psychology and Psychoanalysis.* Dismayed at the infiltration of Greenwich Village by homosexuals, the writer accuses them of turning it into "a place of 'Freak Exhibits.' These are the sexual inverts, members of the third sex who flaunt their traits in the Village, 'Lady Lovers,' teenage girls with their 'wives' roving the dark streets and alleys, clothed in mannish togs, flat-chested, hair slicked back, faces thin and hard with voices as low as a man's."[15] In this context, *freak* describes the allegedly unnatural condition of homosexuality, an affliction that is immediately visible in the subject's appearance and personal demeanor. Like a sideshow curiosity, the homosexual's deviance is prominently displayed on the surface of the body. Treated as a freakish perversion, sexual nonconformity met with condemnation, and in some cases criminal punishment or torturous medical "cures."

McCullers was witness to the increasing tendency for gay people to become visible targets. She references this context when she uses the word *queer* in vague but suggestive ways, often associated with her characters' receptiveness to nonnormative permutations of sex and gender. Her caginess is unsurprising at a historical moment when the word more commonly functioned to legitimate discrimination and physical violence against homosexuals.[16] The frequent appearance of *queer* in McCullers's writing demonstrates an acute awareness of its negative baggage as well as the possibility that individuals or groups of readers might understand it differently. Its multiple valences are related to her own experiences with both the homophobia of the dominant culture and communities that encouraged more diverse forms of sex and gender identification. Much of *Member of the Wedding* was written during World War II, a period of increased sexual freedom in the United States brought about by the separation of families, the growth and diversification of urban populations, and a general atmosphere of social and economic instability.[17] In particular, the uncommon segregation of men and women during wartime provided more opportunities for same-sex relationships and the development of homosexual communities. Both *Member of the Wedding* and *Clock without Hands* acknowledge the dangers of publicly visible sexual deviance, while depicting alternative spaces where those differences might be welcomed and explored.

Mirroring the diffuse proclivities of her characters, in her own life McCullers rejected attempts to link the unpredictable flows of human desire to the categorical definitions suggested by homo- or heterosexuality. Before her husband, Reeves, was drafted into the army, Carson moved with him to New York, one of the primary centers for a flourishing homosexual subculture. There, where her penchant for dressing in men's clothing was well received, she fell in love with a series of women and lived for a time with a "queer aggregate of artists"[18] that included gay poet W. H. Auden, stripper Gypsy Rose Lee, and Richard Wright's interracial family. Yet outside her own unconventional circle of acquaintances, *queer* was used as an accusation of sexual deviance and an excuse for violence.[19] Like the transsexual Gordon Langley Hall, the author perceived a discrepancy between normative gender roles and her own sexual preferences that led her to declare to her friend Newton Arvin, "Newton, I was born a man."[20] This decisive statement seems to echo the popular belief in sexual inversion, which saw the lesbian as a woman possessed by male desires. But McCullers's own sexuality could not be so easily contained, as she was attracted to both men and women and relatively uninterested in being part of a stable heterosexual pair. Claiming to have been born a man, she asserts a masculine authority to determine the nature of her sexual attachments. She was involved in at least one intense, triangulated erotic relationship that included Reeves and composer David Diamond.[21] In addition to sharing her husband's love for Diamond, McCullers was also drawn to women such as Greta Garbo, Katherine Anne Porter, and the Countess Annamarie

Clarac-Schwartzenbach, with whom she had a passionate affair. Similarly intimate, complex, erotically charged relations surface throughout her oeuvre to suggest that, far from being the norm, heterosexuality and its institutions are destabilized by the polymorphous nature of desire itself.

The problem of categorical indeterminacy figures prominently in McCullers's fiction with regard to racial, as well as sexual, difference. McCullers's use of the queer is nuanced by an understanding of the way that racial differences have unevenly affected the history of sexual difference within various communities. Delineating the important future projects for queer studies, Judith Butler writes that "queering" must consider "the differential formation of homosexuality across racial boundaries, including the question of how racial and reproductive relations become articulated through one another."[22] McCullers's fiction offers important insights about the ways in which sex, gender, and racial relations are interconnected without collapsing the distinctions among them. In both *Member of the Wedding* and *Clock without Hands,* the struggle for queer forms of intimacy cannot be separated from the racial hierarchies that divide southern culture in the postwar period. The freak show, which returns each year to delight and appall small-town audiences, is also the return of the repressed, displaying the abject elements that have been banished from visibility but nonetheless endure in furtive or closeted forms.

The Gaze of the Hermaphrodite

Although the adult McCullers frequently dressed in men's clothes and flaunted unconventional sexual preferences much like those of her freakish characters, as a teenager her odd apparel and awkward body drew the contempt of her more feminine classmates, who threw rocks at her because she was "freakish-looking" and "queer."[23] The author's own experiences thus attuned her to the capacity of clothing both to normalize and, when worn inappropriately, to transform normality into freakishness. Fashion could be manipulated to protest rigid social codes, but not everyone had the privilege of engaging in such playful experimentation. Those whose differences could not be neutralized by garments or accessories lived with a fearful relationship to their own bodies. The same kinds of deviance transformed into profitable spectacles at the freak show might provoke persecution and violence outside the carnival tent. In *Member of the Wedding* and *Clock without Hands,* clothing, with its ability to cover over the body's irregularities, holds the powerful allure of normalization for those who worry that they are freaks, but also threatens to unveil their queer tendencies when they are unable to wear it properly.

Many of McCullers's female characters, in particular, identify themselves as freaks because of their inability to perform expected gender roles or successfully don the required accouterments of femininity.[24] Frankie Addams, the boyish twelve-year-old protagonist of *Member of the Wedding,* worries that a summer growth spurt will eventually render her suitable only for display as a sideshow exhibit, for she feels afraid that she is already "almost a big freak."[25] Barefoot and wearing "a pair of blue black shorts" and "a B.V.D. undervest," with "her hair . . . cut like a boy's" (*MW,* 2), Frankie awkwardly attempts to conceal her body's development beneath the childish androgyny of boys' clothing. Inspecting herself in the mirror she determines that "according to mathematics and unless she could somehow stop herself, she would grow to be over nine feet tall. And what would be a lady who is over nine feet high? She would be a Freak" (*MW,* 16–17). Associating femininity with diminutive stature, Frankie anxiously predicts that upon reaching a certain height she will cease to be recognizable in terms of gender categories and become legible only as a freak. Fearful that she will be unable to "stop herself," Frankie equates bodily size with self-control, and excessive growth with moral inadequacy. A female giant is grotesquely inappropriate simply by virtue of her immensity. Her body is a visual signpost indicating perverse desires that could otherwise remain hidden. It is no accident that Frankie imagines a growth spurt that will transform her into a freak, for at the sideshow, where deviance is represented as a visible quality, the bodies of freaks promise to tell all there is to know about identity. At the same time, because these ruminations occur at a point in the novel when Frankie actively objects to the imposition of femininity, the fantasy of growing to gigantic proportions must be a source of desire as well as concern. From this perspective, the female giant's enormity could be seen as liberatory, rather than oppressive. Throughout the narrative, the adolescent Frankie is torn between a queer attraction to all that is freakish and a belief in the social codes that define a "normal" young woman in contrast to the abnormality of the freaks at the sideshow. The novel ends without resolving this tension; however, its conclusion implies that she may be able to transform gender confusion into more productive energies rather than repressing them in favor of a socially acceptable femininity.

Frankie's more conservative fears about her own bodily excess are closely associated with the Freak Pavilion that she, like the young Lula Carson, visits faithfully at the annual Chattahoochee Exposition. Displayed before an audience of astonished onlookers is a collection including a giant, a midget, a fat lady, and a wild man. A particularly heavy crowd surrounds the "Half-Man Half-Woman, a morphidite and a miracle of science" (*MW,* 18) who challenges the assumption that all bodies must be one sex or the other. There is a certain contradiction in this description, between the sexual hybridity implied by the term *morphidite* and the strict sexual segregation of the half man–half woman. An actual morphidite (or hermaphrodite) would possess ambiguous secondary sex characteristics, making classification as male or female a problem. However, in this case, the freak appears to be less a miracle of science than of costume: "[T]he left side was a man and the right side a woman. The costume on the left was a leopard skin and on the right side a brassiere and a spangled skirt" (*MW*, 18). The half man–half woman's clothing creates a superficial appearance of freakishness by implying that it corresponds to a more radical sexual division beneath. If this half man–half woman is truly a morphidite, there is no visible evidence; the freak's indefinite sexual identity appears to exist only at the level of vestment. It is no wonder that Frankie, confused about the first stirrings of her own desire, shudders in fear at the spectacle of man and woman divided into opposing camps, at a tense stand-off within one body. This freak show's negative representation of sexual deviance has little relationship to the bisexuality that McCullers believed was inherent in most human eroticism.[26] The half man–half woman cannot entertain the more dangerous indeterminacy of a third sex that would blur the difference between "man" and "woman." Outside of the sideshow tent, the more ambiguously gendered body surfaces throughout McCullers's fiction in characters such as Cousin Lymon and Miss Amelia in *Ballad of the Sad Cafe;* Singer, Antonapoulos, and Biff Brannon in *The Heart is a Lonely Hunter;* and Captain Penderton and Anacleto in *Reflections in a Golden Eye.* Each combines qualities of masculine and feminine to suggest that sexuality is based on a continuum rather than a strict binary opposition.[27]

For the adolescent Frankie, terrified by the maturation of her own body and hurt by the cruel rejection of her peers, the half man–half woman represents her own unwelcome sexual indeterminacy. The sideshow is a place of fear, where her anxieties are heightened by identification with the freaks rather than assuaged by confirmation of her own normality. Instead of exploring the possibilities of multiple sexualities and genders, she attempts unsuccessfully to assert her femininity by modifying her behavior and clothing. This response is unsurprising given the importance of costume in transforming the half man–half woman into a freak. Replacing the undershirt and shorts of the previous day, which on a more mature woman could be the uniform of a butch lesbian rather than a tomboy, Frankie dresses "in her most grown and best, the pink organdy, and put[s] on lipstick and Sweet Serenade" (*MW*, 46). Along with this change in clothing, a new name, F. Jasmine, heralds her metamorphosis into a young woman whose grace and maturity will replace the old Frankie's tomboy lifestyle. The femininity she so desires is encapsulated in the orange satin gown she buys for her brother's upcoming nuptials, a garment that holds the promise of adulthood and inclusion, the possibility of becoming a "member of the wedding." Because the new dress is such an important component in her imagined transformation from gangly teenager to attractive woman, Frankie repeatedly insists on the beauty of the garment rather than her appearance in it, as if the dress alone had the power to alter or erase the identity of the wearer. Her illusions are challenged by the black housekeeper, Berenice, who reflects critically that the bargain basement evening gown is ill-suited to her charge's boyish appearance: "Here you got on this grown woman's evening dress. Orange satin. And that brown crust on your elbows. The two things just don't mix" (*MW*, 84). Like the freak's visible inability to reconcile masculinity and femininity, Frankie's own body is a freakish meeting ground for gendered contradictions. The excesses of the gown foreshadow Frankie's subsequent exclusion from the heterosexual bliss of her brother's honeymoon: its lurid color is inappropriate to the occasion and it is too large, signaling her unreadiness to assume the part of the mature woman intended to fill out its contours. Instead of transforming Frankie into a woman, the gown highlights the discrepancy between her body's awkward passage from youth to adulthood and the garment's unfulfilled promise of glamour and sophistication.

Although the mis-fit between dress and body proclaims Frankie's failure to acquire a more conventional femininity, other characters in *Member of the Wedding* subvert the normalizing message of the half man–half woman, purposefully manipulating the trappings of one gender or the other to signal a queer resistance to normative heterosexuality. Frankie's counterpart is Lily Mae Jenkins, who successfully utilizes a pink satin blouse to effect a similar metamorphosis. Berenice entertains her incredulous charges with the tale of the effeminate male Lily Mae, who "fell in love with a man named Juney Jones. A man, mind you. And Lily Mae turned into a girl. He changed his nature and his sex and turned into a girl" (*MW*, 76). Lily Mae, who "prisses around with a pink satin blouse and one arm akimbo," wears the exaggerated cues of homosexual effeminacy. While critical of Frankie's attempt to become a woman simply by putting on more mature feminine clothing, Berenice's account of Lily Mae affirms the transformative power of costume. A man who desires another man can voluntarily change from one sex to the other, his metamorphosis announced by hyperfeminine performance and clothing. In Berenice's queer story, gender is a matter of preference and sexual identification is defined through one's choice of erotic attachments; the body literally evolves in conformity with the desires of its inhabitant and the garments that clothe it. "Nature," as Berenice uses the term, connotes one's erotic tendencies rather than its more typical association with those aspects of self that are static and unalterable.

Berenice's story is one example of the instructive range of positions on the relationship between sexuality and gender articulated by the three central characters in *Member of the Wedding*. The wild reach of their imaginations extends well beyond the limited options represented by the freak show. The improbably frequent repetition of the word *queer* throughout this text leaves traces for a reader open to its suggestion that, rather than occupying any singular or normative position, sexuality comprises multiple identifications and erotic possibilities. Although it would be difficult to argue that *Member of the Wedding* is a novel *about* same-sex desire, the repeated use of the queer functions as an open secret for those who wish to explore its more affirmative possibilities.[28] Lori Kenschaft has described the imagined community of readers created by the novel as "lesbian"; however, in the context I have established, *queer* seems a more accurate term because it is generated by the vocabulary of the novel itself. Moreover, it accounts for the wide array of sexual tendencies that are depicted in McCullers's work, many of which do not involve the desire or intimacy between women that the term *lesbian* connotes.[29]

For Frankie, the queer is often associated with unpleasant, tentative forays into the world of heterosexual romance, the "queer sin" she commits with Barney MacKean, a neighborhood boy, and the attentions of a drunken sailor in a smelly hotel that make her "feel a little queer" (*MW*, 68). Such uses of the term make heterosexuality itself queer by revealing how awkward and unnatural its conventions can be. At more affirmative moments, *queer* describes various characters' attempts to imagine a world more accommodating to sexual difference. Often, their fantasies return to the freak as a figure of anxiety and desire. In the kitchen where the novel's primary action takes place, which is "hot and bright and queer," decorated with John Henry's "queer drawings of Christmas trees, airplanes, freak soldiers, flowers" (*MW*, 7), Berenice passes the time with stories of "many a queer thing" (*MW*, 75).[30] Perhaps it is the tale of Lily Mae and the pink satin blouse that inspires Frankie's fantasy of remaking the world to allow for a better correspondence between gendered identification and biological sex, which leads to a heated, unresolved debate between the kitchen's three occupants: "[Frankie] planned it so that people could instantly change back and forth from boys to girls, whichever way they felt like and wanted. But Berenice would argue with her about this, insisting that the law of human sex was exactly right just as it was and could in no way be improved. And then John Henry West would very likely add his two cents' worth about this time, and think that people ought to be half boy and half girl, and when the old Frankie threatened to take him to the Fair and sell him to the Freak Pavilion, he would only close his eyes and smile" (*MW*, 92). In contrast with the tenor of her previous story, Berenice responds negatively to Frankie's proposal by arguing for a fixed and impermeable "law of human sex." While Frankie holds out for the capacity of erotic desire to determine one's sex and gender, which remain open to voluntary reconfiguration "whichever way they felt like and wanted," she nonetheless affirms a necessary equivalence between the two with the conservative assertion that a body must occupy only one side of the binary divide at a time: "boys" or "girls." John Henry offers yet another alternative, in which individuals are a strange mix of tendencies—"half boy and half girl"—that precludes the polarized opposition between male and female altogether. Frankie's threat to take him to the Freak Pavilion reflects her conviction that one cannot be at once male and female without being a freak, suitable only for display before an astonished audience of normally sexed people. Based on her own anxious experiences at the carnival, her reaction to John Henry's hermaphrodite fantasy confirms the official message of the Freak Pavilion, where all deviations from the norm are turned into freakish spectacles. Although Frankie's trepidation about her own queer desires forces her to repudiate John Henry's vision, by the end of the novel she is more receptive to the notion of erotic indeterminacy. Her assumption of the adult name, Frances, may mean that she accepts a typical adolescent femininity, but it may also indicate her openness to more unconventional possibilities, for, as Kenschaft has argued, "'Frances' may be less aggressively boyish than 'Frankie,' but it is nevertheless androgynous when spoken."[31]

Frankie is thus torn between the excitement of awakening sexuality and her desire to pass from the queer ambivalence of "that green and crazy summer" into a more typical relationship between her body and the things that surround it. Her experiences are shared by Jester Clane, the teenage protagonist of *Clock without Hands,* who is tormented by anxiety over his developing erotic attraction to other men. While both resist the pressure towards gender conformity and heterosexual romance, Jester enjoys a larger degree of freedom and social mobility than his female counterpart. But, as a gay male, his position is also more dangerous because of the threat he poses to the rabidly homophobic order of his small southern town.[32] As Gayatri Spivak has written of *The Heart is a Lonely Hunter,* "although women and male homosexuals are both marginal as 'non-serious' versions of the male norm, the woman has a recognized use in the male economy of reproduction, genealogy and the passage of property. The male homosexual, on the other hand, has only the unrecognized use of sustaining as criminal or monstrous the tremendous force of the repressed homoeroticism of the patriarchy."[33] In revealing his identity, the gay man risks unleashing the floodgates of male homosocial panic. Because McCullers speaks of homosexuality more directly in *Clock without Hands*, the queer secret of her earlier novel can be mobilized for more direct criticism of the particular historical and geographical contours of homophobia. However, the clinical term *homosexual* also has the opposite effect of diffusing the more capacious aspects of the queer.

Jester, like Frankie, is a teenager plagued with doubts about his sexuality. The more conventionally attractive of the two, Jester's body still bears an awkward relationship to the clothing that covers it. Initially, he is described as "a slight limber boy of seventeen . . . [who] wore blue jeans and a striped jersey, the sleeves of which were pushed back to his delicate elbows."[34] Dressed in the typical costume of an adolescent boy of the 1950s, Jester's queer difference is implied by his effeminate slenderness and delicacy, a suggestion furthered by his grandfather's affectionate references to him as "Lambones" and "darling." In the company of Jester and his overly solicitous grandfather, the town pharmacist Malone observes that something about Jester makes him seem "a 'stranger.' . . . There was something hidden about the boy and his softness, his brightness seemed somehow dangerous—it was as though he resembled a silk-sheathed knife" (*CWH*, 25). What Jester's conventionally boyish clothing and respectful behavior conceal is the intense shame of his unrequited and deeply queer love for his classmate Ted Hopkins, "the best all-around athlete in the school" (CWH, 42), and his mannish English teacher, Miss Pafford. In a small town that adheres to strict codes of racial, gender, and class segregation, the affluent, white Jester is indeed a "stranger" who will ultimately transgress all of these boundaries in his secretive passion for a black man. As his name implies, he leads a life of deception, but his trickery is deadly serious. Rather than causing harm to others, the softness of his body, the visible evidence of sexual perversion, in fact puts him in danger of the violence that would inevitably accompany the detection of his secret.

If the freak-loving public in *Member of the Wedding* was fascinated by the half man–half woman's challenge to strict gender divisions, sexual panic in the predominantly male world of *Clock without Hands* crystallizes around arguments over the Kinsey Report.[35] While the Freak Pavilion makes deviance visible for a "normal" audience, the Kinsey Report suggests that the freaks' perversions have infiltrated the normal world. Assuming the unbiased tone and methodology of science, Kinsey stripped aside the wholesome domesticity of postwar America to reveal the pervasiveness of homoerotic desires and practices among men. Read eagerly by Jester, Kinsey's study provides reassurance that he is not alone in his desire for other men, but also disturbingly classifies his desire as "homosexual," an appellation laden with connotations of medicalized deviance. When Jester defends the Report's scientific accuracy to his grandfather, the reactionary Judge Clane, the older man objects: "Science my foot. I have been an observer of human sin for close on to ninety years, and I never saw anything like that." Insisting that deviance must be visible in order to be scientifically verifiable, Judge Clane shrugs off the prospect of covert homosexual activity as the fantasy of "an impotent, dirty old man" (*CWH*, 83). Ironically, this hidden desire is precisely the strangeness that Malone perceives in the youthful Jester at the beginning of the novel. It is a secret repeatedly intimated in the dialogue between Jester and his grandfather, but one that cannot be disclosed because of the judge's homophobia and Jester's inability to speak with honesty and purpose.

For Jester, the Kinsey Report's scientific validity is crucial to the affirmation of his normality, for he "was afraid, so terribly afraid, that he was not normal. . . . [H]e had never felt the normal sexual urge and his heart quaked with fear for himself, as more than anything else he yearned to be exactly like everyone else" (*CWH*, 84). Jester's longing "to be exactly like everyone else" reflects a typically adolescent self-loathing. At the same time, his desire for normalcy is not just a phase, but reflects a cultural obsession with conformity characteristic of Cold War America. Jester's terror that he is not normal is merited at a time when homosexuality was regularly linked to criminal activities, insanity, and political insurgency, and was also understood as a pathology requiring medical "cures" such as shock treatment, aversion therapy, and even castration or lobotomy.[36] But the irony of Jester's longing "to be exactly like everyone else" is that nearly "everyone else" in McCullers's fiction is plagued by queer tendencies of their own that cannot be classified as anything like normative heterosexuality. Although the story of Jester's failed love for the mulatto Sherman Pew ends with the promise of closure—"his odyssey of passion, friendship, love, and revenge was now finished" (*CWH*, 202)—his future remains as unfinished as that of the androgynous Frances. For a mainstream audience, this conclusion may imply that Jester has moved from a childish homoeroticism to mature heterosexuality; for the queer reader, however, it suggests that he has begun to accept desire and identification as "crazy and complex" (*CWH*, 202) rather than conforming to predetermined social categories.

The possibilities and dangers of this more diffuse sexuality are multiplied by a profound identification in McCullers's work between sexual and racial oppression, both of which operate by turning some persons into freaks in order to confirm the normative (white) heterosexuality of others. As Thadious M. Davis has argued, "without collapsing the difference of race and gender, McCullers attends in her literary production, with varying degrees of intensity, to race in the representation of women in the South. She assumes the intricate connections of race and gender, particularly in conjoining the two categories and inscribing race in gender."[37] Recognizing common experiences of suffering, queer white characters such as Frankie and Jester are often compelled to identify with their black counterparts. However, McCullers is well aware that their identification is circumscribed by differences between sexual and racial discrimination, the most crucial of which is that queer sexuality may remain undetected, whereas race is the visible signifier of difference that endures in spite of characters' attempts to alter or conceal bodily attributes that make them the targets of discrimination and abuse.

Why Berenice Wanted a Blue Eye

Besides the pinhead and half man–half woman, another Freak Pavilion exhibit described in some detail in *Member of the Wedding* is the "Wild Nigger . . . from a savage island . . . [who] squatted in his booth among the dusty bones and palm leaves and ate raw living rats." Unlike the other freaks, the black man's alterity is undermined by the rumor that "he was not a genuine Wild Nigger, but a crazy colored man from Selma" (*MW*, 17). This speculation implies that *freak* is not an innate quality, but an identity imposed on certain bodies to justify their exclusion from the privileges of normality. The grotesque spectacle of the wild man is believable because it draws on a preexisting equation of blackness with savage deviance. Since that equation is a fiction of the white imagination, the "Wild Nigger" will always be accompanied by rumors of inauthenticity. His prominent position in the account of the Freak Pavilion—where the audience's anxieties about sexual normality are provoked and assuaged by the spectacle of the half man–half woman—draws attention to the intimate relationship between racial and sexual difference in McCullers's fiction. In *Member of the Wedding* and *Clock without Hands,* black characters negotiate, with varying degrees of success, between the diversity of their own communities and a dominant culture that views them as one-dimensional types like the "Wild Nigger" at the Freak Pavilion.

The connection between racial and sexual Otherness is reinforced by Frankie and Jester, who, as they struggle to reconcile their own unconventional erotic urges, are drawn to black characters who have extensive experience with discrimination and injustice. Frankie, who is attracted to the "stir of company" (*MW*, 124) in Berenice's crowded home, identifies particularly with the homosexual Honey Brown, "a sick-loose person" (*MW*, 35) who "feel [*sic*] like he just can't breathe no more" (*MW*, 114). When Honey's family describes him as "a boy God has not finished," initially Frankie "did not understand the hidden meaning. Such a remark put her in mind of a peculiar half-boy—one arm, one leg, half a face" (*MW*, 122).

The image of a freakish half-person gives way to sympathetic identification as she becomes aware of Honey's plight as a black, homosexual man. Imagining a world where race, like gender, is fluid and shifting, Frankie replaces her fantasy of the half-boy's deviant corporeality with one of racial transgression, in which the light-skinned Honey leaves the South and "change[s] into a Cuban" (*MW*, 125).[38] While this is a moment of personal enlightenment, her suggestion is untenable for obvious reasons and the end of the novel finds Honey incarcerated after a drug-induced crime spree. Following a similar pattern of well-meaning ignorance, Jester falls passionately in love with Sherman Pew, his grandfather's young mulatto secretary. Although Sherman showers the white boy with physical and verbal abuse, Jester feels a "creepy thrill" (*CWH*, 67) when he listens to Sherman singing. He responds with envious admiration to Sherman's untruths about his involvement with the Golden Nigerians, a group of radical civil rights activists. Previously ashamed because he believed himself incapable of sexual passion, Jester's feelings for Sherman assure him of his capacity for desire, and fantasizing about the black teenager allows him "to become a man" by having sex with a female prostitute. As we will see, Jester derives personal satisfaction from his love for Sherman, but his unwanted affections cannot counteract the pervasive discrimination that thwarts Sherman's attempts to improve his social and economic situation.

Part of Berenice and Sherman's appeal to white teenagers confused about their own sexual identities is that their bodies, like that of the half man–half woman, resist classification into neatly opposed categories. Berenice's tales of "many a queer thing" involve the trespass of racial as well as sexual boundaries, further evidence that the queer in McCullers's fiction encompasses multiple and intersecting forms of difference. With one blue glass eye that "stared fixed and wild from her quiet, colored face" (*MW*, 3), Berenice herself is a freakish mix of the natural and artificial.[39] The novel's omniscient narrative voice is not entirely sympathetic when it proclaims the eye as the "only . . . thing wrong about Berenice" and professes bemused ignorance: "why she had wanted a blue eye nobody human would ever know" (*MW*, 3). More aesthetic than functional, the prosthetic eye is described as an excessive luxury much like the lurid orange material of Frankie's bargain basement gown or Lily Mae's pink satin blouse. But there is something disingenuous about this criticism, since the eye is Berenice's only claim to the privileges of whiteness. Delighted by situations of racial and gender ambiguity, Berenice is comfortable with the contradictions the eye introduces. Possessed by a woman "who always spoke of herself as though she was somebody very beautiful" (*MW*, 79), the blue glass eye represents a self-confidence independent of dominant aesthetic standards and the racial hierarchies they imply.

In *Clock without Hands* a similar hybridity characterizes Sherman Pew, whose blue eyes are often a source of surprise and confusion. As the visible evidence of miscegenation, Sherman's body becomes a cipher for various characters' own fantasies and anxieties about racial mixing. Jester, who is trying to come to terms with his sexuality, fixates on Sherman as the object of his desire. Jester's grandfather, the racist judge who harbors the "queer" fantasy of reinstating Jim Crow (*CWH*, 155), sees his affection for Sherman as evidence of his own benevolence. Malone, who has just discovered that he is dying of leukemia, encounters Sherman as he cuts through an alley, and he notices the young man's "unnatural appearance": "Once those eyes were seen, the rest of the body seemed also unusual and out of proportion. The arms were too long, the chest too broad—and the expression alternated from emotional sensitivity to deliberate sullenness" (*CWH,* 15). The blue eyes, which appear "unnatural" juxtaposed with dark skin, cause Malone to perceive Sherman as a freak whose entire body is grotesquely disproportionate. Although Sherman does nothing more than look at Malone, the pharmacist "automatically" classifies him as a delinquent, arrogantly assuming the power to make moral determinations based on an initial visual perception. As they stare at one another, "it seemed to Malone that the blaze [in Sherman's eyes] flickered and steadied to a look of eerie understanding. He felt that those strange eyes knew that he was soon to die" (*CWH*, 16). While Sherman couldn't possibly know of Malone's diagnosis, the pharmacist reads his own fears about death into the meeting, imbuing Sherman's alien gaze with an "eerie understanding." This encounter parallels Frankie's visit to the Freak Pavilion early in *Member of the Wedding*, where the exhibits frighten her because they look back at her "as though to say: we know you" (*MW,* 18). Both Frankie and Malone assume the right to stare without consequences. Finding their gazes returned, they interpret the exchange not as evidence of an autonomous subjectivity, but as a source of mysterious and improbable knowledge about themselves. The momentary discomfort occasioned by the realization that the freak is able to look back is powerful and potentially transformative. As we have seen, Frankie will eventually embrace this potential, while Malone will die having learned nothing and asserting that "nothing mattered to him" (*CWH*, 207). The near-collision of Malone and Sherman, in which Sherman's mere presence fills Malone with dread of "something momentous and terrible," serves as a paradigm for race relations throughout *Clock without Hands*, as white men project their fears and desires as attributes of Sherman's person, regardless of his actions.

While Sherman, like Jester, longs for "normality," the crucial difference between them is that Jester can conceal his queer tendencies while Sherman's body makes him a visible target. Unlike Berenice, who is the hub for a circle of family and friends, Sherman's hostility bars him from satisfying personal relationships within the black community. He feels each act of violence against people of color in his own body, the marker of difference that turns him into a freak who is neither black nor white. Sherman's visceral response to news of racial violence is coupled with his desire for a social status that would insulate him from personally experiencing such assaults. He associates respectability with a large vocabulary, which he consistently misuses in his attempts to impress Jester, and the acquisition of luxury items such as expensive whiskey, caviar, and silk bedspreads. Despite boasting of numerous affairs with women, Sherman's true passion is for his possessions, which seem to promise the security and fulfillment he is unable to attain through intimacy with others. But like Frankie and her ill-fitting dress, Sherman's material belongings cannot conceal the unconventional appearance of his body. Unable to secure legitimacy through the ownership of status symbols, Sherman ensures his isolation by treating his peers with disdain. Because he has no place within the privileged company of the white men he serves, or the separate circles of African American citizens, Sherman occupies a dangerous liminal ground between racial communities. Although this racial in-betweenness is itself a category that could become the ground for identification with others, Sherman is unable to perceive it as such. His self-understanding as someone who is monstrously unique is supported by his reception in Milan, where he is progressively excluded from each of the town's segregated social spheres. Eventually he is left with only the terrible alienation of the freak, who is barred from all group affiliations by being the only one of his kind.

McCullers's characters become freaks when their unusual bodily appearances are coupled with exclusion from communal bonds. A consumer culture that offers material possessions as a means of inclusion cannot compensate characters like Sherman or Honey Brown. Whereas Honey literally breaks the law, Sherman commits a more audacious crime against the social order when he buys a house in a white neighborhood. Transgressing the boundaries of Milan's segregated communities, Sherman is matter out of place. A black man who can own rather than be property poses a threat to the white citizens who bomb the house as a means of violently reasserting his difference from them, for their normality can only be secured by transforming him into a dangerous freak. As Robyn Wiegman has argued in reference to lynchings, "differences among men are so violently foregrounded that one can no longer cling to the rhetorical homogeneity attached to the masculine."[40] Sherman's death by lynching makes all too clear the profound gulf that separates him not only from Jester, but from the resentful working-class citizens whose whiteness is their only claim to superiority. Dramatically demonstrating divisions among men, lynching thus belies the false leveling of differences promised by the consumption of commodities and recalls the dramatic racial divisions of the Freak Pavilion. While *Clock without Hands* challenges the existence of anything like a normative masculinity by suggesting that all of its male characters—Malone, dying of leukemia; Judge Clane, disabled by obesity and a stroke; Jester, a closeted queer; Sherman, a mulatto—are freaks, it nonetheless asserts that some forms of freakishness are more dangerous than others and racial categories remain the most damaging of all social divisions. Although they recognize that there is no easy solution to these problems, McCullers's characters often attempt to imagine a world that does not rely on hierarchical distinctions among persons for its social organization.

"A mixture of delicious and freak"

Fantasies, in McCullers's fiction, are the most significant way of envisioning alternatives to corporeal inequalities that fracture communities and stifle personal idiosyncrasies. In this respect, the scene in *Member of the Wedding* discussed earlier, in which Frankie, Berenice, and John Henry "judge the work of God, and mention the ways how they would improve the world" (*MW*, 91) is crucial.[41] The majority of their work takes place in the kitchen, a space for creating what Patricia Yaeger calls "surrealist history," which "makes us encounter the strangeness of a particular historical moment, attacking the familiar, provoking eruptions of the unanticipated Otherness of the everyday."[42] If the world around them is unjustly segregated along racial lines and torn by the persistent buzz of wartime news on the radio, they compensate for inadequacies in their own lives with utopian fantasies of remaking. Each occupant of the kitchen takes a turn weaving a fantasy that reflects individual longings, which sometimes become interwoven with the fantasies of the other two so that "their voices crossed and the three worlds twisted" (*MW*, 92). This model of collective imagining, which can momentarily bridge differences in age, race, and gender among its collaborators, is especially important to the task of dreaming up alternative social worlds. Freaks play a central role in that project.

Frankie's fantasy, discussed above, responds to anxieties about her developing sexual identity by allowing people to change from one sex to another at will. Louise Westling has argued that these progressive ideals are undermined by the novel's conclusion, which requires "Frankie's ultimate submission to the inexorable demand that she accept her sex as female."[43] By placing an undue emphasis on the ending, this reading forecloses the possibilities of the novel's more radically affirmative moments.[44] Moreover, a negative understanding of Frankie's acceptance of femininity ignores the lesbian implications of "the wonder of her love" (*MW*, 151) for her new friend Mary Littlejohn. Frankie's obsession with becoming "a member of the wedding"—the narrative's eponymous organizing concept—might be interpreted as capitulation to a conservative socialization process that encourages young girls to desire nothing more than marriage and motherhood. But instead of longing to replace the bride, Frankie's ultimate fantasy is to become a part of the community formed by Janice and Jarvis. "They are the we of me," Frankie says, connecting the pair to her own split subjectivity. The queer desire to be not a "bride" but a "member" exchanges the normative heterosexuality of the married couple for a triadic relationship, much like those sought by the author in her own life.[45] In both novels, alienated characters long for membership, a mode of identity that is relational, inclusive, and nonhierarchical.

The models of sexuality and race generated by the three inhabitants of the kitchen are fluid and open to many different variations. In Berenice's imagination, "there would be no separate colored people in the world, but all human beings would be light brown color with blue eyes and black hair. There would be no colored people and no white people to make the colored people feel cheap and sorry all through their lives" (*MW*, 91). In this new world free of racial bigotry, both Berenice, with her blue glass eye, and Sherman Pew, born with dark skin and blue eyes, are model citizens: freakish mixtures of black and white, nature and artifice, they point the way towards the abolition of racial hierarchies. Berenice proposes a radical reconfiguration of race that would not simply reverse the terms of white supremacy, but obliterate the entire system by making each person multiracial. The hybridity that causes Berenice and Sherman to be figures of ridicule—and in Sherman's case, violence—would become instead the norm.

But six-year-old John Henry's fantasy is the queerest of all. In contrast with Frankie's fearful experience of the Freak Pavilion, John Henry is enamored of the pinhead, who "skipped and giggled and sassed around, with a shrunken head no larger than an orange, which was shaved except for one lock tied with a pink bow at the top" (*MW*, 18). Unafraid of the freaks, John Henry's declaration that "she was the cutest little girl I ever saw" moves beyond mere acceptance to the possibility of a developing erotic attraction. His delight at dressing in women's clothing brings out his own freakishness by making him look "like a little old woman dwarf, wearing the pink hat with the plume, and the high-heel shoes" (*MW*, 117). A character whose ill-suited clothes make him appear both young and old, male and female, John Henry most completely embodies the freak's potential to provide alternatives to exclusionary norms. Instead of a shameful inability to fit a proscribed role, wearing someone else's clothing generates new and varied possibilities. John Henry's plan for remaking the world is one which, in its disorder and particularity, can incorporate "a mixture of delicious and freak": "[H]e did not think in global terms: the sudden long arm that could stretch from here to California, chocolate dirt and rains of lemonade, the extra eye seeing a thousand miles, a hinged tail that could be let down as a kind of prop to sit on when you wished to rest, the candy flowers" (*MW*, 91). Unable to "think in global terms," John Henry values specificity and flexibility over totalizing models of identity. Like recent articulations of the queer, John Henry's heterotopia is not organized around a consistent, determining logic of identity, but rather in quirky opposition to all that is normal. The long arm and extra eye that allow for a more expansive community, whose vision and reach extend outside the South's stifling regionalism; the excremental appreciation of "chocolate dirt and rains of lemonade"; the hinged tail that recalls our interconnection with the animal world—all suggest a sympathetic appreciation of the body and its many variations. The best that a freak can be, John Henry contracts meningitis and suffers a gruesome death, "screaming for three days [with] his eyeballs walled up in a corner stuck and blind" (*MW*, 152), for often in McCullers's fiction bodily difference must be hidden, normalized, or punished, leaving hope in the dream of something better. However, as the more mature Frances embarks on an exciting new relationship with Mary, she holds onto the queer possibilities suggested by John Henry, whom she remembers "at twilight time or when the special hush would come into the room" (*MW*, 153).

At the end of *Member of the Wedding*, the freak show reappears when Frances and Mary return to the fair, "but [do] not enter the Freak Pavilion, as Mrs. Littlejohn said it was morbid to gaze at freaks" (*MW*, 152). This explanation for their abstinence might indicate Frankie's submission to the older woman's authority, thus serving as evidence of her ultimate normalization. As a docile young lady, Frances has learned to repress her fears and channel her desires more appropriately. But a reading more faithful to the novel's queer secrets would interpret the young women's decision not as a sign of obedience to Mrs. Littlejohn's prohibition, but of their recognition that the world itself is suffused with freaks, that they no longer need the Freak Pavilion to reassure themselves of their own normality. The logic of the freak show, which insists on cordoning off the differences of some to insist on the sameness of everyone else, is precisely the logic that led to Sherman's death and Honey and Berenice's feeling that "we all caught" (*MW*, 114).

Queer and *freak* are terms that counter the binary logic of sexual and racial division staged at the freak show and, by identifying themselves in this way, McCullers's characters are able to express both the "caughtness" that they feel and the possibility of imagining a more just and equitable social world. At a historical moment of especially punitive insistence on normalcy, this vocabulary provides a place to begin imagining a community rooted in heterogeneity rather than sameness, desire rather than proscription, where each member can find in herself "a mixture of delicious and freak." The dream of membership in a society that accepts each individual as such a mixture is an appealing extension of McCullers's own political beliefs. Sensitive to racial injustice and strongly sympathetic to the efforts of civil rights organizers in the South, she wrote frequently of the need for mutual understanding and tolerance between the races, although, as her biographer acknowledges, her "participation was often vicarious . . . and executed largely in her fiction."[46] It is fitting that an author who realized her own political convictions largely through the imagined worlds of her protagonists would create characters who themselves devised alternatives to official politics and history through fantasies spun out in the humble, but absolutely necessary, spaces of the bedroom and the kitchen.

As Gordon Langley Hall would learn, McCullers's own struggle against oppressive social norms, compounded by her chronic illness, caused her to identify with the suffering of others. This ability to find common ground across identitarian categories was the powerful basis for the liberal civil rights movement that emerged on the national landscape during McCullers's most prolific period as a writer. But in the work of an author so aware of the danger of *visible* differences, it is worth asking what her model of social justice would look like. Berenice provides the most compelling antiracist vision in her fantasy of a time when people of color would cease to exist because "all human beings would be light brown color with blue eyes and black hair" (*MW*, 91). In this world where mixture is the norm rather than the exception, everyone is equal because everyone looks the same. It is impossible for Berenice to imagine an end to racism without imposing a new kind of homogeneity. In keeping with this solution, Frankie and Jester survive because their differences can eventually be assimilated in a way that the visible stigma of dark skin cannot. Without becoming heterosexual, each overcomes the deadly isolation of feeling like a freak by accepting the strange urges of their own bodies. The tragedy of Honey Brown, caught up in a self-destructive cycle of drugs and crime, proves that this positive resolution is not available to all. Although at the close of *Member of the Wedding* Frances decides not to enter it, the Freak Pavilion continues to thrive, a concrete reminder that her transformation is an exception, not the norm. The hopeful dream that everyone would discover aspects of freak and queer in themselves rings ironic in a context where success comes to those who can best conceal their deviations from the norm. Echoing the civil rights vision of social justice, McCullers's characters strive to imagine a politics of coalition, where communities are forged across the divisive lines of race, gender, and sexual orientation. Their transcendent vision of "a mixture of delicious and freak" is a product of a time when those alignments seemed possible, as is the unhappy reality that some differences, unfortunately, would continue to matter more than others.

FREAK PHOTOGRAPHY

In her 1976 study, *Literary Women*, Ellen Moers observed a strong resemblance between the work of Carson McCullers and Diane Arbus, "for Arbus's photographs of freaks—her drag queens, lesbians, circus people, adolescents, lunatics, dwarfs, and the rest—look as if they might have been designed to illustrate McCullers's fiction."[1] Moers was struck by similarities in subject matter, but also by a shared propensity to represent the freak as a figure for "the haunted and self-hating self." Her assessment is in accord with my argument that, as the century wears on, freaks are increasingly understood not as alien strangers but as the embodiment of the strangeness within. However, to observe that individual or social disorder is registered in representations of the deviant body is to tell only part of the story. For both McCullers and Arbus, the concern with freaks is motivated by a knowing appreciation for the waning popular culture of sideshows in America. Each woman's depiction of "the haunted and self-hating self" is less a general instance of the female gothic, as Moers would have it, than a preoccupation with different, historically specific forms of deviance. During a time when sexual, racial, and political nonconformity was often forced into the closet, the freak show's iconography allowed McCullers to bring it into dramatic visibility for the purpose of social critique. Whereas McCullers's queer characters live in fear that their perversions are visible like the bodies at the freak show, Arbus's subjects often seem unconcerned, even proud, of the unconventional appearances they cut. As Susan Sontag notes, "the decade of Arbus's serious work coincides with, and is very much of, the sixties, the decade in which freaks went public, and became a safe, approved subject of art."[2] If the 1940s and 1950s were a time of great danger for freaks of all kinds, the 1960s were marked by the celebratory invocation of the freak, who embodied the era's embrace of rebellious nonconformity.

Certain obvious affinities aside, McCullers and Arbus must be distinguished by their locations on opposite ends of the 1960s and by their chosen media, literature and photography. As Walter Benjamin once observed, "it is a different nature which speaks to the camera than speaks to the eye."[3] Often described as a technology of realism, a photograph does not provide an unmediated view of the object before the camera. As I argued in chapter 3, film can teach us to perceive the freak's body differently because of the intense but shifting identification it establishes between the spectator and the cinematic image. Likewise, photography has the potential to make us look awry. Exaggerating the sideshow's tableau-like qualities, the photograph enhances the freak's Otherness because it facilitates a gaze unfettered by confrontation with another living person and the feelings of guilt, responsibility, or pleasure that might ensue. At the same time, more sustained contemplation of the static image, absent the jarring frisson of a live encounter, might also lead to increasing comfort with, and acceptance of, the freak's unique form of embodiment, and hence an acknowledgment of her humanity.

In what follows, I will trace the visual representation of freaks back to the first endeavors to record the human body on film for commercial purposes. The rise of freak shows in the United States corresponds historically with the development of photographic technologies and the emergence of photography as a professional enterprise. Likewise, the most famous freaks of the nineteenth century endure in our cultural memory because their images were captured on film. Few can claim to be unfamiliar with the stirring portraits of conjoined twins Chang and Eng, Tom Thumb, or Jo-Jo the Dog-Faced Boy. The camera's paradoxical capacity to document reality and to deceive the eye made it an ideal device for the representation of freaks, creatures jointly born of biology, fantasy, and commerce. But visual images have also been used to frame the anomalous body in terms of social and medical pathology. As a result, photography would play an equally significant role in transforming freaks into case studies by shifting the gaze from the body's unique and sensational features to its status as a representative type.

From studio portraiture to clinical documentation, early freak photography is an important precursor for Diane Arbus and subsequent artists working with images of embodied deviance. Although many have described Arbus as a photographer of freaks, that reputation has never been connected to her engagement with the history and culture of the sideshow, which is a recurrent point of reference in her writing, her art, and the legends surrounding her life and suicide. If Arbus, like other photographers of the 1960s, was drawn to scenes of social and physical marginality, she links this preoccupation directly to the living remains of freak shows in New York City and its environs. Fascinated by portraits of the great sideshow performers, Arbus frequented the seedy neighborhoods, low-budget carnivals, and cheap rooming houses where freaks had come to rest. There, she befriended them with her camera and brought their pictures to the walls of galleries and art museums. In doing so, she produced a controversial hybrid of public and private, a genre both documentary and aesthetic that forced the bastions of high art into contact with the seamiest zones of popular culture.

Whereas turn-of-the century portrait photographers participated in a larger industry devoted to the commodification of prodigious bodies, Arbus's traffic with freaks was part of the more individuated practice of art photography. In contrast to an earlier generation whose work helped to transform the freak into a celebrity, Arbus earned celebrity status for herself as the photographer of freaks. The arresting quality of the images combined with the anonymity of her captions ensured that the identities of Arbus's subjects would become virtually indistinguishable from the photographer's own name recognition. Ironically, the fame of an artist who devoted her career to escaping the narrow confines of her upbringing would end up eclipsing the lives she attempted to rescue from obscurity. In the wake of Arbus, contemporary artists must contend with this legacy as they bring older visual genres to bear on extraordinary bodies, living and dead, creating their own variants of freak photography.

Freaks on Film

The freak show's ascendancy in the mid-nineteenth century coincided with the birth of photography, and sideshow promoters rapidly learned to exploit the potential of the new visual technology as a publicity tool.[4] Among the most common freak show souvenirs were photographic *cartes de visite,* small images mounted on cardboard, which often included a description of the subject's condition and biography printed on the back.[5] Collected in albums, freak *cartes de visite* might be juxtaposed with portraits of friends and family, eminent citizens, and royalty. These popular and inexpensive mementos helped to transform freaks into celebrities with recognizable names and images. But the very technology that made freaks famous could also turn them into case studies. Medical photography contributed to the pathologization of freaks that would ultimately end many sideshow careers. The photographic representation of disabled, insane, and criminal types was part of a broader movement to define and systematize the science of deviance in the nineteenth and early twentieth centuries.

Freaks have a central, if unacknowledged, presence in the history of photographic portraiture. Mathew Brady, renowned for his photographs of the Civil War and the most illustrious citizens of his time, included freaks among his celebrated clientele.[6] His gallery, where famous images of the conjoined twins Chang and Eng, Tom Thumb and Lavinia Warren, and William Henry Johnson, the "What Is It?" were produced, adjoined Barnum's American Museum in New York City.[7] Alan Trachtenberg describes the affinities between these spaces of commerce and social interaction as "places to see and be seen. And in some measure each was a place of putting on and encountering appearances, a place of illusion and recognition, a place where the very making of illusion could be witnessed."[8] The enterprises of exhibiting curiosities and taking portraits are equally invested in the creation of artifice, as they transform the raw material of the visible world into illusions. From its inception, the camera was recognized for its hallucinatory capacity to distort reality: the same audiences delighted by images of ghosts and fairies also found photography an ideal medium for depicting freaks.[9] At the same time, photography was also valued for its realism, meaning that it was ideally suited to support the claims of sideshow promoters with irrefutable visible evidence of the freak's authenticity. This complementary fusion of illusion and reality made the photograph the fitting counterpart to an establishment such as the American Museum, whose visitors were fully aware that they were entering a space of fantasy and humbug, but at some level longed to believe, if only temporarily, in its truth.

The souvenir *cartes de visite* sold at freak shows were part of the nineteenth-century rage for photographic portraiture. Robert Bogdan writes that "the photo album was the television of Victorian homes. . . . [J]udging by the number of freak images produced, it is safe to say that human oddities were not only fascinating, but quite acceptable as Victorian houseguests—as long as they stayed in their albums."[10] Adopting the conventions of expression, pose, and setting dictated by portrait photography, the *carte de visite* enhanced the freak's wondrous features by situating her within a familiar context: the stiff and respectable midgets Tom Thumb and Lavinia Warren posing with a baby; gentlemen in suits and top hats, indistinguishable from other men except that they have three legs or no limbs at all; a woman standing with her husband in a Victorian parlor, her face covered by a plush, ample beard (figures 19–21). Portraits were the perfect format for other presentational strategies favored by sideshow promoters, the juxtaposition of freak and normal person, or pairs of freaks who embodied opposing extremes of height, weight, or skin color (figure 22). Confirming the freak's reality in a way that a drawing could not, the mass-produced photograph conferred celebrity on the era's most prodigious human curiosities.

The same visual technologies that contributed to the widespread popularity of freaks also hastened their decline. Intended for public consumption, the freak photograph promotes its subject as unique and memorable. By contrast, the clinical photograph employed by correctional institutions depicts the same subjects as case studies intended for professional eyes only. Whereas portraiture establishes the subject's belonging within a particular social class and historical moment,

FIGURES 19–21. Typical examples of *cartes de visite* in which the freaks' unusual bodies are emphasized by the conventionality of pose and setting.

FIGURE 19. The nuclear family in miniature, Tom Thumb and Lavinia Warren with a baby. Photograph by Matthew Brady (?), 1865. © Collection of The New-York Historical Society.

FIGURE 20. Charles Tripp, the Armless Wonder. Photo by Charles Eisenmann, for Barnum and Bailey, 1903. Museum of the City of New York.

FIGURE 21. A bearded lady and her husband surrounded by ornate Victorian furniture. Photograph by Bogardus, 1885. Becker Collection, Syracuse University.

clinical photography aims to track and catalog those who do not belong by virtue of illness, criminality, or poverty. The freak portrait confirms the presence of deviance within the social order; the clinical photograph is part of an institutional apparatus that attempts to document it then push it to the margins.[11] Turning their subjects into representative types, clinical photographs focus on their common features, rather than isolating the anomalies that made them distinct.

Of the many institutional uses for visual documentation, medical images overlapped to the greatest extent with freak photography. According to Martin Kemp, the first generation of medical photographers shared the freak show's interest in severe cases of physical disability: "The most obvious early subjects of pathological and surgical photography involved conditions or deformities that manifested themselves externally in a gross manner, not only because they were easiest to document photographically but also because they attracted the kind of public fascination traditionally evoked by freaks and monsters."[12] Initially devoted to

FIGURE 22. Midget and giant pose together to enhance each figure's extreme proportions, ca. 1865. © Collection of The New-York Historical Society.

recording the isolated or extreme instance, the emphasis of medical photography gradually shifted towards the accumulation of an archive of images, cataloged on the basis of shared rather than unique qualities. By providing a visual record of symptoms and treatment, photographs made an invaluable contribution to the increasing standardization of medical science beginning in the nineteenth century.[13] Whereas the freak portrait used props and setting to heighten the body's sensational features, the medical photograph stripped the body of clothing and adornment to provide an unencumbered view of its abnormality. Diagnosed in terms of recognizable pathologies, freaks lost the aura of mystery and wonder that once made them objects of visual fascination. The freak portrait thus represents an earlier mode of reception based on curiosity and sensation, whereas the clinical and medical photographs reflect a modern commitment to empirical observation and scientific method.[14]

The role of science in changing public understanding of the freak's anomalies from wonders to symptoms is humorously illustrated by a 1956 *New Yorker* cartoon. Three boys at a circus sideshow stand before a man advertised as "The World's Tallest: Wilbur the Giant" (figure 23). The sign, which promotes the giant as a unique and sensational attraction, is undercut by the words of one of the boys, who explains to his companion that the man's gigantism is caused by a pituitary disorder. The cartoon thus pictures the conflict of interest between entertainment and medicine, which provide competing forms of knowledge to describe the same visual evidence. Read historically, this sketch suggests that by the mid-twentieth century a young generation of sideshow viewers would interpret what they saw through the lens of popular medical science. The boy's ability to define the freak in terms of pathology provides reassuring evidence of his own normality. But of course, the line that divides normal from freak is never entirely secure. A resistant reader might interpret this boy's invocation of science as tremulous bravado intended to quell

FIGURE 23. A *New Yorker* cartoon from 1956 that humorously illustrates the ascendancy of pathological understandings of freaks. Here, a clash of competing knowledge systems is represented in the disparity between the freak show's hyperbolic claim that the giant is "the world's tallest" and the medical explanation offered by the young boy. The former requires the attraction to be unique and sensational, whereas the latter relies on a predictable relationship between disease and symptoms. © The New Yorker Collection 1956 Barney Tobey from cartoonbank.com. All rights reserved.

"There's a small gland in the center of the skull called the pituitary, and . . ."

anxiety about his own rapidly growing body. The cartoon might also thematize the tension between the resolute closure of a physician's diagnosis and the unresolved terror aroused by the sight of the prodigious body.

The photography of physical and social deviance creates a visual record that aspires to contain or alleviate the problem it depicts. Whereas clinical photography serves the modern tendency to segregate and institutionalize abnormality, the freak portrait belongs to an era when a greater array of human differences were at least partially incorporated into the social fabric. However, this distinction is less clear-cut than it might seem, for the meaning of visual artifacts often exceeds any attempt to foreclose their significance with official language. The medical photograph is as much a testament to the persistence of disease and suffering as it is to the accomplishments of science; the photography of insanity and criminality bespeaks the eruption of chaos and disarray at the heart of the social order.[15] The freak photograph, like the freak's body itself, ultimately points towards the collapse of categorical distinctions. Indeed, the freak emerges at precisely the moment when familiar explanatory paradigms are rendered inadequate as they confront their failure to account for arresting visual phenomena.

From Hubert's to MOMA: Freaks in the Museum

The photographer who forms the most provocative bridge between older genres devoted to the freakish body and contemporary representations is Diane Arbus. Known as a photographer of freaks, Arbus was also a fan of freak shows, which seemed poised on the edge of extinction by the mid-1960s. As she contemplated the decline of sideshows in New York City, Arbus was inspired by the freak photograph's formal conventions, as well as its potential to become a technology of memory that might preserve residual cultural forms rapidly fading from visibility.

The lure of freaks for Diane Arbus is evident in an essay she wrote in 1966 upon the closing of Hubert's Museum, a basement establishment on Forty-second Street in New York City where a traditional ten-in-one had played for nearly forty years. In "Hubert's Obituary" she describes the camera's role in creating and preserving the history of local sideshows as they are threatened by encroaching gentrification. Arbus is nostalgic for the great freak celebrities conjured up from the past by banners plastered across the museum's walls: "Coming Attractions it would say under the posters, New Acts, Next Week, Weird, Unusual, Primitive. Many of them were not exactly Coming Next Week like it said for the very good reason that they had already gone to a Far, Far Better Place. They were the Great Ones who had been there during Hubert's Forty (nearly forty, that is) Golden Years on 42nd Street, which used to be a very high class street, they say."[16] The anticipatory hype of these faded advertisements contrasts sadly with the passing of the "Golden Years," a glamorous era when freaks performed before "Ladies and Gentlemen in their tiaras and tails. . . . You couldn't even get in without a tie in those days." Times have changed and so have attitudes towards the exhibition of human oddities, on the decline as a result of medicalization and legal intervention. Echoing the sentiments of the *New Yorker* cartoon, Arbus writes, "Medical Science being what it is they don't hardly make 'em like that anymore and the laws prevent pretending or people are rich enough nowadays to hide their relatives away instead of selling them to the carnival like they used to." Countering official views of the freak show's inhumanity, Arbus romanticizes the performers she once knew at Hubert's as the last of several generations of unique talent.

Arbus's elegy charges photography with responsibility for commemorating these cherished figures long after the curtains have closed on their final performances. More than a theatrical venue, Hubert's was also a museum where "the walls were crammed with immortals" whose celebrity was embalmed in photographic images. Now silent and empty, "no one is there except the pictures on the walls of all the people who used to be there." This description of an establishment adorned with memorabilia and alive with history has its ironic counterpart in Arbus's 1968 photograph *Four People at a Gallery Opening,* in which a cluster of elegantly dressed patrons make conversation against a large expanse of conspicuously blank wall.[17] The composition emphasizes the emptiness of the art gallery, where a social elite gathers as much to be seen as to see, and wealthy clients take precedence over the creative product itself. By contrast, the freak museum—cluttered with memories and mementos—celebrates and preserves the art produced within. The loss of Hubert's makes Arbus acutely aware of the photograph's potential to inspire and enhance memory. One of the performers, Presto the Fire Eater, recalled that when the museum closed, Arbus asked for the portraits that had decorated its walls and "walked off with stacks of freak pictures in her arms."[18] A lesson in the history of freak photography, the "immortals" pictured in those old portraits would return to haunt Arbus's own images of deviant and marginal persons.

Four People at a Gallery Opening might serve as a metaphor for Arbus's unorthodox approach to art photography, for her work unsettles the predictable relationship between patrons, venues, and genres. It is fitting that as she aspired to make the transition from commercial to art photographer, Arbus wrote about Hubert's Museum, a sign that she had transgressed the firm boundaries between business and aesthetic production, the elite preserve of MOMA and the degraded terrain of the freak show. Aware of photography's potential as a mnemonic device, her reverence for the portraits on the walls of Hubert's carries over into her own visual documentation of freaks. Turning to Arbus's images themselves will allow more detailed consideration of the striking hybrids she creating by melding the public conventions of portraiture, the private and quotidian world of the snapshot, and the institutional genre of clinical photography. Refashioning these traditions, Arbus brought a once-reviled form of popular culture to the walls of the art museum and impacted significantly the way that freaks would be represented in the future.

The Photographer of Freaks

Despite her own claim that "for me the subject of the picture is always more important than the picture," Arbus clearly understood that photography is not a transparent medium, but an artifact capable of shaping or altering the way we see its content.[19] Looking at old freak photographs, she was aware of the camera's capacity to access details and capture fleeting expressions that could not be perceived by the naked eye. Recalling a portrait of Jean Libbera, who had a vestigial twin growing from his midsection (figure 24), she remarks on its phenomenological difference from the man himself: "I don't know if people really fainted when they saw Jean Libbera. He looked a bit rueful in a poster on the far wall, standing in a tuxedo sweetly holding the hands of his vestigial twin who grew, head inwards, sticking out of his abdomen and wore, the twin did, little patent leather shoes and a diaper to keep him from wetting his pants."[20] More pathetic than horrifying, this description points to the discrepancy between lived experience and still photography, the jarring confrontation with the conjoined bodies themselves, and the extended gaze allowed by photographic representation. Arbus implies that the virtue of the photograph is a permanence that allows the viewer to overcome the initial shock of the extraordinary body and invest the freak with human qualities. The image strikes her less because of the obvious disabilities of its subject than because of the prick of unanticipated details (what Roland Barthes would call the *punctum*) incited by the little patent leather shoes, the diaper, the clasped hands. A similar appreciation for odd and often unflattering perspectives characterizes the shots Arbus would ultimately choose to print from her own contact sheets.

The subjects of Arbus's portraits are so dramatic that they often threaten to overwhelm any consideration of their form, an impression she encouraged by professing a lack of interest in technical matters. Nonetheless, the formal qualities of Arbus's work are one of the key elements that link her images to older genres of freak photography. In freak photography, the prodigious body has always drawn attention away from the image's status as an artifact, encouraging the viewer to

FIGURE 24. This photograph of Jean Libbera, or Laloo, must be the image that Arbus describes in "Hubert's Obituary." Responding to his portrait with pathos rather than horror, Arbus is aware of the photograph's capacity to alter perception. Photograph by Herman Boll, undated. Museum of the City of New York.

conflate the photograph with its referent. Questions about lighting and composition inevitably diminish when the subject is conjoined twins, a microcephalic child, or a hermaphrodite. So interesting is the fact that these extraordinary figures once sat before the camera that the camera's intervention seems irrelevant. But, as we have seen, photographs never simply recorded the reality of freaks; they played an important part in creating a freakishness that represented itself as the real thing.

Arbus photographs are notable for their technical hybridity, combining a square format evocative of the snapshot and the Polaroid with the clarity, precision, and studio ambiance of the first daguerreotype images.[21] In accordance with the conventions of studio portraiture, her subjects are centered within the frame, fully aware that they are being photographed. However, instead of adopting a more typical expression of disinterested composure, they are caught in transitional postures, at unguarded moments when they have forgotten the camera's presence or, as Arbus put it, "in between action and repose."[22] If the portrait commemorates an enduring personal essence, Arbus sought out impermanent gestures captured by the sudden glare of the flash. As Emily Hulick observes, "[W]hen Arbus began to use flash to fix her subject's expression, it becomes apparent the portraits she made are records of one moment only. They do not attempt to provide a complete portrait of a human being over time."[23] Of course, all photographic portraits are records of a single moment, but Arbus was especially uninterested in the impression of timelessness, and she deliberately scanned her proof sheets for expressions that seemed unposed or fleeting.

The harshness of the flash illuminates irregularities or blemishes that might be erased by more gentle lighting, for Arbus was preoccupied with the imperfection of the human form.[24] Rather than concealing the materiality of the body, her camera focused relentlessly on pimples, enlarged pores, stray hairs, stubble, and bruises. Susan Sontag described the deliberate ugliness of Arbus's portraits as a rejection of the aesthetic she had learned as a fashion photographer: "Arbus's work is reactive—reactive against gentility, against what is approved. It was her way of saying fuck *Vogue*, fuck fashion, fuck what's pretty."[25] Arbus was indeed reacting against the constraints of social and artistic convention, but she was also creative, generating images that would change the way we understand the relationship between deviance and normality as it has been conveyed through photographic images. Ugliness, asymmetry, awkwardness were no longer associated only with the photography of social marginality, for anyone could look like a freak if the camera were to catch them at the proper angle.

Arbus's self-conscious disregard for aesthetic ideals is nowhere better expressed than in her famous portrait *A Young Man in Curlers at Home on West 20th Street*. While this image may now seem unextraordinary, it constituted a bold, unconventional statement about gender ambiguity, as well as the generic conventions of portraiture, when it was first printed in 1966. The illumination of the flash divides the frame into dark and light, a visual metaphor for the subject's embodiment of male and female attributes. The hair in curlers, the eyebrows plucked into delicate arches just beginning to grow in around the edges, the half smoked cigarette, the long, painted fingernails and their contrast with the masculine set of the mouth and jawline: every aspect of this young man's appearance bespeaks process rather than permanence. Gender, this portrait suggests, is an elaborate combination of costume and gesture that has no predictable relationship to the sexed body.

Instances of sex and gender ambiguity were among the freak show's favorite obsessions, from hermaphrodites to bearded ladies and transvestites. The radical insight about gender offered by *A Young Man in Curlers* can be illustrated by comparing it with the freak show's more typical representation of gender indeterminacy, the half man–half woman, whose body is divided directly down the middle. As I argued in the previous chapter, s/he is indeed a curious spectacle, but one that does little to unsettle the binary opposition between the sexes, since the male and female zones are clearly delineated by such conventionally gendered signifiers as body hair and masculine clothing on one side; shaved legs, makeup, a breast, and fishnet stockings on the other. The half man–half woman's freakishness rests on the assumption that gendered garments are consistent with the sexed body they conceal, which is, in this case, partitioned into male and female zones. To be half and half thus upholds the Freudian dictum that anatomy is destiny by representing gender as a strictly dualistic system that is the natural expression of one's biological sex.

The distinctive insight about gender offered by *A Young Man in Curlers* is thrown into more dramatic relief when it is juxtaposed with a portrait of the freak Albert-Alberta taken at Hubert's Museum by Arbus's teacher, Lisette Model (figure 25). Together they illustrate Arbus's departure from the work of her mentor in how she chose to translate the freak show's concern with sexual deviance into photographic representation. Fully dressed for performance, Model's Albert-Alberta is at once male and female, a condition confirmed by the polarized division of

FIGURE 25. *Albert-Alberta, Hubert's Forty-second Street Flea Circus, New York.* Lisette Model, 1945. This photograph of the half man–half woman illustrates the sideshow's more conventional understanding of the sexual freak, whose body is divided vertically down the middle. By relegating male and female to distinct longitudes, the potential for a more radical understanding of sexual ambiguity is diffused. © The Lisette Model Foundation, Inc. 1983. Used by permission.

his/her body, clothing, and makeup. As Model accounts for this curious figure, "[h]e was a Parisian, he had been a woman until the age of thirty-five, with four children, and when the fourth child was born, he slowly but surely turned into a man . . . he had still one female and one male breast."[26] In her story, the transformation from female to male is gradual, passive, and permanent. Model describes Albert-Alberta during an interview in which she also distinguishes her work from that of her most famous student by professing a distaste for freaks.[27] In contrast to Arbus's enthusiasm for Hubert's, Model claims that Albert-Alberta was the only performer of any photographic interest to be found in the museum. Listing her differences from Arbus, she stated, "I have never photographed homosexuals. I have never photographed lesbians. I have never photographed freaks. [This] is not what I was interested in."[28] This series of disavowals creates pejorative links among homosexuality, lesbianism, and freakishness. Model avoids any association with such categorical perversions by explaining Albert-Alberta's body in terms of individual idiosyncrasy. Claiming that Albert-Alberta "slowly but surely turned into a man," she represents hermaphroditism as a mysterious and irreversible transformation. Looking at the photograph itself, it seems plausible that Albert-Alberta's costume might be a strategy for expressing multiple sexual identifications and, by extension, the wearer's refusal to limit desire to members of one sex. But Model forecloses the unmentionable possibility of bisexuality by denying that Albert-Alberta's condition represents anything other than a biological anomaly. By contrast, Arbus's photographs of cross-dressers and transsexuals resist the freak show's overly schematic portrayal of the relationship between sex and gender. Whereas Model's photograph is closer to the studio aesthetic of the traditional freak portrait, Arbus pictured similar subjects relaxing in the contexts where she had found them. Their differences cannot be definitively segregated from an otherwise normal world, nor isolated within one part of the body; they are neither sanitized to appear "just like us" nor cordoned off as unique and irreplicable anomalies.

Whereas the freak portrait positions its subjects against a staged backdrop, Arbus penetrates the intimate domestic spaces of bedroom, boudoir, and kitchen, turning environment into an extension of individual personality. Like her human subjects, these interiors are not composed for the camera, but unmistakably in use, cluttered with the garbage, kitschy decorations, appliances, shabby furniture, and other paraphernalia of everyday life. Arbus's portrait of Eddie Carmel, *A Jewish Giant at Home with His Parents in the Bronx, N.Y.*, makes exemplary use of setting. This image recalls the tradition of freak *cartes de visite*, where giants emphasized their enormity by posing in the company of midgets or average-sized persons.[29]

His shoulders stooped as if to avoid brushing the ceiling, Carmel looms above his parents, who look up with expressions of awe, and perhaps dismay, at the enormity they have created. In place of a nondescript studio backdrop is the Carmel living room in the Bronx, where the young man's enormous body appears out of proportion to the space and its furnishings. His plight is enhanced by the banality of the context—the furniture draped in ill-fitting slipcovers, scattered papers and Kleenex tissues, lampshades encased in protective plastic, a cheap alarm clock on an end table, and a mottled carpet. The distinctively working-class milieu of the Carmel home contrasts with the grandiosity typical of giants who become sideshow personalities. Carmel is a freak because there is no place that can accommodate the massive expanse of his body, a point emphasized by the fact that he is in his house, yet so dramatically not at home. The misfit between Eddie Carmel's immense form and the proportions of his living room transforms him into a freak. Yet his freakishness, as it is represented in this photograph, is of a different order than that of the sideshow giants, for it bespeaks the pain and loneliness that result from an incongruity between the body and its most intimate surroundings.

Because Arbus considered photographs to be a technology of memory, she might have been gratified by a 1999 radio documentary produced by Carmel's cousin Stacy Abramson.[30] The program employs a montage of disparate voices belonging to members of the Carmel family. Their recollections pivot around the Arbus portrait, which inspires and facilitates the painful work of reconstructing his past. A second cousin born after Carmel's death commented that she first learned of her famous relative when she found his portrait included in the Arbus monograph. According to another family member, "[H]e loved that picture. . . . . [H]e used to laugh at it. He'd say, 'Isn't it awful to have midget parents?' " Family members recount a life filled with loneliness, disappointment, fear, and physical suffering. Forced to turn his dream of becoming a comedian into a stint as a freak show giant, Carmel outgrew his friends, relatives, and house, and eventually the capacity of his own body to support itself. Yet the portrait allowed him to view his circumstances differently, to understand his situation as a humorous trick of perspective rather than an existential condition. It also enabled his family to discuss his life and death for the first time. Aware of the camera's capacity to rip freaks from their surroundings and turn them into case studies, the Carmel family tells stories to resist that dehumanizing tendency, fleshing out the image provided by the Arbus photograph.

I have argued that, within the tradition of freak photography, the clinical anonymity of the medical photograph inverts the *carte de visite*'s promotion of the freak as an individual and a celebrity. Each image of grandiosity is haunted by the fact that, stripped of the spectacular edifice of the freak show, the performers would become cases, documented by the physician's camera, the image filed away in a medical archive. The medical image shears away all signs of personality by focusing exclusively on the manifestation of disorder. Often the face, the most important register of individuality, is obscured or cut out of the frame altogether. Although many of Arbus's subjects could easily become the anonymous cases of clinical photography, she refuses to erase the particularities of the body or to remove them from the spaces and belongings that distinguish them as individuals. A striking example is her portrait *Mexican Dwarf in His Hotel Room.* In the style of a medical image, the subject—whose name is Morales, although he remains anonymous in the caption—is unclothed, a towel spread across his genitals. Instead of the blank, unfocused gaze of a specimen, the dwarf looks directly and complacently at the camera. He wears a hat perched at a jaunty angle and drapes his arm casually across the bedside table, where a bottle of liquor and a glass rest within easy reach. This image led Sontag to remark critically that "far from spying on freaks and pariahs, catching them unawares, the photographer has gotten to know them, reassured them—so that they posed for her as calmly and stiffly as any Victorian notable sat for a studio portrait with Julia Margaret Cameron. A large part of the mystery of Arbus's photographs lies in what they suggest about how her subjects felt after consenting to be photographed. Do they see themselves, the viewer wonders, like *that*? Do they know how grotesque they are? It seems as if they don't."[31] Dismayed at Arbus's disregard for the conventions of portrait photography, Sontag objects that persons who should rightly be the specimens of institutional photography are inappropriate as the focus of portraiture. As we have seen in the previous section, during the Victorian era freaks commonly sat for studio portraits, a practice that was eliminated, in part, by the rise of clinical photography. Arbus's work represents less a flagrant perversion of the genre than a return to some of its original content overlaid with her own distinctively contemporary imprint. The archive has been opened, and its subjects have taken lodgings in New York's cheap hotels; they are performing in bars and sitting on park benches. Arbus's photographs find them lounging in revealing poses, apparently at ease with their bodies. Sontag insists that these abject figures should know they are grotesque in the eyes of others; Arbus violates recent convention by picturing them expressing confidence in their own legitimacy as the subjects of portraiture.

But Morales's relaxation says more than this, for it suggests the intimate connection between photographer and sitter that is typical of much of Arbus's work.[32]

The portrait's slightly asymmetrical arrangement draws the eye to the unoccupied space in the bed that could easily have been hers a moment earlier. We cannot know whether the photographer sat up, equally unclothed, to shoot this snapshot of her companion. Nonetheless, the image's erotic undertones are palpable as it emphatically denies that only more conventionally proportioned bodies can be comfortable or sexually appealing in a state of undress.[33] Poking out from beneath the towel, Morales's slightly swollen foot is foreshortened so that it appears just below his groin, where it intimates an erect, phallic virility. Rather than attempting to normalize or conceal his body, Morales's relaxed pose asks the viewer to question a world that would designate him as a monster or have us avert our eyes in his presence.[34]

Arbus made her most powerful intervention in the genre of clinical photography with a series shot at an institution for the developmentally disabled. The last photographs taken before her suicide, they project a sense of community that is absent from much of her work, so often focused on isolated individuals or gatherings in which persons appear estranged from one another. In this series, Arbus's subjects, whom she called "retardates," are clustered in groups, where they relax and play with blissful disregard for the photographer. These images recall Lewis Hine's photograph of two "idiot children," a tiny, microcephalic boy standing next to a girl whose massive, oddly formed head is outlined against a broad expanse of sky (figure 26).[35] In another time and place, the two children might have been exhibited as human curiosities. Shot in 1924, Hine's image documents the movement of the developmentally and physically disabled into institutions. The transformation from "freaks" to "idiots" or "morons" (as they were called in contemporary parlance) who pose with the same blank passivity as sideshow attractions does not necessarily suggest progress. Unlike the monumental stillness of the Hine photograph, Arbus's subjects are in motion, turning somersaults, holding hands, walking. In contrast to the sharp clarity of her previous portraits, these images capture the blur of exuberant activity. The expressive energy that suffuses their movements counteracts the view of medical texts and photographs of the period, which typically saw persons with Down syndrome as irredeemably damaged. This is precisely the kind of institution Arbus criticized in "Hubert's Obituary," where rich people "hide their relatives away instead of selling them to the Carnival." Arbus refused to allow the inmates to remain hidden. She did not grant them visibility in the manner of the freak portrait, with its stiff pose and exaggeration of physical disability, or the medical photograph, with its disregard for personality, but in a state of contentment with the body and its capacity for play.

Arguably, these final subjects are not freaks at all, for they have found a space

FIGURE 26. *Institution. Morons in Institutions,* Lewis Hine, 1924. The setting for
Diane Arbus's Untitled series is reminiscent of this Hine photograph, although the vibrant
motion of her subjects differs dramatically from the stasis of Hine's children. Courtesy
George Eastman House.

that can accommodate their atypical bodies and behaviors. There is no one to gaze
at them and no profit to be made through their exhibition. Yet they are fixtures
within the canon that has earned Diane Arbus a reputation as a photographer of
freaks. As I have suggested, there are reasons, both historical and generic, for describing Arbus in these terms. A collector of freak paraphernalia and a freak show
aficionado, she is the connecting link between the sideshow as a degraded form of
popular culture and a current generation of art photographers focused on the deviant body. But other, more troubling explanations for why Arbus might be called
the photographer of freaks require further scrutiny.

The first has much to do with the biographical details that have become im-
possibly entangled with interpretations of Arbus's work.[36] Indeed, the mythology
that has grown up around the artist's life has been so insistently associated with her
photography that Arbus herself has come to be understood as a freak. Much of the
blame for this confusion lies with Patricia Bosworth's unauthorized 1984 biography, which speculates at length about Arbus's feelings of alienation from her family and peers, her unconventional sexual proclivities, and her attraction to all
things freakish.[37] However, well before the publication of *Diane Arbus,* critics

had trouble viewing the freaks in Arbus's work as anything other than projections of the artist's own psychic trauma. The effect is to diminish Arbus's artistic accomplishments as well as the real suffering that eventually led her to take her own life. Her suicide in 1971 ensured that subsequent interpretations of her work, already as controversial as it was critically acclaimed, would be shadowed by the fact of untimely death, as has been the case with female authors such as Sylvia Plath and Anne Sexton. Catherine Lord writes caustically of the Bosworth biography, "[T]he photographs are 'explained' by constructing Arbus herself as a freak, and their power, from which she derives their value as art, is legitimated by her suicide."[38] As Lord suggests, this disturbing conflation of biography and art is highly gendered, for critics have been particularly unable to consider the work of women artists as anything other than a form of self-expression that emerges unmediated from life experience. The point is not that Arbus's life story is irrelevant, for it has become a fixture of her celebrity as a freak photographer, but that the significance of her work extends well beyond the confines of naïve biographical criticism.

The second reason Arbus has come to be known as the photographer of freaks has to do with the 1960s culture of celebrity. Andrew Ross describes the achievement of 1960s art photography: "[R]esonating with the documentarist call for cinema verité, photography in the sixties zeroed in on the everyday, the vulgar, the freakish, in short, the anti-aesthetic. In this respect, the new photography presented a broad critique of the cult of art photography which had decorously framed the everyday in a distancing, noninterventionist way."[39] Arbus's work was an undeniable part of this rejection of the aesthetic dictates of art photography. The ironic consequence of this new interest in the marginal and the quotidian was that instead of drawing attention to social problems, it often turned the subjects of photography into trademarks that ensured the artist's own name recognition. Arbus contributes to this troubling dynamic by choosing not to identify her subjects, branding them with captions like "the Mexican Dwarf," "the Jewish Giant," and "Hermaphrodite with Dog." Such monikers, so like the stage personae imposed on freak performers, draw attention to the artist's power to title and categorize, guaranteeing that hers is the only proper name linked to the visual image.

Moreover, Arbus's celebrity bespeaks her historical distance from a time when sideshows were commonplace and photographs of freaks were regularly available as cheap souvenirs. The original freak photographs, produced in concert with the institutions of popular amusement and medical or criminal documentation, focused attention on the subjects, not the photographer. Looking nostalgically at such images, Arbus could draw inspiration from their form and content, but she could not replicate the circumstances of their use and circulation. By the 1960s, freak photographs did little to enhance the financial or professional situation of their subjects, who were marked with the indelible signature of the photographer-as-celebrity. The portrait of Eddie Carmel may have helped his family to remember him, but on the wall at MOMA and reproduced in the Aperture volume, it ensured Arbus's acclaim as a photographer of giants. In short, the meaning of freak photography inevitably changes when it is shorn of its original context. Viewed in this light, Arbus's assertion that "there are things which nobody would see unless I photographed them" looks somewhat different, for its emphasis rests as much on the photographic *I* as on the *things* that might otherwise remain invisible. In the new culture of celebrity born in the postwar years, the cost of Arbus's renown as a photographer of freaks is precisely the history she claimed she most wanted to preserve.

Since the 1960s it has become commonplace to understand each individual as a combination of freak and normal, a condition so aptly captured in Arbus's juxtaposition of the banal details of everyday life with the truly strange qualities latent just beneath the surface. If earlier photographic genres fixated on the freak's abnormality, Arbus's work reminds us of the photograph's capacity to find freakishness in the most normal subjects. We are all familiar with the prick of misrecognition that comes from looking at a snapshot that catches us at an odd angle; Arbus had an especially acute talent for translating that uncanny experience into something concrete and communicable to others.

And yet, to say that we are all freaks provides too easy and unsatisfying an answer to the more troubling questions raised by an Arbus photograph. Despite her professed interest in the lives of her subjects, Arbus's celebrity has had the ironic effect of conflating their identities with hers. Freaks are so clearly created as much from imagination as from the blunt matter of the body that they are always in danger of becoming *merely* symbols of the artist's own dark interiority. Any image that too readily allows us to move from the fact that *freak* is a constructed identity to conclude that everyone has a freak within threatens to erase the lives laid bare by the camera's eye.

The Next Generation
Arbus photographs have lost much of their capacity to shock, for they have been absorbed into the archive of vernacular images and replaced by the work of even more controversial documentarians of the body such as Robert Mappelthorpe and Joel Peter Witkin.[40] The critical legacy unwittingly instigated by Arbus, in which the photographer's freakish subjects are understood as an extension of "the haunted and self-hating self," has been embraced with particular enthusiasm by

Witkin. Arbus's photographs appear tame beside Witkin's macabre tableaux, which feature dead, mutilated, or congenitally disabled bodies wearing makeup, masks, and disguises in a profane union of stagy artificiality with the gruesome materiality of the human form. If Arbus manipulated the conventions of portraiture and medical photography that have governed representations of the freak since the nineteenth century, Witkin pays homage to a more ancient tradition of associating freaks with the divine, the mystical, and the diabolical. But he also traces his artistic career back to an early assignment photographing the Coney Island freak show. "The freak show became my home, my real environment filled with living fantasies," he wrote. When it closed for the season, "I began to create my own environments of personal fantasy to photograph."[41] The real subject of his photographs, which include many of the stock characters of the ten-in-one—conjoined twins, dwarves, hermaphrodites, and people without limbs—is the artist's own psychic landscape.[42] The borders of a Witkin photograph function as a theatrical proscenium surrounding bodies elaborately adorned with costumes, props, and scenery. Carrying the culture of photographic celebrity to its limits, Witkin is the undeniable auteur of these images, which draw attention to the artist's construction of the mise-en-scène and his alteration of the photographic surface at every stage of the developing process. By tearing and scratching the negative, spattering the image with paint and ink, or coating it with a wax encaustic, the artist inserts numerous layers of mediation between the artifact and the subjects that once posed before the camera. In Witkin's hands, the freak becomes entirely metaphorical, removed from both the context of everyday life and the freak show that the artist claims as inspiration.

In some sense the medical photographs, the freak *cartes de visite,* and the Hine portrait, with their matter-of-fact focus on bodily disability, are far more unsettling than a Witkin. Sepia-toned photographs of limbs grown massive and misshapen with elephantiasis, the bodies of conjoined twins, the scars of Civil War veterans continue to be moving, for they represent the failure of medical science to alleviate such conditions and the camera's audacity in daring to preserve them on film. Contemporary viewers have grown accustomed to understanding freaks as artistic projections, and it is the impersonality of the camera's eye that now repels.

The conventions of medical photography, which sought to close a chapter in the visual history of freaks by turning wonder into pathology, are evoked and reconfigured in the photographs of Rosamond Purcell, which document the contents of physicians' archives and natural history museums where the remains of human anomalies have been stored. Her work takes the fascinating remnants of the human form—a wax model of Madame Dimanche, a nineteenth-century woman with a ten-inch horn growing from her forehead; a plaster cast of Chang and Eng; the skeleton of a hydrocephalic child—and transforms them into art. Manipulations of light, color, and composition confer beauty on objects that were once scrutinized by the cold eye of science. In *Hydrocephalic Child Whose Skull Opened Like a Flower,* a skeleton with an enormous, shattered skull is awash in an ethereal golden light that makes it look as if it were floating against a soft purple background. The tired cliché ("like a flower") is reinvigorated by its unlikely combination with the harsh sounds of the medical diagnosis. The sentence fragment captions a scene that is at once serene and terrible, a reminder of the body's remarkable variability and extreme frailty. A black-and-white photograph of a giant's skeleton is disorienting because it is cropped in the style of a three-quarter-length portrait (figure 27). Although dramatic lighting and shadow give this figure a monumental cast, it is impossible to know that the skeleton is larger than the

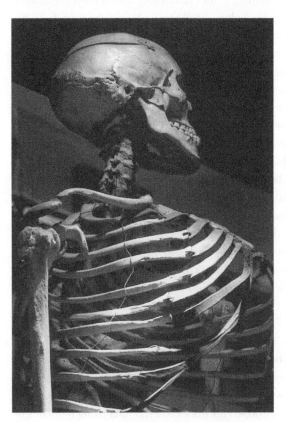

FIGURE 27. "Skeleton of a 7' 6" giant from Kentucky, identity unknown, estimated age twenty-two to twenty-four years; purchased 1877, Mutter Museum, College of Physicians, Philadelphia, Pennsylvania." Although the play of light and shadow gives this form a monumental quality, the caption provides the only indication that this skeleton is larger than ordinary. Photograph by Rosamond Purcell, 1993. Courtesy Rosamond Purcell.

norm, for it lacks any of the comparative indices typically included in the visual iconography of giants. Only the caption reveals that this was the frame of a person seven feet, six inches in height, with severe curvature of the spine "causing an unnatural protrusion of the rib cage." An artifact from the Mutter Museum at the College of Physicians in Philadelphia, this image recalls the genre of medical photography, but also an older tradition in which the remains of freaks were exhibited long after death. The virtue of both images lies in Purcell's skillful exploitation of the photograph's capacity to change the meaning of what we see, transforming pain and disability into beauty. At the same time, she provides little context for interpreting these inanimate forms, bathed in the luminous glow typical of more conventional museum pieces. It is entirely possible to appreciate the photographs' aesthetic accomplishment without reflecting on the history of displaying freaks, alive or dead, for profit and entertainment. This is a history that should not be forgotten, even as photographers seek new and less exploitative ways of picturing the disabled body.

In extreme contrast to the aestheticized stasis of Purcell's photographs are Zoe Leonard's portraits of Jennifer Miller, a woman with a beard. In *Pin-up #1*, the nude Miller lies suggestively across a dark, plush expanse of cloth (figure 28). The frisson of this image arises from the contrast between Miller's voluptuous feminine form and her generous beard and underarm hair. Miller's pose exploits the contrast between her own sexual ambiguity and the utterly stereotypical femininity of the pinup girl. Her expression is confident and seductive as she offers her body to the camera. This photograph pushes beyond Arbus's insistence that the freak is an appropriate subject of portraiture to confirm that she may be beautiful and alluring. Of course, unlike hydrocephaly, gigantism, or other disabilities, a beard is, to a certain extent, a voluntary enhancement of the body's potential. As I will discuss at greater length in the epilogue, Miller has taken a consciously feminist stance by refusing to shave, wax, or undergo electrolysis to remove her facial hair. In this, her situation differs significantly from the painful and unavoidable forms of embodiment represented in many other photographs discussed in this chapter.

The juxtaposition of the Purcell and Leonard photographs draws attention to the two divergent paths freaks have taken in the late twentieth century. On the one hand, many of the extreme congenital disabilities that once afflicted freak performers have been tackled by medical science. That their effects can now be seen only in photographs and rare instances where human remains are still exhibited to the public has had ironic consequences. People with disabilities, no longer photographed as freaks, now confront the problem of social and political

FIGURE 28. Bearded
Lady Jennifer Miller
appropriates the classic pose
of a pin-up girl, bringing
together the traditions of
erotic photography and
freak portraiture in Zoe
Leonard's *Pin-up #1
(Jennifer Miller Does
Marilyn Monroe)*, 1995.
Courtesy Paula Cooper
Gallery, New York.

invisibility and must seek new, less exploitative ways of gaining the public eye. On the other hand, Miller's pose is a sign that other types of freakishness have become ever more a matter of choice and style. Once a reviled identity, some now proudly claim the title of freak as a personal or collective mode of self-identification.

Miller's inviting smile is a saucy rejoinder to Sontag's question, "Do they see themselves . . . like *that*?" But instead of the depressing leveling of differences that Sontag predicted on the photographic horizon, freaks continue to inspire provocative and varied artistic responses. Perhaps the lesson in this is that visual representation cannot easily be translated into the language of moral criticism. Like freaks, photographic images sometimes confound description; at once strange and familiar, they record a split second that can never be recaptured in life, but is preserved indefinitely in the visual record. Freak photographs inevitably mean something different when detached from their original context as a part of the publicity apparatus of the sideshow, yet they continue to *be* meaningful and their impact on a contemporary generation of art photographers is apparent. Arbus is the link between those photographers who lived and worked during the time when sideshows were commonplace and those whose work gestures back to its style and subjects. Taken together, their work indicates that photography, which flirts constantly with the borders of illusion and reality, memory and history, the dead and the living, might, for better or for worse, be the ideal technology for representing freaks.

FROM SIDESHOW TO THE STREETS
Performing the "Secret Self"

TOURIST: What do you call yourselves that for?

HIPPIE: Because we admit it—compared to everybody else, we're freaks.

TOURIST: As long as you behave yourselves, there's nothing wrong.

HIPPIE: I'm not putting bad connotations on the word *freak*. I'm just . . .

TOURIST: Doesn't the word *freak* itself have bad connotations?

HIPPIE: Well, it's whatever you think about it.

This dialogue between an earnest hippie and a couple of tourists, which takes place early in Michael Wadleigh's film *Woodstock* (1970), perfectly captures the changing status of the freak in the 1960s. As this intercultural exchange unfolds on the left side of the screen, the right side tracks over the seemingly endless caravan of cars, motorcycles, and RVs all making the pilgrimage to Woodstock. The split screen implies that the times, they are a-changin', that the world of the well-meaning, straight vacationers will soon be overrun by a younger generation, one requiring a new vocabulary to speak of radical changes in lifestyle, values, and political views. As Abe Peck recalls, at Woodstock "the music became a soundtrack for tribal neighborhoods—freaks, bikers, college towns of mud, blankets, and tents."[1] His inclusion of freaks among other countercultural groups is indicative of the term's transformation from a brand of misfortune and suffering to a mode of affirmative self-identification.

Woodstock provides one example of the shifting significance of all things freakish in the turbulent years of the 1960s and early 1970s, when freaks proliferated at music festivals and in rock lyrics, crucial indexes of the era's social and political upheaval. Spokespersons for a new generation, Frank Zappa encouraged fans to "Freak Out," Jimi Hendrix brandished a "freak flag," and Crosby, Stills, Nash, and Young "felt like letting my freak flag fly." Rock festivals at Monterey, Woodstock, and Altamont provided the meeting grounds for a generation of freaks that grew their hair long, liked their music loud, and invited the world to follow Timothy Leary's lead and "Turn On, Tune In, Drop Out."[2] The countercultural appropriation of *freak* has certain affinities with the term's more traditional connotations, for it continued to signify extreme deviations in appearance and behavior. But the difference—the kernel of misunderstanding in the *Woodstock* dialogue quoted above—is that young people of the 1960s voluntarily adopted the name *freak* as a banner of rebellion against the authority of parents, schools, and government. Continuing the developments described in the previous two chapters, in which freaks increasingly become aspects of self, members of the counterculture called themselves *freaks* to describe their own alienation from mainstream society. Suddenly, everyone had a stranger within who could be released through consciousness raising, mind-altering substances, travel, or meditation. And although the rebels of the 1960s would mellow with age, the innovations in style and vocabulary that they introduced transformed the meaning of *freak* forever. It is important to consider how and why that meaning changed because any contemporary understanding of the history and culture of freaks is inevitably filtered through our knowledge of this era.

In the 1960s, the term *freak* acquired meanings as contradictory as the counterculture itself. Identifying oneself as a countercultural freak could be both a serious quest for alternatives to the conformity of the dominant culture and a gesture of self-indulgence.[3] The women's movement would call attention to the irony of the rebels' talk of free love and sexual liberation and their reliance on traditional gender divisions that required women to serve as mothers, cooks, and homemakers. "We were twisting and smoking and thieving and using the lingo and having a very good time," radical lesbian Jill Johnston writes of the sixties, "but still we were experiencing the fringe benefits of a man's revolution which meant basically more and better women to fuck and more shit on the women's heads for doing everything they always did as well as taking care of the new pleasure oriented freaks."[4] Despite the professed radicalism of the countercultural freaks, they often failed to introduce progressive solutions to the social order they condemned while remaining ignorant of the contradictions in their own attitudes.

Elaborating some of the historical changes described in the last chapter, I will begin by exploring the general range of meanings that accrued around the term *freak* within the counterculture and beyond. Not surprisingly, freaks appear most prominently at the radical extreme, in the writings of yippie revolutionaries Jerry Rubin and Abbie Hoffman. Rejecting conventional forms of activism, their flamboyant, highly stylized strategies of resistance frequently center on the figure of the freak, whose performative antics transform the serious business of courtrooms, schools, and streets into sideshows.[5] I will argue, in the second part of this chapter, that the counterculture's appropriation of the freak sets the stage for

Leslie Fiedler's *Freaks: Myths and Images of the Secret Self.* As much spiritual autobiography as social history, *Freaks* was acclaimed by mainstream reviewers when it was published in 1978 and remains the most comprehensive analysis of freaks in literature and popular culture. Nonetheless, it has been virtually ignored by academics, who have allowed critical silence to speak for itself.[6] My own analysis will break that silence, situating Fiedler's treatment of freaks as an outgrowth of his attempt to comprehend the tumultuous events of the sixties. As compensation for his disaffection with a young generation of radicals who called themselves freaks, Fiedler returns to a time when human prodigies were treated with reverence and wonder. He looks nostalgically to the past to conclude that something was lost as freaks evolved into dissidents, rock stars, and comic book characters. Whereas the counterculture invested the freak with newfound political significance, Fiedler objects to the politicization that, in his eyes, threatened to rob freaks of the mythical stature that made them powerful. What lies behind his critique is a desire to preserve the freak as the "secret self," the embodiment of his own deepest fears and longings. But these differences should not mask the fact that Fiedler's *Freaks* is characterized by many of the same underlying contradictions that trouble the work of his more radical contemporaries. As each attempts to dismantle traditional masculine forms of authority, he claims the status of freak, thus reaffirming his own importance within a new order that values the marginal and the outcast. By identifying with or as freaks, they conveniently erase the privilege that they continue to wield, while announcing themselves as spokespersons for those who have been forgotten or silenced.

Styles and Obsessions

Looking back at the preceding decade, sociologist Daniel Foss wrote in 1970, "It may disturb some Americans to discover that a number of youths (as of 1967–1968) have been referring to themselves with pride as 'freaks,' or that expressions such as 'it's freaky man' or 'that really freaked me out' are used in a positive sense. But that is part of the whole point."[7] Foss addresses a mainstream audience of "Americans," much like the tourists in *Woodstock* who, imbued with the conformist values of the early Cold War era, understand *freak* to be an insult or accusation. For those who prize normality above all else, the notion that *freak* would be a label assumed with pride needs considerable justification. As Tod Gitlin explains, the counterculture adopted *freak* as a strategy for turning charges of deviance into grounds for resistance: "If you were bashed over the head and labeled a freak, well then, you were reminded why you had felt like a freak and gravitated towards drugs and weirdness in the first place."[8] Instead of accepting the stigma attached to the term, rebellious young people embraced freakiness as a sign of social dissidence in much the same way that sexual minorities have recently appropriated the term *queer.*

Transformed into a chosen identity, *freak* also became an active verb that indicated one's enthusiasm for uncommon tastes and practices (Dennis Hopper in *Easy Rider:* "I never thought of myself as a freak, but I love to freak") or a more negative excess (Jerry Rubin in *Do It!:* "[W]e barged right into the exclusive little lounge. The professors *freaked out,* spilled soup all over their suits and ran for cover. We began liberating the place").[9] Turning *freak* into an activity, the counterculture emphasized the fact that, historically, freaks have relied as much on performance as on the raw material of the body. Whereas the sideshow typically concealed the freak's performative qualities by presenting her as natural and authentic, the hippies proudly announced themselves as practitioners ready to "freak," as well as to "groove," "trip," "dig," and "zonk." Writing of hippie lingo, Stuart Hall has noted, "[T]he slogans are striking, linguistically, especially for two aspects: their emphasis on the continuous-present tense—'grooving,' 'balling,' 'tripping,' 'mind-blowing,' etc. and their prepositional flavour—'turn *on,*' 'freak-*out,*' be-*in,*' 'love-*in,*' 'cop-*out,*' 'put *on,*' *up*tight,' 'where it's *at.*' The style of phrasing appears to be *existential* and *situational.*"[10] In other words, *freak* is both an identity and a series of activities. It is both reactive, forged in opposition to the mainstream world of "straights," and productive, involving participation in a subcultural community.

At once an act and a condition, the designation *freak* proclaimed the counterculture's purposeful embrace of marginality. Beyond its association with rebellion, it would be difficult to define *freak* more precisely, for it is one instance of the deliberately vague language of youth subculture.[11] Logic and specificity were dismissed as the dominant culture's attempts to regulate freedom of expression. As Tom Wolfe describes this circumvention of meaning in *The Electric Kool-Aid Acid Test,* "*Thing* was a major abstract word in Haight-Ashbury. It could mean *any*thing, isms, life styles, habits, leanings, causes, sexual organs; *thing* and *freak; freak* referred to styles and obsessions, as in 'Stewart Brand is an Indian freak' or 'the zodiac—that's her freak,' or just to heads in costume. It wasn't a negative word."[12] In his manifesto of yippie rebellion, *Revolution for the Hell of It,* Abbie Hoffman explains his resistance to definition as an oppositional stance: "This reluctance to define ourselves gives us glorious freedom in which to fuck with the system. We become communist-racist-acid-headed freaks, holding flowers in one hand and bombs in the other."[13] Categorization is inherently oppressive because it seeks to compartmentalize and divide, constraining the freedom prized by the counterculture's spokespersons, who urged their followers to "do your own thing." Pairing flowers and bombs is one example of Hoffman's affirmation of paradox. "Accept contradictions," he writes, "that's what life is all about. Have a good time."[14] The embrace of opposites and the intentional subversion of vocabulary are some of the connotations that begin to circulate around the varied and nebulous word *freak* in the 1960s.

As it became a common vocabulary word, *freak* was also used to describe countercultural "styles and obsessions." Sociologists Daniel Foss and Ralph Larkin explain that "the 'freak' culture early on idealized emancipation from repetitive, routine activity, 'living by the clock,' 'preprogrammed' careers, keeping up appearances subsuming the conventional practice of incessant cleaning and the consumption of countless products marketed for this purpose with the intention of maintaining living quarters and personal appearance—or odor—in perpetual readiness for inspection by impersonal outsiders, and other activities which might be concerned by stretching the term 'compulsive.'"[15] Their catalog underscores the fact that countercultural resistance was often concerned less with politics than with matters of individual lifestyle.[16] Seeking alternatives to the domestic arrangements of their parents' generation, young people migrated from suburbs and small towns to urban centers, concentrating in neighborhoods such as the East Village in New York City or San Francisco's Haight-Ashbury district, where they attempted to realize the ideals of free love and communal living. New fusions of folk, soul, and rock music evolved as the fitting accompaniment to political protests, orgies, and dropping acid.[17] As Gitlin describes it, "freak culture was a pastiche, stirring together intoxicating brews from extracts of bygone tradition."[18] Hippie style was a colorful, eclectic mixture of other cultures and periods: the slang of the black hipster; the moccasins, beads, and headbands of the American Indian; Mexican huaraches and blankets; an orientalist mélange that included the *I Ching*, the sitar music of Ravi Shankar, Nehru jackets, and fragments of Zen Buddhism and meditation.[19]

While I have been using *freak* as a synonym for *hippie*,[20] numerous compound words containing *freak*—LSD freaks, speed freaks, Jesus freaks, violence freaks, structure freaks—described those whose behavior, particularly drug consumption or sexual habits, was perceived as excessive even by the loosened standards of the counterculture. *Freak* was also a favorite term among groups on the radical fringes of the counterculture who, by the late 1960s, had become disillusioned with both the New Left and the alternative lifestyles of the hippies. Two of the most colorful and prolific of these figures, Abbie Hoffman and Jerry Rubin, began their careers as political activists within the civil rights and antiwar movements.

Impatient with the failure of peaceful protest to produce noticeable change and prompted by incidents of police brutality and the escalating conflict in Vietnam, freaks engaged in more dramatic struggles against "the system" in the late 1960s and early 1970s. The writings of these revolutionaries reveal both the freaks' radical political possibilities and their most extreme excesses.

Freak is a particular favorite in the work of Jerry Rubin, who is labeled "the P. T. Barnum of the revolution" on the opening page of his 1970 collection, *Do It!*[21] A veteran of Berkeley's free speech movement and chair of the Vietnam Day Committee, Rubin developed increasingly sensational styles of insurgency towards the end of the 1960s. Advocating immediate and intense forms of revolutionary activity, he writes that the goal of the Vietnam Day Committee "was to create crises which would grab everybody's attention and force people to change their lives overnight."[22] Rubin employs *freak* to decry the dominant culture's institutions and values. In *Do It!* he denounces higher education as oppressive and hypocritical, indicating his disdain for normative standards by spelling the word as *freek.*

In place of the sideshow, Rubin and Hoffman orchestrated "be-ins" and "happenings"; the streets, the mall in Washington, D.C., and the floor of the New York Stock Exchange became the stage for a new kind of radical freak performance. Groups like the Diggers, the yippies, and Up against the Wall Motherfucker eschewed organized political opposition in favor of spectacular public interventions that they termed "guerilla theater." Performance was a crucial aspect of the expressive politics of the 1960s, and freaks used public spaces and channels of communication as stages for the dramatization of their resistance to the serious business of politics, commerce, and education.[23] In contrast to the hippies' romance with the "natural," the technologically sophisticated yippies were skilled at attracting and managing media attention. Aware that news does not simply happen, but is made, Hoffman writes, "The impression that we are media freaks is created by our ability to make news. MEDIA is communication."[24] The capacity of media freaks to make news was proven when battalions of police were detached to protect Chicago's reservoirs after the yippies joked about putting LSD in the water supply during the 1968 Democratic National Convention.[25]

While the yippies' performative antics were loosely inspired by political concerns, other radicals advocated the revolutionary potential of "freaking out" itself. Such was the case with Frank Zappa, whose Mothers of Invention *Freak Out* album (1967) included the following invitation on its inside jacket: "On a personal level, *Freaking Out* is a process whereby an individual casts off outmoded and restricting standards of thinking, dress, and social etiquette in order to express

CREATIVELY his relationship to his immediate environment and the social structure as a whole. . . . We would like everyone who HEARS this music to join us . . . become a member of *The United Mutations* . . . FREAK OUT!"[26] Capitalizing on the
term's radical currency, Zappa embraced freakiness as a sign of artistic rebellion.
Somewhat ironically, he invited fans to rebel through consumerism, to become
freaks (to FREAK OUT) by buying and listening to the album.[27] As George Lipsitz
argues, Zappa's politics are more "alternative than oppositional." His brand of
freakiness is symptomatic of the tensions and continuities between countercultural
style and political activism: on the one hand, freaking out is the logical extension of
the expressive politics advocated by the New Left; on the other, it is not invested in
any program beyond the advocacy of performative weirdness "on a personal level."

The counterculture's problematic flirtation with marginality often had very
real adverse consequences for those who already lived on the margins. Com-
munes and group homes provided an escape from the constraints of conventional,
middle-class life, but as hippies and radicals moved into places like Haight-Ashbury or the East Village, they often antagonized or drove out the disadvantaged
residents already living in those neighborhoods. The freaks' rhetoric of inclusive-
ness thus frequently stood in contrast to the exclusions that characterized their actual practices. These limitations are exemplified by Jerry Rubin's description of
longhairs: "[W]e are a new minority group, a nationwide community of longhairs,
a new identity, new loyalties. . . . Long hair turns white middle-class youth into
niggers. Amerika is a different country when you have long hair. We're outcasts.
We, the children of the middle class, feel like Indians, blacks, Vietnamese, the
outsiders of Amerikan history."[28] Rubin's own feelings of alienation from the
mainstream cause him to identify with the ongoing legacy of racism within
the United States (or "Amerika") and its connections to an imperialistic foreign
policy. Though his long, unkempt hair may indeed have challenged bourgeois
standards of hygiene and grooming, as well as the rigid differentiation of gender
roles, the naïveté of such easy identifications is now obvious. For despite what
they may have felt, the position of young white people who chose to grow their
hair is hardly equivalent to that of inner-city African Americans or Vietnamese
peasants. In fact, their movement to the margins was rarely welcomed by those
who were already there and were impatient with the freaks' romanticized vision of
themselves as outsiders. Long hair and voluntary poverty allowed the countercul-
turalists to appropriate the experiences of dispossessed groups, but were hardly
adequate to the hard work of dismantling "the system" they decried.

Although long hair symbolized men's resistance to traditional codes of masculinity, it did not necessarily lead to a desire for gender equality. In particular, the

"militant mutation of the hippie" that Jane and Michael Stern label a "Freek" was known for his relentless masculinism. Of the counterculture's dubious gender politics, the Sterns write, "while other rebel groups had their high profile females . . . [Freeks'] girlfriends got even less respect than hippie chicks, because ants-in-the-pants freek guys were generally too angry, too stoned, or too engaged in taunting authority to appreciate fresh-baked bread and other such 'womanly' contributions that hippie girls used to make to the movement."[29] The Freek might loudly proclaim his dissidence while invoking conventional forms of male privilege or active prejudice against women and homosexuals. This sort of hypermasculine radicalism is evident in the freaks created by underground comic book artists such as Bill Griffith, Robert Crumb, and Gilbert Shelton. Born in the 1960s, Shelton's swinging bachelors, the Fabulous Furry Freak Brothers, have endless appetites for raunchy sex and illegal drugs. The Freak brothers' effeminate garb—long hair, colorful clothes, and jewelry—is balanced out by their aggressively macho libidinal activities. Their adventures, which involve repeated scrapes with the law and other figures of authority, are always punctuated by romps with the many vapid, busty women who stray across their path.

As hippies morphed into freaks and the Greatest Show on Earth moved out of the circus tent and into the streets, the meaning of *freak* exploded exponentially.[30] No longer only a stigma marking those at the extreme margins of society, *freak* gained new centrality in the mouths of peaceniks, radicals, and activists. As a verb, *freak* became an activity that one could choose to perform or not, an identity one could selectively embrace or put aside. The many associations the word accrued in the sixties continue to impact subsequent understandings of the freak's significance. Some of the contradictions now inherent in the term are shared by Leslie Fiedler's *Freaks,* which, until recently, has served as the authoritative reference to the history and culture of the sideshow. Reading Fiedler's work in the context of this historical moment will reframe key aspects of his interpretation of the "secret self" and help to cement the connection between the sideshow freak and the countercultural freak.

Fiedler's Counterculture

Leslie Fiedler introduces *Freaks* by remarking on the term's changed status in the wake of the 1960s: "We live at a moment when the name 'Freaks' is being rejected by the kinds of physiologically deviant humans to whom it has traditionally been applied," he writes. "Meanwhile, the name Freak which they have abandoned is being claimed as an honorific title by the kind of physiologically normal but dissident young people who use hallucinogenic drugs and are otherwise known as 'hippies,' 'long hairs,' and 'heads.'"[31] His observation that "this development expresses itself as a kind of politics" frames the study that follows as an outgrowth of and an engagement with political events of the preceding decade. Nonetheless, Fiedler's critics have often described his intellectual trajectory in terms of a retreat from the more serious political commentary of the early essays collected in *An End to Innocence*. Both Morris Dickstein and Donald Pease have observed that, after absenting himself from the radicalism of the 1960s, Fiedler somewhat disingenuously attempts to rewrite himself into the decade's revolutionary activities with *Being Busted*, which chronicles his arrest and charge with possession of marijuana.[32] There, his claim to insight about the new generation of students is legitimated by the professed political dissidence of his own youth in the 1930s, as well as his more recent victimization by an invasive government apparatus. But in keeping with a more general silence among literary critics, neither Pease nor Dickstein mentions *Freaks* in his assessment of Fiedler's scholarly career.

The failure of academics to subject *Freaks* to sustained critical analysis is surprising (or perhaps utterly unsurprising), given its undeniable popular success. It outsold his widely read classic, *Love and Death in the American Novel*, received favorable reviews in periodicals—from *Hustler* and *High Times* to the *New York Times Book Review*—and brought him into such nonliterary venues as the TV talkshow circuit and panels on medical ethics. As Feidler described it, literary critics recoiled from his "deliberately unfashionable book," which they considered "a flagrant betrayal of what they felt to be their essential professional function and mine: to defend the standards of High Culture, indeed, of civility itself, against the onslaught of the leveling and hopelessly vulgar culture of the marketplace."[33] At a moment when literary criticism was concerned almost exclusively with matters of textuality, Fiedler, self-styled intellectual renegade, claimed to have crossed the line of academic respectability by taking on so degraded a subject as freaks. Rather conveniently, this account of his exclusion from academic circles only lends credence to Fiedler's sense of himself as perpetually marginalized by his own scandalous disregard for the conventions of his profession.

Its author's self-aggrandizement aside, *Freaks* was a prescient work that anticipated many of the current preoccupations of cultural studies. Not only did Fiedler connect his interest in freaks to recent upheavals in national politics, but he described his method as motivated by a cultural politics that attempted to bridge the divide between elite and popular forms. In his 1969 essay, "Cross the Border—Close the Gap," he makes his most explicit argument against conservative aesthetic hierarchies: "The notion of one art for the 'cultured,' i.e., the favored few in any given society—in our own chiefly the university educated—and another subart for the 'uncultured,' i.e., an excluded majority as deficient in Gutenberg skills as they are untutored in 'taste,' in fact represents the last survival in mass industrial societies (capitalist, socialist, communist—it makes no difference in this regard) of an invidious distinction proper only to a class-structured community."[34] Anticipating the charges of bad taste to be leveled against *Freaks*, Fiedler attributes such judgments of aesthetic value to an antidemocratic class system. With "Cross the Border" he recognizes cracks in the apparatus designed to maintain the authority of a cultural elite. Fiedler predicts the increasing obsolescence of critics who insist on their traditional function as gatekeepers of artistic discrimination, while proposing that those who could embrace the changing cultural climate confronted exhilarating possibilities.

Freaks is Fiedler's most sustained effort to put his theory of cultural criticism into practice. Arguing that freaks have always been a staple of the Western literary imagination, he probes the relationship of canonical arts and letters to ancient myths and religious practices, as well as more modern forms of popular culture. The paucity of scholarship on this topic, he claims, is less a sign of its irrelevance to American literature than the failure of literary critics to do justice to their object of study. He makes this point twenty years earlier in the introduction to *Love and Death* (1960), where he writes, "American literature is distinguished by the number of dangerous and disturbing books in its canon—and American scholarship by its ability to conceal this fact. To redeem our great books from the commentaries on them is one of the chief functions of this study."[35] Linking the disturbing qualities of American literature to the terror and thrill of the sideshow, *Love and Death* contains many of the underlying themes of *Freaks* in embryonic form, such as the observation that "[o]ur literature as a whole at times seems a chamber of horrors disguised as an amusement park 'fun house,' where we pay to play at terror and are confronted in the innermost chamber with a series of inter-reflecting mirrors which present us with a thousand versions of our own face."[36] What had been a metaphor for American literature in *Love and Death* became a reality in *Freaks*, which studied the cultural history of popular amusement itself. Calling the literary tradition a sideshow, Fiedler implies that American fiction contains an untapped reservoir of terrors and thrills, and, likewise, that the study of mass entertainment can provide access to underlying truths about American culture.

The shudder of abjection evoked by so many works in Western literature, and the relationship between literature and the lived history of human curiosities are the subjects of *Freaks*. But Fiedler's treatment of that history is motivated by changing conceptions of the freak during the turbulent years that preceded the book's publication. Looking back, Fiedler saw affinities between the deviant body's challenge to social norms and the expressive politics of the New Left. Noting how countercultural dissidents eagerly took on the freak's marginality, Fiedler suggests that the mythic appeal of his subject matter might be harnessed in the service of activism: "[S]omething has been happening recently in the relations between Freaks and non-Freaks, implying just such a radical alteration of consciousness as underlies the politics of black power or neo-feminism or gay liberation" (15). Inspired by recent emancipatory movements for racial, gender, and sexual equality, other marginalized groups (such as the mentally or physically disabled) might organize under the banner of *freaks* to combat discrimination and forge new political coalitions. Yet Fiedler hesitates to pursue the implications of his argument because a resistance organized around the term *freak* "remains a politics without a program, unlike the analogous efforts of those once called 'niggers' and 'colored' to rebaptize themselves first 'Negroes,' then 'blacks'; or of former 'ladies' and 'girls' to become 'women'; or of ex-'faggots' and 'dykes' to transform themselves into 'gays'" (13). In contrast to the coalescence of minority groups into political units, freaks have not been able to organize around shared experiences of oppression.

Whereas identification as a freak may be an inadequate basis for political mobilization, the idea allows Fiedler to connect his survey of canonical Western arts and literature to contemporary events and popular culture. Prefiguring certain assumptions of cultural studies in the 1980s and 1990s, Fiedler questions class-specific judgments of taste and treats mass culture as a legitimate subject of scholarly analysis. However his more inclusive gestures are compromised by an ambivalence about the political radicalism unfolding around him, an insecurity about whether to assume the role of participant-observer or disapproving critic. Like the radicals described in the preceding section, Fiedler's identification with freaks provides him with a device for claiming his own marginality in a context that grants new validity to the outcast. In doing so, he delegitimizes the political claims of minority coalitions and replaces them with an investigation of his own fantasies and desires, which he represents as universal aspects of the human condition. Confronted with the spectacle of freaks moving off the sideshow platform and into the streets, Fiedler uses Freudian psychoanalysis to justify his retreat into a nostalgic recollection of childhood visits to the freak show. To contemplate the primal emotions stirred by the sideshow freak proves far less threatening than taking seriously the demands for social and political parity made by marginalized groups in the 1960s and early 1970s.

Remembrances of Freaks Past: Fiedler's Secret Self

Throughout *Freaks* the analysis of the timeless appeal of corporeal Otherness continually collapses into self-analysis, for the volume is also intended to probe the author's own subjectivity, to explore the passage of his youth and preserve the self-rending trauma of its loss. The bodies of freaks, Fiedler claims, paradoxically tell us what it means to be "fully human" (347) and evoke collective fears and desires that challenge our fundamental beliefs about the boundaries of the human. His description of the spectator's experiences repeatedly slips between the personal and the universal. As it does so, his own painful but necessary encounter with deviance becomes the paradigm for an archetypal human response, and his interest in the cultural transformation of freaks from objects of sacred wonder to pity is confused with nostalgia for a younger, more innocent self. Twenty years after his call for maturity in *An End to Innocence,* Fiedler returns to the untutored experiences and impressions of childhood to understand the power of the freak show; likewise, the freak show becomes a way of reviving childhood anew. Given his alienation from the counterculture, Fiedler's longing for a return to youthful innocence can only be read as compensatory. He associates infancy with the irretrievable sensation of wholeness, dimly recalled through encounters with extreme forms of bodily Otherness at the freak show. The primal fantasies summoned up by the sideshow freak are presented as a more enduring and meaningful alternative to the counterculture's freaks.

Fiedler's retreat from the political is exemplified by his treatment of Tod Browning's film *Freaks,* which became a cult classic in the 1960s. Within Fiedler's *Freaks,* Browning's *Freaks* is a transitional artifact marking not only the historical movement of the sideshow from stage to screen, but a bridge between the 1930s and the 1960s, between the author's childhood innocence and his desire to conjure it up through the act of remembering. In the introductory chapter, Fiedler claims that his own *Freaks* "represents a belated tribute to that great director and his truly astonishing film, since I can no longer disentangle my earliest memories of actual Freaks—encountered, I suppose, somewhere back of the boardwalk at Coney Island, the smell of fresh buttered corn and frying hot dogs in my nostrils—from the nightmare images he evoked. . . . And his movie has played and replayed itself in my troubled head so often that merely recalling it, I call up again not only its images but the response of my then fifteen-year-old self" (18–19). For Fiedler, Browning's film is a Proustian mnemonic for recapturing the disjointed smells and sensations of a past only barely held together by narrative. As the precise details of time and place give way to the fuzzy speculation of memory, the experience of watching a film blurs into the childhood encounter with living freaks. Moreover, the process of recollection takes on the attributes of a film that plays and replays in some darkened interior space as its images imprint upon and entangle with the viewer's own subjectivity. Recalling freaks, as they are filtered through Browning's representations of them, Fiedler also recalls his distant childhood, which can function as a substitute for the more unsatisfying activities of young people in the 1960s. So potent are these memories that by the end of *Freaks* Fiedler has revised his claim to have confused Browning's film with his childhood visits to the carnival ten-in-one, instead implying that he was born *after* freak shows had vanished from American popular culture: "For many of us, in fact, *born after the movie house had replaced the tanbark* as the dream place of the Freak fancier, his celluloid side show was the first we ever knew" (289, emphasis added).

The sideshow's disappearance from American culture collapses into its erasure from the author's own memory. Despite his considerable interest in the lives of the freak performers themselves, Fiedler describes the waning of the sideshow primarily in terms of personal loss. His own experience of its absence melds with his chronicle of the vanishing ten-in-one: "[A] sense of the Freak show as an unworthy survival of an unjust past spread everywhere in the early twentieth century so that for a while it seemed as if those of us now living might well represent the last generations whose imaginations would be shaped by a live confrontation with nightmare distortions of the human body." Almost more important than the extinction of the sideshow itself is the aging generation of survivors who were once moved by the spectacle of freaks and are still able to summon them up through memory. The representation of freaks in film cannot replace the encounter between two human beings that could only take place across a sideshow platform. Its dissolution "implies a trauma as irreparable as the one caused by the passage of the dialogue between the King and Fool from court to stage: a trauma which is, in fact, a chief occasion for this book" (16). It is not the fleshly encounter between freaks and normals that is the scene of an originary trauma, but its passing, which can only be worked through in the extended narrative charted by Fiedler's study.

Fiedler's *Freaks* is structured by attempts to recuperate that traumatic loss. Although it is framed by recent historical events—the rise and wane of the counterculture—the work is organized into chapters based on types of human oddity, each of which evokes a predictable range of human responses across time and space. Rather than a chronicle of progress or decline, the structure of *Freaks* tells a story of psychic continuity. Assuming the role of sideshow barker, Fiedler leads the reader from one category of freak to the next, describing them in the psychoanalytic terms of childhood trauma. Our responses to dwarfs and giants, he explains, are stirred by youthful memories of scale in which parents loom above us. Hermaphrodites recall the inadequacy of the binary division of the sexes into male and female, while androgynous figures such as bearded ladies are associated with "the dream of polymorphous-perverse satisfaction" (186). Conjoined twins remind us that we are all inextricably bound to other human beings. At a more profound level they evoke echoes of the mirror stage, the original confrontation with one's own body simultaneously doubled and severed from its surroundings. Human skeletons signify the inevitability of death, while fat ladies represent "eros without guilt or limit or satiety or exhaustion" (136). In short, the bodies onstage reflect back the viewer's own deepest desires and insecurities about the integrity of the self and its relationship to the world. Such responses are universal because they are tied to archetypal forms that undergird all human experience. In order to access the most profound truths about what it means to be human, any historical analysis must be preceded by a consideration of "psychic need" that seeks "prototypes neither in history or anthropology, nor in embryology or teratology, but in depth psychology, which deals with our basic uncertainty about the limits of our bodies and our egos" (27). Fiedler understands "depth psychology" as the study of archetypal patterns imprinted at a preconscious level, and it is within this realm that he effects his escape from the historical context that was his inspiration into the more enduring strata of myth.[37]

Nostalgia is the governing emotion in *Freaks*, which gestures to a distant past when human oddities were more readily available. These were not the annoying hippies loitering on any street corner or park bench, but true prodigies whose bodies evoked a shudder of recognition and disavowal. *Freaks* is a work suffused with longing for a time when such figures were treated with wonder and reverence, responses that reside now only at the deepest levels of the psyche. Fiedler's nostalgia is driven by a sense that encounters with freaks once gave rise to an originary wholeness that has been lost as we have learned to interpret them in terms of pathology, rather than sources of awe. But if the longing for an "equivocal and sacred unity" (19) exists on a psychic register so profound and irrational that it defies representation, how is Fiedler authorized to access and render it in textual terms? Such speculation is possible only if the author assumes that his own fantasies and nightmares are representative. The problem with *Freaks* is that the blurring of self into Other too often means only that the Other becomes subsumed within the "secret self" mentioned in the work's subtitle. Interpreted though the lens of a diluted Freudian psychoanalysis, the freak at certain moments is little more than a double or a projection of the psyche's own internal contradictions.

For Fiedler, freaks are inherently sexualized, for they evoke submerged desires that are otherwise available only in fantasies. In particular, they stir the longing for union with an alien Other: "[A]bnormality arouses in some 'normal' beholders a temptation to go beyond looking to *knowing* in the full carnal sense the ultimate Other. This desire is itself felt as freaky, however, since it implies not only a longing for degradation but a dream of breaching the last taboo against miscegenation" (137). Although Fiedler is referring here to prohibitions against racial miscegenation, his notion that all human eroticism is founded on an attraction of opposites—the more different the more forbidden and passionate the attraction—is implicitly heterosexual. Indeed, his entire description of freaks' sexual appeal presupposes not only a heterosexual, but a masculine sensibility. It speaks in the voice of a male libido that longs to be engulfed in abundant feminine fleshiness, as if this were a universal desire. The discussion of giants, for example, moves from the observation that there are few actual giants in the world to the Freudian claim that our interest in them comes from "memories of having once been cuddled against the buxom breast and folded into the ample arms of a warm, soft Giantess, whose bulk—to our 8-pound, 21-inch infant selves—must have seemed as mountainous as any 600-pound Fat Lady." The cherished memory of being mothered is imprinted within the lusty drives of adult men who wish to "rediscover in our later loves the superabundance of female flesh which we remember from our first . . . a satisfaction we all project in dreams, though we may be unwilling to confess it once we are awake" (131). Such passages answer the question about the sources of Fiedler's knowledge about archetypes. His own desires form the basis for his theory of natural human drives, allowing him to dismiss those (men) who reject them as out of touch with the substance of their own fantasies.

Unabashed about attributing his erotic predilections to a residual infantile sexuality, Fiedler betrays an animosity towards women who assert themselves as something other than objects of male desire. Assuming an explicitly male reader in his chapter on hermaphrodites, he writes, "[T]hough we no longer believe that women, however wicked, can make men sterile, we still fear that some can cause impotence" (178). This is particularly the case in modern permutations of the "witch," whose aim is to destroy the male ego, and who has been adopted "as a role model by mysandrist radical feminists" (179). Feminism, rendered cultish and irrational by the evocation of witchcraft, is associated not with attempts to empower women, but with the belittlement and denigration of men. Likewise, Fiedler writes of bearded ladies, "certain neo-feminists are trying to 'normalize' such members of their sex—or at least to make us perceive them even with whiskers full grown not as monstrous but as leaders in the fight to liberate all women from traditional, and presumably debasing, sex roles. Nonetheless," he concludes smugly, "I would guess that even now more Bearded Ladies choose careers as Freaks than as revolutionaries" (143).[38] This statement jars with Fiedler's more insightful criticism of a beauty industry aimed at freakifying the female body. Having registered his individual protest against gender oppression, he objects to the spectacle of organized resistance, particularly when it involves crowds of angry women. While freaks are rich terrain for exploring personal desires and anxieties, they cannot become the basis for, or an element of, any collective form of political protest. Because the power Fiedler ascribes to freaks derives largely from heterosexual male fantasies, he objects particularly to any attempt to unsettle conventional relations between the sexes by empowering women.

It is no accident that he accuses women of leveling the loudest and most objectionable campaign for civil rights, for he sees their demands as a threat to the heterosexual masculinity so important to the freak's phantasmic allure. Not only had the feminist movement radicalized women, but the general atmosphere of social upheaval had the distressing effect of feminizing dissident young men. The unfortunate connection Fiedler imagines among expressive politics, male effeminacy, and the total breakdown of the social order is most evident in his essay "The New Mutants," which describes the events of the 1960s as "the abandonment of the classroom in favor of the Dionysiac pack, the turning from *polis* to *thiasos*, from forms of social organization traditionally thought of as male to the sort of passionate community attributed by the ancients to females out of control."[39] As they participate in this frightening mob, a new generation of young men is emasculated. Not only have advances in birth control "placed paternity at the mercy and whims of women,"[40] but changing styles of dress and behavior have blurred the boundaries between male and female in unseemly ways, for young men "have embraced certain kinds of gesture and garb, certain accents and tones traditionally associated with females or female impersonators; which is why we have been observing recently (in life as well as fiction and verse) young boys, quite unequivocally male, playing all the traditional roles of women: the vamp, the coquette, the whore, the icy tease, the pure young virgin."[41] Finally, he connects the free love of countercultural freaks to bodily contamination and moral depravity, asking, "[H]ow can we bring ourselves to applaud without reservation a group of believers who offer us a kind of salvation, to be sure, a way out of the secular trap in which we have been struggling, but who are themselves ridden by superstition, wracked by diseases spread in the very act of love, dedicated to subverting sweet reason through the use of psychedelic drugs and the worship of madness, committed to orgiastic sex and doctrinaire sterility, pursuing ecstasy even when it debauches in murder, denying finally the very ideal of the human in whose name we have dubbed our species *homo sapiens*?" (382). Paradoxically, while Fiedler argues that our attraction to freaks is the most profound expression of our humanity, he contends that freaks in their embodied form are carriers of disease and perversion who betray the human. In the end, his professed longing for the fleshly encounter with freaks is belied by disgust at those who attempt to transform the affirmation of deviance into a lifestyle. The same might be said of the radicals discussed earlier, who fantasize about living next to, sleeping with, and becoming the Other, but often balk at the hard work of realizing that project.

This reticence returns us to Fiedler's hasty retreat from the promise of an alliance between struggles for social equality and the study of deviant bodies, for any self-consciously political representation would inevitably shatter the freak's ability to inspire wonder and fear. Towards the end of *Freaks* he even casts a dubious eye on his own project, intimating that all attempts at visual or written interpretation "inevitably betray the mystery of Freaks" (318). If a group of persons such as dwarves attempted to organize politically, "who would have heard them then above the millions of students demanding peace and parity, more millions of blacks clamoring for political power, or the cries of the largest oppressed group of all, women" (89). In the wake of the 1960s, Fiedler confronts a scene where everyone is a revolutionary and the particularity of each group's position is lost in the dim of oppositional voices. It is not that he has any inherent objection to those demands; much of his writing is sympathetic to the marginal and the outcast. But in an atmosphere where each coalition insists on the right to represent itself, Fiedler is distressed to witness his role as their spokesperson diminish in importance.

The counterculture's reinvigoration of freaks, which inspired and fueled Fiedler's study, ultimately gives way to his disillusionment with the politics of such generational upheaval. Although he begins by analyzing the new politicization of freaks, Fiedler subsumes the political into the domain of myth and psychology in an effort to protect the "quasi-religious awe" that he associates with the deviant body. For if *freak* were to become a political designation, the freak could no longer stand as a pure signifier of the author's own "secret self," his deepest fears and desires, his longing for a lost wholeness irrevocably shattered by his entry into the adult world. Echoing the position of the victimized longhair, *Freaks* thus valorizes a masculine subject that takes a certain pleasure in understanding himself as always fragmentary, lacking, empty. Ultimately it is this desire to preserve the self-rending experience of loss that propels the work forward, as its pessimism about the possibilities of collective social change validates the author's own irretrievably divided subjectivity.

The Afterlife of Freaks

It is fitting that the subtitle of Fiedler's work describes freaks as "myths and images of the secret self." Represented as universal human archetypes, these fantasies bear the distinctly autobiographical imprint of the author's own psychology. As was the case with radicals Abbie Hoffman and Jerry Rubin, Fiedler's search for freaks at the margins of society collapses into self-exploration often followed by uncritical identification with the Other. Not surprisingly, what they find within is a deviance that allows longhaired dissidents and aging English professors to claim the same oppositional status as the dispossessed. As *freak* became something anyone could be, an aspect of all human subjectivity, the suffering and isolation of those who had previously worn that label diminished in importance.

The expanded significance of the freak had consequences for popular culture and cultural criticism alike. Not only were the radical freaks accused of "selling out," but *freak* itself became a commodity. Of course, freaks have been exhibited for profit for many centuries, but as *freak* evolved into a valued sign of individual hipness it presented a new set of marketing opportunities. Many of the artists and musicians who earned their fame denouncing the greed and excess of the culture around them also grew rich as a result of their success. The counterculture, which had coalesced in protest against the materialism of an older generation, became a style for sale in the form of mass-produced souvenirs, accessories, and clothing. One remarkable example appeared in a *Teen* fashion spread, which instructed its readers about how to "freak out": "be as far out and nonconformist as you dare. Exaggerated makeup is a must for freakettes. Tricolored op art designs decorate Linda's fair face. Janis, in a one-piece bathing suit, is daubed head to foot in luminescent paints. Jeannie, who looks better in a leopard skin than a leopard, has painted the words 'Freak Out' on her legs. Carol is wearing the new mini skirt she's too shy to wear on the street. Cam's shift was cut from a lace window curtain and Frank's slacks from a chintz couch cover."[42] Caught up in the banalities of adolescent trendiness, *freak* loses both its radical countercultural status and any connection to the unfortunate beings who continue to be exhibited at sideshows. Thirty years later, freak iconography decorates lunch boxes, T-shirts, and refrigerator magnets, and a trade in previously owned freakabilia is thriving on the eBay Web site.

Such developments inspired Fiedler to write *Freaks*, his attempt to recapture a past that had been overshadowed by the freak's politicization in the 1960s and commercialization in the 1970s. Though flawed in many ways as a scholarly analysis, Fiedler's work is an important and largely unacknowledged precursor to the cultural studies approaches that would flourish in the 1980s and 1990s. The interest in popular culture and frank treatment of eroticism and fantasy that allowed Fiedler to claim the status of intellectual dissident among an earlier generation now provide some of the most important and familiar topics of scholarly investigation. In the foreword to a 1996 collection of essays, Fiedler comments on the changed climate that made the academic study of freaks possible: "It seems that my deliberately unfashionable book has opened the way for an innovative yet mainstream volume on a once iconoclastic subject that is nevertheless published by a university press, suitable for classroom use, and appropriate to both an interdisciplinary academic audience as well as the general reader."[43] Behind a characteristic immodesty, Fiedler accurately assesses the transformations that have made formerly reviled aspects of culture into a vital area of research, teaching, and publication.

Ironically, despite the questionable gender politics and overt animosity towards the women's movement he expresses in *Freaks,* Feidler's insights anticipate certain developments in feminist scholarship, such as the interest in the grotesque body inspired by the English translation of Mikhail Bakhtin's *Rabelais and His World.* Building on Bakhtin's argument for the revolutionary potential of carnival, critics observed that the grotesque may pose an affirmative challenge to the idealized classical body and the normative social order it enforces. And could there be any more literal incarnation of the Bakhtinian grotesque than the freak's unruly, asymmetrical body? Remarking on a lengthy tradition of coding the grotesque as feminine enabled feminist scholars both to criticize the association of women's bodies with the horror and shame of the abject and to see the grotesque as a source of powerful, disruptive potential.[44] At various moments in *Freaks,* Fiedler himself writes with sensitivity about oppressive gender norms that cause women to feel disgust at their own bodies. For example: "[W]hen young women find what they are taught to regard as 'excess hair' growing between their breasts, on the upper lips, in their armpits or on their legs, they may doubt their full femininity as well as their full humanity. A whole industry, indeed, has grown up by exploiting their fear: advertising painless electrolysis, sure-fire depilatories, and dainty mini-razors for women eager to de-freakify themselves before a night of partying or a day at the beach" (32). If hirsute freaks stir anxieties about the freakish potential of our own bodies, the beauty industry capitalizes on that fear by encouraging women to perceive certain physical attributes as defects.

While women are the primary target of the cosmetic industry, Fiedler per-

ceived that the rigid division of the sexes affects men and women alike. The freak
show hermaphrodite is an extreme example of the continuum between male and
female that he saw as characteristic of all human sexuality. Drawing on medical literature, he writes, "[T]he study of intersexuality reinforces a prior conviction that
none of us is (or at least it would be useful to act as if none of us were) exclusively
male or female, but rather, to one degree or another, bisexual. Certainly there is a
prima facie case for this point of view, in the area of 'gender' at least, since gender
identity and role are clearly matters of convention, socially determined and reinforced" (195). In the early 1990s, feminism and queer theory would seize on hermaphroditism as evidence that human sexuality is far more varied than the binary
opposition between male and female allows. If gender had previously been recognized as a social construction, the hermaphrodite suggests that sex is also the
product of culture rather than nature.[45] Inspired by the breakdown of gender
roles taking place everywhere around him, Fiedler sees in the freak show prototypes of the more multiple and fluid forms of identity promoted by the counterculture. These more radical insights about sex and gender coexist somewhat
paradoxically alongside his more strident denunciations of women's liberation and
the effeminacy of male hippies. While Fiedler himself would not be the one to
work through these contradictions, they have made his writing available to critics
committed to linking the freak's nonconformity with progressive theories of gender and sexuality.

The consequences of the freak's proliferation in the wake of the 1960s defy simple
evaluative judgments. Freaks are turned into yet another consumer item, but also
the grounds for a more expansive and politically conscious cultural criticism. Both
are aspects of the broader development I have attempted to chart over the course
of act 2, which has documented the freak's increasing assimilation as an aspect of
individual and group dynamics. Once seen as that which was radically Other, in
the middle decades of the twentieth century freaks became symbols of the contradictions and strangeness within. This turn of events coincides with cultural critics' increasing turn towards Freudian psychoanalysis, with its vision of a subject
irretrievably divided against itself, and the counterculture's interest in the untapped hallucinatory aspects of consciousness lying just beyond the doors of
perception. For Carson McCullers, the Freak Pavilion's opposition between deviance and normalcy gave way to a recognition of all people as "a mixture of delicious and freak." Reserving her strongest criticism for racial divisions based on
visible bodily differences, she devised characters who struggle to imagine alternatives in which each individual's inevitable hybridity could be tolerated and affirmed.

Diane Arbus earned a reputation as a photographer of freaks, a celebrity who turned the subjects of her art into extensions of herself. Her work opened the way for photographers like Joel Peter Witkin to describe his images of freaks as projections of individual fantasy. It is not surprising that both McCullers and Arbus make an appearance in Leslie Fiedler's *Freaks,* a work of cultural criticism that echoes the shifting focus of art and literature towards the "secret self." While, as I have argued, McCullers, Arbus, and Fiedler all were knowledgeable about and engaged with the freak show's history, the overwhelming thrust of their work is the reincorporation of freakishness back into the authorial consciousness. As the sideshow's curiosities are taken up by art and literature, the freak is assimilated as a double, Other, or effect of subjectivity. This movement can result in self-absorption of the kind we see in *Freaks*, or a greater understanding of the way that individual disaffection may be attributed to an oppressive social context. Recognizing freaks as a problem generated by one's own culture, rather than imported from elsewhere, makes it possible to approach that problem from within. Instead of continuing in this vein, however, act 3 will chart a surprising turn of events in which the freak's absolute alterity is asserted anew, but in the service of a very different set of motivations than those that inspired the classic freak show impresario.

☞ *ACT THREE*

ACT THREE

THE BLACK LOOK AND
THE "SPECTACLE OF WHITEFOLKS"
Wildness in Toni Morrison's Beloved

> *"Freaky," said Milkman. "Some freaky shit."*
> *"Freaky world," said Guitar. "A freaky, fucked-up world."*
> TONI MORRISON, *Song of Solomon*

Few readers of Toni Morrison's *Beloved* (1987) recall that early in the novel Sethe, Denver, and Paul D visit a carnival freak show. The black customers who approach the fairgrounds are "breathless with the excitement of seeing whitepeople loose: doing magic, clowning, without heads or with two heads, twenty feet tall or two feet tall, weighing a ton, completely tattooed, eating glass, swallowing fire, spitting ribbons, twisted into knots, forming pyramids, playing with snakes and beating each other up." These loose "whitepeople" are the carnival's main attraction, freaks who boast feats of strength and agility, amazing extremes of shape and size, and bodies that press at the very boundaries of the human.[1]

All too soon, this compelling description is revealed as the fickle promise of a publicity agent. But the carnival's failure to live up to the wonders anticipated by its advertising, and the obvious racism of its employees, are of little consequence for the black visitors determined to enjoy its pleasures: "[T]he barker called their children names ('Pickaninnies free!') but the food on his vest and the hole in his pants rendered it fairly harmless. In any case it was a small price to pay for the fun they might not ever have again. Two pennies and an insult were well spent if it meant seeing the spectacle of whitefolks making a spectacle of themselves." Enduring the insults of a resentful carnival staff, the black spectators are thrilled by the unprecedented sight of white performers on display for their entertainment. For once, instead of being the object of surveillance, the black fairgoer is a member of the audience who has paid to point and stare. Despite the performers' hostility—"One-Ton Lady spit at them" and "Arabian Nights Dancer cut her performance to three minutes instead of the usual fifteen she normally did"—or perhaps because of it, the black audience draws together, a sense of community reinforced through their perceived differences from the freaks onstage.

Paul D takes particular enjoyment in the experience of the carnival. An ideal consumer, he buys candy for Sethe and Denver and gawks at the freaks' spectacular bodies.[2] But his credulity reaches its limits when he confronts an ordinary black man playing the part of a wild African savage. Otherwise willing to suspend his disbelief, Paul D vehemently rejects the conventions of spectatorship that should dictate his reception of the show: "When Wild African Savage shook his bars and said wa, wa, Paul D told everybody he knew him back in Roanoke."[3] It is not surprising that the only black person in the troupe is masquerading as a wild African savage, the role of dangerous exotic predictably assigned to nonwhite carnies. By claiming familiarity with this man, who is not from savage Africa but Roanoke, Paul D disrupts the fiction of his absolute alterity as well as the apparently solid boundary between spectator and performer.

This richly evocative confrontation is diffused in the film version of *Beloved* (Jonathan Demme, 1999), which faithfully reproduces the dialogue but in so muted a form that its significance is lost. Speaking amidst the noise of the crowd, Paul D's words are reduced to a lighthearted aside rather than a powerful intervention in the fairgoers' enjoyment of the spectacle. The carnival scene has been treated with similar neglect in the extensive body of criticism devoted to Morrison's fiction. This chapter will argue that the scene provides an important key to understanding *Beloved* as well as adding complexity to the analysis of racial freaks that has been evolving throughout this book. As Morrison once remarked, her fiction is intended to provide "the kind of information you can find between the lines of history. . . . It's right there in the intersection where an institution becomes personal, where the historical becomes people with names."[4] In what follows, I read *Beloved* as a novel that gives voice to stories about the freak show that otherwise lurk "between the lines of history." When Paul D locates the wild African savage within a familiar context, he translates the institution of human exhibition into something of personal consequence for each member of the community. The freak show's treatment of race—the combinations of exotic costuming and pseudoscientific ballyhoo described in chapter 2—might seem so obvious that it virtually goes without saying. But if the black man masquerading as a wild African savage is such a crude and self-evident manifestation of racial stereotyping that it hardly needs interpretation, the reactions of audiences to such performances are less easily explained.

Paul D's response to the spectacle has numerous counterparts in memoirs and legends about carnival life. This chapter will consider a number of historical analogues to the encounter fictionalized in *Beloved*, in which the wild man's act is disrupted by the unruly behavior of audience members. Analysis of these interruptions provides an alternative perspective on the portrait of freak shows that has emerged in preceding chapters, for it shifts the interpretive focus from their content to their reception. The interruption draws attention to the role of spectators, who did not simply absorb the tableaux of bodies exhibited before them, but responded actively to what they were seeing. Historical evidence about spectatorship reveals that freak shows offered a particularly unconvincing form of racial performance, that, when it came to wild men and savage tribes, audiences seem to have regularly discounted the truth of what they saw. Indeed, in the age of the confidence man epitomized by Barnum's maxim, "a sucker is born every minute," it appears that one of the primary pleasures of viewing a racial exhibit was to disclose its fraudulence.[5] Spectators' desire to unmask the racial freak as a hoax did not mean that they questioned the exhibit's underlying assumption of white supremacy, but their reactions betray that, in their eyes, the natives of Africa or Asia assumed a dubious status akin to Martians, mermaids, or missing links. Even when the exotics were what they claimed to be—Igorots from the Philippines, African Pygmies, Ubangi women—they were subject to impudent prodding by customers who had to touch to believe. However, for an audience of African Americans who bore the burden of such racial stereotypes, the delight of revelation was magnified, for it was a moment when, catching white showmen in the act, they could briefly seize control of representation.

This is the information "between the lines of history" that Morrison summons up in her scene of carnivalesque reversal and unmasking, which occurs immediately before the mysterious Beloved's appearance and is of great consequence to the events that follow. The episode, in which the collective identity of the spectators is broken down and reconfigured, becomes a paradigm for the narrative's broader concern with the difficulty of forming alliances among persons who have endured intense suffering. As the audience of ex-slaves at the freak show draws together, it reveals a troubling aspect of communities that have the potential to heal, but rely on the exclusion of even more marginalized others in order to identify as a group.

Under Morrison's pen Paul D's meeting with the wild African savage unveils the pernicious fiction of racist stereotypes, but not of race itself. Ultimately, the arsenal for collective healing is stored as a form of racial memory transmitted bodily from one generation to the next. Like freaks, Morrison's characters are defined entirely in corporeal terms; emotions are projected outwards onto the contours of their bodies, which are so often scarred, wounded, or disabled. Ancestral traumas pulsate in the blood of their offspring and memories materialize as rememories so concrete a person can bump into them.[6] Morrison's preoccupation with physicality distinguishes her from the positions articulated in act 2, where freaks point to the need for a common humanity that transcends superficial differences between spectators and the unfortunate figures onstage. Whereas there the freak's physical deviance represents individual or collective disorder, in *Beloved,* the body is a foundation for the formation of communal bonds and the exclusion of outsiders. If Morrison disputes the false opposition between freak and normal, she insists on other intractable differences: race enables the black spectator to identify with the wild African savage, and race precludes identification with the other freaks. *Beloved* ends by denying that those who bear the legacy of slavery in their bodies could unite with those who do not on the basis of a mutual humanity. The side-show freak, whose properties are soon transferred onto the freakish Beloved, is a figure for the impossibility of that union.

The Black Look and the "spectacle of whitefolks"

Paul D's spirited interruption of the freak show is a fictional rendition of numerous historical accounts in which a wild man's act is stopped short by the antics of an unruly spectator. The episode, as Morrison describes it, draws attention to the contours of the racial freak's performance and reception as it occurred in the past; in turn, a sustained consideration of historical evidence offers insight about the scene's significance to the novel. The wild man was a stock sideshow personality, along with other common types such as fat ladies, tattooed people, giants, and midgets. As shown in chapter 1, during the period of their greatest popularity, freak shows consistently trafficked in representations of non-Western races that combined pedagogy and entertainment, pseudoscientific jargon and fantastic hyperbole. In doing so, they offered simplified answers to the pressing concerns about race that would have provoked their predominantly white audiences, already anxious about the consequences of slavery and its aftermath, great waves of seemingly inassimilable immigrants, and imperial expansion.[7] As James W. Cook Jr. writes of Barnum's famous "What Is It?" the "scientific" questions raised by an African American man advertised as a missing link "quickly spilled over into even more controversial questions of racial definition, politics, and property."[8] Freak show savages equated race with a monstrous deviance made clearly legible on the surfaces of the body. The interior of the tent or dime museum mapped the differences between freak and normal in concrete spatial terms: the physical separation between the onlooker and the figures on the exhibition platform announced itself as a vast, existential divide between spectacularly individuated deviance and the comfortable anonymity of normalcy. As the black body was transformed into a hypervisible spectacle, the audience aspired to blend together into a transparent,

FIGURE 29. Unnamed
man posing as a freak show
savage. Courtesy Theatre
Arts Collection, Harry
Ransom Humanities
Research Center, the
University of Texas at
Austin.

homogenous whiteness. Those most anxious about their own status as citizens ap-
plauded the reassuring vision of nonwhite bodies that absolutely could not be assimilated.[9]

Indeed, whether foolish and docile or wild with rage and bloodlust, the racial
freak's dominant message is the unassimilability of the dark-skinned body (figure
29). I use the terms "racial freak" and "wild man" interchangeably to refer to a particular kind of exhibition that linked the spectacle of ferocious wildness to racial
and national difference. As W. C. Thompson explained in his 1905 memoir, *On the
Road with a Circus*, "[T]he original circus wild man, the denizen of Borneo, was
white, but his successors have almost invariably had dark skins."[10] The pre-
dictability of such connections between wildness and dark skin is confirmed by

FIGURE 30. Hiram and
Barney Davis, the micro-
cephalic brothers first
exhibited as Waino and
Plutano, the Wild Men of
Borneo. Courtesy Theatre
Arts Collection, Harry
Ransom Humanities
Research Center, the
University of Texas at
Austin.

journalist Scott Hart, who remarked in 1946, "[M]ost Wild Men from Borneo are
amiable Negro boys from about the circus lot who are trained to growl, flash a set
of fake tusks and eat raw meat. . . . The Wild Man is always from Borneo. The
Bear Woman is from the darkest wilds of Africa. The Pinheaded Man is from the
jungle-ridden regions of Somewhere."[11] The formulaic print "ethnographies"
that often accompanied these exhibits associated wildness with remote geographical locales. A pamphlet on Waino and Plutano, the original Wild Men of Borneo,
for example, informed the reader, "Borneo is an island so large that England, Ire-
land, and Scotland might be set down in the middle of it. The interior of this vast
island is a dense forest, inhabited by a race of humanity very little different from
the animal creation."[12] Couched in pedagogical terms, such explanatory narratives perpetuated commonly held assumptions about the physical and cultural
Otherness of non-Western and nonwhite people (figure 30).

In contrast to the presentation of physically disabled freaks, who might answer questions, lecture the audience about their unusual bodies, or demonstrate their capacity to perform everyday activities, the wild man was deliberately inarticulate and undomesticated, his snarls and roars a sign of his absolute inability to communicate through language. "I was all stripped 'cept around the middle and wore a claw necklace; had to make out as if I couldn't talk. 'Twas mighty tiresome to howl and grin all day," recalls a former wild man quoted in Thompson's memoir.[13] Sometimes eating raw meat, biting the heads off live animals, or drinking blood, the wild man's voracious and indiscriminate appetites attested to his preference for the raw to the cooked. Often described in the terms of popular evolutionary science as a "missing link," the wild man was said to come from a lost species located somewhere on the developmental chain between human and beast. While such acts were a regular part of low-budget traveling carnivals like the one described in *Beloved*, they were equally popular in more reputable venues such as world's fairs and museums. There, they were greeted with interest by scientific professionals and respectable citizens such as lawyer George Templeton Strong, who noted in his diary in 1860 that he had "stopped at Barnum's on my way downtown to see the much advertised nondescript, the 'What-is-it.'"[14] In short, while the venue and tenor of the performance might vary, the exhibition of nonwhite persons as wild men, cannibals, and missing links was an acceptable source of entertainment and knowledge for spectators across the social spectrum (figure 31).

Authenticity was always an important part of the freak show's promotional rhetoric, which advertised exhibits as LIVE! TRUE! REAL! GENUINE! Despite such hyperbolic claims of veracity, the exotic act was the most easily and regularly fabricated of all attractions. More often than not, those advertised as Zulu warriors, Wild Men from Borneo, and Dahomeans were actually people of color from nearby urban locales.[15] As William C. Fitzgerald observed in an 1897 article on sideshows, "Certainly it is far easier and cheaper to engage and 'fit-up' as the 'Cuban Wonder' an astute individual from the New York slums, than to send costly missions to the Pearl of the Antilles in search of human curiosities."[16] Former sideshow managers and employees unapologetically recall how they participated in the fabrication of ethnographic freaks. Indeed, the creation of a wild man is a recurrent chapter in the formulaic genre of the carnival memoir. Hart tells the following story:

On a platform before the tent a tense, narrow-cheeked man related how the unfortunate individual from Borneo knew the whereabouts of neither father,

FIGURE 31. This
publicity poster for
the What Is It? provides a
sense of Barnum's intended
clientele. Dressed in the
respectable garb of the
middle class, this group,
which includes women and
children, implies that the
entertainment provided by
the American Museum is
suitable for the whole
family. © Collection of The
New-York Historical
Society.

mother, nor home, and that five thousand dollars would be paid anyone
providing such information.

Inside the tent, a fat rural woman said, "Oh, ain't that awful!" A child
asked, "You reckon he can get out?" But when dinnertime came, the Wild
Man was taken to meet a distinguished local circus fan and his wife. In the
ensuing pleasantries, he created a very happy social impression.

With professional awareness, however, the Wild Man failed to mention
that he came from South Carolina.[17]

Hart's anecdote exploits the discrepancy between the barker's deliberately mysti-
fied rhetoric and the mundane, but quite respectable, activities of the wild man
upon leaving the display platform. Others are less sanguine about the arrangement between performers and their managers. Thompson describes the career of
Calvin Bird, "a negro who hailed from Pearson, GA [who] toured most of the
country, mystifying all who saw him and sending them away impressed with a conviction that he was all he was represented to be. Not until he appeared at a Syracuse hospital with a request that his horns be removed was the secret of his

unnatural appearance disclosed. Under his scalp was found inserted a silver plate, in which stood two standards. In these, when he was on exhibition, Bird screwed two goat horns."[18] In contrast to the comfortable arrangement between Hart's wild man and his promoters, Bird suffered bodily harm for the sake of his act. Far from demonstrating that he was a missing link, this elaborate ruse proved the wild man to be all too human, the victim of abusive surgeons and greedy showmen. Illustrating his remark that "the life of the professional wild man is an unhappy one at best," Thompson adds the story of a black man from Baltimore who ran out of money while visiting Berlin and "enlisted as an untamed arrival from Africa with a small American circus then playing abroad. He endured the torture he was compelled to undergo for a month and then stole away to a hospital"[19] to recuperate from the forced diet of raw horse meat and blood and the chill of performing during cold weather dressed only in a loincloth.[20]

Such anecdotal evidence bespeaks the pragmatic, and often cruel, opportunism of sideshow managers, who cared far less about the authenticity promised in their advertising than the lucrative consequences of maintaining a steady supply of unique and varied attractions. Accounts of their fraudulence are numerous and unsurprising: after all, it was the showman's job to create illusions that amused and deceived his customers, and the wild man conformed to prevailing beliefs about racial inferiority. The standard was set by Barnum, who began his career by exhibiting a racial freak, an elderly, disabled slave named Joice Heth who claimed to be the 161-year-old nurse of George Washington. A black woman whose body was contorted with age and years of hard labor was easily transformed into a sensation through Barnum's skillful publicity campaign. When an autopsy following Heth's death revealed her to be no more than eighty, Barnum deflected controversy by professing himself the victim of a hoax devised by Heth and her former owners.[21] Barnum's autobiographical writings provide different and somewhat contradictory accounts of these events, but they are consistently uninterested in proving that Heth was what she claimed to be. In some versions, Barnum conspires with Heth to deceive the public, while in others he is innocent, but in each version he establishes humbug as the rule rather than the exception in the showman's trade.[22]

These examples attest to the performative gap between black actor and stage persona, but also to the frequency with which that disjuncture recurred in narratives about the freak show. As I have argued, the freak show's theatrical conventions induct actors and audiences into a carefully orchestrated relationship, albeit one that was frequently violated by misbehavior on both sides of the velvet rope.[23] In *Beloved*, the ex-slaves experience the carnival, with its "spectacle of whitefolks," as a temporary release from their more ordinary interactions with the white citizens of Cincinnati. The freaks, in turn, feel little obligation to behave professionally when they confront an audience that they deem inferior. The performers' crude disdain is met by the customers' rude jeers and laughter. Facing off in a venue where rowdy, indecorous behavior was the norm, spectators and performers apparently felt free to modulate their behavior in response to one another, climaxing in the open exchange of hostilities between marginalized groups.

The festive, unrestrained atmosphere of carnival often gave rise to the kind of disruptive misbehavior that Morrison describes. While it is not particularly surprising to find that racial freaks were local people of color tricked out in costume, more striking is the evidence that *audiences* seemed so rarely to believe what they saw. For instance, having viewed the "What Is It?" at Barnum's Museum, Strong opined, "Some say it's an advanced chimpanzee, others that it's a cross between nigger and baboon. But it seems to me clearly an idiotic negro dwarf, raised, perhaps, in Alabama or Virginia. The showman's story of capture (with three other specimens that died) by a party in pursuit of the gorilla on the western coast of Africa is probably bosh."[24] Strong distinguishes his own capacity for prudent discrimination from the speculations of other observers and the showman's fantastic account of peril and adventure. As the episode from *Beloved* suggests, even Paul D—a customer determined to enjoy the pleasures of carnival—questions the implausible spectacle of a black man performing as an African savage. Such moments of resistance are to be found across diverse groups of patrons, but the most powerful accounts are of the kind Morrison describes, in which a black spectator looks with suspicion and disbelief at a racist performance, refuses to enter into its fiction, and loudly enjoins the audience into collective incredulity. In his 1913 biography, circus veteran George Middleton offers a neat parallel to Paul D's encounter with the wild African savage: "In the side show we have a big negro whom we had fitted up with rings in his nose, a leopard skin, some assagais and a large shield made out of cows' skin. While he was sitting on stage in the side show, along came two negro women and remarked, 'See that nigger over there? He ain't no Zulu, that's Bill Jackson. He worked over here at Camden on the dock. I seen that nigger often.' Poor old Bill Jackson was as uneasy as if he was sitting on needles, holding the shield between him and the two negro women."[25] Like Paul D, the women in Middleton's anecdote disrupt the exhibition, shattering the fourth wall by speaking directly to the stage. The interpellative gesture of recognition— "I know you!"—dispels the illusion of the wild man's absolute alterity, relocating him within the community of onlookers. Instead of a Zulu, he is Bill Jackson; rather than hailing from Africa, he is a dock worker from New Jersey. The account derives its humor from the transformation of the shield intended as a sign of tribal savagery into a barrier protecting the guilty man from the female customers he was supposed to terrorize.

Such instances are best understood by turning from an analysis of the *content* of freak exhibition to questions of *spectatorship*. The racism of wild men and cannibal acts is crude and obvious, but why were audiences so eager to interrupt these performances? Theories of cinematic reception help to explain the shifting and unpredictable relationship between the spectator and the visual image.[26] Eric Lott has productively applied these insights to an analysis of minstrelsy, where he describes the experience of cinema as "a destabilized structure of fascination, a continual confusion of subject and object" in which "we successively identify, across gender lines, with logical screen representatives of ourselves (heroes, victims), then with seeming adversaries (villains, killers), and so on."[27] Like a film narrative, the freak show implicitly situated the viewer in a particular relationship to its content; however the response of actual spectators did not always conform to structural expectations.[28] The black fairgoer faced problems of identification akin to those of the black film viewer: confronted by representations of African Americans ranging from the uninteresting to the degrading, she had to identify across racial boundaries or forgo the visual pleasures of identification altogether.

Film theory is a useful point of entry for understanding the shifting contours of reception, for it provides the most sustained consideration of the random ways in which any given spectator will identify with, repudiate, or otherwise respond to narrative cinema. Yet such theories have only limited ability to account for live performance. In the scenes I have described, the flash of identificatory insight is followed by a cry that utterly disrupts the action taking place onstage and invites the rest of the audience to join in a ritual of communal disbelief. It is impossible for the wild man to continue beyond the moment of recognition, for his act depends on the illusion of his absolute inscrutability. Only during a live encounter can the viewer's response register with and alter the course of the dramatic action. In fact, an important ingredient in the audience's enjoyment of freak shows seems to have been precisely this capacity to deconstruct the visual evidence presented to them. Although the reasons for their satisfaction would inevitably vary from one viewing constituency to another, interruption, misidentification, and the possibility of fraudulence contributed considerably to the shows' appeal.

The pleasures of unmasking are part of a broader nineteenth-century preoccupation with the figure of the confidence man. His reliance on trickery and deception was the unsavory counterpart to the Horatio Alger story of legitimate success gained through hard work and ingenuity. Neil Harris attributes the effi-cacy of P. T. Barnum's hoaxes to a public that appreciated "the sheer exhilaration of debate, the utter fun of the opportunity to learn and evaluate, whether the sub-ject was an ancient slave, an exotic mermaid, or a politician's honor. Barnum's audiences found the encounter with potential frauds exciting. It was a form of in-tellectual exercise, stimulating even when the truth could not be determined."[29] Ferreting out deception at the freak show doubtless gratified audiences by prov-ing their ability distinguish between a scam and the real thing. George Templeton Strong takes manifest pride in recognizing the What Is It? as an ordinary African American and not a missing link. But the particular scenes of recognition of con-cern to my argument deal more specifically with racial boundaries and identifica-tions *among* African Americans, who were both viewers and performers. An audience of ex-slaves contemplating the spectacle of a black man performing as an African savage would have a particularly savvy understanding of how slippery the-atrical representation could be. To hail the savage as "one of us" was a dangerous move because it threatened to equate the African Americans with the barbarism of Africa, but to stop the savage in his tracks gave the lie to that equation, demon-strating the power of the black look back.

In the context of *Beloved,* the moment of recognition is significant because it anticipates the novel's attempt to reverse the terms of slavery by shifting attention from the spectacle of the oppressed black body to a black viewer whose gaze im-plicates "whitefolks" as the architects of that peculiar institution. Assuming the interchangeability of one dark-skinned person for another, the freak show repre-sents the black body as inherently readable in terms of primitive exoticism. At the same time, it undercuts this assumption by acknowledging that the wild man is only readable as "wild" through an elaborate combination of costume and per-formance. Invoking the same stereotypes that made the wild African savage at the freak show possible, Stamp Paid reflects, "Whitepeople believed that what-ever the manners, under every dark skin was a jungle. Swift, unnavigable waters, swinging, screaming baboons, sleeping snakes, red gums ready for their sweet white blood" (198). The same logic that associates all black bodies with the bes-tiality of the jungle allows a man from Virginia to masquerade as a savage in a performance that just might be convincing to white audiences. When a canny spectator like Paul D reveals it as a feeble ruse, the infrastructure of racism itself, which assumes the inherent savagery of all black persons, threatens to crumble. Consistently challenged by the behavior of the slaves themselves, this system of belief requires constant vigilance and a ceaseless supply of new evidence to grant it the status of truth.

172

The scientific method is represented in *Beloved* as the corrupt means by which racial bigotry is maintained and given legitimacy as empirical fact. As I demonstrated in chapter 2, showmen and professionals alike used the rhetoric of science to prove the truth of racial difference. Thus Sethe recalls Schoolteacher's instructions to his pupils "to put her human characteristics on the left; her animal ones on the right. And don't forget to line them up" (193).[30] Schoolteacher, a merciless overseer and even more pernicious pedagogue, begins his chilling lesson with the same assumptions that undergirded Barnum's What Is It?—that the black body combines human and animal attributes—then proceeds to use scientific reasoning to detect and categorize those features. The scheme of classification Schoolteacher has devised is all the more horrifying because of the neat alignment of columns, a testament to the potential of empirical data to authorize popular racism. Naming this character Schoolteacher emphasizes the educational function of such taxonomies, which do not simply establish the "truth" of racial inferiority, but guarantee the transmission of that truth from one generation of slaveholders to the next. The encounter with Schoolteacher prompts Sethe to ask her ailing mistress to define *characteristics* for her, to which Mrs. Garner replies, "a thing that's natural to a thing" (195). This statement encapsulates the circular logic of the slave system, which naturalizes the association of blackness with certain mental and psychological deficiencies that are used, in turn, to legitimate the bondage of black people.

It is hardly necessary for Morrison, writing in 1987, to prove that the association of slaves with atavistic savagery is profoundly unnatural. Her contribution is to take the dynamic staged at the carnival, in which black viewers contemplate with delight "the spectacle of whitefolks making a spectacle of themselves" as a starting point for examining the way that slavery makes whiteness itself a visible quality.[31] The condition of human bondage encourages terrible and otherwise inexplicable acts within the slave community (such as the abandonment or murder of one's own children) but is even more damaging to those who create and enforce that system. Thus Stamp Paid thinks about how the jungle associated with blackness "spread, until it invaded the whites who had made it. Touched them every one. Changed and altered them. Made them bloody, silly, worse than even they wanted to be, so scared were they of the jungle they had made. The screaming baboon lived under their own white skin; the red gums were their own" (198–199). Stamp Paid asserts that there is nothing natural about the jungle made by those who fear the consequences of their own barbarism. From this perspective, Schoolteacher's insistence that the columns of characteristics be precisely aligned is clearly a defense against the realization that the anarchic jungle lurks within himself, a byproduct of his cruelty that must be staved off through the imposition of orderly logic. Likewise, Paul D's recognition that the wild African savage is an acquaintance from Roanoke does not simply lift the burden of barbarism from the black body, but it relocates that savagery as the brainchild of the whitefolks who manage the carnival's attractions.

The sideshow savage embodies the abject characteristics attributed to blacks to justify the persistence of inequalities after slavery and secure the purity of whiteness as his obverse. When Paul D disputes the truth of the wild man's mysterious demeanor, he also reveals the fragility of the association between blackness and bestiality, for if "African" is a fictive designation for the nationality of the man before them onstage, then surely *wild* and *savage* are equally fictitious identities. But the carnival freak's parodic wildness bespeaks a more profound and terrifying disorder. The trauma of slavery cannot be resolved by one lighthearted moment of reversal: some months later, Paul D will betray Sethe when he responds to the story of the infanticide by telling her, "You got two feet, Sethe, not four" (165), an accusation that becomes the grounds for their estrangement. Implying that Sethe's behavior is more animal than human, Paul D refuses to comprehend the impossible situation that drove her to murder her own child as a preferable alternative to relinquishing her to the approaching slavecatchers.[32] He invokes a form of wildness that has nothing to do with Africa, but is nonetheless all too real. This unfeeling remark is also the occasion for Paul D to remember that he and the other young male slaves at Sweet Home plantation regularly had sex with calves, a practice that likewise blurs the distinction between human and beast. "How fast he had moved from his shame to hers," Paul D thinks later, as he recalls the shared experience of suffering that initially drew him to Sethe but subsequently became painfully divisive.

Intended as an insult, the reminder that Sethe has "two feet" must also invoke the journey to freedom she made late in her pregnancy when, unable to use her swollen feet, she crawled on her hands and knees in a desperate effort to save her unborn infant and reach her children. The extreme horrors of slavery make it difficult, if not impossible, to pass definitive moral judgments about what constitutes properly "human" activity. The wildness mimicked by the freak show's African savage spreads with infectious power through the novel, punctuating scenes of terror like "the wildness that shot up into the eye the moment the lips were yanked back" (71) to accommodate a bit into the mouth; or Schoolteacher's reaction to the scene of carnage resulting from Sethe's effort to save her children, that "now she'd gone wild" (149). The wildness exhibited by these slaves cannot be seen as the antithesis of the slaveowner's civility, but as a mirror that reflects the

174

way that slavery has contaminated everything, threatening to dissolve moral categories and meaning itself.

Freaking Beloved

The freak show episode in *Beloved* is about more than the spectacle of whitefolks; it also provides a paradigm for reading the group dynamics that are continually reworked throughout the rest of the novel as the ex-slaves struggle to define the contours of community. The carnival sequence dramatizes the powerful, ongoing process of identity formation which, as I argued in the introduction to this book, is called into question with particular force during visits to the freak show. The consolidation of that lumpy cluster of affiliations called identity occurs not only through the positive identification of self, but by casting off the negative and undesirable elements that constitute the nonself. Nevertheless, the boundaries of identity, whether individual or collective, must be continually affirmed or reconfigured in response to external challenges. As Eve Sedgwick describes it, "to identify *as* must always include multiple processes of identification *with.* It also involves identification *as against;* but even did it not, the relations implicit in *identifying with* are, as psychoanalysis suggests, in themselves quite sufficiently fraught with intensities of incorporation, diminishment, inflation, threat, loss, reparation, and disavowal."[33] At the carnival, two disenfranchised groups confront one another with derisive animosity. The ex-slaves leer and point at the freaks, while the freaks respond with unconcealed disdain. What happens at this freak show is less a confusion about the boundaries of *individual* self and body often attributed to encounters with prodigies like conjoined twins, hermaphrodites, and persons with extra or missing limbs than a confusion about the boundaries of *group* identity. *Beloved* acknowledges similarities between these marginalized communities based on shared suffering that their members are unable to recognize from within the context of their particular experiences of degradation: the bodies of freaks and slaves, conceived as the property of others, bar them from the comforts and privileges of a humanity that exceeds the limits of corporeal identity. In other words, the extreme visibility of dark skin or severe disabilities ensures that the slave and the freak will experience the body as a prison that they cannot escape. Unable to perceive their potential affinities, each camp consolidates the boundaries of its own group identity through the rejection of an even more abject collectivity.

The visit to the fair recalls the group dynamics responsible for Sethe's eighteen-year ostracism and establishes the possibility of her eventual reincorporation into the community.[34] Optimistically called a carnival, this traveling amusement park, which is actually "a lot less than mediocre (which is why it agreed to a Colored Thursday)" (48), has little in common with the ebullient grotesqueries that Bakhtin described as "carnivalesque." Nonetheless, it maintains one of the most important features of Bakhtinian carnival, the ritualistic inversion of hierarchies and unsettling of power relations. And like the festive reversals recounted by Bakhtin, these category confusions are only temporary, serving more as a safety valve to ensure the stability of the dominant order than contributing to its overthrow; however, they anticipate the more enduring transformations that will occur around the freakish appearance and disappearance of Beloved herself.[35]

As I have noted, the carnival and the freaks that are its central attraction are a poor shadow of the wonders promised by its promotional advertisements. Regardless of its rude employees and mediocre entertainment, "it gave the four hundred black people in its audience thrill upon thrill upon thrill" (48). Far from irrelevant, the carnies' insulting behavior actually contributes to consolidating the bonds of community among the black customers. Denver, long the object of an exclusionary gaze, takes particular pleasure in being "surrounded by a crowd of people who did not find her the main attraction." As she stands with Paul D and Sethe watching the midget dance, the collective experience of looking "made the stares of other Negroes kind, gentle, something Denver did not remember seeing in their faces. Several even nodded and smiled at her mother" (48). Having encountered persons even more marginal than themselves, the group of onlookers is able to invite Sethe and Denver back into its fold. In a classic pattern of scapegoating, the freaks replace mother and child as the reviled outsiders against which the community affirms its bonds.

But this passing gesture of inclusion is hardly a promising step towards the creation of a more functional and supportive community, for it relies on the spectators' cruel sense of superiority to the freaks. The fat white lady who spits at the audience is amusing because "her bulk shortened her aim and they got a big kick out of the helpless meanness in her little eyes." She becomes an object of humorous derision when her enormous body renders her gesture of disrespect inconsequential. But the "helpless meanness" the black fairgoers detect in her eyes must be understood as the product of earning her livelihood sitting onstage, where she must endure stares, prodding, and impudent questions. The fat lady's weight imprisons her in much the same way as does the slave's black skin. *Beloved* demonstrates how the extreme rage engendered by prolonged psychological and physical cruelty may erupt in many ways, including violent aggression between one injured party and another. Although the ex-slaves are conditioned to find pleasure in unlikely places, the "big kick" they get from the fat lady's impotent meanness seems less like the deep, liberating belly laugh of Bakhtinian carnival than the barely repressed hostility that Freud attributed to defensive forms of humor.[36] I argued in chapter 3 that laughter in Tod Browning's *Freaks* was more a hysterical response to the freaks' challenge to bodily integrity than a sign of amusement; similarly, the audience's reaction to the freaks in *Beloved* must be linked to recollections of the fact that, as slaves, they were once subjected to the denigrating gaze of whitefolks and the abuse that inevitably accompanied it. "People I saw as a child," Sethe remarks later to Paul D, "who'd had the bit always looked wild after that" (71). The absurd performance of the wild African savage may invite laughter, but may simultaneously stir more unpleasant memories of a wildness born of fury, humiliation, and physical pain.

Although she too has felt the pain of being the "main attraction," Denver cannot find the grounds to identify with the carnies' unenviable situation. But the connections Denver is unable to imagine are anticipated by Morrison's use of descriptive language. Denver buys sweets from a refreshment concession "manned by a little whitegirl in ladies' high-topped shoes" (48).[37] The apparent paradoxes in this sentence attest to the plight of a child who must work for a living. The table is "manned," implying a form of labor inappropriate for a young girl whose adult's shoes literalize the burden of responsibilities beyond her years. Forced to stand in someone else's shoes, this pathetic figure, at once man, girl, and woman, is a prototype for Denver, who will also have to compensate for her mother's neglect by working for a living. She too will venture into an adult world wearing clothes that don't fit her. These encounters between fairgoers and carnies, overlaid with hostility and misunderstanding, intimate similarities between the two groups that cannot be perceived by their participants. At this point in the narrative, an awareness of these common bonds is unavailable to the insiders themselves, although it is latent within Morrison's allusive prose.

Freaks are beings whose fantastic bodies defy categorization, who are found, in the most literal sense, on the platforms of sideshows, dime museums, and the carnival midway. I designate Beloved a freak to foreground the links between slaves and carnies and to describe the profound indeterminacy of her identity (who is she and where does she come from?), which cannot be disassociated from the otherwise inexplicable physical metamorphoses that she undergoes throughout the course of the narrative. Her presence encourages the development of a healing community among the ex-slaves of Cincinnati, but also leaves the uncomfortable possibility that the formation of communities always depends on the scapegoating of an even more abject group. Although the freaks' fantastic bodies are long gone by the close of the novel, as is Beloved's equally spectacular embodied form, Morrison's text cautions that the solidification of collective bonds may take place at the expense of less visible, but no less haunting, others. The destructive potential of community is an ongoing concern in Morrison's fiction, from the citizens of Lorrain, Ohio, in *The Bluest Eye* (1970), who allow Pecola Breedlove's self-hatred to reach tragic proportions, to the Bottom's rejection of Sula Peace in *Sula* (1973), to the deadly confrontation between the men of Ruby, Oklahoma, and the women in the convent in *Paradise* (1998).

Whereas the carnival freaks briefly and grudgingly unsettle racial hierarchies by allowing black customers to occupy the position of spectators, the appearance of Beloved, a real freak whose bizarre attributes—unlike those of the wild African savage—are never explained or diffused, enables the community to begin working through the traumatic events that continue to haunt their relations to one another. The particular significance of the carnival excursion for Sethe is reinforced by the manifestation of Beloved directly afterwards. Although the embodied Beloved first appears in the chapter following the excursion, her emergence from the river coincides temporally with the visit to the carnival itself, as if the freak show, with its temporary reversals, had somehow produced a more enduring and significant oddity outside its gates. The link between Beloved's materialization and the freak show is suggested by Sethe's initial response, an immediate need to urinate so intense and prolonged that she feels like a freak herself: "Just about the time she started wondering if the carnival would accept another freak, it stopped" (51). The amount of liquid Sethe produces is so copious that she relates it to the breaking water of Denver's birth. It is no accident that Sethe's identification with the freaks occurs in a passage that also mentions the newborn Denver, her own absent mother, and the stranger who will turn out to be her murdered older daughter, Beloved, come back to life. This associative chain implies that relations between enslaved mothers and daughters are akin to the alienating relations of the freak show, where some persons are stripped of autonomy and self-determination as their bodies become the property of others.[38] Sethe's body registers the import of the meeting long before she realizes the identity of the mysterious stranger. Her visceral reaction anticipates the intense bond she will develop with Beloved, which substitutes corporeal sensations for desires and memories that cannot be given verbal expression.[39]

The identification between Beloved and the carnival freaks continues as the bizarre circumstances of her appearance and nature confound rational explanation. Beloved's supernatural qualities have led many critics to interpret her as a ghost and, indeed, the notion of ghostly haunting is appropriate for describing the persistence of the traumatic memories that she invokes, as well as the spectral presence that haunts the house on Bluestone Road until Paul D arrives.[40] But this infantile phantom is substantially different from the fully embodied woman who appears after the freak show. The terms *ghost* and *freak* are useful for distinguishing between these two distinctive manifestations, separated from one another by the experience of carnival. Calling the materialized Beloved a freak draws attention to her association with the disempowered persons on display at the sideshow, a connection embedded at the level of figurative language that pushes us to acknowledge affinities between oppressed groups. Moreover, Beloved is a freak because of the unavoidable fact of her body. The intangible quality of ghostliness is inadequate to describe the warm, greedy, desiring sentience of the stranger who moves Sethe so deeply. As I will demonstrate, *Beloved* is a novel relatively uninterested in interiority as such, for it projects the emotional states of its characters onto the surfaces of the human form.

The associative links between motherhood, freaks, and community in *Beloved* are prefigured by Pilate, the most powerful female character in Morrison's *Song of Solomon* (1977). Having fought her way out of her dead mother's body, the newborn baby emerges without a navel, her smooth belly a sign of her detachment from the woman who engendered her. Alienated from one community after another, Pilate is dismayed to find that her oddity is unmarketable: "Even a traveling show would have rejected her, since her freak quality lacked that important ingredient—the grotesque. There was really nothing to see. Her defect, frightening and exotic as it was, was also a theatrical failure. It needed intimacy, gossip, and the time it took for curiosity to become drama."[41] Similarly, Beloved's freak qualities are not shocking or sensational; they manifest slowly as her difference becomes apparent to the members of Sethe's family and the close-knit society that surrounds it.

Like the carnival freaks, Beloved embodies apparently unresolvable contradictions. She is simultaneously childlike and a grown woman, sick and glowing with health, innocent and fully sexualized, strong and feeble. When Sethe worries about Beloved's weakness, Paul D responds suspiciously that she "[c]an't walk, but I seen her pick up the rocker with one hand" (56). The disparity between Sethe and Paul D's assessments of Beloved indicates how closely their perceptions of her physical body stem from a more profound sense of her significance to each of their lives. She appears frail and childlike to Sethe, who longs to protect the daughter she was forced to murder; she takes the form of a powerful sexual aggressor to Paul D, who fears the disruption of the tentative new life he has made at the house on Bluestone Road.

Beloved's paradoxical embodiment of frailty and inexplicable strength is a prototype for the physical transformations the other women in the novel will undergo. Akin to the carnival freaks, whose oddities are most commonly defined in terms of deviations in shape and size—"twenty feet tall or two feet tall, weighing a ton," or hardly anything at all—the women at 124 shrink and grow in unexpected ways. The rapidity and excess of these corporeal changes suggest that they in fact describe emotional states. In *Beloved* something like the unconscious, where unspeakable and unresolved traumas reside, registers in the external contours of the female form. Early in the novel, Sethe is described as a "quiet, queenly woman," whose emotional fortitude, which enabled her to escape slavery, survive prison, and raise a daughter alone, is conveyed by her powerful, statuesque corporeality. The scars that traverse her back, a "sculpture . . . like the decorative work of an ironsmith too passionate for display" (49), recall wounds that have healed but have left permanent traces of violence and injury. Likewise, Denver's fleshy face and "far too womanly breasts" bespeak a body developed beyond its years. Paul D notices Denver's mature breasts precisely at the moment when she tearfully describes the isolation she and her mother have endured, her excessive size reflecting the emotional growth required of the young girl during years of ostracism from the surrounding community. The unmistakable signs that Denver *has a body*—her tears, hunger, thirst, and pouting—demand her mother's affection in a manner almost unbearable to Sethe, who has been conditioned by enslavement to maintain a distance from her own offspring. Referring to the dangerous love for her own children in corporeal terms, she tells Paul D, "I was big . . . and deep and wide" (162). As Beloved insinuates herself into the household, she will challenge the monumentality of both Sethe and Denver, whose statuesque bodies bespeak strength of character but also a dangerously isolated individuation.

As Beloved's needs take their toll on Sethe and Denver, the burden is manifest physically in the shrinking and weakening of their bodies. Initially replicating the joyful excess of the carnival outing, Sethe spends her life savings "to feed themselves with fancy food and decorate themselves with ribbon and dress goods" (240), but as the money runs out, Beloved, with her "basket-fat stomach" (243), continues to expand, demanding "sweets although she was getting bigger, plumper by the day" (239). Beloved's untoward appetites are literally devouring Sethe. Even as they starve, Sethe clothes the household in "carnival dresses" made from gaudy materials that connect the reversals within the carnival gates to the reversals occasioned by Beloved's appearance: as Beloved expands, Sethe shrinks; as Beloved fills with vitality, Sethe droops listlessly; and the young Beloved "looked the mother, Sethe the teething child" (250). Threatening to overpower the dwindling bodies within them, the excess of the brightly colored garments signals the dangers of excessive, self-consuming desire in a house once devoid of color.

As Beloved grows, Sethe becomes thin and fragile. Sethe's desire for Beloved is dangerous because it overpowers her concern for her living daughter and her own well-being. Denver observes that "the flesh between her mother's forefinger and thumb was thin as china silk and there wasn't a piece of clothing in the house that didn't sag on her" (239). Just as the ghostly Beloved once appeared "thin" to Paul D, the formerly monumental Sethe is frail and weak with hunger, her body literally eaten away by the "thickness" of her love. Similarly, Denver, at one time physically mature for her age, also shrinks, not only growing thinner but also shorter and smaller: "[T]he sleeves of her own carnival shirtwaist cover[ed] her fingers; hems that once showed her ankles now swept the floor" (243). While Denver's weight loss is a consequence of starvation, her shrinking cannot be explained except as a literalization of her dwindling importance in her mother's eyes. Finally, in "a dress so loud it embarrassed the needlepoint seat" (247), Denver ventures out into the community to seek help. Her previous attempt to establish relationships outside her family by enrolling in Lady Jones's makeshift school was greeted with a telling invitation: "Come in the front door, Miss Denver. This is not a side show" (102). Lady Jones makes an important distinction between active participation and staring; she challenges Denver to negate the alienating dynamics of the sideshow by crossing the threshold and joining the group inside. Denver's second attempt at reintegration is more successful because the community is more willing to acknowledge her effort, responding with the contrition and generosity that it was unable to muster in the past.

Ultimately, the efforts of the entire community are required to counteract Sethe's assertion that she doesn't need the world outside. The crowd of women who gather in front of her house on Bluestone Road witness Sethe reliving the traumatic event in which she took the life of the infant Beloved to protect her from the approaching slavecatchers. This time, however, she turns her rage outward, brandishing an ice pick at the solitary white man who approaches the house on horseback. Sethe's actions banish Beloved in her embodied form. A process that began with the visit to the carnival ends with the integration of the onlookers (the group of women) with the object of their gaze, as Sethe plunges off the porch into the crowd, "running into the faces of the people out there, joining them and leaving Beloved behind" (261). Abandoning Beloved indicates that Sethe is ready to move beyond both the deadly repression of the past that took shape as the "thin" baby ghost and the excesses of dwelling on the past embodied by the grown, "basket fat" freak, Beloved. The point is not that the terrible trauma is resolved at this moment but that Sethe's burden cannot be shouldered alone. Individuality and self-reliance are not the antidotes to the unfreedom of slavery in *Beloved,* which concludes that its wounds can be salved only through the formation of new kinds of collectivity. Sethe has made the first step towards reentry into a group that, in turn, seems ready to acknowledge her crime as their own. In this, the community recognizes that Beloved is not simply the incarnation of Sethe's individual acts, but of the greed, barbarism, and wildness of slavery itself, a freak child born of their collective suffering.

Like any freak, a being who relies as much on the spectator's imaginative work as the prodigious contours of her body, Beloved is part of a fragmented story that shifts depending on the teller. Finally, it is forgotten, for "remembering seemed unwise" (274). But like conjoined twins, the double meaning of the novel's final injunction, "this is not a story to pass on," remains. Countless readers have pondered the meaning of this ambiguous warning: Is Beloved's a story to be shared with others, to "pass on" from one generation to the next? Or is it a story to leave behind, to "pass on" as one moves towards something else? This dual process of identification and dissociation is suggested by the image of the "photograph of a close friend or relative" evoked in one of the novel's final paragraphs that, "looked at too long—shifts, and something more familiar than the dear face itself moves there" (275). This uncanny experience, in which the image of a loved one momentarily becomes the "more familiar" reflection of the self, is akin to the moment at the freak show when identity is shattered and reconfigured by encounters with persons so strange that they confuse our very sense of self and other. This tentative recognition that the shifting boundaries of self and body might merge with others is a crucial stage in the development of a collectivity that can embrace, as well as wound and exclude.

Reclaiming Wild

Baby. Grown woman. Ghost. Memory. Forgotten past. Wound. Healer. Beloved, as many have remarked, is a figure for the impossible but necessary task of working through collective loss.[42] That process involves healing and forgiveness, but too often also entails the scapegoating of another more unfortunate and dispossessed group. Beloved is also a freak, for freaks are at once living persons and the bodily projection of our most profound individual and collective traumas. It is impossible to see a freak unmediated by the desires and anxieties that filter our perception of extreme alterity. Early in the novel, the black audience at the carnival was not ready to recognize its misfortunes mirrored in the unhappy performers onstage. Seeking entertainment and forgetting, they resisted finding images that recalled their own exploitation and instead simply reversed the terms by loading derision onto the freaks. Although freaks and slaves have both suffered the experience of imprisonment within their bodies, the characters in *Beloved* identify only with the racial freak. Later, as Sethe stands before them in much the same position, they are able to acknowledge her suffering as a necessary and painful part of their own past, literally reincorporating her into the group. Recalling Mrs. Garner's simple definition of *characteristic* as "a thing that's natural to a thing," the community affirms race as the grounds for their identification with one another and their rejection of outsiders, whether they be well-meaning abolitionists or the bigots responsible for the jungle so vividly described by Stamp Paid. In banishing Beloved, they are also banishing the specter of the white man on horseback, the abolitionist Mr. Bodwin, whose benevolence must be rejected along with the slaveowners' cruelty.[43] The grotesque Sambo figurine that decorates the Bodwins' kitchen implicates him in the same representational system that created the wild African savage.

Any reader tempted to resolve these racial antagonisms by resorting to a common humanity would do well to heed the words of Guitar in *Song of Solomon* when he asserts that "white people are unnatural. . . . [T]he disease they have is in their blood, in the structure of their chromosomes."[44] Guitar has learned Schoolteacher's lesson that race is a biological fact, which can be measured scientifically because it is lodged, like a pathogen, in the body's cellular matter. Patently ridiculous freaks like the wild African savage attest to the fraudulence of these lessons; the cruelty and abuse exchanged between black spectators and white performers remind us of the lesson's palpably real effects. Set loose in the world, they emerge from the mouth of a man like Guitar, who has no other vocabulary to articulate his rage at unprovoked violence against black citizens. When each group views the other's difference as the product of an intractable nature, there is little possibility for mutual recognition. The reconsolidation of communal bonds initiated by the freak show will take place without challenging more profound racial divisions, lodged firmly in place through the crimes of history. Ultimately, while the meaning of the freak show's invocation of racial essences is called into question, the fact that those essences exist is not. In crucial respects, Bodwin is more like the white carnies and the slavecatchers than like the community that shares his abhorrence of slavery and, as a result, he cannot play a part in their ritual of testimonial and healing.

Beloved ends not with a moment of divisive rage but with the possibility of recovery as the community turns inward to shelter its own members. In a final reminder of the excursion to the fair, as Paul D sits by Sethe's bedside to comfort her he "examines the quilt patched in carnival colors" (272), an image that knits together many disparate lives and the pain they endured in a commemorative pattern. Unlike the carnival dresses bought with Sethe's life savings, which represented a retreat into the past at the expense of the future, the patches signify the acknowledgment of the past as it is woven into something useful to those alive in the present. As they become part of the quilt, the pieces lose their particularity, each making its own significant and colorful contribution to the pattern.

This pattern continues as Beloved returns to haunt the pages of Morrison's next novel, *Jazz*, in the form of a disheveled, speechless woman named Wild. As Morrison described her to an interviewer, "The woman they call Wild . . . could be Sethe's daughter Beloved. When you see Beloved towards the end, you don't know; she's either a ghost who has been exorcised or she's a real person pregnant by Paul D, who runs away, ending up in Virginia, which is right next to Ohio." Morrison's next sentence, "But I don't want to make all these connections," does not undo what went before, but insists on the necessary ambiguity of both wild women, whose significance must be conjoined in part through the reader's own imaginings.[45] Like the wild African savage of the freak show, who is at once familiar and exotic, Wild is both known and mysterious, a living woman who suffers pain and hunger and the stuff of local fantasy, "a used-to-be-long-ago crazy girl." But unlike the carnival wild man, whose wildness is as fictive as his African nationality, Wild roams freely through the cane fields of Virginia (and perhaps from one text to another), haunting those she encounters with the possibility that the boundary between their civility and her savagery is less than stable. As Michael Taussig suggests in his reading of ethnographic writing about South America, wildness is more than the antithesis of Western rationality and order; it represents the threat, at once terrifying and enticing, of the dissolution of signification itself: "[Wildness] is the spirit of the unknown and the disorderly, loose in the forest encircling the city and the sown land, disrupting the conventions upon which meaning and the shaping function of images rest."[46] This chapter has treated wildness largely in terms of its performative dimensions in an age of confidence men and Barnumesque entertainment. Taussig's observations recall a more serious definition of wildness as the place where reason and order come to an end. Both meanings of wildness pertain to Morrison's fiction. Its more frightening and irrational forms are born of slavery, and the legacy of racism and poverty that survives in its wake. This wildness is not to be found in nature, for it is the product of human history and institutions.

By evocatively linking Wild to Beloved, Morrison suggests that her past is connected to the collective trauma of enslavement that haunts U.S. history and endures in the embodied memories of its citizens. Most of *Jazz* takes place among a generation removed from slavery. Set in 1920s Harlem, the novel focuses on Wild's son Joe Trace as he is caught up in a drama of passion, adultery, murder, and forgiveness. An undomesticated, antimaternal figure, Wild is the apparent antithesis to the urban dwellers of Manhattan. At the same time, although they do not know each other, she seems to have transmitted the pain and disorder of her own life to her offspring. Neat categorical oppositions between past and present, madness and sanity, threaten to become unmoored as wildness bursts forth at the heart of civilization in Joe's murderous desire for Dorcas, Violet's irrational rage at Dorcas's corpse, the incurable eruptions of Dorcas's skin. Beloved, reincarnated, or simply relocated as Wild, thus perpetually returns to remind the community of what remains outside, inhabiting the abject spaces rejected by even the most marginal persons, but unwilling, or perhaps unable, to go away.

MATERNAL IMPRESSIONS

One is not born a woman, but, rather, becomes one.
SIMONE DE BEAUVOIR, *The Second Sex* (1952)

> *Organisms are not born, but they are made.*
> DONNA HARAWAY, "The Promises of Monsters" (1992)

> *A true freak cannot be made. A true freak must be born.*
> *(Olympia Binewski)*
> KATHERINE DUNN, *Geek Love* (1989)

Near the end of *Beloved*, Ella, who has always "considered love a serious disability," comes to identify with Sethe based on a similar experience of suffering.[1] After having been repeatedly raped by the white father and son she calls "the lowest yet," she gave birth to a "hairy white thing [that] lived five days without making a sound" (258–259), a freak baby that embodied the brutal conditions of its conception. Ella's fear that her dead child might, like Beloved, return uninvited into her life enables her to cast aside years of resentment and come to her neighbor's aid. In the previous chapter, I argued that, like freaks themselves, Morrison's characters are all body, for conditions typically understood in terms of interiority are externalized as unhealed wounds, scars, and disabilities. Memories endure in material form as "rememories," which conjure up a past so tangible that one can collide with it years later. Rememories are not only accessible to those who lived through the events themselves, but can be transmitted bodily from one generation to the next. Hence Beloved, born in the 1860s to an American slave, can access the trauma of the Middle Passage. In keeping with this notion of embodied memory, disabled children bear the imprint of the unnatural events surrounding their conception.

The inscription of prenatal experiences upon the gestating infant's flesh is not simply a fictional device for describing the infectious potential of powerful expe-

186

riences. Until the late eighteenth century, the concept of maternal impression, which held that pregnant women had the ability to imprint their unspoken fears and desires onto the fetal body, was a legitimate medical theory.[2] It was both a way of policing women by threatening that their crimes would become visible for all to see and an acknowledgment of the tremendous power they held over the reproductive process. Long after it was refuted by science, the theory endured as a form of popular wisdom and a sensational explanatory device to answer one of the sideshow's favorite questions: Where do freaks come from? The freak presupposes the need for stories of origin, whether they attribute her anomalies to exotic geographical locales or a sequence of bizarre events surrounding her birth and conception. In contemporary American literature, there is no more unique and gut-churning answer to this question of origins than Katherine Dunn's 1989 cult novel, *Geek Love*. As it tells the story of a family of carnival freaks, *Geek Love*'s crude language and sick twists of plot fascinate and repel, a mixture of responses much like those aroused by the classic freak shows themselves. Describing it variously as "undistinguished" and "brilliant," "a sort of literary laxative" and "a visceral toxic shock," critics struggled to make sense of the novel, and to decide whether it merited analysis at all.[3] Because its concern is not just freaks, but also the freak show, with all of its traditional sensationalism and excess, *Geek Love* is the requisite text for the final chapter of *Sideshow U.S.A.* Although N. Katherine Hayles has described its characters as "embodied metaphor," I will argue that, like the sideshow's original performers, the freaks in *Geek Love* defy any such coherent meaning.[4] Having devised a cast of fantastically grotesque freak characters, the novel's primary challenge is to find a vocabulary and narrative mode suitable to accommodate them. Transporting the residual culture of the traveling carnival into the late twentieth century, its plot unfolds across an American landscape where open fields have been replaced by strip malls and live performance must compete with mechanical reproduction.[5]

Narrated in the first person by a hunchback, albino dwarf named Olympia Binewski, *Geek Love* is a saga of three generations of carnival freaks. The freak show's traditional preoccupation with genealogy is introduced into a contemporary context where reproductive technologies have altered the relationship between sex and procreation, the fetus and the maternal body. But even in this brave new world of contraceptive choices, artificial insemination, fetal screening, and abortion, women continue to bear the exclusive responsibility for creating freaks. Indeed, in this novel "true freaks," which can only be conceived biologically, must contend with the possibilities and limitations of reproduction in both a narrative and a corporeal sense. Forged through the vagaries of maternal impression, freaks' bodies bear witness to ancestral memory. The Binewski clan springs from Lillian and Al Binewski, seasoned circus performers who devise the ingenious plan of breeding their own freak show by dosing Lil with drugs and exposing her to massive amounts of radiation. In addition to Olympia, their progeny include conjoined twins Electra and Iphegenia, telekinetic Chick, and Arturo, a boy born with flippers in place of arms and legs. Tensions among these idiosyncratic family members escalate until the carnival is consumed by a fire that kills everyone except three generations of women, Lil, Olympia, and Olympia's daughter, Miranda. This story is interwoven with a secondary narrative concerning the relationships among the survivors. Miranda, who was abandoned as a baby because her only disability—a small, curly tail—wasn't spectacular enough to make her a freak, grows up knowing nothing of her ancestry. A medical illustrator, she feels compelled to draw anomalous bodies without knowing why. Olympia lives nearby, where she can watch over Miranda and Lil while keeping her identity concealed from them.

Geek Love is one of several novels about freaks written in the last two decades of the twentieth century. As I have argued throughout this book, when freaks become scarce within popular culture they appear with greater frequency in representations. In the 1980s and 1990s, they are found in the fiction of John Irving, Elizabeth McCracken, Barbara Gowdy, Ursula Hegi, Harry Crews, Kevin Baker, and many other contemporary authors. This chapter will begin by situating Geek Love vis-à-vis this recent surge of fictional narratives about freaks by comparing it with three representative texts—Darin Strauss's Chang and Eng (2000), the Polish brothers' film Twin Falls Idaho (1999), and Ursula Hegi's Stones from the River (1994). Sympathetic to its disabled protagonist(s), each asserts the humanity they share with their nondisabled peers and condemns a society that stigmatizes them as freaks. From this perspective, the existence of freaks has more to do with bigotry than the accidents of the body that make some people look different from others. The world would be a better place, they propose, if we could become more tolerant of a greater spectrum of physical variation while learning to make judgments about personal value on the basis of something other than appearance. By contrast with these rather uncontroversial views, Geek Love's characters embrace their differences, speaking disdainfully of the "norms" who pay to view them. Although the performers featured in the Binewski Fabulon are all disabled—the form of freakishness most firmly connected to the body and discourses of authenticity—they see their disabilities not as impediments, but as talents that make them superior to the boring and undistinguished masses that pay to attend the carnival.

Because *Geek Love* presents *freak* as a bodily essence imparted to a select group from birth, reproduction is one of the novel's governing obsessions. In the second part of this chapter I will consider that obsession by turning to the role that maternal impression played in classic freak shows at the turn of the century. *Geek Love* incorporates this residual belief into its own form and content by relating it to the explosion of biotechnical research in the early 1980s. This growing knowledge about genetics promised to change the way we conceive of human identity by proposing that many traits formerly attributed to social conditioning should be explained in terms of biology.[6] *Geek Love* uses the freak as a limit case to explore the impact of this biotechnological understanding of the human organism. Whereas once the theory of maternal impression focused on the unruly powers of female imagination, *Geek Love* draws on molecular biology to describe a very similar scenario of genetic, matrilineal transmission. Constitutionally different from norms, freaks are proud and fiercely protective of their exclusive status. When the end of the novel reveals that it is a long letter written by a mother to her daughter, *Geek Love* itself becomes a type of maternal impression. That is, the story of Miranda's origins—which reveals that she is a freak—unfolds much like a strand of DNA that carries the imprint of, and is passed along to her through, the maternal body. The act of reading is meant to unite historical and genetic identity by confirming that she is something she always knew she was supposed to be. Born freaks were considered so valuable that their bodies were often preserved even in death, and Lil keeps her "failures," those children so severely disabled that they died in utero or soon after birth, enshrined in glass jars. *Geek Love* might be seen as Dunn's narrative "failure," a tale so bloated with monstrosities it threatens to collapse under their collective weight.

Born Freaks

As Olympia's epigrammatic statement attests, the authentic "born freak" is the doyen of the sideshow world. Juxtaposed with the memorable words of Simone de Beauvoir and Donna Haraway, who represent two generations of feminist thought devoted to proving that sex and gender are cultural constructions, it signals a return to understanding the body as a foundation for human identity. "A true freak cannot be made. A true freak must be born."[7] This claim, which would have been unsurprising in 1889, has an ironic ring in 1989, when *freak* is a voluntary sign of nonconformity for some and an intolerable slur for others. In either case, *freak* is understood as a social construction. Why, then, would Olympia announce that the true freak is a product of biology rather than culture? By insisting on her absolute and intractable Otherness, she denies the more conventional belief that a common humanity subtends even the most extreme differences between one body and another. Moreover, she reverses the terms so that *freak* becomes a desired identity, elevated above the homogenous banality of the normal. Her words reveal the potential of the freak as a narrator: Olympia's diminished stature not only brings her closer to the ground, but causes her to understand the world differently from those who are normal and would like to believe that she wants nothing more than to be just like them. On the contrary, Olympia is proud to be a freak; her only regret is that, unlike her brothers and sisters, she was never sensational enough to merit an act of her own.

As with *Geek Love*, a freak is the first-person narrator of Darin Strauss's *Chang and Eng*, a novel about the original Siamese twins. Taken from their home in rural Siam in 1885 as young boys, Chang and Eng were brought to the United States, where they embarked on a profitable career as human curiosities, became successful landowners, married, and raised two families (figure 32). Like many other accounts written during their lifetime and after, Strauss's focuses on the peculiar-

FIGURE 32. Chang and Eng, the original Siamese twins, posing with two of their children, ca. 1865. © Collection of The New-York Historical Society.

ities of their courtship and marriage to sisters Adelaide and Sarah Yates.[8] What makes *Chang and Eng* distinctive is that its story unfolds from the perspective of only one of the twins, the more sober and introspective Eng, who from his earliest moments of consciousness longs for separation from his weaker and less intelligent brother. The twins could not be more different in temperament, for Chang is personable and vivacious, while Eng is shy and often resentful of others. Chang drinks too much and has poor health, whereas Eng is abstemious and strong. Although much of their livelihood comes from exhibiting themselves as freaks, Eng is tormented by the indignities of show business. His problems are compounded by his growing love for Chang's wife, Adelaide. An unwilling witness to the couple's passionate sexual activities as well as their frequent quarrels, Eng is consumed by a desire to steal his brother's spouse and escape his own unhappy marriage.

As Mark Twain was well aware when he presented readers with his literary double bill of *Pudd'nhead Wilson* and *Those Extraordinary Twins,* conjoined twins present interesting formal and thematic provocations to the novel, a genre committed to the development of a stable individual subjectivity. According to D. A. Miller, the nineteenth-century novel produced a "subject whose private life, mental or domestic, is felt to provide constant, inarguable evidence of his constitutive 'freedom,' but also to, broadly speaking, the political regime that sets store by this subject."[9] What happens to the sanctioned freedom of the narrative subject when his body is fused with another? Twain's pair, whose "natures differ a good deal from each other," run into a series of comic mishaps stemming from their agreement that each twin must relinquish control over the body to his brother on alternating days. Each protagonist's individuality is compromised by the fact that he does not have exclusive agency over his actions. Likewise, the protagonist of *Chang and Eng* is incapable of absolute individuation, although his personality is quite distinct from that of his brother. He is also barred from complete participation in the activities that typically bring resolution to the bildungsroman—self-realization, marriage, and subsumption into the cherished privacy of family life. Social rituals crucial to the nineteenth-century novel are disrupted by characters whose bodily integrity is so dramatically compromised. However, instead of exploiting these curious generic problems, Strauss normalizes Eng by representing him as an autonomous individual who has the misfortune to be attached to another person. His subjectivity appears to be generated not by his unique physical condition, but in spite of it. The reader is granted access to Eng's fantasy life only to find it overcome by desire to have conventional sexual relations in private. Within the dull fictional universe of *Chang and Eng,* eroticism is governed by bourgeois social norms, even for those whose bodies make the realization of convention impossible. Ultimately, the complex life histories of the real Chang and Eng are reduced to the tragedy of an untenable desire for separation and normalcy.

This somewhat paradoxical desire to achieve individual wholeness through cleavage, which could only be a fantasy for Chang and Eng due to the limitations of nineteenth-century medical knowledge, is realized in the 1999 film about conjoined brothers, *Twin Falls Idaho* (Polish brothers). Unlike *Chang and Eng*'s commitment to the individuation of its protagonist, the film conveys the remarkable unity of the Falls brothers, Blake and Francis, through private gestures and whispered conversations. Unable to hear what they are saying, the spectator confronts the limits of her ability to comprehend an intimacy born of physical and psychological attachment. Since a visual medium is the obvious choice for depicting the spectacular qualities of conjoined twins, the representation of the brothers' intense connection through sound, or its absence, is an inventive manipulation of film's formal properties. The twins' apparently seamless union is disrupted when they meet Penny, a prostitute who sparks the desires of Blake, the stronger of the two. So repugnant is the idea of his brother's attraction to this woman that Francis is afflicted with fits of vomiting during the night of their first meeting. Rejecting the birthday cake he has eaten earlier, his body resists the notion of incorporating an outsider into their solitary companionship. Francis's response to Penny inverts the more predictable outcome of an encounter with conjoined twins, who might be expected to arouse alarm and disgust in the individuals who see them.[10] When the three eventually spend the night together, the film continues to challenge our expectations about this relationship. Penny begins to kiss Blake but stops abruptly when she realizes that Francis is watching them with a gaze of curiosity and resentment. Francis's look prevents Penny from satisfying her curiosity about their conjoined bodies by reminding her that each brother possesses a subjectivity of his own. Unlike the sideshow, where the freak is obliged to endure the stares and probing hands of spectators, the bedroom is depicted as a space that requires mutual respect and accountability. But Penny's sympathy is an exception; far more often, under the eyes of cruel strangers the twins become the objects of a gaze that reduces them to freaks.

Despite these promising insights, *Twin Falls Idaho* is unable to bear the imaginative burden of realizing the erotic entanglements of conjoined twin brothers. Conveniently, Francis becomes fatally ill and must be separated from Blake by emergency surgery. At the film's close, Penny travels to the circus where the twins once performed to find Blake alive but devastated at the loss of his arm, his leg, and his brother. Standing in the place of his lost companion, Penny promises Blake a happy ending and the two limp slowly down a dusty, sunlit road as the camera pulls back in a gesture of closure. The bittersweet conclusion of *Twin Falls* does not celebrate the fact that, absent his other half, Blake is at last free to be an individual. Nonetheless, this film attests to the difficulty of envisioning a long-term arrangement that so dramatically defies social norms. As long as Francis is in the picture, any relationship with Penny can only be a freakish perversion, and the story cannot find its ending without eliminating the brother who obstructs the consolidation of heterosexual romance.

In both *Chang and Eng* and *Twin Falls Idaho,* desire disrupts the union of conjoined twin brothers, leading one of them to aspire to the individuation that would grant him access to a conventional male-female relationship. The former responds to this problem by representing its narrator as a character who is just like other people despite his unique body; the latter, by transforming the body to bring it into alignment with narrative expectations. A third alternative is presented in Ursula Hegi's 1994 novel, *Stones from the River.* Set in the small town of Burgdorf, Germany, during the era of Nazism, the story's protagonist is Trudi Montag, a dwarf whose status as a partial outsider gives her particular sympathy for the Jews she shelters from persecution. But there are limits to her compassion: her fear of being labeled a freak causes her to avoid any association with those who are more severely disabled than she. During the war, Trudi embarks on a short-lived relationship with Max Rudnick, who dies during the bombing of Dresden. In addition to losing Max, her grief is multiplied because she must mourn alone, having kept her affair a secret from the townspeople who have always deemed her unworthy of romantic love. As the town's inherent prejudices heighten to grotesque excess under the Nazi regime, it is represented as far more freakish than the diminutive protagonist: "Trudi knew that beneath the sheen of normalcy the town was a freak. She could see the ugliness, the twistedness, made even more evident by the tidiness, the surface beauty."[11] In *Stones from the River, freak* is a pejorative term that describes violations of the trust and decency necessary to any functional community. The town becomes a freak because its citizens betray the most basic foundations of the social contract, revealing that hatred and prejudice lie just behind the thin façade of civility. Against this backdrop, Trudi stands out as a decidedly nonfreakish character. Despite the chronic pain of her disability, she suffers far more from the cruelty of those around her. *Stones from the River* thus preserves the negative connotations of freakishness, using it as a term to condemn the community for treating Trudi as less than human.

In each of these fictions, the protagonists' bodies position them decidedly outside the norm. However, they object strenuously to being perceived as freaks, going to great lengths to assimilate in spite of their unusual appearances. Freaks, these narratives suggest, are produced not through the accidents of birth but the tension between their bodies and their inhospitable surroundings. The fact that they are ostracized or treated as curiosities is evidence of a disordered social environment. In other words, *freak* is a category invented by communities unable to arrive at more imaginative ways of accommodating the great range of human physical variation. The reader and the film viewer are invited to dissociate themselves from the perverse social order represented within these texts, to identify instead with the disabled protagonists in their struggle against the lonely and dehumanizing stigma of being branded a freak.

Geek Love deviates from this position by elevating *freak* to a prized identity, one that is determined by biology rather than culture. Although Olympia Binewski is as alienated as Trudi Montag or the conjoined twins, she responds neither by longing to be like everybody else nor by discovering freakishness within the normal, but by rejecting normalcy altogether. Her pithy remark that "a true freak must be born" returns to the traditional values of carnival, which sees the born freak as the aristocrat of the ten-in-one.[12] Instead of envying the society that excludes them, the Binewski family pities the norms for their banality. *Freak* is a proud title that can only be legitimately claimed by those who are disabled from birth. But it is also a genetic identity that can be transmitted from parent to child, though sometimes lying dormant in the cells of those who appear to be normal but know they are not. "I've wished I had two heads. Or that I was invisible. I've wished for a fish's tale instead of legs. I've wished to be more special," sighs Miranda, who is ignorant of her Binewski ancestry but expresses a penchant for freakishness nonetheless (34). Although she knows nothing about her origins, her body yearns to be strange and exceptional.

This understanding of *freak* as an inherent quality is the foundation for the novel's experimentation with character and subjectivity. At a moment when cultural critics seek to decouple identity from the body, to insist that race, gender, and other key categories of self-understanding are social constructions, *Geek Love* takes precisely the opposite tack. Identity for the Binewskis is as much a product of corporeal matter as it is of personal history or psychology. Detailed knowledge of the body is the basis for intimacy between one family member and another. For example, after revealing that she never had a close relationship with her sisters, Olympia provides an exacting account of their internal physiology: "[T]hey had separate hearts but a meshing bloodstream; separate stomachs but a common intestine. They had one liver and one set of kidneys. They had two brains and a nervous system that was peculiarly connected and unexpectedly separate" (51). With a surgeon's precision, Olympia replaces a representation of the twins' character(s) with this road map of their organs and circulatory system. Because the novel proceeds without ever disclosing very much about the twins' motivations and desires, this literal catalog of their body's insides must suffice for a more familiar description of interiority. In this, the passage returns to the rhetoric of the classic freak show, where an account of the extraordinary body is often a substitute for more penetrating biographical detail.

In dramatic contrast to narratives that emphasize normalcy beneath the skin, *Geek Love* revels in a difference that permeates the freak through and through, saturating language, subjectivity, and personal relationships. Freaks speak in distinctive ways, for their unique physical makeup drives them to use a peculiar vocabulary crafted to represent their unorthodox views of the world. If *Stones from the River* preserves the negative significance of the word *freak* in order to condemn the community that has ostracized its protagonist, *Geek Love* asks how the freak's alien vantage point would affect her use of language. "How deep and sticky is the darkness of childhood," Olympia reflects, "how rigid the blades of infant evil, which is unadulterated, unrestrained by the convenient cushions of age and its civilizing anesthesia" (106). Her unsentimental description of childhood is as encrusted with adjectives as the freak is burdened with excess of flesh. Wrought in terms that are at once crude and lyrical, the visceral imagery and alliteration of this passage give the words themselves a palpable resonance that turns abstractions like childhood and age into tangible qualities.[13] Freaks think in this way because their subjectivity is inherently different from that of norms. Olympia speculates that "even if I had begun as a norm, the saw-toothed yearning that whirls in me would bend me and spin me colorless, shrink me, scorch every hair from my body, and all invisibly so only my red eyes would blink out glimpses of the furnace thing inside" (241). Her passions confirm her as a freak from the inside out, possessed of a psyche so contorted that it would be capable of reshaping her body, were it not already bent and stunted.

As the plot unfolds, the freaks' beliefs and activities prove to be as twisted as their bodies, recalling a lengthy tradition in which the disabled form is the external sign of a perverse or corrupt character.[14] Access to the freaks' interiority reveals that they are jealous, vindictive, and needy; above all, they harbor deep prejudices against the inferior humans they call the "norms." Because bodily essentialism is the basis for distinguishing between freak and norm, reproduction is one of the most charged issues in the novel. And because only women are capable of the reproductive processes that create authentic freaks, the female body is an object of great interest and concern. Ultimately, women are responsible for the biological continuity of the Binewski family line and the preservation of family history. They also suffer most profoundly from the consequences of such a rigid and deterministic linkage between identity and corporeal matter.

Of Woman Born

Once the born freak is returned to her vaunted status, pregnancy and reproduction assume profound importance as the only means of creating more authentic freaks. *Geek Love*'s experimentation with language and character is effected by recycling many of the freak show's historical preoccupations, particularly its reverence for biological authenticity. The novel's strategic importation of these concerns into a contemporary setting can be best understood by returning to sideshows of the past, which relied on a reproductive discourse to describe the freak's place within the social order. They did so by invoking the theory of maternal impression, which focused attention on the female body and its dangerous but awesome procreative capacities. In the 1980s, as developments in genetic engineering become popular knowledge, *Geek Love* returns to that theory to reanimate the link between biology and identity. In the context of late-twentieth-century reproductive politics, genes take the place of the imagination as the creative force that allows mothers to transmit freakishness from one generation to another.

In the late nineteenth and early twentieth centuries, the freak show's extensive discussion of reproduction intersected with contemporary concerns about racial purity. This is not surprising, given that the freak show's greatest popularity coincided with slavery and its aftermath, a policy of imperial expansion, and major waves of immigration into the United States, all of which entailed greater degrees of contact among different races and nationalities. The debates about the consequences of racial miscegenation that raged during the early decades of the twentieth century were echoed in the sideshow's interest in the biological origins of freaks.[15] The annexation of foreign territories and the arrival of new immigrants from Eastern Europe and Asia caused social conservatives to worry about the contamination of pure, American bloodlines. Theodore Roosevelt advocated the need to "keep out races which do not rapidly assimilate with our own," while exhorting hearty Anglo-Saxon couples to reproduce in order to stave off the threat of "race suicide."[16] By linking questions of racial and national identity, breeding and patriotism, the president's writings made procreation a matter of public policy.

The immigrant's alien qualities were manifest in exaggerated form in the figure of the freak who claimed to come from the far reaches of the globe. The freak's visible anomalies only exacerbated popular belief in the deviance of non-Western people, whose differences (always described in terms of abnormality) were understood in biological, as well as cultural, terms. For working-class and immigrant audiences anxious about their own potential to assimilate, the freak's extreme racial and geographical Otherness provided the reassuring confirmation of their status as white Americans. At least in theory, if not in practice, their own differences would fade into irrelevance when confronted by the spectacle of absolute alterity on the sideshow platform.

However, unlike the immigrant who, in the eyes of nativist detractors, represented an alarmingly prolific collectivity, the freak's threatening potential to produce more freaks was safely dispelled by her claim to singularity. Created through an irreplicable chain of circumstances, the freak's value hinged on her status as a unique mistake of nature. Born of normal parents and capable of producing normal offspring, the freak was an aberration rather than the first member of a deviant race. Anxiety about containing the freak's reproductive capacities could have amusing consequences, such as the confusions of a broadsheet advertising the Albino Family from Madagascar (figure 33). The copy claims that this group, which includes a mother, father, and three children, are "born of perfectly black parents." The referent for this phrase is ambiguous, since both generations of albinos could not be born of the same dark-skinned parents. Obviously a consequence of the advertisement's cheap and hurried production, this error also bespeaks a reluctance to characterize freaks as a new racial category, which would be the implication of proposing that black lines of descent could suddenly become white through the accidents of birth. If all of the albinos come from one set of parents, perhaps their whiteness is confined to one, anomalous generation. Within the sideshow's reproductive discourse, the human prodigy assuaged eugenicist concerns because of her convenient impotence, or, at the very least, inability to reproduce in her own image.

When Roosevelt introduced concerns about reproduction into public discourse, he focused on the importance of mothers to the nation's health and longevity. Worried that the better classes might be overwhelmed by weak and inferior strains, he proposed that the foremost patriotic duty of all American women was to bear the right kind of children.[17] Immigrant mothers were viewed with particular alarm because of their alleged fecundity, which threatened to dilute America's wholesome stock through the rapid introduction of foreign blood.[18] The freak show mirrored this anxiety about the maternal role in reproduction by holding mothers responsible for creating abnormality. As Marie-Helene Huet has demonstrated, the equation between the maternal imagination and monstrosity

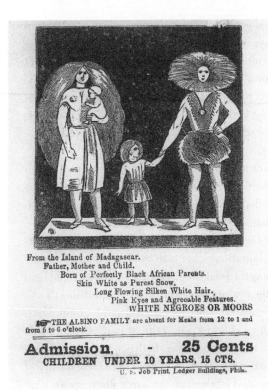

From the Island of Madagascar.
Father, Mother and Child.
Born of Perfectly Black African Parents.
Skin White as Purest Snow.
Long Flowing Silken White Hair.
Pink Eyes and Agreeable Features.
WHITE NEGROES OR MOORS

☞THE ALBINO FAMILY are absent for Meals from 12 to 1 and from 5 to 6 o'clock.

Admission, - 25 Cents
CHILDREN UNDER 10 YEARS, 15 CTS.

U. S. Job Print. Ledger Buildings, Phila.

FIGURE 33. The Albino Family from Madagascar. This handbill illustrates an anxiety about the freak's reproductive capacities. Although it pictures father, mother, and two children, the copy claims that all are "born of perfectly black African parents." The impossible suggestion that all of the members of this family came from the same parents wards off the more threatening prospect of a race of freaks able to reproduce in their own image. © Collection of The New York Historical Society.

extends back within Western culture as far as the writings of Aristotle. "Instead of reproducing the father's image, as nature commands, the monstrous child bore witness to the violent desires that moved the mother at the time of conception or during pregnancy."[19] According to Huet, interest in the maternal capacity for monstrous procreation waned during the Romantic period, an age that devoted more attention to the male artist's potential to create monstrous works of the imagination. But in the realm of popular culture, where residual beliefs and practices are conserved, the theory of maternal impression endured, acquiring added significance in the era of eugenics and American nativism.

Warning pregnant women against entering the sideshow tent, freak lore posited a direct connection between the freak's anomalies and flights of maternal fancy. The very sight of a freak might be enough to deform the gestating fetus. Likewise, the freak's abnormality was regularly described as the consequence of a trauma experienced by the pregnant mother. For example, one pamphlet traced the hirsutism of Lionel the Lion-Faced Boy to the fact that his mother had witnessed his father being mauled to death by a lion. Joseph Merrick, the Elephant

Man, attributed his condition to an injury his mother received from a circus elephant.[20] The armless Ann E. Leak Thompson claimed that she was born that way because her pregnant mother had been surprised by the sight of her father coming home drunk with his coat thrown over his shoulders, his arms concealed in its folds (figure 34).[21] Robert Bogdan argues that, compared to earlier, religiously inspired accounts of the freak's origins, the theories of maternal impression were "more humane and harmless, for they castigated neither the child nor the parent."[22] But Bogdan makes his case only by ignoring the problematic role of gender in these explanatory models, which lay the blame squarely on the inappropriate and perverse maternal imagination. While they do not propose to punish women for destructive flights of fancy, they are part of a longstanding tradition that credits fathers with normal, healthy reproduction (defined in part by the child's approximation of paternal features) and blames mothers for the production of monstrous anomalies.[23] The story of Ann Thompson, for instance, deemphasizes the husband's recurrent drunkenness and violence (and the inevitably unhappy

FIGURE 34. Ann E. Leak Thompson, who claimed that she was born armless because her pregnant mother saw her father coming home drunk with his coat slung over his shoulders, concealing his arms. Courtesy Theatre Arts Collection, Harry Ransom Humanities Research Center, the University of Texas at Austin.

consequences for his spouse), while bringing his wife's potent and destructive anxiety to the fore. Assumed to be normal at the time of conception, the fetus was vulnerable to being disfigured by the very body that nurtured it during gestation. In an era of nativist xenophobia, the freak is thus a figure of unresolved contradiction: details about birth and genealogy confirm the freak's difference from the immigrant, but also reinforce prevailing prejudices against foreigners by linking the anomalous body to geographical Otherness. Behind the prodigious bodies onstage are mothers, whose unruly imaginative powers take physical form in the birthing of freak children.

Geek Love brings the freak show's longstanding preoccupation with family and procreation together with contemporary questions about genetics and reproductive politics. Leaving behind the racial component of turn-of-the-century sideshows, Dunn's novel focuses exclusively on disability as a source of freakishness. Not all disabled bodies in *Geek Love* are freaks, but all freaks rely on congenital disabilities for their spectacular combination of physical and performative talents. The Binewski freaks are the undeniable products of maternal impression in that the pregnant Lil deliberately poisons herself in the hope of giving birth to freaks. In keeping with classically gendered dichotomies, the Binewski men are associated with operations of the mind, while women do the physical work of reproduction; Lil bears children under the aegis of Al, the architect and administrator of her treatment. And faithful to the freak shows that inspired it, *Geek Love* downplays the father's genetic contribution while dwelling on the mother's procreative capacities. The novel's multiple reproductive scenarios, which include Lil and Al's breeding experiments, as well as the pregnancies of Olympia and the twins, explore the pleasures and suffering that can take place only within the maternal body.[24] It is around the relationship between mothers and daughters that the novel's commitment to a notion of genetic essentialism is most fully realized. Only mothers are capable of reproducing more authentic freaks, and freakishness is as much a fact of biology as it is of performance.

Like its classic antecedents, the Binewski Fabulon offers fairgoers a combination of human curiosities, living and dead. The Chute, "A Museum of Nature's Innovative Art," is a trailer lined with Lil's "failures," the dead infants she keeps enshrined in glass jars. Of course, these freak babies are not simply the accidents of nature; a sign above the jars explains that they are "HUMAN. BORN OF NORMAL PARENTS." The story of their origins is part of their sensational appeal, for the fact that their parents were not freaks makes them all the more miraculous. "You must always remember that these are your brothers and sisters," Lil tells her living children, emphasizing the importance of knowing and honoring their ancestry. Alive or dead, family members are determined according to biology, rather than their participation in the rituals of kinship. Significantly, Lil charges her daughters with the task of preserving the family's reproductive legacy: "The twins and I were expected to share responsibility for the jars if anything happened to Lil," Olympia comments. "This burden wasn't even mentioned to Chick or Arty" (54–55). Not only are women required to perform the physical labor of reproduction and mothering, but they are also the bearers of familial memories, which are preserved in the most literal sense by caring for the remains of the dead.

If the female body is the sole means of creating new human prodigies, men in *Geek Love* can only replicate compensatory versions of themselves. This is the lesson of the Arturan cult, whose initiates work for the privilege of having their limbs amputated in the image of their armless and legless leader, Arturo. The cultists are not true freaks because they are merely inferior copies of the original. Their goal is not to be unique but to look like everybody else. As a result, despite his power and charisma, Arturo's project is doomed because he can only produce clones of himself instead of the surprising new variations on the human body valued by the freak show. If reproduction, at its best, is an act of generosity in which the maternal body devotes itself to creating something unique, replication is the most extreme form of egotism. By establishing a firm difference between the cult members and the Binewski family, the novel distinguishes the born freak from those who are merely disabled. One cannot become a freak though superficial alterations in appearance, for it is an identity that resides at a deep cellular level.

Threatened by the female body's ability to reproduce freaks, Arty takes drastic measures to secure his own power by controlling the sexual activities of his sisters. Aware that their body immediately suggests the erotic possibilities of multiple orifices and partners, the twins invent new ways to capitalize on their appeal, both onstage and off. Alienated from narratives of heterosexual romance that privilege privacy, true love, and female virginity, Elly and Iphy willingly offer sexual favors to anyone capable of paying their considerable fees. Arty is enraged to find that his sisters have been prostituting themselves, but he objects even more strenuously when they try to eliminate the resulting pregnancy. His efforts to dominate their bodies by force provide a lesson in the dangers of unwanted motherhood, which leaves its mark according to the freak show's logic of maternal impression. If reproduction can potentially generate fantastic variations on the theme of the human form, enforced pregnancy has disastrous consequences for mothers and children alike. After preventing the twins from having an abortion, Arty has Elly—the stronger and more rebellious half of the pair—lobotomized, leaving Iphy to care for the limp torso of her sister, as well as the developing fetus. Iphy's condition is pitiful, her every move a "painful progress" as she attempts to walk "with her swollen belly pulling her forward while she struggles to balance the flabby monster that sprouts from her waist" (272–273). Such descriptions link the burden of Elly's insensate body with the burden of unwanted pregnancy: like the passive and drooling Elly, the fetus is a parasitic, alien presence entirely dependent upon the care of the host. Iphy's energy is consumed by nurturing others whose lives literally cannot be extricated from her own.

Geek Love's equation of enforced motherhood with monstrosity is clear when the twins give birth to the hideously fat Mumpo, a baby "who lay like a big sagging pumpkin in the blankets. He was a bottomless craving and he was cunning" (301). Mumpo, who eats constantly but "only shits once every three days and then not much" (309), approaches allegorical proportions, for he embodies a grotesquely selfish mode of consumption that threatens to devour the exhausted bodies of his mothers. Olympia's description is worth quoting at length for its strikingly unromantic approach to the most sentimental of relationships, that of infant and mother(s): "[The twins] grew frail and bony except for the four breasts that ballooned every three hours in time for Mumpo to wake. He bellowed before he even opened his eyes, roaring until the gap was crammed with raw tit. Then he vacuumed the bag until it draped flat over the protruding ribs of his mothers, and bellowed for the next tit until all four milk bags were drained and limp. . . . Mumpo grew, spreading around himself in looping, creased pools of pinkness that pulsated with his breathing" (310). This passage reduces the mother-child relationship to the blunt matter of bodies engaged in the instinctual drive for survival: the maternal breast, so often idealized for its voluptuous, nurturing capacities, is transformed into "raw tit," a "milk bag" that is mechanistically filled and drained during feeding, while the fragile innocence of the suckling infant is refigured as a frightening and malignant agency. Incapable of doing anything but eating, Mumpo is reduced to the "looping, creased pools of pinkness" of the intestinal cavity itself.

True to the sideshow's conventions, Mumpo is indeed the product of maternal impressions that might be more properly described as "maternal oppressions." His ceaseless hunger and rapidly expanding flesh are the horrifying result of Arty's attempt to dominate the body and minds of his sisters, for they have imprinted the traumatic experience of pregnancy onto his shapeless body. At Dunn's freak show, the purpose of maternal impression is not to condemn mothers, but to affirm the necessity of women's sexual and reproductive freedom in order to prevent the creation of monsters. In a context that celebrates abnormality, monsters are defined

less by their prodigious bodies than by the horrifying circumstances of their production. At the root of the word *monster* is the Latin *mostrare,* "to show": Mumpo
is a monster because he is a legible sign of disorder and injustice in the social
world created by authorial rather than divine agency. The final conflict between
the twins, in which Iphy and Elly fatally wound each other and their son, represents the logical outcome for the persistent denial of corporeal integrity—the
body that turns on itself. Eventually the twins, who have never been granted control over their own physicality, exert the only agency left to them—murder and
suicide.

The story of Mumpo bears a striking resemblance to a poem written by Cynthia MacDonald in 1972, one year before the *Roe v. Wade* decision legalized abortion. About the consequences of unwanted maternity, "The Insatiable Baby" also
employs economic imagery to render the mother-child relationship in impersonal
terms: "The insatiable baby sucked on its mother. / As the book said, supply increased with demand; / So the baby grew enormously." The unexpected language
of supply and demand used to describe the suckling baby opens up the question of
who will profit from the transaction. Clearly the mother is not the beneficiary: as
the freak child grows rapidly to the size of a six-year-old, but remains "Baby-
featured, baby-limbed," he begins to consume the body that nourishes him. He is
provided with an artificial breast that pumps milk into his body, but in the end neither baby nor mother can survive: "The metal milk disagreed: both died, / She inside him, curled like an embryo."[25] Written at a moment when abortion was a
dangerous, criminal procedure, MacDonald's poem draws upon the freak show to
raise feminist questions about the burdens and obligations of motherhood. The
neat parallels between Dunn and MacDonald's twin narratives about maternity
gone awry draw attention to the sideshow as a place that capitalizes on reproductive disasters.

At one extreme of the novel's reproductive concerns, the conjoined twins treat
sex as a financial exchange rather than an activity related to procreation or love. At
the other is Olympia, whose unsightliness precludes the relationships that could
be most meaningful—the intimacy of a sexual partner and the bond between
mother and daughter. In *Geek Love,* the clichéd idea that love is blind is laughable; if character and body are one and the same, there is no chance for a romance
that would transcend the limitations of corporeality. Like Trudi Montag of *Stones
from the River,* Olympia is perceived as someone who could never experience romantic love or be an object of sexual desire. Whereas Hegi proves that these assumptions are false by finding Trudi a lover, Dunn's character bears them out.
Olympia endures the terrible isolation of an ugliness that bars her from all forms

of erotic attention. "I have certainly mourned for myself," she writes. "I have wallowed in grief for the lonesome, deliberate seep of my love into the air like the smell of uneaten popcorn greening to rubbery staleness" (309). Giving voice to her loneliness represents something of a break with tradition. When freak shows in the past exhibited ugly individuals such as Grace McDaniels, the Mule-Faced Woman, descriptions of their monstrous features were typically balanced by references to their flawless manners, grace, or romantic success. True to what Leslie Fiedler called "the eros of ugliness," McDaniels was rumored to be so attractive to men that she entertained numerous marriage proposals before settling happily with her chosen mate (figure 35).[26] The profane combination of ugliness and erotic allure, rough features and smooth etiquette, exploits the freak show's favored strategy, the juxtaposition of opposites. Not so for Olympia, whose irregular appearance ensures that she will always be alone.

Denied the physical intimacy of sex, Olympia is artificially inseminated with Arty's sperm by the fantastic, telekinetic powers of her brother Chick. If the twins' unhappy pregnancy results in the useless and flaccid Mumpo, Olympia's desire for

FIGURE 35. Grace McDaniels, the "Mule-Faced Woman." Although she was exhibited because of her uncommon ugliness, McDaniels was rumored to have rejected several marriage proposals before settling with a devoted husband. In this, she embodies the freak's paradoxical combination of repellence and allure. Undated. Museum of the City of New York.

motherhood has a more favorable outcome in the beautiful Miranda. Not surprisingly, Miranda's only flaw is a small curled tail, the predictable imprint of a mother who is a skilled and articulate storyteller, a teller of tales. Arty, who never knows he is the father, forces Olympia to give up the new baby to foster care because she is not sensational enough to perform as a freak. Having inveigled her way into pregnancy, Olympia is denied the right to decide whether she will raise her own child. Instead, she watches Miranda grow up in an orphanage, where the girl is taught that her tail is "punishment for [her] mother's sins" (32). The theory of maternal impression persists, for all that Miranda knows about her mother's identity is that her body is marked from birth by the maternal crimes that preceded it. Whether there may be some truth to this lesson within the novel's own logic is never entirely clear: Olympia is a jealous, vengeful person but also a loving mother and daughter, and the bearer of family history. Miranda is left to decide whether her tail is a gift or a stigma. After the carnival comes to a fiery end, Olympia establishes a connection to her daughter by bequeathing Miranda the story of her origins. In death, she offers Miranda the possibility of telling a less tragic sequel to the Binewski family story, a tale (and tail) indelibly imprinted in the body's cellular composition. However, like her tail, the tale of the Binewskis seems more like a genetic inheritance than a product of memory and storytelling. When history is understood in biological terms it may be impossible to tell it differently or alter its course.

"Some hooked structure in her cells"

The narrative body of *Geek Love* is the testimonial that Olympia has left to her daughter in the hope that knowledge about her past will enable her to make informed choices about her future. Specifically, she must decide whether to keep the tail she was born with or have it removed. Although she came of age knowing nothing of her family history, Miranda's behavior implies that the attraction to freakishness is a genetic inheritance. Her career (she *draws* prodigious bodies) has a punning relationship to her ongoing affinity for all that is freakish (she is *drawn* to prodigious bodies). As Olympia speculates, "it may be that the impressions of her infancy are caught somehow in the pulp of her eyes, luring her. Or there may be some hooked structure in her cells that twists her towards all that the world calls freakish" (15). Miranda's life story, or something more innate, "some twist in her genetic coil" (25), might be the key to explaining her proclivity for physical deviance. Absent the carnivalesque environment so central to her family's history, the only way to explain her taste for freaks is that it derives from some more essential facet of her nature. If the men who leer at her and "want to pump her full of baby juice" (18) when she dances at a strip club called the Glass House invest her tail with one set of meanings, her genetic history provides an alternative understanding of the appendage she calls "her specialty." It tells her that the penchant for freakishness is inherent, and that no amount of social conditioning will be able to erase its irresistible lure. As Olympia puts it, "she is part of, and the product of, forces assembled before she was born" (40). Normality is not her primary orientation, but the mundane and uninteresting counterpart to an originary freakishness imparted to her at birth. By the terms of Olympia's original definition, Miranda is a true freak despite the fact that she has never performed as one.

Recording her life story in this manner, Olympia memorializes her own death and carries out her mother's charge to commemorate her unique family history. In her letter, she writes her daughter into a narrative that would otherwise have remained untold: "I can't be sure what [it] will mean to you, or the news that you aren't alone, that you are one of us" (348). This sentence echoes the climatic wedding feast of Tod Browning's *Freaks*, in which, to her horror, the beautiful Cleopatra is welcomed by the freaks as "one of us." In *Freaks*, becoming "one of us" is a punishment, for by the end of the film Cleopatra is transformed into a hideous chicken woman; likewise, in *Geek Love* Miranda's life story connects her to a legacy of violence and pain, but it is a past that she has, in some sense, always desired.

Despite its resonance with *Freaks*, the end of *Geek Love* seems like an explicit attempt to rewrite Tod Browning's film, to imply that sometimes becoming "one of us" might not be a punishment but a privilege. Olympia is unable to predict what her daughter will do with the knowledge that she is "one of us," but asks that Miranda take the remains of her ancestors, "open our metal jars and pour all the Binewski dust together into that big battered loving cup that first held Grandpa B. Bolt us to the hood of your travelling machine and take us on the road again" (347). The loving cup is yet another gesture back to *Freaks*, where drinking from a communal chalice is part of the ritual that initiates Cleopatra into the world of freaks. In the case of *Geek Love*, the loving cup is not a sign of alienation or unwanted inclusion, but hope for restored community. Listening to the often painful stories told by these freaks, we are asked to imagine becoming "one of us" not as a tragedy but as a lucky break. Moreover, the mingling of dust suggests that, in the end, the specificities of any one body are irrelevant. Such yearning for collectivity differs from the insistent individuation that characterized *Chang and Eng* or *Twin Falls Idaho*, where the heterosexual couple (made up of two discrete individuals) is the norm towards which all desire gravitates. Olympia's final request for the body's immolation is an alternative to the history of those unfortunate freaks—

Julia Pastrana, Joseph Merrick, Joice Heth, Saartje Bartman—whose corpses were preserved for dissection or exhibition after their deaths.

In "Katherine Dunn in Her Own Words," an autobiographical section following the novel's conclusion, the author draws parallels between her own life experiences and those of her characters. One way of reading this coda might be to conclude that anyone, in moments of awkwardness or difficulty, could feel herself to be a freak like the characters of *Geek Love*. At the same time, the reader is never invited to participate in the community of freaks. Like Morrison's *Beloved*, *Geek Love* takes the uninitiated inside of a damaged and marginalized collectivity, asks her to acknowledge their suffering, then bars her from membership. Dunn's strategy of reversal is powerful, for it effectively shows the appeal of inclusion within the carnival community, as well as the potentially violent consequences of appearance-based discrimination. But unlike *Beloved,* which uses this device to condemn any too-easy sense of liberal, biracial identification, the purpose of *Geek Love's* essentialism is more murky. The Binewskis are as bigoted and insular as any separatist group that bases its isolation on a sense of superiority towards others. They speak disdainfully of the "horror of normalcy" (223), describing nonfreaks as "assembly line items" distinguishable only by their clothes (282). Any identification that may begin to develop between the reader and the novel's uncommon narrator comes untethered at moments when we are reminded of Olympia's deeply ingrained prejudices towards the world of norms.

A saga of three generations of women, *Geek Love* seems sensitive to the injustice of sexual double standards and the contradictions in contemporary attitudes about the maternal role in reproduction and parenting. At the same time, the novel's critique is undercut by its incessant reduction of women to the sexual and procreative capacities of their bodies. When one character values another only by virtue of what her body can do, women have few options besides prostitution, pregnancy, and motherhood. Its more affirmative vision of a society that appreciates its members for their unique qualities is never balanced by any attempt to break down divisive categories founded on physical differences. These characters are capable only of loving those who are just like them, forming a community limited by the insular genetic ties of family. The Binewski sisters' incestuous love for Arturo bespeaks an inability to desire others outside of the intimate family circle. Because identity is determined genetically from birth and the Binewskis bond only with one another, there is no incentive to understand or collaborate with those who look or believe differently. Lacking the "hooked structure" that determines Miranda's penchant for freakiness, why would anyone be drawn into the discriminating, often petty world inhabited by these characters? When Olympia instructs her daughter to "take us on the road again" (348), we can only hope that Miranda will break the family cycle and come up with other ways of relating to those who are unlike her. But there is good reason to doubt that she will be successful since so many of the qualities that we would describe as the products of history or social environment are, in the logic of *Geek Love*, genetically programmed.

Returning to the antiessentialist claims at the opening of this chapter, freaks might be seen as a test case for exploring the limits of social construction in an age of biotechnical engineering. Confronting the most extreme instances of disability may give us pause to think again about the extent to which those bodies are made, rather than born. According to an antiessentialist logic, disabilities are produced by culture, by social conditioning that teaches us to segregate deviance from normality and shapes the world in its own image. According to *Geek Love*, the freakishness of certain bodies is determined from within, by innate qualities that make some of us freaks, others merely norms. But at the same time that its freak characters celebrate the genetic origins of their identities, *Geek Love*'s plot suggests the problems with such a view. Whereas the born freak provides a fascinating point of departure for experimentation with language and literary form, she is less successful as a basis for community. Those who believe that they are superior by virtue of biology have no incentive to collaborate in the formation of a more diverse and tolerant social order. Prejudices against the disabled are reversed but not eliminated.

Geek Love is a fitting text for the final chapter of a book that begins with the freak show itself and follows its movement into print and audiovisual representation. The novel's plot revives the freak show's most repugnant beliefs: that freak is an identity bound to an inherent bodily essence, that freaks are as jealous, egotistical, and greedy as their twisted bodies, and that they cannot live outside of the carnival without causing violence and social disorder. But its narrative proves an equally important point, that freak shows continue to inspire bold and unexpected forms of literary experimentation. *Geek Love* may not provide a road map to a brave new world, but it is a more interesting novel for its failure. We close it feeling that we might not want to live next door to a freak, but we would certainly stay up late reading the story of her life.

Freak shows have survived because of a tenacious capacity to invent and then recycle their successes. *Sideshow U.S.A.* will conclude with just such a return, by moving back to the freak show as a form of live performance. In the 1980s, coinciding with the publication of Dunn's novel, a new generation of entertainers revived the freak show, taking its traffic in deviance as an opportunity for queers, perverts, and radicals of many stripes to flaunt, rather than conceal, their unconventionality. As these marginal identities become increasingly visible, disability—once the most vaunted freak quality—threatens to vanish from sight.

>Don't leave now! The best is yet to come!
>This double movement will set the stage for the grand finale,
>a description of live freak shows that should not be missed!

EPILOGUE
Live from New York

During two long days of jury duty in the summer of 1999 I fell into conversation with one of the other panelists, a hip but seemingly unremarkable fellow named Fred, who lived in the East Village and worked as a Web designer. But as we talked more, he revealed that, though computer geek by day, his passion was reserved for his second job as the Great Fredini, a sideshow performer who juggled, ate fire, and hammered nails into his nose. Raised by show people, he had worked as a carnival entertainer for most of his life and had his own variety program currently running at Coney Island. My chance meeting with the Great Fredini might serve as a paradigm for the experience of researching this book. While I have uncovered many dusty treasures in libraries, archives, and museums, I have also met their living counterparts in Times Square, at Coney Island, and on the Bowery, where they persist despite the strenuous efforts of Mayor Rudolph Giuliani to eliminate them.[1] Times have changed, and TV talk shows, reality programs, late-night pornography, and science fiction may have claimed the cultural position once occupied by freak shows, but they have stubbornly reemerged in their old neighborhoods in forms strikingly faithful to the past, attracting a loyal following of artists, children, rebels, and enthusiasts.

It is most appropriate, then, that this book close by considering the resurgence of live freak shows in New York, a phenomenon that includes Dick Zigun's Coney Island Circus Side Show, the Bindlestiff Family Cirkus, and the work of performance artist Jennifer Miller. Not only are these sideshow-inspired performances saturated in carnival tradition and history, but their architects are often familiar with recent scholarship on freak shows and conversant in cultural studies and poststructuralist theory. Interpretation, citation, and critique are an integral part of some contemporary freak shows, which have incorporated the process of theoretical explication into their programs. Research on this living subculture requires a method more ethnographic than textual. As I have discovered, the accomplishments of its articulate and self-conscious participants merit a mode of analysis that leaves a place for them to speak about their own work, as well as my responses to

210

it. I have spent the last three years in New York City as both a fan and a researcher of the contemporary freak show, and this book concludes with an account of my most interesting discoveries. These final pages will introduce you to the sideshow revival, but with a cautionary note that many of the more troubling aspects of the freak show's history remain unresolved.

Over the course of the twentieth century, we have seen freak shows prosper in almost every possible representational medium, from live performance to CD-ROM. Their longevity has been coupled with repeated predictions of impending demise, announcements that human exhibition is no longer tolerable, and that freaks themselves are facing rapid extinction or have simply chosen other lines of employment. In 1920, an article in *Variety* asked, "Where Are Freaks of Yesteryear? Not Many Left Sez Carny Exec." The *World Telegram* quoted a frustrated talent scout, who observed, "In 39 years with the circus business, I've never seen the freak crop so puny! New York with its supposedly screwy people! Bah!"[2] A 1947 issue of the *New York World* ran the headline "Freaks Still Attract Curious Stragglers on Coney Island's Midway, but the Mule Face Boy and the Turtle Girl Are Losing Their Popularity"; the *New York Journal American* announced in 1961, "World of Midgets Shrinks—Only 7 Left in Circus"; and a 1995 story in the *Los Angeles Times* headlined "Hard Times for Human Blockhead" reported on the financial insolvency of the Coney Island freak show, which faced the prospect of being replaced by a McDonald's.[3]

Such predictions say less about the freak show's demise than its restless plasticity, a determined evolution and reinvention that is almost always coupled with nostalgia for more prosperous times. Aware that scarcity or impending extinction are certain crowd pleasers, freak shows advertise not only the rarity of individual attractions, but the more general enterprise of human exhibition itself as a threatened practice. This is not to deny that freak shows have faced serious challenges from censors, medical practitioners, and advocates of the disabled. They have never again seen the popularity they enjoyed in the late nineteenth century during the apogee of amusement parks, circuses, and other modes of live mass entertainment. The fact that freak shows still exist at all attests to their flexibility, a willingness to mutate in response to shifting cultural norms while preserving enough of the original format to remain immediately recognizable. These mutations have emerged in a variety of media, from comic books to art photography, independent films to TV talk shows, CD-ROMs, Web sites, and kitschy products like lunch boxes and refrigerator magnets decorated with sideshow banners. Freak paraphernalia enjoys a thriving trade on eBay, where collectors peddle everything from home videos of the TV series *Freaks and Geeks* to reproductions of nineteenth-century freak *cartes de visite*.

Among the most successful of mainstream contemporary appropriations is the critically acclaimed 1997 Broadway musical *Sideshow,* loosely based on the lives of conjoined twins Daisy and Violet Hilton. A fervent longing not to be seen as freaks leads the sisters to seek love, marriage, and careers as Hollywood stars, only to be cruelly exploited by the world outside the carnival. At their most despairing moment, Tod Browning appears onstage to offer them a part in the film *Freaks,* confirming that they will always be perceived as freaks, whether or not they work as sideshow curiosities. The musical assimilates the admittedly unhappy lives of the Hilton sisters—who were exploited by relatives and managers and eventually died in poverty—into a maudlin tale of thwarted romance.[4] Utterly conventional in their desires and aspirations, the twins in *Sideshow* experience their bodies as a prison that impedes their profound wish for normalcy. They want nothing more than individuation, which would free them to pursue their dreams of heterosexual courtship and marriage. The musical's take on freak shows is underscored by a chorus that punctuates the activities of the main characters. Their clothing, which alternates between the varied and colorful costumes of freaks and drab, anonymous garb that causes individual bodies to blend together, implies that *freak* is a matter of performance, that despite superficial differences we are all "normal" inside. Although Tod Browning plays a part, it is the role of the villain; *Sideshow* is profoundly unfaithful to his belief that freaks' distinctive bodies require unconventional erotic and social arrangements. Instead, the musical congratulates itself on moving beyond the inhumanity of the freak show to recognize that beneath the inconsequential casings of our bodies all people are essentially the same.

I have described *Sideshow* at some length in order to contrast it with more innovative and historically perceptive reconfigurations of the freak show. The most appropriate capstone to this book is not this banal, moralistic translation of the freak show into a Broadway musical, but a new crop of live freak shows that have struggled on the margins of performance art and popular culture for the last ten or fifteen years. In conclusion, this book returns to New York, home of the great freak venues of an earlier era—Coney Island, Hubert's, Barnum's American Museum—to consider how and why contemporary artists are recuperating an antiquated form. However, it will also probe the limits of this inspired appropriation, which relies on an ironic and politically progressive audience, while erasing the more unsavory aspects of the freak show's history.

Coney Island U.S.A.

In the mid-1980s the Coney Island Circus Side Show was resurrected on Surf Avenue, one of the main side streets running perpendicular to the Boardwalk at

Coney Island. Now a run-down neighborhood where open-front shops overflow with cheap toys, clothes, and household goods, it is difficult to see evidence of the bustling resort that once was Coney Island, a place where New Yorkers thronged on hot summer days to enjoy the beach, the promenade, dance halls, and amusement parks (figures 36 and 37).

At the turn of the last century, freaks were an important part of Coney Island's landscape. Visiting the resort in 1881, José Martí remarked on the "fifty-cent museums where human monsters, freakish fish, bearded ladies, melancholy dwarfs, and rickety elephants, ballyhooed as the biggest elephants in the world, are shown."[5] Likewise, during her career as a journalist, Djuna Barnes wrote frequently of such Coney Island attractions as a man with a hole in his torso, a giant operating a test of strength, "the sideshow with its fat lady and its human enigma," an ethnographic exhibit of Somali Islanders, "chocolate-colored savages . . . whooping and dancing," and the ossified man who would later make a cameo appearance in *Nightwood*, a novel populated by circus people, freaks, and all manner of indeterminate or incomplete beings.[6] In his cultural history of Coney Island, John Kasson views freaks as the paradigmatic embodiment of the resort's

FIGURE 36. Surf Avenue in 1905, when Coney Island was a bustling seaside resort. Photograph by Adolph Witteman. Museum of the City of New York. The Leonard Hassam Bogart Collection.

213

FIGURE 37. Surf Avenue in 2000, on the afternoon of the Puerto Rican Day Parade. Photograph by Sam Adams.

unbounded, carnivalesque atmosphere: "As in traditional carnivals and fairs, the grotesque was prominently represented, symbolizing the exaggerated and excessive character of Coney Island as a whole. Midgets, giants, fat ladies, and ape-men were both stigmatized and honored as freaks. They fascinated spectators in the way they displayed themselves openly as exceptions to the rules of the conventional world. Their grotesque presences heightened the visitors' sense that they had penetrated a marvelous realm of transformation, subject to laws all its own. The popular distorting mirrors furnished the illusion that the spectators themselves had become freaks. Thus Coney Island seemed charged with a magical power to transmute customary appearances into fluid new possibilities."[7] Fun houses with distorting mirrors, trick floors, and slides, and rides called the Human Toboggan, the Human Roulette Wheel, and the Human Pool Table were participatory attractions where the visitor's body became part of the entertainment. Freaks found their ideal home in a place of sensation and excess where, for a short time, anyone could experience fusions of the human and the mechanical, or become exceptionally short, tall, fat, or weightless.[8]

At the end of the twentieth century, a new generation of entertainers attempted to bring Coney Island's history back to life. During the summer months, the Coney Island Circus Side Show runs a continuous sequence of acts that includes contortion, snake charming, juggling, fire eating, and—for an extra price—the final blow off, a video clip of a woman giving birth, the literal (if pre-dictably disappointing) rendition of the carny's famous maxim, "There's a sucker born every minute." Banners splashed with bold colors and oversized block print advertise the extraordinary attractions in traditionally hyperbolic terms—LIVE! UNIQUE! SHOCKING! UNBELIEVABLE! Once inside the dimly lit space, the audi-ence sits on wooden bleachers to watch stunts performed with well-worn props. Reviewing the history of Coney Island, it is easy to forget that seaside resorts do not run themselves, but rely on countless workers whose labor enables the cus-tomers to escape the drudgery of their own lives. The labor behind the ten-in-one was impossible to ignore on the humid summer day when I attended Coney Island's Circus Side Show. During my visit the entertainers appeared hot and annoyed, shooting flecks of perspiration and spittle into the audience as they delivered their lines, or languidly going through the motions, their eyes glazed with boredom.

Although it has been called a "postmodern freak show," there is very little of the "post-" about this production, except perhaps its nostalgic and self-conscious cita-tion of an earlier tradition. In fact, what makes the Coney Island Circus Side Show interesting is its understanding of the past. The brainchild of Dick Zigun, who has a master's degree in theater arts from Yale, the Side Show is coordinated under the auspices of a nonprofit arts organization called Coney Island U.S.A. Once funded by the NEA, its grant was dropped during cutbacks in the early 1990s. Zigun is no P. T. Barnum; unlike the great sideshow impresarios of old, he is uninterested in making money. "We're the only nonprofit sideshow in history," he says proudly, justifying his project on the grounds that it resurrects an important indigenous practice. Sideshows, as he describes them, are "a New York City art form."[9]

Despite his admiration for the sideshow's history and respect for its perform-ers, Zigun insists that he is uninterested in rigid fidelity to the original form. Aware that freak shows have survived the twentieth century precisely because of their malleability, he remarks, "The last thing we want to do is create a sideshow that is exactly preserved the way you might have seen one traveling with a carnival down south in the mid-1950s." And, in truth, while it maintains an appealing grittiness, most of the objectionable content of earlier freak exhibits has been excised from the current Coney Island show. Noticeably absent are all references to ethno-graphic curiosities and racial freaks. In place of born freaks are performers who juggle knives, eat fire, escape from straight jackets, and wrap themselves with snakes. While traditionally each act would have been assigned to a separate player, these contemporary performers are skilled at multitasking. Indeed, on the day I visited the show, a single man, drenched in perspiration and resentful in tone, grudgingly performed almost all of the stunts in the cycle.

A striking exception was Koko the Killer Clown. A rotund, developmentally disabled dwarf, Koko was the only performer I saw at Coney Island who might have earned a job as a freak in earlier days. Although his appearance is hardly spectacular, he is a reminder that freak shows once displayed persons with physical and developmental disabilities. Lumbering onstage with his face slathered in black and white grease paint, Koko delivered a loud, atonal monologue as he struggled to make balloon animals. My response, shared by other audience members, was distinct discomfort. We could not laugh, for, despite Koko's concerted efforts, there was nothing funny about what we were seeing and the very act of looking, of being there at all, suddenly made us feel complicit in his degradation. Despite Zigun's insistence that Koko is proud and happy with his role, his disability raises questions about consent because he seems so unaware of how he is perceived by the audience. He produces neither laughter nor thrills, but a palpable unease, as a combination of shame and distaste radiates through the crowd. The source of our revulsion must be the way that Koko, unlike the other performers, recalls the aspects of past freak shows that would be most intolerable to a contemporary viewer. Some line between individual agency and exploitation has been crossed, and the spectator who has paid for the pleasure of looking becomes an unwitting accomplice.

Although he denies that he wants to recreate the sideshow exactly as it once was, Zigun points to Koko and two other entertainers who have performed at Coney Island—bearded lady Jennifer Miller and Michael Wilson, the Illustrated Man (now deceased, his body was heavily covered in tattoos)—as evidence of the project's authenticity. Annoyed by critics who dismiss his outfit as "not much more than magic acts," he contends that these individuals, who combine physical anomalies with dramatic performance, are genuine freaks. Zigun is also relatively uninterested in most academic scholarship on freak shows. He takes particular exception to the work of Robert Bogdan, because he believes it to be overly critical of freak shows. Zigun asks, "Who's exploitative, the critic who condemns the performer [or] the producer of the show who pays him a salary?" Recalling Bogdan's treatment of Otis the Frog Man, Zigun claimed that the Coney Island Side Show allowed Otis "to finish his career with a lot of dignity" by revamping his act after the controversy in upstate New York. He proudly notes that the Coney Island Circus Side Show "is the last traditional ten-in-one, which is the proper format for a sideshow, left anywhere in the country." Indeed, the seedy atmosphere of Coney Island and the slightly unsavory feel of its sideshow may be the most constituent elements of its fidelity to a past that it claims to cite and reconfigure. Writing about freak shows at a historical remove, it is tempting to romanticize, or simply to forget, the deep discomfort that accompanies the act of paying to look at another person's body for pleasure, thrills, or simple curiosity. Coney Island activates memories of the important, and often neglected, place that freak shows occupy in the history of New York's popular culture, a history punctuated by injustice and exploitation, as well as enjoyment and profit.

Williamsburg U.S.A.

If the Coney Island Side Show attempts the authentic resurrection of an indigenous art form, a small group of artists in the Williamsburg neighborhood of Brooklyn have appropriated the freak show's episodic structure, while revamping its content for its young, self-consciously hip, urban followers. A fashionable suburb in the mid-nineteenth century, Williamsburg became home to working-class immigrants who moved from the Lower East Side when the bridge opened in 1903. Now it is an eclectic, low-rent neighborhood populated by Hassidic Jews, more recent immigrants from Latin America, and artists who can no longer afford to live in Manhattan or more gentrified parts of Brooklyn.[10] Based in Williamsburg, the performers featured in the Bindlestiff Family Cirkus and Circus Amok are decidedly queer and politically radical, commitments that distinguish them from the more apolitical Coney Island Side Show. In addition to tackling current debates within local and national politics, they fervently support freedom of expression, both sexual and artistic.

Addressing fans and performance artists around the country in winter 1999, *The Roustabout Reporter,* newsletter for the Bindlestiff Family Cirkus, offered biting commentary on Mayor Rudolph Giuliani's "Quality of Life" program:

> Under the current regime of New York City's Mayor Giuliani, artists, vendors, variety entertainers, and street performers are being harassed and attacked. Clubs and cabarets continue to be shut down over cabaret license infractions and superficial charges, and parks and sidewalks no longer allow street life or live entertainment.
>
> New York City is being applauded for the "improvements." Don't let this happen in your town.[11]

Mayor Giuliani's plan to cleanse New York City has been widely criticized by artists and free-speech advocates as an assault on the sexual subcultures that congregated within the commercial and public spaces targeted for elimination. Consistent with its anticensorship politics, the Bindlestiff Family Cirkus program includes raunchy sexual humor as well as displays of nudity and cross-dressing.

217

Calling itself a "Family" circus is an ironic jab at conservative notions of "family values," since most of its content is addressed to a sexually mature audience. Regular features are a safe-sex lecture in which the ringmistress, Philomena, threads a condom through one nostril into her mouth and blows it into a bubble, and an invitation to a brave audience member to drop his or her pants onstage in exchange for a prize. Presiding over the evening's entertainment is Scotty, aka the Blue Bunny, a tall, full-bodied man dressed in black tights, outrageously high platform boots, and a series of cropped jackets (made alternately in blue fur, blue spangles, or blue spandex) with large rabbit ears sewn into the hood. In the denouement, the Blue Bunny performs a striptease until, wearing only a silver-spangled loincloth, he douses himself with a jug of cheap red wine. Another sensation is a plate-spinning act performed by Philomena and Mr. Pennygaff, the clown. The episode begins unremarkably with Mr. Pennygaff balancing sticks topped by spinning plates on various parts of his body. It becomes outrageous when Philomena drops to the floor and turns upside-down with her legs over her head, revealing that she is naked underneath her skirt. Capping one of the sticks with a lubricated dildo, Mr. Pennygaff inserts it (with the plate still spinning) into Philomena's vagina. Such wildly funny exploits are coupled with more traditional circus fare: musical numbers, a trapeze artist, juggling, fire eating, clowns, and an escape act. The Cirkus program varies from one season to the next, as numbers by its permanent cast are interspersed with vignettes and stunts by visiting performers.

Nudity, cross-dressing, camp performance, and explicit sexuality are consistent themes at the Bindlestiff Family Cirkus. Unlike classic sideshows, which might have included figures of gender confusion such as a half man–half woman or a bearded lady, the Bindlestiff Cirkus represents a plurality of gendered styles, targeting a knowing, gay-friendly audience. Using the sideshow's episodic format to combine flamboyant campiness with bawdy sexual humor, the Bindlestiffs stitch together the affinity between *freak* and *queer* intimated in the fiction of Carson McCullers. The questions about desire and sexual practices that are often implied but rarely discussed at more conventional freak shows are foregrounded by the Bindlestiffs' appropriation of the ten-in-one's malleable format.

Although their content is far from the family-oriented entertainment of a P. T. Barnum, the Bindlestiffs adopt the form of the circus sideshow. At the end of a century dominated by mechanical reproduction, they hailed a renewed interest in live performance: "In the mid 90's the sideshow rose from its dusty place in our cultural attic, enhanced with rock and roll aggressiveness and marketing. Were we starting to search for something more visceral? Now, at the end of the millennium we see a rise in live shows again—theatre of all kinds. Could it be that we as a culture are getting over our fascination with the second hand thrills that television and interactive media offer? Has our love affair with the moving image, nearly a century old, faded? . . . An increase in leisure time and expendable income has already differentiated this end of the century from the last. However, vaudeville, circuses and sideshows have experienced a popularity akin to that of their prime 100 years ago."[12] The Bindlestiffs announce the return of the sideshow, as fin-de-siècle audiences tire of the impersonal and desensitizing effects of mass media. Having come full circle from the moment when Tod Browning captured a generation's most well-known freaks onscreen, the Bindlestiffs see themselves as harbingers of a revived enthusiasm for live theater, with the sideshow at its center. Their goal is to take freaks out of the domain of mechanical reproduction by reintroducing the unpredictable fleshly encounters integral to their carnival origins. They look to the past not with nostalgia, but as enthusiastic collectors who will salvage what is useful, revamp it "with rock and roll aggressiveness and marketing," and offer it to theatergoers eager for something more immediate and tangible.

As we have seen, classic sideshows gained (or mocked) legitimacy by promising to educate as well as entertain. Their pedagogical function was carried out by "professors" and "doctors" who delivered lectures, answered questions, and sold reading material. The Bindlestiffs' Autonomadic Bookmobile is a sophisticated, postmodern variant of this tradition. At this concession stand, theatergoers can purchase Bindlestiff souvenirs like T-shirts and posters alongside volumes of literature and poststructuralist theory by such authors as Jean Baudrillard, J. G. Ballard, Michel Foucault, and Paul Virilio. Its inventory attests to the contemporary freak performers' interest in the relationship between theory and practice, as well as their anticipation of an audience of young artist-intellectuals who understand the shows more as avant-garde theater than cheap thrills. The Cirkus presumes that it will be viewed with an ironic appreciation akin to camp reception, a mode of spectatorship that combines knowing distance with devoted fandom. Criticism is an integral part of the performance itself, which invites the viewer to become a participant-observer in an encounter no longer invested in drawing firm boundaries between freak and normal.

Bearded Lady and Revolutionary

A fixture of the Williamsburg circus subculture, the radical activist and performance artist Jennifer Miller might just be Leslie Fiedler's worst nightmare. In chapter 6, I quoted Fiedler's unfavorable characterization of those "neo-feminists" whose affirmation of female facial hair led him to conclude defensively, "I would guess that even now more Bearded Ladies choose careers as Freaks than as Revolutionaries."[13] As both a revolutionary and a woman with a beard who has self-consciously claimed the sideshow tradition, Jennifer Miller defies this opposition (figure 38). Now in her late thirties, Miller recalls growing up in a progressive household unconcerned with "issues of beauty and appearance."[14] When her beard first appeared twenty years ago, she could not imagine using any of the painful and expensive remedies available to remove it.[15] Out as a lesbian and a woman with a beard, Miller moved into the world of the circus and performance art instead of going to college. As the most well-known circus performer in New York, Miller participates in a number of theatrical ventures, including the Coney Island Circus Side Show, occasional appearances at the Bindlestiff Cirkus, one-woman shows, and her own troupe, Circus Amok. She has also made money by juggling in the subway, appeared twice on the Jerry Springer show, been photographed in the nude by Annie Liebowitz, and is the subject of a feminist documentary called *Juggling Gender* (Tami Gold, 1992).

Aside from Koko, Miller is the only performer in the Coney Island Circus Side Show with a physical anomaly that once would have designated her a born freak.

FIGURE 38. Jennifer Miller performing as MC for Circus Amok, June 2000. Photograph by Sam Adams.

Unlike Koko, who raises troubling questions about consent, Miller's act borrows the freak show format to couple entertainment with political consciousness raising in the form of entertainment. As a character called Zenobia, she delivers a sideshow-style spiel with an overtly feminist spin. If spielers have traditionally exaggerated the freak's abnormal qualities, Miller uses her monologue to create bonds with women in the audience and situate the beard in the context of broader cultural attitudes towards hair. In this, she turns a rhetorical mode intended to produce distance into a way of connecting with the spectators. Calling herself a woman with a beard rather than a "bearded lady," she explains to the crowd, emphasizes that she is not a freak but an extreme example of a common condition that affects many, if not most, women. "The world's full of women who have beards. Or at least they have potential," she tells them. "If only they would reach out, if only they would fulfill their potential instead of wasting time and money on the waxing, the shaving, the electrolysis, the plucking." Miller's goal is to empower women to refuse time-consuming, expensive, and painful beauty regimens, or at least to recognize them as choices rather than necessities. She encourages female spectators to identify with her, to see her as unremarkable, while contemplating their own potential for freakiness. Addressing mixed groups of men and women, she reminds them that "historically, hair has belonged to people who have power. You got the hair club for men, can't stand to be without his strength. It goes all the way back to Samson and his big mane of power; that's why the men don't want women having so much in too many places." Miller resists the notion that her beard is a freakish anomaly by situating it within an analysis of enduring, patriarchal systems of meaning that have associated facial hair and other male secondary sex characteristics with power and privilege.

As Zenobia, Miller participates in, and critically reconfigures, a tradition of exhibiting women with excess hair as sideshow attractions. Bearded ladies have typically been figures of exaggerated femininity whose facial hair stood out in jarring contrast to their voluminous gowns, jewelry, and elaborate hairstyles (figure 39). It is not surprising that Fiedler looked back at these freaks with nostalgia as he contemplated the rise of a radical women's movement, for, by representing themselves as unique curiosities, they upheld the normality of the binary opposition between the sexes. As Chris Straayer has noted, for men the beard is one of the developments that confirms the onset of normal, adult sexuality, "a reward at the end of horrifying (male) adolescence, a solidification after that messy stage of bodily transformations. Secondary sex characteristics are *supposed* to offer relief after prolonged worries about whether our childish bodies will deliver the 'appropriate' sexes or ultimately expose us as 'freaks.'"[16] A woman with a beard unsettles the

FIGURE 39. Madame
Clofullia, the Bearded Lady
of Switzerland, ca. 1860. In
this more traditional image,
the bearded lady's lavish
gown, jewelry, delicate pose,
and coifed hair attest to her
femininity, which is interrupted only by the thick
growth that covers her chin.
© Collection of The New-
York Historical Society.

assumption that human biology provides definitive confirmation of a dualistic
gender system in which, upon reaching maturity, all bodies settle neatly into the
categories of male and female. As we have seen, Fiedler aligns freaks with the
bodily confusions of childhood, which for adults are relegated to the subconscious
realm of dreams. Decked out in feminine garb and safely cordoned off as a freak
of nature, a bearded lady at the sideshow might stir those latent fantasies, but Jennifer Miller asserts that she is neither a freak nor the stuff of someone else's psychic refuse.

A woman with a beard who performs as a freak and a radical activist is thus ideally positioned to dispute received notions about sex and gender in a manner that
coincides forcefully with contemporary feminist, queer, and transgender politics.
Impatient with the Coney Island Side Show's lack of political content, Miller recognizes that there are clear limitations to what she can accomplish there in her
role as Zenobia. Regardless of her powerful spiel, Miller is still exhibiting herself
at Coney Island, a location laden with the history, artifacts, and living embodiments of the freak show tradition. The male spectators who channel their anxiety
by shouting at her to "take it off" attempt to normalize her, either by proving that

she is a man or by subjecting her to the treatment that sexist men reserve for humiliating women. Their misbehavior is produced, in part, by the venue itself, since freak shows are places that encourage such indecorous, disruptive outbursts. They draw crowds by promising lurid spectacles, not critiques of patriarchy, capitalism, or the sex-gender system. Contained within such a traditional format, Miller's act inevitably loses some of its radical potential, for doubtless many come away having seen her (and her message) as merely freakish, rather than having had their consciousnesses raised.

Miller compensates for the more unsatisfying aspects of the Coney Island Side Show with her own nonprofit, queer performance troupe, Circus Amok. Many of the group's participants are gay and lesbian, and, as in the Bindlestiff Family Cirkus, cross-dressing and exuberant camp performance are crucial elements of its style. But Circus Amok differs from the Bindlestiff Cirkus by soliciting audiences across the spectrum of race, age, and class. Whereas the Bindlestiffs play in venues that cater to ironic young hipsters, Miller's group actively pursues unconventional crowds with free, daytime performances in low-income, multiethnic neighborhoods. For two weeks each summer, the Circus appears in parks and playgrounds around New York, where it combines political theater with more traditional circus acts such as people on stilts, clowns, acrobatics, and juggling. Instead of making its sexual politics explicit, the Circus allows them to meld with a generally outrageous performance style. Numerous costume changes reveal a complete disregard for differentiating men from women or upholding the sex-gender correspondence. In an act called "The Rope of Death," for example, a male clown mounts a tightrope, where he sheds a layer of clothing one piece at a time, balancing precariously all the while. Underneath his baggy Chaplinesque suit he is wearing a full-skirted women's gown, to which he adds a pair of high-heeled shoes. The balancing act may be read as a metaphor for the laborious and unstable construction of gender; the "rope of death" is anchored by cast members at either end, their struggle suggesting the extreme difficulty of keeping the entire system in the air. Miller is a particularly ambiguous figure who participates in almost every episode, sometimes wearing a dress, sometimes a tuxedo, and often one of many colorful nongendered outfits. Since there is no point in the fast-paced program when the audience is invited to ask about her beard or her sex, Miller's multiple personae become just one aspect of the show's deliberate confusion of bodies and costumes (figure 40).

Because it never overtly connects camp and cross-dressing with sex radicalism, the Circus attracts audiences that might be alienated by a more direct statement of its sexual politics. Instead, queer sexual performance becomes a subtext

FIGURE 40. The
performers in Circus Amok
dramatize the concentration
of the nation's wealth among
an increasingly small per-
centage of the population.
Non-gender specific cos-
tumes and clown makeup
add to the provocative
confusion of gender and sex
that the group encourages.
Jennifer Miller can be seen
in the middle of the group.
Photograph by Sam Adams.

for Circus Amok's explicit dramatization of controversies within local and national politics. The show responds to current events with topical episodes that change from one year to the next. In 1998, it satirized Mayor Giuliani's "quality of life" campaign with a skit about jaywalking and decried environmental racism with twenty-foot-tall puppets representing the asthma that afflicts so many inner-city residents. The following summer's program continued to shower the mayor with ridicule, repainted the puppets in a tribute to Amadou Diallo (the African immigrant shot forty-one times by the NYPD), and added a skit about Y2K that poked fun at millennial hopes and fears. The 2000 season featured an acrobatic parody of New York's senatorial race between Hillary Clinton and congressman Rick Lazio and a sketch about the increasing concentration of the nation's wealth among the richest 10 percent of the population. In the tradition of political street theater, these episodes criticize established figures of power and authority, using a combination of entertainment and criticism to heighten the spectators' awareness about issues of civic concern.

The entire panoply of Miller's dramatic endeavors was brought together in March 1999, in a one-woman show called *Morphadike*, which played at Dixon

Place, a nonprofit performance space committed to feminist, alternative, and experimental theater. Like her other shows, *Morphadike* is structured episodically, with acts that include juggling, eating glass, and escape from a straight jacket, as well as more self-conscious critical interventions. Yet another alignment of freak and queer, its title combines the sex-gender ambiguity of the freak show "morphidite" with Miller's own lesbian (dyke) identification. In one act, she delivers the Zenobia monologue, which becomes self-reflexive once removed from its freak show setting and recycled as part of a one-woman show. In the context of other acts, Zenobia, the woman with a beard, is not the definitive expression of Miller's person, but one among many different roles she chooses to play. Another noteworthy episode is "A Short Talk," in which Miller recites passages from cultural anthropologist Barbara Kirschenblatt-Gimblett's "Objects of Ethnography," an essay about how persons and things are transformed into ethnographic artifacts. As she quotes the critical text, Miller holds up a hula hoop, moving her head into and out of its frame as an ironic illustration of Kirschenblatt-Gimblett's point about how the ethnographic mode constructs insiders and outsiders, self and other.[17] With a nod to 1960s countercultural freaks, Miller reads from Alan Ginsberg's "Howl" while crunching on a lightbulb. In another number she gyrates to the sounds of "Come See the Freaks," the theme song from the Broadway musical *Sideshow,* while keeping numerous hula hoops spinning around her hips. Rolling her eyes and moving with exaggerated gestures, Miller transforms the melodramatic strains of *Sideshow* into ironic commentary.[18] In short, *Morphadike* incorporates many of the modes of freak presentation described in this book, from sideshows to ethnographic exhibits, the counterculture, literary, critical, and popular representations. As Miller effectively demonstrates, the meanings of these representations are not fixed and they need not be exploitative, regardless of their original intentions. An inherently unruly, interactive form, the freak show's significance changes depending on the audience and context of reception.

Miller has succeeded in transforming her body and her penchant for the sideshow tradition into a political statement. A woman who couples energy and charisma with a progressive social vision, Miller deserves a good deal of credit for her accomplishment. However, it also has to do with the particularities of her body. Of the three traditional freak categories—race, disability, and unusual talents—she fits into the second two. As I have argued, racial freaks and ethnographic displays are off the menu of contemporary sideshows for obvious reasons. Likewise, the uneasy reactions to Koko are evidence that most contemporary audiences would recoil at the thought of exhibiting a person with disabilities as a freak. Miller's difference, which might loosely be defined as a disability, does not produce the same discomfort. This is partly because she is such a dynamic figure, but also because her anomaly fits into a context that tolerates, and even embraces, sexual and gender ambiguity. This is not to deny that Miller has endured her share of ridicule and prejudice. *Juggling Gender* includes one scene in which she is harassed on the street by a man who wants to touch the beard and then rub his face aggressively against hers. But she has been able to rework those negative experiences because she has found a place within a subculture where bisexuals, transgenders, and queers are at the vanguard of radical sexual politics.

As the accidents of the body converge with personal charisma, commitment, and a welcoming community, Miller has been able to turn stigma into a powerful statement. The contemporary freak show has become a particularly appealing point of reference for gay subculture, which has long been accused of freakish deviance. At the beginning of the new millennium, *freak* seems more like an option than a constraint. One of the primary distinctions between Barnum's ensemble and its twenty-first century counterparts is that freaks are no longer valuable commodities. While, as I argued in chapter 6, the new meaning of the word *freak* may be traced to broader cultural changes inaugurated in the 1960s, the most recent shift in the freak show's significance seems largely due to its nonprofit status.[19] Taken out of the marketplace, freak shows cannot be a way for one person to make money by exploiting another. The practice of human exhibition has been transformed by losing the very commercial basis that brought it into existence.

However, sideshow nostalgia is not equally attractive to every marginalized group that might once have been exhibited as freaks. Among the human attractions he observed in 1881, José Martí wrote of "a poor Negro who, for a miserable wage, sticks his head out of a hole in a cloth and is busied day and night eluding with grotesque movements the balls pitched at him." Obviously designed for humorous effects, this concession requires the customer to treat the black man as an object in order to enjoy his struggle to avoid being hit by the ball. Speculating on the unfortunate man's "miserable wage," Martí reminds the reader of his status as a worker and a human.[20] Looking back at a time when such sadistic amusements were commonplace, there seems little of value to salvage or recuperate. One century later, poet Robert Hayden echoed this sentiment when he spoke in the anguished voice of a tattooed circus freak: "Born alien, / homeless everywhere, / did I, then, choose bizarrity, / having no other choice?" The man's voluntary ornamentation of his bodily surfaces reflects his more enduring sense of displacement. The colorful tattoos can be read as a figure for the visible stigma of black skin, which causes him to feel as if imprisoned within "a gilt / and scarlet cage." Seeing

this deviant spectacle provides curious onlookers with a reassuring measure of
their own normality:

> Hundreds have paid
> to gawk at me—
> grotesque outsider whose
> unnaturalness
> assures them they
> are natural, they indeed
> belong.[21]

The lure of the freak's marked body is its ability to define the terms of inclusion
and exclusion, community and alienation. But by putting these insights in the
mouth of the tattooed man himself, the poem conveys not the comforts of normality, but the pain of injustice based on "colored" skin.

The word *freak* and the history of human exhibition are treated with an equivalent degree of caution by people with disabilities. In her survey of "nasty words,"
Simi Linton emphasizes the importance of context for determining the significance of a certain charged vocabulary words: "*Cripple, gimp,* and *freak* as used by
the disability community have transgressive potential. They are personally and
politically useful as a means to comment on oppression because they assert our
right to name experience."[22] In certain strategic situations, *freak* can be critically
reappropriated as a gesture of empowerment and political solidarity. But for poet
Kenny Fries, who writes, "*Freak, midget, three-toed / bastard.* Words I've always
heard," it is a jarring insult imposed on him by able-bodied strangers.[23] "Why
doesn't the word *freak* connect me easily and directly to subversion?" asks Eli
Clare, a writer who identifies herself as queer and disabled. "The end of the freak
show didn't mean the end of our display or the end of voyeurism. We simply
traded one kind of freakdom for another."[24] In the words of these disabled authors, the freak show is less a source of nostalgic inspiration than an expression of
the discomfort of living with a body always marked as Other.

Our show must come to an end, then, with the uneasy juxtaposition of opposing views: one that sees freaks and the freak show revival as a source of creative
possibility; another that is all too aware of its continued capacity for exploitation
and injustice. As we enter a new century, we might look back a hundred years to
recall that an iconic figure of American children's literature, the Wizard of Oz, was
a carnival barker. Born in Omaha and given the unwieldy name Oscar Zoroaster
Phadrig Isaac Norman Henkle Emmanuel Ambroise Diggs, he shortened it to

Oz.[25] Fortuitously for our story, the remaining initials spell the name of a freak show regular: "PINHEAD." Fearful of being associated with the pinhead's feeble intellect, the Wiz hides behind a screen of illusory humbug that causes all to believe he is a powerful magician. The motley crew of scarecrow, lion, tin man, and homeless girl who confront him in the Emerald City look a lot like a freak show, with their hybrid combinations of animal, human, and machine. All of the members of this unlikely band perceive themselves to be fragmentary or incomplete in some way. Hopeful that the Wizard can make them whole, they are dismayed to find that he is a fraud. "I have been making believe," he tells them.[26] This is a disappointing confession from a man who claimed awesome powers. But it also contains a kernel of truth, for although they haven't yet realized it, he has shown the travelers that they already posses the very qualities they most desire.

It should be perfectly clear by now that "making believe" has always been the work of the freak show. Fraudulent, thrilling, exploitative, and sometimes deeply moving, sideshows are places where unlikely individuals come together to contemplate the strangers within and the strangers without. Often those who hope to see the freakishness of others are unsettled to feel a shock of recognition as the bodies onstage remind them of their own tenuous grasp on normality. And those who look down from the platform repeatedly remind us that the things they want and do are not so very unusual after all. These shifting relationships between self and other, sameness and difference, are at the heart of our most fundamental sense of identity, both individual and collective. For precisely this reason, the freak show has become one of the enduring images Americans have used to locate themselves in the world and in relation to others, spinning a rich fabric of literary and artistic production as a result. As I hope to have shown, the sideshow may be located on the margins but, for those of us who appreciate the danger and promise of "making believe," it is invariably the most popular and profoundly affecting attraction of all.

CHAPTER ONE

1. Bogdan, *Freak Show*, 280.
2. Ibid., 279.
3. For example, Dick Zigun, manager of the Coney Island Circus Side Show, has a master's degree in theater arts from Yale. Zigun conceives of the sideshow as a dramatic art and calls his own rendition a "postmodern freak show." All of the freak performers I have met in New York have read some cultural criticism, although some like it more than others.
4. Gamson is the author of a book about the representation of sexual difference on TV talk shows, *Freaks Talk Back: Tabloid Talk Shows and Sexual Nonconformity*. I am indebted to Gamson for this enviable turn of phrase, which will recur throughout my own study as an apt way of describing a pattern in which the freak's injunction to silence is inevitably met by unruly vocal outbursts on the part of both audiences and performers.
5. Schenkar, *Signs of Life*.
6. Bogdan, *Freak Show*, 3.
7. Butler, "Performative Acts and Gender Constitution," 270.
8. Thompson, *On the Road with a Circus*, 68.
9. Twain, *Those Extraordinary Twins*, 237.
10. Grosz, "Intolerable Ambiguity," 55.
11. Mitchell, "Lady Olga," 95.
12. McCullers, *Member of the Wedding*, 18.
13. For feminist readings of the psychoanalytic concept of identification, see Butler, *Bodies that Matter* and *Gender Trouble;* and Fuss, *Identification Papers*.
14. McCullers, *Member of the Wedding*, 18.
15. Fiedler, *Freaks*. Fiedler's understanding of freaks as metaphors for the "secret self" may explain his misquotation of the McCullers passage I cite, to which he adds the sentence *"We are you!"* after the phrase *"we know you."* This easy slippage from knowledge of to identification with the Other is characteristic of Fiedler's study as a whole, which will be analyzed in greater detail in chapter 6.
16. Fuss, *Identification Papers*, 5.

17. Fiedler, *Freaks,* 22.

18. On the Freudian criticism of New York Intellectuals such as Lionel Trilling, Alfred Kazin, Irving Howe, Phillip Rahv, and Leslie Fiedler, see Leitch, *American Literary Criticism.*

19. Fiedler, *Love and Death,* 38. Likewise, Lionel Trilling, the most influential literary critic of his generation, writes, "For literature, as for Freud, the self is the first object of attention and solicitude. The culture in which the self has its existence is a matter of liveliest curiosity, but in a secondary way, as an essential condition of the self, as a chief object of the self's energies, or as representing the aggregation of selves" ("Freud: Within and beyond Culture," 103).

20. Davis, *Enforcing Normalcy,* especially chapter 2. On the emergence of the concept of normalcy in the United States, see Thomson, *Extraordinary Bodies*

21. This question is indebted to the work of postcolonial critics who have interrogated the relationship between colonizer and colonized in very similar terms. In particular, see Bhabba, *The Location of Culture;* Chow, *Writing Diaspora;* and Spivak, *In Other Worlds* and *A Critique of Postcolonial Reason.*

22. Although *freak* came to be associated with the business of human exhibition in the nineteenth century, the *OED* provides the word with a much more lengthy etymology. First used in 1563, its various meanings include "A sudden, causeless change or turn of mind; a capricious humor, notion, whim, or vagary." "A monstrosity, an abnormally developed individual of any species." And, beginning in 1967, "One who 'freaks out.'"

23. See, for example, Bogdan, *Freak Show;* Drimmer, *Very Special People;* Fiedler, *Freaks;* Gould and Pyle, *Anomalies and Curiosities of Medicine;* Mannix, *Freaks;* Thompson, *The History and Lore of Freaks;* Thomson, "Introduction: From Wonder to Error," 1–19, and *Extraordinary Bodies.*

24. *The Tempest,* 2.2.31–32.

25. On the history of the mass entertainment industry in the United States, see Adams, *The American Amusement Park Industry;* Dennett, *Weird and Wonderful;* Kasson, *Amusing the Million;* Peiss, *Cheap Amusements;* and Rydell, *All the World's a Fair.*

26. Brown, *The Material Unconscious;* Gleason, *The Leisure Ethic.*

27. On the life and career of P. T. Barnum, see Adams, *E. Pluribus Barnum;* Harris, *Humbug;* Kunhardt, Kunhardt, and Kunhardt, *P. T. Barnum;* and Saxton, *P. T. Barnum,* as well as Barnum's own biography, *Struggles and Triumphs.*

28. Fitzgerald, "Side-Shows." For an analysis of the topicality of Wild West shows, which regularly featured freaks alongside stock figures such as cowboys, Indians, and maidens in distress, see Slotkin, "Buffalo Bill's 'Wild West.'"

29. "A Goddess of Discord."

30. As late as 1960, Diane Arbus photographed Hezekiah Trembles, a black man performing as "The Jungle Creep" at Hubert's Museum in New York's Times Square. This photograph, which follows a traditional freak show convention of linking dark skin with

exotic jungles and savage bestiality, originally appeared in *Esquire* and is reprinted in Arbus, *Diane Arbus.*

31. On minstrelsy in the nineteenth century, see Hartman, *Scenes of Subjection;* Lott, *Love and Theft;* and Toll, *Blacking Up.* Rogin's *Blackface, White Noise* and Lott's work on the twentieth century reveal how the dynamics of minstrelsy extend well beyond the original form. Nonetheless, compared to minstrelsy, freak shows have been able to survive *as such* because of the greater variety among their cast of characters and their broader understanding of difference.

32. Stewart, *On Longing;* Thomson, *Extraordinary Bodies.*

33. The work responsible for inaugurating a wealth of scholarship on carnival is Bakhtin's *Rabelais and His World.* Bakhtin's notion of the grotesque has played an important role in theoretical writings about freaks and other extreme forms of bodily difference. A number of feminist critics have argued that Bakhtin's notion of carnival implicitly associates the female body with grotesque excess, while neglecting to address issues of gender. See, for example, Russo, *The Female Grotesque.* For an earlier influential analysis of women, carnival, and the grotesque, see Davis, "Women on Top," in *Society and Culture in Early Modern France,* 124–151. A feminist reading of freaks and the grotesque is also offered by Braidotti, "Mothers, Monsters, and Machines," in *Nomadic Subjects,* 76–94. On class and gender in relation to the grotesque, see Kipnis, "(Male) Desire and (Female) Disgust." On race and the grotesque, see Cassuto, *The Inhuman Race.* On the distinction between *grotesque* and *disabled,* see Davis, *Enforcing Normalcy.* On the *grotesque* as an aesthetic category, see Harpham, *On the Grotesque.*

34. Stewart, *On Longing,* 108.

35. Mitchell, "Lady Olga," 95–96.

36. Harris, *Humbug.*

37. *World Fair Freaks and Attractions, Inc. v. Hodges,* 267 So. 2d 817 (1972).

38. The connections between bad taste and class traced by this book are particularly indebted to Kipnis's *Ecstasy Unlimited* and Ross's *No Respect,* as well as Bourdieu's foundational study, *Distinction.*

39. Bogdan, *Freak Show,* 81.

40. Dunn, *Geek Love,* 7.

41. Dime Store Oddities box, Theatre Collection, Harry Ransom Humanities Center, University of Texas.

42. On the institutionalization of people with disabilities, see Linton, *Claiming Disability;* Longmore, "People with Disabilities"; Starr, *American Medicine;* and Trent, *Inventing the Feeble Mind.*

43. Stiker, *A History of Disability,* 192.

44. Ellison, *The Invisible Man,* 3 (emphasis added).

45. Sone, *Nisei Daughter,* 158.

46. Kingston, *Tripmaster Monkey*, 293.
47. Eliot, Introduction to *Nightwood*, xvi.

CHAPTER TWO

1. Fellows, *This Way to the Big Show*, 296.
2. For accounts of the development of racial science, see Degler, *In Search of Human Nature;* Haller, *Outcasts from Evolution;* Gilman, *Difference and Pathology;* Gould, *The Mismeasure of Man;* and Stepan, "Race and Gender."
3. See Berlant's introduction to *The Anatomy of National Fantasy*, 1–17.
4. Bledstein, *The Culture of Professionalism*, 90.
5. Nasaw, *Going Out*.
6. DiMaggio, "Cultural Entrepreneurship." As Lawrence Levine has argued in *Highbrow/Lowbrow*, during the nineteenth century the divide between high and low cultural spheres widened. The efforts of the first generation of accredited scientists to distinguish their work from that of amateur showmen, explorers, and armchair travelers are part of the process of defining the legitimacy of the high against the messy amateurism of the low.
7. See Bogdan, *Freak Show;* and Thomson, "Introduction: From Wonder to Error" and *Extraordinary Bodies*.
8. Adams, *E Pluribus Barnum*, 30. On Barnum, see also Harris, *Humbug*.
9. Thomson, *Extraordinary Bodies*, 64.
10. Bradford and Blume, *Ota Benga*. On Verner's career as a Presbyterian missionary, see Crawford, "Pioneer African Missionary."
11. Bradford and Blume, 187.
12. Ibid., 181.
13. The uncropped version is included, without analysis, in Harvey Blume's "Ota Benga and the Barnum Perplex."
14. Bradford and Blume, *Ota Benga*, 255.
15. Verner, *Pioneering in Central Africa*, 276.
16. Crawford notes that Verner's "language became more professional and anthropological rather than evangelical, as he tried to use the knowledge acquired in his rich and frustrating years in the Congo." "Pioneer African Missionary," 55.
17. Verner's reverence for the rich and powerful, and his propensity for name dropping, is evident in an unpublished manuscript, "Thomas F. Ryan as A Benefactor of a Carolina Boy. How the Great Financier Made the Dreams of an African Explorer Come True."
18. Hinsley, *Savages and Scientists*, 286. Bradford and Blume write of Verner's frustrated efforts to dispense of the artifacts he had collected and turn his African adventures into a career. The unenthusiastic responses of professional curators, naturalists, and anthropologists "struck Verner hard. A note of resentment, an edge of bitterness creeps into his letters, despite the cordial, nearly obsequious language. Verner felt

that his lack of academic credentials prevented him from getting the treatment that Professor Starr, for example, would receive." *Ota Benga,* 163–164.

19. On the What Is It? exhibit, see Cook, "Of Men, Missing Links, and Nondescripts"; and Lindfors, "P. T. Barnum and Africa."

20. Editorial, *New York Tribune,* 13 September 1906, Wildlife Conservation Society Archives, New York Zoological Park.

21. "Negro Ministers Act to Free the Pygmy," *New York Times,* 11 September 1906, quoted in Bradford and Blume, *Ota Benga,* 262.

22. Cited in Horowitz, "Animal and Man," 445.

23. Bledstein, "Spaces and Words," in *The Culture of Professionalism,* 46–79; and Levine, "Order, Hierarchy, and Culture," in *Highbrow/Lowbrow,* 169–242.

24. Horowitz, "Animal and Man." On the history of zoos and their relationship to other strategies of containing and preserving nature, see Wilson, *The Culture of Nature.*

25. Horowitz, "Animal and Man," 451 (emphasis added).

26. Bradford and Blume, *Ota Benga,* 171.

27. Hornaday, *Minds and Manners,* 67.

28. Ibid., 83.

29. Verner, *Pioneering in Central Africa,* 277.

30. Benjamin Reiss writes of African American intellectuals' struggle against the insulting representations of blackness found at the freak show and similar sites of popular entertainment in *The Showman and the Slave.* See also Reed, *"All the World Is Here!"*

31. In their distaste for science, these religious men take a position opposite to that of African American intellectuals like W. E. B. DuBois, who used the language and methods of scientific rationality to further the struggle against racism.

32. "Bushman's Champions Angry," *New York Tribune,* 12 September 1906, Wildlife Conservation Society Archives, New York Zoological Park.

33. Cited in Bradford and Blume, *Ota Benga,* 262.

34. "Still Stirred about Benga," *New York Times,* 23 September 1906, Wildlife Conservation Society Archives, New York Zoological Park.

35. On the African American identification with Africa at the turn of the century, see Fierce, *The Pan-African Idea;* Gilroy, *The Black Atlantic;* Gruesser, *Black on Black;* Magubane, *The Ties That Bind;* McCarthy, *Dark Continent;* and Williams, *Rethinking Race.*

36. In *All the World Is Here!* Christopher Robert Reed describes a similar ambivalence among African American intellectuals reluctant to be associated with racist images of Africa at the Chicago World's Fair.

37. On the involvement of African Americans in missionary work in Africa, see Gruesser, *Black on Black;* Jacobs, *Black Americans* (especially Jacobs, "The Historical Role of Afro-Americans," 5–32); and Williams, "William Henry Sheppard." See also Williams, *Black Americans.*

38. "Ota Benga Now a Real Colored Gentleman," *New York Daily Globe,* 16 October 1906. Cited in Bradford and Blume, *Ota Benga,* 275.

39. Ibid., 220.

40. "Civilization," *North American,* 17 or 18 September 1906. Cited in Bradford and Blume, *Ota Benga,* 269.

41. Blume and Bradford, *Ota Benga,* 273–274.

42. Rosaldo, *Culture and Truth,* 70.

43. Saxton Temple Pope, *Hunting with the Bow and Arrow* (San Francisco: Jas. H. Barry, 1923), quoted in Eloesser, "Saxton Temple Pope, M.D.," 849.

44. On the pervasiveness of the "antimodern impulse" in the United States at the turn of the century, see Lears, *No Place of Grace.* In *Manliness and Civilization,* Gail Bederman explores the rhetoric of modernity's enervating effects on manhood.

45. Kinsley, "Untainted Life," 100.

46. The most extended account of Ishi's life is provided in the biography written by Theodora Kroeber, *Ishi in Two Worlds.*

47. Kroeber, *Ishi in Two Worlds,* 129.

48. Ibid.

49. Letter to Professor Waterman, 6 September 1911, Lowie Museum archives, University of California, Berkeley.

50. Kroeber, *Ishi in Two Worlds,* 169.

51. Miller, "Indian Enigma," 97.

52. "Stone Age Indian Hauled from Forests' Depths by Savants," *San Francisco Evening Post,* 5 September 1911, Lowie Museum archives, University of California, Berkeley.

53. After his release from the Bronx Zoo, Ota Benga attended the Hippodrome accompanied by Verner. There, the African's response to the show was also observed and recorded by reporters (see Bradford and Blume, *Ota Benga,* 273). During the late nineteenth and early twentieth centuries, it was not uncommon to take non-Western people to theatrical performances for the purpose of observing and recording their reactions. Such excursions seem designed to gauge the distance between the visitors' underdevelopment and the enlightenment of the Western audience, to study the capacity of the foreign onlookers to understand the complexities of performative representation taking place on the stage with the assumption that they lacked the necessary sophistication to appreciate what they saw.

54. Wallace, "Ishi," 108.

55. From the beginning, writing about Ishi expressed an interest in his sexual history. Ishi grew to maturity surrounded only by his immediate family. Was he a virgin? Or had he practiced incest in the interests of survival? Did abstinence result in the magnification of desire or its absence? Pope reflects briefly on Ishi's undeveloped sexual knowledge. The subject receives greater speculation in Theodora Kroeber's biography, where she comments on his reticent behavior towards women and its relation to "sex starvation" (220–221). Recent accounts demonstrate an increasingly explicit preoccupation with

the topic. The most extreme versions are Henry Beissel's play, *Under Coyote's Eye,* in which Ishi has an incestuous relationship with his sister, and the fictionalized encounter between Ishi and a prostitute in the HBO film, *The Last of His Tribe* (Harry Hook, 1992).

56. Kroeber, "Ishi, the Last Aborigine," 121.

57. Kroeber, "It's All Too Much for Ishi," 111.

58. Hinsley, *Savages and Scientists,* 35; Levine, in *Highbrow/Lowbrow,* makes a similar point about the Smithsonian's early history (156–158).

59. Kroeber, *Ishi in Two Worlds,* 121–123.

60. Karl Kroeber argues that the contribution of Boasian anthropology, which disputed the progress-oriented paradigm of its European counterparts, may be partially explained by the fact that many of its early practitioners, including Boas himself, were immigrants. For a number of eminent anthropologists of this period, "the understanding and describing of native cultures was part of the process of naturalizing themselves as Americans—of finding themselves at home in an America created by dispossession of native cultures." *Artistry in Native American Myths,* 13.

61. Degler, *In Search of Human Nature,* 62.

62. See Kuper, *The Invention of Primitive Society,* on the necessity of primitivism to the evolution of anthropology as a discipline.

63. Kroeber, "Ishi, the Last Aborigine," 123.

64. For a discussion of Kroeber's influence on the anthropological study of human nature, see Degler, "In the Wake of Boas," in *In Search of Human Nature,* 84–104.

65. Of course there is an equally significant tradition of using anthropometry to confirm the inferiority of the Indian. See Gould, *The Mismeasure of Man,* chapter 2.

66. Pope, "The Medical History of Ishi," 232.

67. Ibid., 234.

68. Waterman, "The Yana Indians," 157.

69. Unpublished comments of Dr. Elsaesser to Marshall Kuhn. Marshall Kuhn papers, Bancroft Library, University of California, Berkeley. This memory was recorded decades after Dr. Elsaesser's encounter with Ishi and may be shaped by fantasies about the wild Indian's perfection. Interview with Elaine Dorfman, 1977–78.

70. Quoted in Eloesser, "Saxton Temple Pope, M.D.," 848.

71. Leslie Fiedler was among the first to comment on this tradition in his classic essay, "Come Back to the Raft Ag'in Huck Honey" (in *End to Innocence*). For more contemporary scholarship on the male bonding tradition in American literature and culture, see Bederman, *Manliness and Civilization;* Leverentz, *Manhood and the American Renaissance;* Nelson, *National Manhood;* and Wiegman, *American Anatomies.*

72. Wiegman, *American Anatomies,* 158.

73. By the time of his death, Ishi's public appeal had greatly diminished. After four years in civilization, the wild man who lived at the university's museum was hardly a breaking story, and the more he adapted to modern life, the less spectacular he became. In

fact, within a few years of his appearance, newspapers were breaking stories that Ishi
was not the last of his tribe, with headlines such as "Ishi Is Not the Last of Lost Tribe:
Stockmen and Ranchers of Deer Creek Country Find Traces of Aborigines" and "Ishi's
Squaw Seen Hunting for Mate: Parties Searching Underbrush Near Oroville for Wife
of Lone Survivor." Lowie Museum archives, University of California, Berkeley.

74. "Ishi's Death—A Chico Commentary," 242.

75. Editorial, *Portland Oregon Telegram,* 30 March 1916, Lowie Museum archives, University of California, Berkeley.

76. After his death in 1916, Ishi was largely forgotten until the post-World War II period,
when he was reintroduced by the publication of Theodora Kroeber's best-selling *Ishi
in Two Worlds.* In that volume, Kroeber provides the most complete account of Ishi's
life. Kroeber is able to write Ishi's experiences into a coherent narrative through considerable speculation, informed by more contemporary anthropological perspectives
of the 1960s that supplement her late husband's Victorian sensibilities. The Kroeber
biography takes liberties similar to *Ota Benga: The Pygmy in the Zoo* by novelizing
aspects of a life unavailable to an author who never knew Ishi and had relatively scant
information at her disposal. The popularity of this engaging account and the surge of
interest in Native American cultures since the 1960s have brought renewed attention
to Ishi's story, resulting in a flood of representations that I call "Ishimania." To name
only selected examples of a long list, Ishi has been the subject of plays by Henry Beissel
(*Under Coyote's Eye*), Gerald Vizenor (*Ishi and the Wood Ducks*), Preston Arroweed,
and Gary Weimberg (*Ishi, the Last Wild Indian*); fictional accounts by Kroeber herself
(a children's book called *Ishi, the Last of his Tribe*), Gerald Vizenor (*Manifest Manners,* and *Trickster of Liberty*), Kathleen Allan Meyer (*Ishi*), Richard Burrill (*Ishi:
America's Last Stoneage Indian*), David Petersen (*Ishi, the Last of His People*), and
Leanne Hinton (*Ishi's Tale of Lizard*); works of art by Peter Voltos (*Mr. Ishi*), Frank
Tuttle (*What Wild Indian?*), Jean La Mar, and Brian Tripp; and films by Harry Hook
(*The Last of His Tribe,* 1992) and Jeff Riffe (*Ishi, the Last Yahi,* 1996); and a series of
interviews by past Sierra Club president and activist Marshall Kuhn.

77. On Kroeber's response to Ishi's death and autopsy, see Thomas, *Skull Wars.*

78. Thomson, *Extraordinary Bodies,* 57. On the irrelevance of sentience to the freak's appeal, see Stewart, *On Longing,* 111. For a compelling analysis of the life and death of
P. T. Barnum's first attraction, Joice Heth, see Reiss, "P. T. Barnum."

79. The Eskimos brought from Greenland to New York by the Peary expedition suffered
a similar fate. When four of the six died of tuberculosis, they were dissected and their
remains stored in the American Museum of Natural History. Kenn Harper's *Give Me
My Father's Body* tells the story of Minik, one of two survivors, who discovered that his
father's remains had not been buried as he had been deceived into believing at the
time, but placed on display at the museum.

80. Kroeber, *Ishi in Two Worlds,* 238.

CHAPTER THREE

1. Dwight Taylor, quoted in Skal and Savada, *Dark Carnival,* 168.

2. In *The Politics and Poetics of Transgression,* Stallybrass and White argue that, beginning in the eighteenth century, Western bourgeois subjectivity is formed through the rejection of degraded carnivalesque elements, which resurface as phobic eruptions of disgust, fear, and desire. As Taylor describes it, Fitzgerald's overreaction fits this model perfectly. If the twins' doubled body confuses the distinction between self and other, vomiting is a phobic symptom of the refusal to incorporate a foreign element into the self.

3. Fitzgerald was raised in a family that had class aspirations but lacked the financial means to realize them. Despite attending Princeton and winning the affections of the moneyed southern belle Zelda Sayre, he was perpetually anxious about his social and economic status, particularly during the period he spent as a Hollywood screenwriter. These anxieties frequently gave way to wild alcoholic binges during which he became violent and abusive and frequently lost consciousness. It seems hardly accidental that the freaks appeared to the author in the midst of such an episode, as if they were the embodiment of his own carnivalesque excesses. This incident appears in muted form in Fitzgerald's short story, "Crazy Sunday." In the story, the freaks enter the commissary as the young author attempts to work through his ambivalent feelings about being an employee of the Hollywood film industry.

4. Quoted in Skal and Savada, *Dark Carnival,* 179. Numerous other sources refer to this incident as an emblem of the extreme responses the film evoked in its contemporaries. See, for example, Brosnan, *The Horror People,* 66; Morris and Viera, "*Freaks:* Production and Analysis"; and Norden, *The Cinema of Isolation.*

5. Skal and Savada describe Freaks as "a commercial disaster," at a cost of $316,000. It lost the studio $164,000, "more than the entire budget of *The Unholy Three,* the film that had made Browning's name at the studio" (*Dark Carnival,* 181).

6. Ibid., 5.

7. As I will argue in greater detail below, this is a transitional moment in the film's depiction of the sideshow performers. Up to this point it resists portraying the disabled characters as "freaks," but when Cleo interpellates them as such, their behavior becomes increasingly sinister and monstrous. In keeping with this two-part structure, I have tried to use the term *freaks* only when the film represents them in this way. Otherwise, I refer to them as disabled actors or performers in order to preserve the distinction between the performative identity *freak* and the more complex personhood of the performer.

8. Concerns about class were characteristic of Browning's work from the beginning. Although they may be contextualized most neatly by reference to the national economic depression of the 1930s, Browning himself lived out those years in financial security after having struggled with poverty in his youth. Despite the fact that he became a

successful Hollywood director, biographical evidence suggests a lifelong uneasiness with wealth and the privileges that accompanied it.

9. Unlike the obviously fictive antagonists of Universal's popular monster movies, such as *Dracula* (also directed by Browning, in 1931), *Frankenstein* (James Whale, 1931), and *The Mummy* (James Whale, 1931), *Freaks* cast stars whose monstrous bodies collapsed the distinction between actors and the roles that they played. The brutal realism of bodies without limbs, bodies that were too skinny, too small, too bald, or too hairy was a far cry from the deliciously scary creatures of more typical horror films. Despite the fear that the Universal monsters provoked while on screen, there was never any doubt that they were played by actors, with the help of makeup and special effects.

10. Fiedler, *Freaks,* 18.

11. Skal and Savada, *Dark Carnival,* 229. In addition, *Freaks* has influenced such filmmakers as Luis Buñuel, Max Ophuls, Federico Fellini, and Ingmar Bergman. It was adapted for the stage by French director Genevieve de Kermabon in a critically acclaimed 1988 production featuring disabled actors. References to *Freaks* have appeared in Robert Altman's *The Player,* the films of David and Jennifer Lynch, and *The Simpsons.* It is undoubtedly a cinematic forebear for trash film impresario John Waters. Browning made a brief appearance in the 1997 Broadway musical *Sideshow,* the story of conjoined twins Daisy and Violet Hilton, who were part of the cast of *Freaks. Freaks* is also the subject of a comic book series by Jim Woodring and F. Solano Lopez loosely based on the film. Memorabilia such as T-shirts, stills, lobby cards, and videos are part of a thriving trade on eBay.

12. On this tradition, see Brottman, *Offensive Films;* and Hunter, *Inside Teradome.*

13. The notion of a residual cultural form is borrowed from Raymond Williams, who writes of "experiences, meanings and values, which cannot be verified or cannot be expressed in terms of the dominant culture" because they belong to "some previous social formation." Williams, "Base and Superstructure," 415.

14. Before he began to direct his own films, Browning was an assistant to D. W. Griffith during the making of *Intolerance,* a film that Miriam Hansen describes as resistant to the conventions of classical Hollywood cinema. There are continuities between the unconventionality Hansen detects in *Intolerance* and the formal inconsistencies of *Freaks.* See Hansen, *Babel and Babylon. Freaks* also has clear formal and thematic affinities with the exploitation genre, extensively examined in Eric Schaefer's *Bold! Daring! Shocking! True!*

15. In his MPAA biography, Browning offered the following description of the start of his career: "Circus came to town—he got a colored boy, then fixed up a 'wild man' sideshow act, and he landed a job." Browning file, Margaret Herrick Library, Beverly Hills, CA.

16. Gunning, "The Cinema of Attractions," 58.

17. Gunning, "An Aesthetic of Astonishment," 120.

18. Ibid., 124.

19. See Allen, *Vaudeville and Film,* for a discussion of the factors that influenced the replacement of variety acts and historical documentary by narrative in early film.

20. Skal, *The Monster Show.*

21. An important exception is Miss Jane Barnell, the bearded lady, who commented retrospectively that the film was "an insult to all freaks everywhere and [she was] sorry she acted in it. When it was finished, she swore she would never again work in Hollywood." Mitchell, "Lady Olga," 97.

22. Linda Williams argues that the Muybridge photographs offered audiences "an unanticipated pleasure attached to the visual spectacle of lifelike moving bodies." Encoded in that pleasure was an understanding of gender difference. It seems equally true that Muybridge invited spectators to distinguish between normative and deviant types of motion, thus implanting an interest in the movement of the disabled body among the first generation of film spectators. Williams, *Hard Core,* 37–43.

23. Goldbeck and Gordon, *Freaks,* 56.

24. Stewart, *On Longing,* 55.

25. See Butler, *Horror in the Cinema;* Hawkins, "'One of Us'"; Laskas, "Program Notes"; and Thomas, "Freaks."

26. From a feminist perspective, this disruption is more problematic as Cleo, the acquisitive, sexually aggressive woman is depicted as a monstrous giant against the tiny body of the passive, devoted Frieda. *Freaks* certainly does seem intent on cutting women down to size—hence Cleo's shrunken, legless figure at the end of the story. See Russo, *The Female Grotesque,* 92.

27. Goldbeck and Gordon, *Freaks,* 38. After hearing Randian's one incomprehensible line of dialogue it is clear why he was replaced by the more articulate Johnny Eck in this scene, which involves an extended conversation between the three characters.

28. Robbins, "Spurs," 26.

29. Ibid., 27.

30. Ibid., 28.

31. Goldbeck and Gordon, *Freaks,* 5.

32. Ibid., 24.

33. Ibid., 47.

34. Ibid., 106.

35. Gaylyn Studlar has written persuasively of the connection between Chaney's protean screen persona and the freak show in *This Mad Masquerade.* The crucial difference between Chaney and the disabled actors of *Freaks* is that he maintained a clear demarcation between the grotesque characters he played onscreen and the modest, retiring figure he presented when not acting a part. This split between on- and offscreen personae is more akin to classic monster film stars such as Bella Lugosi and Boris Karloff than the actors in *Freaks,* whose cinematic roles melded with their lives offscreen.

36. As Joan Hawkins has suggested, this joke belies the threatening possibility of a homoerotic reversal in which Joseph would be attracted to Hercules: like the conjoined

twins, the blurring of the boundaries of self into Other raises the question of nonnormative sexual relations.

37. Russo and Brottman both point out that the image of the chicken is "the totemic representation of the freaks" (Russo, *The Female Grotesque*, 91; Brottman (citing Russo), *Offensive Films*, 28), a claim they support with numerous examples of chicken imagery that pervade the film. The chicken woman gestures towards the most degraded of all carnival folk, the geek, whose performance consists of biting the heads off of live chickens.

38. Bogdan, *Freak Show*, 204–210, and on Tom Thumb's marriage to Lavinia Warren, 148, 154–156. Also on Tom Thumb weddings, see Stewart, *On Longing*, 119–124.

39. Such an engagement is the subject of the 1997 Broadway musical *Sideshow*, based on the lives of Daisy and Violet Hilton, who long for romantic love and instead are cruelly exploited by men who want to transform their double wedding into a profitable spectacle.

40. On *Freaks* as horror film see Borst, "Reevaluating a Screen Classic"; Butler, *Horror in the Cinema;* Dyer, "Freaks U.S.A., 1932"; Hawkins, "'One of Us'"; Laskas, "Program Notes"; Mayersberg, review of *Freaks;* Quigley, "Freaks with Feeling"; and Rosenthal and Kass, *The Hollywood Professionals.* On freaks as social criticism, see Russo, *The Female Grotesque*, 86–93; and Thomas, "Freaks."

41. Quoted in *Toronto Film Society Notes* 16 January 1967. *Freaks* folder, MOMA film clippings archive, New York.

42. Hanson, *Freaks*, 325.

43. In the Tod Robbins novel *The Unholy Three* (also the source for a Browning film) a midget (also played in the film by Harry Earles) inspires the same disrespectful laughter in the sideshow audience. Filled with barely repressed rage, he eventually gets his revenge by becoming a thief and murderer.

44. Quoted in Skal, *The Monster Show*, 152.

45. On the integral connection between laughter and horror see Paul, *Laughing Screaming.*

46. Brottman, *Offensive Films*, 55. Brottman offers a thoughtful and sustained analysis of laughter in the film. However, she inaccurately connects the hysterical laughter of the characters in *Freaks* with the laughter of Bakhtinian carnival. Whereas laughter in *Freaks* is a neurotic reaction arising more from horror and anxiety than from pleasure, carnivalesque laughter, as Bakhtin describes it, is inclusive and exuberant. At the center of Bakhtin's analysis is Rabelais, who, he argues, drew on Renaissance theories in which "the characteristic trait of laughter was precisely the recognition of its positive, regenerating, creative meaning." Bakhtin, *Rabelais and His World*, 71.

47. Freud, *Jokes*.

48. See Freud, "Analysis of a Phobia."

49. Bogdan, *Freak Show*, 94–118.

50. Russo, *The Female Grotesque*, 88.

51. Browning was forced to add this epilogue, which is supposed to function as a "happy ending," after audiences were horrified by the sight of Cleo's mutilated body at the end of the film.

52. Russo, *The Female Grotesque*, 92.

53. On the gendered violence of horror film, see Berenstein, *Attack of the Leading Ladies;* Clover, *Men, Women, and Chain Saws;* Creed, *The Monstrous Feminine;* and Williams, "When the Woman Looks."

54. John Thomas, quoted in *Toronto Film Society Programme* 9 (22 March 1982): 4.

55. Moreover, Browning's films are replete with the castratory wounding of the male body, not the female. While he rarely depicts powerful or resourceful female protagonists, the violent mutilation of the woman's body is out of keeping with Browning's typical concerns.

CHAPTER FOUR

1. Carr, *The Lonely Hunter*, 519.

2. For a more complete account of Hall's life in Charleston, see Sears, *Lonely Hunters: An Oral History of Lesbian and Gay Southern Life, 1948–1968* (Boulder, CO: Westview Press, 1997), chapter 5; and "Race, Class, Gender, and Sexuality in Pre-Stonewall Charleston: Perspectives on the Gordon Langley Hall Affair," in *Carryin' On in the Lesbian and Gay South,* ed. John Howard (New York: New York University Press, 1997), 164–200.

3. Carr, *The Lonely Hunter*, 519.

4. In *Between Men,* Eve Sedgwick argues that the heroine in the Western literary tradition often functions as the conduit for an intimate, erotically charged struggle between two male competitors. McCullers's own complex erotic life more than once placed her at the apex of such a triangulated affair, and in what follows I will propose that there may be pleasure not only in the homosocial bond between men, but in the woman's position as intermediary.

5. Bigelow, "Carson McCullers," 257. Critics who have argued that McCullers's characters symbolize universal human alienation include Carr (*Understanding Carson McCullers*), Hassan (*Contemporary American Literature, 1945–1972*), Lubbers ("The Necessary Order"), Paden ("Autistic Gestures"), Rubin ("Carson McCullers"), and Sadler ("'Fixed in an Inlay of Mystery'"). Among those who acknowledge the depiction of homosexuality in McCullers's work but make similar claims for universality are Adams (*The Homosexual as Hero*), Bigelow ("Carson McCullers"), and Whatling ("Carson McCullers"). See Logan's introduction to *Critical Essays on Carson McCullers* for a useful overview of McCullers criticism.

6. Patricia Yaeger, in *Dirt and Desire,* has also recently argued that McCullers's fiction is far more historically and politically engaged than critics have recognized. For a discussion of McCullers's postwar drama as social criticism, see Logan and Horvath, "Nobody Knows Best."

7. This perceived homogeneity was, of course, countered by the particularity of many Americans' lives. Recent analyses of urban life, youth culture, and sexual and racial minorities indicate that the postwar years were far more complex and tumultuous than has previously been acknowledged. See, for example, the essays in Foreman, *The Other Fifties;* and Meyerowitz, *Not June Cleaver.*

8. Carr, *The Lonely Hunter,* 1, 127.

9. Using a somewhat different vocabulary, Rubin wrote of McCullers's fiction, "[I]t isn't that freaks are commentaries or criticisms on normality; they are normality" ("Carson McCullers," 118).

10. As Judith Butler describes the earlier significance of the term, "'queer' has operated as one linguistic practice whose purpose has been the shaming of the subject it names or, rather, the producing of a subject through that shaming interpellation" (*Bodies That Matter,* 226).

11. Warner, introduction to *Fear of a Queer Planet,* xxvi.

12. Kazin, "Djuna Barnes's *Nightwood.*" Kazin is responding to a cautionary remark made by T. S. Eliot, who, in his introduction to the book, wrote that "to regard this group of people as a horrid sideshow of freaks is not only to miss the point, but to confirm our wills and harden our hearts in an inveterate sin of pride" (xvi).

13. Cited in Katz, *Gay/Lesbian Almanac,* 577.

14. Ibid., 620.

15. Quoted in Spencer, *Homosexuality in History,* 340.

16. On homosexuality during the postwar period, see Corber, *In the Name of National Security* and *Homosexuality in Cold War America;* D'Emilio, *Sexual Politics, Sexual Communities;* D'Emilio and Freeman, *Intimate Matters;* Lewes, *Male Homosexuality;* and Spencer, *Homosexuality.*

17. According to D'Emilio and Freeman, the social circumstances of World War II contributed to the development of gay and lesbian communities in major cities such as New York and San Francisco. Despite the repressive atmosphere of the Cold War, these subcultures continued to expand and flourished during the 1960s. See Corber, *Homosexuality in Cold War America;* D'Emilio, *Sexual Politics, Sexual Communities,* part 1; and D'Emilio and Freeman, *Intimate Matters,* part 4. On the rise of queer urban spaces in the modernist period, see Boone, "Queer Sites in Modernism."

18. So named by poet Louis Untermeyer, who recalled attending "a gay (in both senses of the word) occasion at which Auden and Gypsy Rose Lee were present" at the home McCullers shared with Auden and George Davis. Quoted in Carr, *The Lonely Hunter,* 199.

19. Indeed, this violence has been so pervasive that "queer bashing" is one of the compound words listed under *queer* in the OED. While it is difficult to trace a precise genealogy of the term, it is clear that *queer* was used almost entirely as a negative label during McCullers's lifetime. For brief reference to previous pejorative uses of *queer,* see Berlant, "Queer Nationality"; Butler, *Bodies That Matter;* Duggan, "Making It

Perfectly Queer"; Spencer, *Homosexuality;* and Warner, introduction to *Fear of a Queer Planet.* George Chauncey details the significance of *queer* between 1890 and 1940, when it was used by male homosexuals to differentiate themselves from the more effeminate "fairies." According to Chauncey, *queer* did not become a derogatory term until the mid-twentieth century. See Chauncey, *Gay New York.*

Lori Kenschaft argues that "[i]n 1946, when *Wedding* was published, 'queer' (like 'gay') was a code word known to many 'in the life' but few outside; it was frequently used to identify oneself to another discreetly, under the public eye but without public knowledge." "Homoerotics and Human Connections," 221. Despite Kenschaft's assertion that *queer* functions as a code among insiders, historical evidence indicates that it was also widely used during this period to condemn the innate abnormality of the homosexual. Just three years later, an article on homosexuality as deviant perversity entitled "Queer People" would appear in a publication as mainstream as *Newsweek.*

20. Quoted in Carr, *The Lonely Hunter,* 159.
21. Carr's biography chronicles the numerous queer erotic arrangements the McCullers couple engaged in during the course of their relationship. Unfortunately, Carr's descriptions are frequently tinged with condescension or homophobia. She writes, for example, "Having sexual problems himself which he could not resolve, Reeves was incapable of coping with his wife's sexual inclinations or of *helping her to become more heterosexually oriented.* Carson was completely open to her friends about her tremendous enjoyment in being physically close to attractive women. She was as frank and open about this aspect of her nature *as a child would be in choosing which toy he most wanted to play with"* (*The Lonely Hunter,* 295, emphasis added).
22. Butler, *Bodies That Matter,* 229. On the necessity of a more complex analysis of racial difference within queer theory, see Eng, "Out Here and Over There," 41–42; Sedgwick, "Queer and Now"; Seidman, "Deconstructing Queer Theory" 116–141; and Warner, introduction to *Fear of a Queer Planet.* Rosemary Hennessey has noted the neglect of class-based analysis among queer critics in "Queer Visibility in Commodity Culture."
23. Carr, *The Lonely Hunter,* 29.
24. This is the standard argument of feminist scholarship on McCullers, which concentrates on her female characters' resistance to feminine behaviors and expectations. See for example, Moers, *Literary Women;* Westling, *Sacred Groves and Ravaged Gardens;* and White, "Loss of Self," 125–142. The limitation of this argument is that, by focusing exclusively on female characters, it neglects the relations among men and between men and women in McCullers's fiction, which put pressure on traditional gender categories in more radical ways.
25. McCullers, *Member of the Wedding,* 2. Subsequent references cited parenthetically in text as *MW.* This anxiety is shared by Frankie's counterpart Mick Kelly in McCullers's first novel, *The Heart is a Lonely Hunter.* Anticipating Frankie's tortured relationship to the freak show, Mick's friend Harry Minowitz attempts to quiet her doubts about

her excessive growth with a less than comforting reassurance: "Once I saw a lady at the fair who was eight and a half feet tall. But you probably won't grow that big" (94).

26. See Carr, *The Lonely Hunter,* 169, 171, and 296, for examples of McCullers's theory of bisexuality as it was manifest in her own life.

27. In this, McCullers's fiction prefigures recent descriptions of the transsexual body as a site where rigid distinctions between sexes and genders break down. See Butler, *Gender Trouble;* Fausto-Sterling, *Sexing the Body;* Garber, *Vested Interests;* Prosser, *Second Skins;* and Stone, "The *Empire* Strikes Back." These critics see the transsexual/transgender not as freakish anomalies, but as evidence that human sexuality is more varied than the categories of male/female allow. Elizabeth Grosz connects the transsexual's ambiguity more directly to the practice of exhibiting sexual freaks in "Intolerable Ambiguity."

28. See Miller, *The Novel and the Police,* on the relationship between the "open secret" and the novelistic form. As Kenschaft rightly points out, "a reader who was unfamiliar with gay slang circa 1940 would miss certain implications of McCullers's texts, even though those texts could reasonably be read and interpreted without that knowledge" ("Homoerotics and Human Connections," 222).

29. Kenschaft acknowledges that "few of McCullers's characters are adequately described as homosexual: They are an adolescent girl falling in love with an engaged couple, an Amazonian woman infatuated with a bird-like man, a married man who never consummates the marriage but is entranced by his wife's desire for other men" ("Homoerotics and Human Connections," 226–227). As these examples attest, *lesbian* may be too specific a category to describe either the polymorphous desires of McCullers's characters or the unpredictable identifications of her readers.

30. In addition to these references to the "queer," see pages 2, 4, 22, 23, 27, 34, 85, 94, 116, and 141 for other examples.

31. Kenschaft, "Homoerotics and Human Connections," 228.

32. See Sears's *Lonely Hunters* for oral histories documenting the experiences of gay men in the South during the Cold War/pre-Stonewall era.

33. Spivak, "A Feminist Reading," 136.

34. McCullers, *Clock without Hands,* 24. Subsequent references cited parenthetically in text as *CWH.*

35. For analyses of the social function and reception of the Kinsey Report in postwar America, see Chauncey, *Gay New York;* D'Emilio and Freeman, *Intimate Matters;* Ehrenreich, *The Hearts of Men;* Lewes, *Male Homosexuality;* and May, *Homeward Bound.*

36. Recent studies of homosexuality during the Cold War period demonstrate a conflation of the demonized identities of the homosexual, the Communist, and the alien. See for example, John D'Emilio, *Making Trouble;* Corber, *In The Name of National Security* and *Homosexuality in Cold War America;* and Edelman, "Tearooms and Sympathy," in *Homographesis,* 148–170.

37. Davis, "Erasing the 'We of Me,'" 207.

38. This is an ironic suggestion, given the desire of southern plantation owners for the annexation of Cuba before the Civil War. In their eyes, Cuba provided an opportunity to extend the system of plantation slavery beyond U.S. borders. To propose that Honey change into a Cuban invokes the history of the South's imperial designs.

39. Davis argues that Berenice's differently colored eyes offer "a sense of the unexpected in human nature" ("Erasing the 'We of Me,'" 208), however the prosthetic eye is hardly natural. Rather, it suggests a more radical incentive to expand or explode the category of "human nature" by incorporating the inorganic and the mechanical.

40. Wiegman, *American Anatomies*, 82.

41. See Kenschaft, "Homoerotics and Human Connections," for a similarly affirmative reading of community in the café scenes from *The Heart is a Lonely Hunter* and *Ballad of the Sad Café*.

42. Yaeger, *Dirt and Desire*, 160.

43. Westling, *Sacred Groves and Ravaged Gardens*, 127.

44. See also Logan and Horvath ("Nobody Knows Best"), who read the stage version of *Member of the Wedding* as a story of Frankie's normalization, which, they argue, is an allegory for the conformity of postwar American culture.

45. Yaeger underestimates the radical potential of membership when she describes Frankie's desire to join the conjugal pair as "silly and eccentric" (*Dirt and Desire*, 178). Like many other critics, she reads the end of the novel as a containment of its more transgressive possibilities: "Frankie moves to the white suburbs and is instructed to find a nice white beau her own age. Frankie's job as a southern grown-up is to take her proper place in a narrow identity quadrant—a grid dividing men from women and blacks from whites—with divisions so rigid that they separate people, absolutely, along the axes of gender and race" (181).

46 Carr, *The Lonely Hunter*, 39.

CHAPTER FIVE

1. Moers, *Literary Women*, 109.

2. Sontag, *On Photography*, 43.

3. Benjamin, "A Short History of Photography," 202.

4. On the role of photography at the freak show, see Bogdan, *Freak Show;* and Thomson, *Extraordinary Bodies*.

5. Darrah, *Cartes de Visite;* and Linkman, *The Victorians*.

6. Bill Brown has considered the relationship between Brady's war and freak photography in "Monstrosity," in *The Material Unconscious*, 200–202. Although Brady may have been the most famous photographer to include freaks among his customers, Charles Eisenmann was the most prolific freak photographer. See Darrah, *Cartes de Visite;* and Mitchell, *Monsters of the Gilded Age*.

7. For a short discussion of Barnum's use of photography as a promotional device, see Kunhardt, Kunhardt, and Kunhardt, *P. T. Barnum*, 168–169.

8. Trachtenberg, *Reading American Photographs,* 39.

9. According to Miles Orvell, Victorians did not assume that photography was a realist medium. Instead they often exploited its potential for illusion, artifice, and distortion. See "Photography and the Artifice of Realism," in *The Real Thing,* 77. Bogdan describes various strategies used by photographers to enhance the freak's extraordinary qualities, including manipulation of the mise-en-scène, camera work, and developing process. *Freak Show,* 11–16.

10. Bogdan, *Freak Show,* 12.

11. John Tagg describes these images' recognizable visual style, which includes "the body isolated; the narrow space; the subjection to an unreturnable gaze; the scrutiny of gestures, face, and features; the clarity of illumination and the sharpness of focus; the names and number boards. These are the traces of power, repeated countless times, whenever the photographer prepared an exposure, in police cell, prison, consultation room, asylum, Home or school" (*The Burden of Representation,* 85).

12. Kemp, "'A Perfect and Faithful Record,'" 146. For a similar argument, see Fox and Lawrence, *Photographing Medicine.* Evidence for the initial convergence of freak and medical photography is found in Stanley B. Burns, M.D., *A Morning's Work.* Many of the early medical photographs collected in this book are indistinguishable from freak photographs of the same period except for their more explicit nudity.

13. Kemp, "'A Perfect and Faithful Record,'" 122.

14. Ibid., 124. Like commemorative portrait photography, the first medical photographs borrowed the conventions of artistic portraiture. It was not until the end of the nineteenth century that discrete conventions of medical photography were established. For an overview of this history, see Fox and Lawrence, *Photographing Medicine.*

15. Sekula, "The Body and the Archive," 7.

16. Arbus, "Hubert's Obituary," in *Diane Arbus.* All quotations from pages 80–81.

17. Regrettably, the Arbus estate denied permission for her images to be reproduced here as part of an ongoing effort to control critical reception of her work. However, all of the photographs discussed in this chapter are published in the Aperture monograph *Diane Arbus.*

18. Cited in Bosworth, *Diane Arbus,* 280.

19. On the formal elements of Arbus's photography, see Hulick, "Diane Arbus's Expressive Methods." Hulick uses a detailed description of Arbus's darkroom, contact sheets, and prints to reconstruct and analyze her image-making process.

20. Arbus, *Diane Arbus,* 80.

21. Of the traditional aspects of Arbus's style, Ann Thomas writes, "tight, rendered with pristine clarity and the kind of attention to detail found in the daguerreotype process, her photographs have the sharpness and textural distinctions of an earlier generation of photographers from the States, such as Paul Strand, Ansel Adams, Walker Evans, and Edward Weston" (*Lisette Model,* 147).

22. Bosworth, *Diane Arbus,* 9.

23. Hulick, "Diane Arbus's Expressive Methods," 114.

24. As Carol Armstrong has noted in "Biology, Destiny, Photography," the overriding subject of Arbus's photography is the flaw, the particularity derived from the inherently imperfect process of human reproduction.

25. Sontag, *On Photography,* 44.

26. Interview, quoted in Thomas, *Lisette Model,* 149.

27. For a discussion of the relationship between Arbus and Model, and comparison of their work, see Thomas, *Lisette Model,* chapter 9. Another fitting comparison with Model's portrait would be Arbus's *Naked Man Being a Woman,* in which the subject poses, like Albert-Alberta, against a backdrop of theatrical curtains. As the title implies, the man is completely undressed; gender ("being a woman") is a performative attribute conveyed entirely by the attitude of the body itself rather than its covering. For a reading that connects *Naked Man Being a Woman* to Arbus's early career as a fashion photographer, see Schloss, "Off the (W)rack."

28. Interview, quoted in Thomas, *Lisette Model,* 149.

29. In his study of freaks, Leslie Fiedler reads this portrait in terms of its representation of Jewishness: "Both [Arbus's] title and treatment strip the Barnum and Bailey show giant, who lived from 1938 to 1972, of all identity except his Jewishness. And precisely this gives an added frisson to the picture, since in legend Giants are the most goyish of all Freaks—typified by the monstrous Goliath sent against the frail champion of the Jews, the boy-man David. Yet to compound the irony, American-born children of East European immigrants do customarily tower over their parents, though not to so exaggerated a degree" (*Freaks,* 118). Fiedler's gloss is useful because it shows how the caption, by making reference to Carmel's Jewishness, amplifies the photograph's ambiguity. Slipping back and forth between the fantastic and the mundane, the giant is simultaneously a mythic figure and the extreme instance of a very common intergenerational phenomenon.

30. The documentary aired on National Public Radio's *All Things Considered* on 6 October 1999.

31. Sontag, *On Photography,* 35–36.

32. The willing participation of Arbus's subjects distinguishes her work from that of Weegee, with whom she is often associated. Weegee tended to intrude voyeuristically upon subjects, who rarely knew they were being photographed. By contrast, Arbus engaged her subjects and made their complicity the visible matter of her work.

33. As disability activist and photographer David Hevey describes affirmingly, "It is not clear what went on between Arbus and Morales . . . but the eroticism of the image cannot be denied. Not only is the so-called 'dwarf' distinctly unfreaky in his three-quarters nakedness, he is positively virile!" (*The Creatures That Time Forgot,* 60). Hevey's celebration of Morales's virility is part of a larger critical-aesthetic project that uses photography to reverse the "enfreakment" of the disabled body by showing its

multiple dimensions, including its capacity for eroticism, labor, and artistic creation. Nonetheless, it is striking that, for Hevey, the affirmation of virility makes Morales "unfreaky," as if restoring masculine potency to the disabled body could resolve the problems with its social and political misrepresentation.

34. Writing of a penchant for photographs of dwarves among 1960s photographers such as Arbus, Garry Winogrand, and Les Krims, Jonathan Green concludes, "[T]he most radical subject for the sixties was the ultimate minority: the traumatized self. And the most persistent image of that trauma was the dwarf. The dwarf became the dominant image for alienation, for the grotesque and the repulsive. He was the walking human contradiction: part myth, part person, the visual embodiment of all our cultural fears of disease, difference, and deformity" (*American Photography,* 120). But this is an inaccurate characterization of Arbus's photographs of dwarves, for her subjects do not seem alienated but at home in their bodies and their surroundings. Moreover, it is difficult to read these images as abstract symbols since they are firmly anchored in time, space, and the details of daily life.

35. Noting this similarity, Sontag wrote that the Hine's *Idiot Children* "could be a late Arbus photograph" (*On Photography,* 46). In many ways this photograph, which hearkens back to many of the freak show's voyeuristic tendencies, is uncharacteristic of Hine's work. Devoted to progressive social reform, Hine believed visual images could be instrumental in educating the public.

36. For examples of this critical approach, see Czach, "Diane Arbus, Sylvia Plath, and Anne Sexton"; Lester, *Suicide in Creative Women;* and Malcolm, "Aristocrats." Carol Schloss uses biographical evidence more successfully to link Arbus's early career in fashion photography with her subsequent work in "Off the (W)rack."

37. According to Bosworth, Arbus frequented sideshows and traveling carnivals, and she was mesmerized by Tod Browning's *Freaks,* which she watched over and over again following its re-release in 1962. Bosworth speculates that as a young girl, Arbus anticipated her peculiar adult interests by riding the subways in search of strange passengers (particularly exhibitionists), and she makes numerous intimations about Arbus's sexual attraction to and possible consummation with her freakish subjects.

38. Lord, "What Becomes a Legend Most," 244.

39. Ross, *No Respect,* 113. On sixties photography, see also, Green, *American Photography,* chapter 8.

40. In addition to these well-known examples, Mark Dery, in *The Pyrotechnic Insanitarium,* labels the work of contemporary photographers such as Rosamond Purcell, Max Aguilera-Hellweg, and Gwen Aiken and Allen Ludwig the "New Grotesque."

41. Witkin, "Revolt against the Mystical," 50. Merging mythological monsters, freaks, and all manner of perversions, Witkin writes, "A partial listing of my interests: physical prodigies of all kinds, pinheads, dwarfs, giants, hunchbacks, pre-op transsexuals, bearded women, active or retired side-show performers, contortionists (erotic), women with one breast (center), people who live as comic book heroes, Satyrs, twins

joined at the foreheads, anyone with a parasitic twin, twins sharing the same arm or leg, living Cyclopes, people with tails, horns, wings, fins, claws, reversed feet or hands, elephantine limbs, etc. Anyone with additional arms, legs, eyes, breasts, genitals, ears, nose, lips. Anyone born without arms, legs, eyes, breasts, genitals, ears, nose, lips. All people with unusually large genitals. Sex masters and slaves. Women whose faces are covered with hair or large skin lesions and who are willing to pose in evening gowns. Five androgynes willing to pose together as Les Demoiselles d'Avignon. Hairless anorexics. Human skeletons and human pincushions. People with complete rubber wardrobes. Geeks. Private collections of instruments of torture, romance; of human, animal, and alien parts. All manner of extreme visual perversions. Hermaphrodites and teratoids (alive and dead). A young blonde girl with two faces. Any living myth. Anyone bearing the wounds of Christ."

42. Like the Arbus estate, Witkin denied permission to reproduce his photographs here. The reader is referred to *Witkin* for examples of his work.

CHAPTER SIX

1. Peck, *Uncovering the Sixties,* 178. Using a similar vocabulary, sociologist Daniel Foss described the festival: "Perhaps 450,000 youths established a provisional Freak utopia with untrammeled group solidarity, dope, sex, and music" (*Freak Culture,* 200).

2. Stuart Hall offers an extended close reading of this phrase, which he describes as the "one slogan which came as near as anything to symbolising the Hippie way of life" ("The Hippies," 173).

3. For accounts of the divided legacy of the counterculture, see Feigelson, *Underground Revolution;* Gitlin, *The Sixties;* Lipsitz, "Who'll Stop the Rain?"; Morgan, *The Sixties Experience;* Savran, "Revolution as Performance," in *Taking It Like a Man,* 104–160; and many of the essays in Sayres et al., *The Sixties without Apology.*

4. Johnston, *Lesbian Nation,* 43.

5. Stephens, *Anti-Disciplinary Protest.*

6. Even a book-length study of Fiedler's criticism includes only four pages on *Freaks,* concluding with a condemnation of the counterculture. Criticizing Fiedler's attempt to trace a genealogical link between the history of freaks and 1960s radicalism, the author writes, "[T]o be abnormal by choice is, at best, a form of slumming that lacks even the misguided nobility shown by the young upper-class liberal who takes a job in a factory or as a migrant worker" (Winchell, *Leslie Fiedler,* 143).

7. Foss, *Freak Culture,* 132.

8. Gitlin, *The Sixties,* 216.

9. Jerry Rubin, *Do It!* 103.

10. Hall, "The Hippies," 173.

11. Hall describes the hippies as embracing "a way of life which rejects and despises, precisely, the language and act of interpretation" ("The Hippies," 170).

12. Wolfe, *The Electric Kool-Aid Acid Test,* 10.

13. Hoffman, *The Best of Abbie Hoffman,* 17.
14. Ibid., 20. Gitlin connects such deliberate nonreferentiality to the state of mind induced by hallucinogenic drugs: "Stoned consciousness darted, flowed, went where it wanted to go, freed of rectilinear purpose and instruction. Routine talk seemed laughable; weird juxtapositions made perfect sense; sense that made no sense at all" (*The Sixties,* 203).
15. Foss and Larkin, "Lexicon of Folk Etymology," 369.
16. On the difficult relationship between New Left politics and the counterculture, see Feigelson, *Underground Revolution;* Gitlin, *The Sixties;* Lipsitz, "Who'll Stop the Rain?"; and Stephens, *Antidisciplinary Protest.*
17. Hoffman, *The Best of Abbie Hoffman,* 101. As Gitlin describes them, "lyrics became more elaborate, compressed, and obscure, images more gnarled, the total effect nonlinear, translinear. Without grass, you were an outsider looking in" (*The Sixties,* 201). See Lipsitz, "Who'll Stop the Rain?" on the connections among rock music of 1960s, political protest, and social upheavals. On the particular innovations of Bob Dylan, see Gitlin, *The Sixties;* and Dickstein, *Gates of Eden.*
18. Gitlin, *The Sixties,* 215.
19. See Stephens's "Consuming India," chapter 3 in *Anti-Disciplinary Protest;* or Hall, "The Hippies," on the hippies' penchant for orientalism.
20. Many commentators on the sixties use the words *freak* and *hippie* interchangeably. See Feigelson, *Underground Revolution;* and Stern and Stern, *Sixties People.*
21. Rubin, *Do It!* 3.
22. Ibid., 37.
23. Savran, *Taking It Like a Man,* 138.
24. Hoffman, *The Best of Abbie Hoffman,* 83.
25. Jezer, *Abbie Hoffman.*
26. As Leslie Fiedler argues in *Freaks,* Zappa provides one example of the freak's ubiquity in underground newspapers, rock lyrics, slogans, and the comics (or *komix*) of dissident artists such as Robert Crumb, Bill Griffith, Gilbert Shelton, and S. Clay Wilson.
27. Stephen Miller notes in "Performing Quotations" that irony is characteristic of Zappa's style.
28. Rubin, *Do It!* 93–94.
29. Stern and Stern, *Sixties People,* 173.
30. I am grateful to the participants on two email discussion lists—H-AMSTUDY and SIXTIES-L—for numerous suggestions about the frequent and varied use of *freak* in the 1960s and 1970s.
31. Fiedler, *Freaks,* 13–14. Subsequent references cited parenthetically in text.
32. See Dickstein, *Gates of Eden;* and Pease, "Leslie Fiedler." Likewise, in *Cultural Conservatism,* James Seaton charges Fiedler with retreating into the same professed innocence that he condemned in other liberal intellectuals of the late 1940s and early 1950s.

33. Fiedler, foreword to Thomson, *Freakery,* xvi, xiii–xiv.
34. Fiedler, "Cross the Border—Close the Gap," 287. Fiedler did not always denounce cultural hierarchies with such enthusiasm. His early political essays, written for liberal journals such as *Commentary, Partisan Review,* and *Encounter,* express the disdain for popular culture shared by the first generation of New York Intellectuals. Andrew Ross convincingly documents the tensions between Fiedler's Cold War liberalism and his contempt for the aesthetics of the Popular Front in "Reading the Rosenberg Letters," in *No Respect,* 15–41.
35. Fiedler, *Love and Death,* 11.
36. Ibid., 27.
37. In an earlier essay, he defines archetype as "a coherent pattern of beliefs and feelings so widely shared at a level beneath consciousness that there exists no abstract vocabulary for representing it, and so 'sacred' that unexamined, irrational restraints inhibit any explicit analysis" (*End to Innocence,* 146). For commentary on Fiedler's movement from history to myth in other contexts, see Goodheart, "Leslie Fiedler and the Mythic Life," 30–45; Pease, "Leslie Fiedler"; Reising, *The Unusable Past;* and Seaton, *Cultural Conservatism.*
38. In the epilogue I consider the art of Jennifer Miller, a bearded lady who is freak, feminist, and "revolutionary."
39. "The New Mutants," 196.
40. Ibid., 201.
41. Ibid., 205.
42. Quoted in *Sixties People,* 163.
43. Fiedler, foreword to Thomson, *Freakery,* xvi.
44. A partial list of critics inspired by Fiedler, Bakhtin, or a combination of the two includes Braidotti, *Nomadic Subjects;* Russo, *The Female Grotesque;* and Wolff, *Feminine Sentences.*
45. For example, Judith Butler turns to genetics in *Gender Trouble* to argue that the range of chromosomal sex options extends far beyond the limits of the male/female opposition. See also Fausto-Sterling, *Sexing the Body;* Judith Halberstam's analysis of transsexuality in *Female Masculinity;* and Jay Prosser, *Second Skins.*

CHAPTER SEVEN

1. In my opening quotation from *Song of Solomon,* of course, the two black men are not using the term *freak* in reference to the sideshow. They are invoking the tradition of the African American toast in which freaks are figures of monstrous (often sexual) excess. The world is "freaky" and "fucked up" because they can find no more precise way to explain a bewildering, and potentially overwhelming, spiral of violence against members of their own community. While the two uses of *freak* may seem unrelated, the following exploration of Morrison's fiction will reveal continuities between the

term's different connotations. On freaks in African American toasts, see Jackson, *"Get Your Ass in the Water."*

2. In her reading of this scene, in "Absence, Loss, and the Space of History," Emily Miller Budick accuses Paul D of macho posturing. While his actions may betray elements of self-aggrandizement, his generosity towards Sethe and Denver is infectious, encouraging other members of the black community to behave similarly. While Paul D alone cannot heal Sethe's wounds, he begins the important process of her reintegration into the community.

3. Morrison, *Beloved*, 47–49. Subsequent references cited parenthetically in text.

4. Schappell, "Toni Morrison," 105. Walter Benn Michaels, in "'You who never was there,'" reads *Beloved* as an allegory for contemporary American understandings of history, in which the past endures in the present in the form of ghosts, who are the literary equivalent of "culture." Culture, in Michaels's controversial argument, boils down to an antiracist racial essentialism. This chapter will connect Morrison's commitment to essentialism to her evocation of the freak show.

5. On the confidence man, see Halttunen, *Confidence Men and Painted Women;* Harris, *Humbug;* Lindberg, *The Confidence Man in American Literature;* and Orvell, *The Real Thing.*

6. On Morrison's concept of rememory, see Rushdy, "'Rememory.'"

7. On black-white racial anxiety and the emergence of freak shows in the 1840s, see Cassuto, "The Racial Freak, the Happy Slave, and the Problems of Melville's Universal Man," in *The Inhuman Race*, 168–216. Bluford Adams describes the development of an increasingly hierarchical understanding of race in Barnum's exhibits in "'A Stupendous Mirror of Departed Empires': The Barnum Hippodromes and Circuses," in *E Pluribus Barnum*, 169–192.

8. Cook, "Of Men, Missing Links, and Nondescripts," 140.

9. Thomson, *Extraordinary Bodies.*

10. Thompson, *On the Road with a Circus*, 69.

11. Hart, "How Circus Freaks Are Made," 49–50.

12. *What We Know about Waino and Plutano.*

13. Thompson, *On the Road with a Circus*, 70.

14. Strong, *The Diaries*, 211.

15. See Bogdan, *Freak Show;* and Rydell, *All the World's a Fair* on the fabrication of ethnographic freaks.

16. Fitzgerald, "Side-Shows," 409.

17. Hart, "How Circus Freaks Are Made," 49.

18. Thompson, *On the Road with a Circus*, 70–71.

19. Ibid., 70.

20. The cruelty of showmen eager to exploit the racial freak's potential is also the subject of Eudora Welty's short story "Keela, the Outcast Indian Maiden," in which Lee Roy, a diminutive black man with a club foot, is kidnapped by a traveling carnival and forced

to perform as a savage woman. As Steve, formerly the barker for this act, describes, "it was supposed to be a Indian woman, see, in this red dress an' stockin's. It didn't have on no shoes, so when it drug its foot ever-body could see. . . . When it come to the chicken's heart, it would eat that too, real fast, and the heart would still be jumpin'" (76). With the figure of "Keela," Welty demonstrates how tenuous the freak's claim to authenticity could be, for not only do nonwhite races slip interchangeably into one another, black easily becoming Indian, but so do genders.

21. On Joice Heth, see Adams, *E Pluribus Barnum;* Harris, *Humbug;* and Reiss, *The Showman and the Slave.*

22. See Adams, *E Pluribus Barnum,* for an analysis of different versions of Barnum's autobiography.

23. The freak show's embrace of authenticity seems, on the surface, to differentiate it from the equally popular nineteenth-century form of blackface minstrelsy, which exploited the difference between the white performer and the black character he was playing. Bill Brown, in *The Material Unconscious,* describes the relationship between minstrelsy and the freak show in evolutionary terms, as "a transition from performative subjectivity to unperformed abjection" (214), that is, from the parodic theatricalization of blackface to the static essentialism of the ethnographic curiosity. Whereas the explicit intention of blackface minstrelsy is to mimic blackness (generally by those who are not themselves black), the freak show represents the intractable savagery of black bodies as an empirical fact. This is a plausible description of the racial exhibit's intended effects, however such intentions are complicated by the examples I have presented, which attest to the sideshow as a venue just as invested in performance, parody, and dialogue between audience and performer as blackface minstrelsy.

24. Strong, *The Diaries,* 211.

25. George C. Middleton, quoted in Bogdan, *Freak Show,* 176.

26. I am referring to the well-known debates among feminist critics inaugurated by Laura Mulvey's "Visual Pleasure and Narrative Cinema," which assumes that the gender of the spectator dictates her identification with the screen image. Subsequent criticism, too copious to cite in a note, has demonstrated that spectatorship is far more complicated and varied than Mulvey's direct correlation would suggest.

27. Lott, *Love and Theft,* 124.

28. Manthia Diawara, in "Black Spectatorship," has acknowledged the black viewer's particular difficulty identifying with the spectatorial positions established by classic cinematic narratives, as well as the elision of questions of race from debates about cinematic spectatorship. On race and resistant viewing practices, see also Bobo, *Black Women as Cultural Readers;* Felix and Roach, "Black Looks"; Freidberg, "A Denial of Difference"; hooks, *Black Looks;* and Mercer, *Welcome to the Jungle.* Ed Guerrero has applied theories of the gaze to Morrison's fiction in "Tracking 'The Look.'"

29. Harris, *Humbug,* 75. See J. Cook, *The Arts of Deception,* for an excellent complement to Harris's analysis of Barnum.

30. This scene is consistent with Budick's contention that counting and numerical formations are important in *Beloved* for both enslavers and the ex-slaves who need to make a place for themselves in the free world. Elaborating on the dual significance of counting, she writes, "[T]his book pulls us toward the problematics of what (and who) counts as family and as history, indeed, even what counts as human" ("Absence, Loss, and the Space of History," 130).

31. The imperative to make whiteness visible, thus robbing it of claims to transcendence and universality, is also crucial to Morrison's critical project, *Playing in the Dark,* one of the first works of literary criticism to take whiteness as a starting point for an analysis of race.

32. The necessity of learning how to listen to Sethe's story is at the heart of Doris Sommer's reading of *Beloved* in *Proceed with Caution.*

33. Sedgwick, *Epistemology of the Closet,* 61.

34. In *Race, Gender, and Desire,* an analysis of Morrison's earlier fiction, Eliot Butler-Evans proposes that the desires of her black female protagonists are often in tension with the communities that surround them.

35. There is an ample body of criticism that debates whether Bakhtinian carnival is a source of revolutionary potential or social containment. See Davis, *Society and Culture in Early Modern France;* Dentith, *Bakhtinian Thought;* Eagleton, *Walter Benjamin;* and Stallybrass and White, *The Politics and Poetics of Transgression.*

36. Freud, *Jokes.*

37. I also read this moment as a revision of the painful scene in *The Bluest Eye,* when Pecola buys candy from a white shopkeeper who recoils at the prospect of taking money from her hand.

38. Many critics have emphasized the primacy of the mother-daughter relationship in *Beloved,* but Morrison herself claims that the murdered child could have been male with much the same effect. On the significance of this female bond, see Liscio, "Beloved's Narrative"; Rushdy, "Daughters Signifyin(g) History"; and Wolff, "Margaret Garner." Undoubtedly, Morrison does seek to revalorize female experience and female storytellers, but her emphasis rests more on the difficulties of motherhood than on a foundational bond between mother and daughter. In fact, relations between mothers and sons are at the center of fictional works such as *Song of Solomon* and *Jazz.* See her discussion of motherhood in Cecil Brown's interview for the *Massachusetts Review.*

39. Jean Wyatt, in "Giving Body to the World," argues that typically metaphorical relations are literalized by the characters in *Beloved,* who experience the materiality of language inscribed upon their bodies.

40. For the most sustained discussion of Beloved's ghostly status, see Gordon, *Ghostly Matters,* 183.

41. Morrison, *Song of Solomon,* 148–149.

42. Melancholia does not figure prominently in this analysis, but is a useful critical paradigm for understanding the way that *Beloved,* inflected with realist detail, also describes the fantastic haunting of a group traumatized by a past with which it has not yet been able

to come to terms. For psychoanalytic readings of the novel that make this argument, see Lawrence, "Fleshly Ghosts and Ghostly Flesh"; and Luckhurst, "'Impossible Mourning.'" In *Ghostly Matters,* Avery Gordon also discusses Morrison's interweaving of history—the fictionalized story of Margaret Garner—with the magical realism of a ghost story, a strategy that allows her to narrate events that could not be accessed through more conventional historical or sociological methods.

43. Analyzing *Beloved* as a critique of contemporary liberalism, James Berger argues for Bodwin's complicity in *After the End.*

44. Morrison, *Song of Solomon,* 156–157.

45. Carabi, interview with Toni Morrison, 39.

46. Taussig, *Shamanism, Colonialism, and the Wild Man,* 219.

CHAPTER EIGHT

1. Morrison, *Beloved,* 256.

2. On the relationship between mothers and monstrous births, see Crawford, *Marvelous Protestantism;* Daston and Park, "Unnatural Conceptions"; and Huet, *Monstrous Imagination.*

3. Dobyns, "Hoping for Something Worse"; Giunti, Review of *Geek Love;* Kaveney, "Grossed Out"; Smith, "Nature Playing"; Steinberg, "Geek Love"; and Young, "Delights of Decadence."

4. Hayles, "Postmodern Parataxis."

5. In the afterword to *Geek Love,* Dunn comments that after the publication of her second novel, *Truck,* she concluded that she "didn't know how to write" and devoted herself to a project of self-education that involved "rediscover[ing] my own American language" (353–354). At the level of plot and vocabulary, *Geek Love* reflects Dunn's ten-year saturation in Americana.

6. Haraway, *Modest Witness.*

7. Dunn, *Geek Love,* 20. Subsequent references cited parenthetically in text.

8. The conjoined brothers' romantic enterprises were the subject of many a humorous commentary by their contemporaries, including Mark Twain's "Personal Habits of the Siamese Twins," which described their double marriage as one of "exceeding sociability which is touching and beautiful to behold, and is a scathing rebuke to our boasted civilization" (298). For further analysis of the metaphorical significance of conjoined twins in Twain's writing, see Gilman, *Dark Twins;* Shell, "The Judgement of Solomon," in *Children of the Earth,* 3–23; and Sundquist, *To Wake the Nations.*

9. Miller, *The Novel and the Police,* x.

10. Recall, in chapter 2, the infamous story of F. Scott Fitzgerald, who rushed outside to vomit after Daisy and Violet Hilton joined him at his table in the MGM studio commissary.

11. Hegi, *Stones from the River,* 473.

12. According to sideshow lore, this hierarchy was realized in concrete financial terms.

Each performer was assigned a different monetary value, with born freaks such as conjoined twins making a significantly better income than more run-of-the-mill performers. An article in *Circus Scrap Book* lists the salaries of the most famous freaks, placing
the conjoined Tocci twins at the top, making $1,000 a week and Ossified Men at the
bottom, making between $30 and $200. Coup, "Freaks and Fakes," 15.

13. Hayles effectively captures this aspect of Dunn's style when she writes, "[I]n a literal
sense, the body of the text is constructed from the bodies of the text" ("Postmodern
Parataxis," 414).

14. Davis, *Enforcing Normalcy;* Mitchell and Snyder, *Narrative Prosthesis;* Norden, *Cinema of Isolation;* Thomson, *Extraordinary Bodies.*

15. On nativist anxiety about miscegenation, see Gossett, *Race;* Gould, *The Mismeasure of
Man;* Higham, *Strangers in the Land;* and Michaels, *Our America.*

16. Quoted in Dyer, *Theodore Roosevelt and the Idea of Race,* 129.

17. Roosevelt, "The Parasite Woman; the Only Indispensable Citizen," 140–151, and
"Birth Reform, from the Positive, not the Negative Side," 152–167.

18. Irving, *Immigrant Mothers.*

19. Huet, *Monstrous Imagination,* 1.

20. Graham and Oehschlaeger, *Articulating the Elephant Man,* 16.

21. See Bogdan, *Freak Show,* 110, 219.

22. Ibid., 111.

23. For an analysis of the contemporary social consequences of blaming the mother for fetal anomalies, see Daniels, "Fathers, Mothers, and Fetal Harm."

24. Hayles also examines the novel's representation of reproduction, which she reads in
terms of a postmodern anxiety about the potential of advanced genetic science to alter
human DNA. While her analysis highlights the novel's preoccupation with the uneasy
relationship between technology and the human body, she does not connect the concern about reproduction with the repeated acts of violence against and domination of
the female body that are crucial to my own reading.

25. MacDonald, "The Insatiable Baby," 66.

26. Fiedler, *Freaks,* 170.

EPILOGUE

1. Mayor Giuliani's regime has been characterized by sensationalistic and controversial
measures intended to transform the culture of New York City by banishing sex shops,
cracking down on jaywalkers, street vendors, and taxi drivers, and charging museums
that receive city funding with indecency.

2. Mowery, "Situation Normal!"

3. Robinson, "Freaks Still Attract Curious Stragglers"; Maloney, "World of Midgets
Shrinks"; Berak, "Hard Times for Human Blockhead."

4. For more accurate biographical information on the Hilton sisters, see Bogdan, *Freak
Show,* 166–173; and Pingree, "The 'Exceptions That Prove the Rule.'"

5. Martí, "Two Views of Coney Island," 166. Thanks to Laura Lomas for this reference.

6. Barnes, "If Noise Were Forbidden at Coney Island," 145.

7. Kasson, *Amusing the Million,* 50–53.

8. Indeed, according to Robert Bogdan, a number of freak celebrities settled in Coney Island after growing tired of life on the road. *Freak Show,* 56.

9. Dick Zigun, personal interview, February 1998.

10. Jackson, *The Encyclopedia of New York.*

11. "Warning! Entertainers Everywhere Beware," 3.

12. "Vaudeville Sweeping the Nation," 1.

13. Fiedler, *Freaks,* 143.

14. Jennifer Miller, personal interview, 29 January 1998.

15. In a newspaper interview, Miller described a few painful incidents when she was forced to shave in order to get a job: "It was hard, really hard, shaving. . . . I cried and cried" (Smith, "Step Right Up!" C23).

16. Straayer, *Deviant Eyes, Deviant Bodies,* 173–174.

17. Kirschenblatt-Gimblett, "Objects of Ethnography."

18. When *Sideshow* played on Broadway, Miller's friend Kennedy Fraser took her to see the production and wrote an article about her reaction, "Seeing the Bearded Lady as Statement, Not Sideshow." With *Morphadike,* Miller appropriated the funny and at times insulting experience of seeing a musical in which a bearded lady was played by a man.

19. My concern with this transformation explains why I am relatively uninterested in more high-concept, for-profit enterprises like the Jim Rose Circus.

20. Martí, "Two Views of Coney Island," 168.

21. Hayden, "The Tattooed Man," 160–162.

22. Linton, *Claiming Disability,* 17.

23. Fries, "Excavation," 146.

24. Clare, *Exile and Pride,* 85.

25. Baum, *The Wonderful Wizard of Oz.*

26. Ibid., 264.

Bibliography

Adams, Bluford. *E Pluribus Barnum: The Great Showman and the Making of U.S. Popular Culture.* Minneapolis: University of Minnesota Press, 1997.

Adams, Judith A. *The American Amusement Park Industry: A History of Technology and Thrills.* Boston: Twayne, 1991.

Adams, Stephen. *The Homosexual as Hero in Contemporary Fiction.* New York: Barnes and Noble Books, 1980.

Allen, Robert. *Vaudeville and Film, 1895–1915: A Study in Media Interaction.* New York: Arno, 1980.

Arbus, Diane. *Diane Arbus: Magazine Work.* Ed. Doon Arbus and Marvin Israel. New York: Aperture, 1984.

Armstrong, Carol. "Biology, Destiny, Photography: Difference according to Diane Arbus." *October* 66 (fall 1993): 29–54.

Bakhtin, Mikhail. *Rabelais and His World.* Trans. Helene Iswolsky. 1968. Bloomington: Indiana University Press, 1984.

Barnes, Djuna. "If Noise Were Forbidden at Coney Island a Lot of People Would Lose Their Jobs." 1914. Reprint, in *New York,* ed. Alyce Barry, 142–149. Los Angeles: Sun and Moon, 1989.

———. *Nightwood.* 1937. Reprint, New York: New Directions, 1961.

Barnum, P. T. *Struggles and Triumphs.* 1869. Reprint, New York: Arno, 1970.

Baum, L. Frank. *The Wonderful Wizard of Oz.* 1900. Reprint, annotated by Michael Patrick Hearn, New York: Clarkson N. Potter, 1973.

Bederman, Gail. *Manliness and Civilization: A Cultural History of Gender and Race in the United States, 1880–1917.* Chicago: University of Chicago Press, 1995.

Beissel, Henry. *Under Coyote's Eye: A Play about Ishi.* Toronto: Playwrights Canada, 1980.

Benjamin, Walter. "A Short History of Photography." In *Classic Essays on Photography,* ed. Alan Trachtenberg, 199–217. New Haven: Leete's Island, 1980.

Berak, Barry. "Hard Times for Human Blockhead." *Los Angeles Times,* 19 August 1995, A1.

Berenstein, Rhona J. *Attack of the Leading Ladies: Gender, Sexuality, and Spectatorship in Classic Horror Cinema.* New York: Columbia University Press, 1996.

Berger, James. *After the End: Representations of Post-Apocalypse.* Minneapolis: University of Minnesota Press, 1999.

Berlant, Lauren. *The Anatomy of National Fantasy: Hawthorne, Utopia, and Everyday Life*. Chicago: University of Chicago Press, 1991.

Berlant, Lauren (with Elizabeth Freeman). "Queer Nationality." In *The Queen of America Goes to Washington City: Essays on Sex and Citizenship,* 145–174. Durham, NC: Duke University Press, 1997.

Bhabba, Homi. *The Location of Culture.* New York: Routledge, 1994.

Bigelow, Pamela. "Carson McCullers." In *Gay and Lesbian Literature,* ed. Sharon Malinowski, 256–259. Detroit, MI: St. James, 1994.

Bledstein, Burton J. *The Culture of Professionalism: The Middle Class and the Development of Higher Education in America.* New York: Norton, 1976.

Blume, Harvey. "Ota Benga and the Barnum Perplex." In *Africans on Stage: Studies in Ethnological Show Business,* ed. Bernth Lindfors, 188–202. Bloomington: Indiana University Press, 1999.

Bobo, Jacqueline. *Black Women as Cultural Readers.* New York: Columbia University Press, 1995.

Bogdan, Robert. *Freak Show: Presenting Human Oddities for Amusement and Profit.* Chicago: University of Chicago Press, 1988.

Boone, Joseph. "Queer Sites in Modernism: Harlem/The Left Bank/Greenwich Village." In *The Geography of Identity,* ed. Patricia Yaeger, 242–272. Ann Arbor: University of Michigan Press, 1996.

Borst, Ronald V. "Reevaluating a Screen Classic." *Photon* 23 (1973): 29–33.

Bosworth, Patricia. *Diane Arbus: A Biography.* New York: Avon, 1984.

Bourdieu, Pierre. *Distinction: A Social Critique of the Judgment of Taste.* Trans. Richard Nice. Cambridge, MA: Harvard University Press, 1984.

Bradford, Philips Verner, and Harvey Blume. *Ota Benga: The Pygmy in the Zoo.* New York: St. Martin's, 1992.

Braidotti, Rosi. *Nomadic Subjects: Embodiment and Sexual Difference in Contemporary Feminist Theory.* New York: Columbia University Press, 1994.

Brosnan, John A. *The Horror People.* New York: St. Martin's, 1976.

Brottman, Mikita. *Offensive Films: Toward an Anthropology of Cinema Vomitif.* Westport, CT: Greenwood, 1997.

Brown, Bill. *The Material Unconscious: American Amusement, Stephen Crane, and the Economies of Play.* Cambridge, MA: Harvard University Press, 1996.

Brown, Cecil. Interview with Toni Morrison. *Massachusetts Review* 36.3 (fall 1995): 455–473.

Budick, Emily Miller. "Absence, Loss, and the Space of History in Toni Morrison's *Beloved.*" *Arizona Quarterly* 48.2 (summer 1992): 117–138.

Burns, Stanley B., M.D. *A Morning's Work: Medical Photographs from the Burns Archive and Collection, 1843–1939.* Santa Fe, NM: Twin Palms, 1998.

Burrill, Richard. *Ishi: America's Last Stoneage Indian.* Sacramento, CA: Anthropology, 1990.

Butler, Ivan. *Horror in the Cinema.* New York: A. S. Barnes, 1967.

Butler, Judith. *Bodies That Matter: On the Discursive Limits of "Sex."* New York: Routledge, 1993.

———. *Gender Trouble: Feminism and the Subversion of Identity.* New York: Routledge, 1990.

———. "Performative Acts and Gender Constitution: An Essay in Phenomenology and Feminist Theory." In *Performing Feminisms: Feminist Critical Theory and Theatre,* ed. Sue-Ellen Case, 270–282. Baltimore: Johns Hopkins University Press, 1990.

Butler-Evans, Eliot. *Race, Gender, and Desire: Narrative Strategies in the Fiction of Toni Cade Bambara, Toni Morrison, and Alice Walker.* Philadelphia: Temple University Press, 1989.

Carabi, Angels. "Interview with Toni Morrison." *Belles Lettres* 9.3 (spring 1994): 38–39ff.

Carr, Virginia Spencer. *The Lonely Hunter: A Biography of Carson McCullers.* Garden City, NY: Doubleday, 1975.

———. *Understanding Carson McCullers.* Columbia, SC: University of South Carolina Press, 1990.

Cassuto, Leonard. *The Inhuman Race: The Racial Grotesque in American Literature and Culture.* New York: Columbia University Press, 1997.

Chauncey, George. *Gay New York: Gender, Urban Culture, and the Making of the Gay Male World, 1890–1940.* New York: Basic Books, 1994.

Chow, Rey. *Writing Diaspora: Tactics of Intervention in Contemporary Cultural Studies.* Bloomington: Indiana University Press, 1993.

Clare, Eli. *Exile and Pride: Disability, Queerness, and Liberation.* Cambridge, MA: South End Press, 1999.

Clover, Carol. *Men, Women, and Chain Saws: Gender in the Modern Horror Film.* Princeton, NJ: Princeton University Press, 1992.

Cook, Jr., James W. *The Arts of Deception: Playing with Fraud in the Age of Barnum.* Cambridge, MA: Harvard University Press, 2001.

———. "Of Men, Missing Links, and Nondescripts: The Strange Career of P. T. Barnum's 'What Is It?' Exhibition." In *Freakery: Cultural Spectacles of the Extraordinary Body,* ed. Rosemarie Garland Thomson, 139–157. New York: New York University Press, 1996.

Corber, Robert. *Homosexuality in Cold War America: Resistance and the Crisis of Masculinity.* Durham, NC: Duke University Press, 1997.

———. *In the Name of National Security: Hitchcock, Homophobia, and the Political Construction of Gender in Postwar America.* Durham, NC: Duke University Press, 1993.

Coup, W. C. "Freaks and Fakes." *Circus Scrap Book* 1.8 (April 1930): 7–18.

Crawford, John R. "Pioneer African Missionary: Samuel Philips Verner." *Journal of Presbyterian History* 60.1 (spring 1982): 42–57.

Crawford, Julie. *Marvelous Protestantism: Miraculous and Monstrous Births in Post Reformation England.* manuscript, n.d.

Creed, Barbara. *The Monstrous Feminine: Film, Feminism, Psychoanalysis.* New York: Routledge, 1993.

Czach, Marie. "Diane Arbus, Sylvia Plath, and Anne Sexton: Astringent Poetry and Tragic Celebrity." *History of Photography* 19.2 (summer 1995): 100–106.

Daniels, Cynthia R. "Fathers, Mothers, and Fetal Harm: Rethinking Gender Difference and Reproductive Responsibility." In *Fetal Subjects, Feminist Positions,* ed. Lynn M. Morgan and Meredith W. Michaels, 83–98. Philadelphia: University of Pennsylvania Press, 1999.

Darrah, William C. *Cartes de Visite in Nineteenth-Century Photography.* Gettysburg, PA: William C. Darrah, 1981.

Daston, Lorraine J., and Katharine Park. "Unnatural Conceptions: The Study of Monsters in Sixteenth- and Seventeenth-Century France and England." *Past and Present* 92 (August 1981): 20–54.

Davis, Lennard. *Enforcing Normalcy: Disability, Deafness, and the Body.* New York: Verso, 1995.

Davis, Natalie Zemon. *Society and Culture in Early Modern France.* Stanford: Stanford University Press, 1975.

Davis, Thadious M. "Erasing the 'We of Me' and Rewriting the Racial Script: Carson McCullers's Two *Member[s] of the Wedding.*" In *Critical Essays on Carson McCullers,* ed. Beverly Lyon Clark and Melvin J. Friedman, 206–219. New York: G. K. Hall, 1996.

Degler, Carl N. *In Search of Human Nature: The Decline and Revival of Darwinism in American Social Thought.* New York: Oxford University Press, 1991.

D'Emilio, John. *Making Trouble: Essays on Gay History, Politics, and the University.* New York: Routledge, 1992.

———. *Sexual Politics, Sexual Communities: The Making of a Homosexual Minority in the United States, 1940–1970.* Chicago: University of Chicago Press, 1983.

D'Emilio, John, and Estelle Freeman. *Intimate Matters: A History of Sexuality in America.* New York: Harper and Row, 1988.

Dennett, Andrea Stulman. *Weird and Wonderful: The Dime Museum in America.* New York: New York University Press, 1997.

Dentith, Simon. *Bakhtinian Thought: An Introductory Reader.* New York: Routledge, 1995.

Dery, Mark. *The Pyrotechnic Insanitarium: American Culture on the Brink of the Millennium.* New York: Grove, 1999.

Diawara, Manthia. "Black Spectatorship: Problems of Identification and Resistance." *Screen* 29.4 (fall 1988): 66–76.

Dickstein, Morris. *Gates of Eden: American Culture in the Sixties.* New York: Basic Books, 1977.

DiMaggio, Paul. "Cultural Entrepreneurship in Nineteenth-Century Boston: The Creation of an Organizational Base for High Culture in America." In *Rethinking Popular Culture: Contemporary Perspectives in Cultural Studies,* ed. Chandra Mukerji and Michael Schudson, 374–397. Berkeley: University of California Press, 1991.

Dobyns, Steven. "Hoping for Something Worse." *New York Times Review of Books,* 2
April 1989, 11.

Drimmer, Frederick. *Very Special People.* New York: Amjon, 1973.

Duggan, Lisa. "Making It Perfectly Queer." In *Sex Wars: Sexual Dissent and Political Culture,* ed. Lisa Duggan and Nan D. Hunter, 155–172. New York: Routledge, 1995.

Dunn, Katherine. *Geek Love.* New York: Warner Books, 1989.

Dyer, Peter John. "Freaks U.S.A., 1932." *Monthly Film Bulletin* August 1963: 110–111.

Dyer, Thomas G. *Theodore Roosevelt and the Idea of Race.* Baton Rouge: Louisiana State
University Press, 1980.

Eagleton, Terry. *Walter Benjamin: Towards a Revolutionary Criticism.* London: Verso, 1981.

Edelman, Lee. *Homographesis: Essays in Gay Literary and Cultural Theory.* New York:
Routledge, 1994.

Ehrenreich, Barbara. *The Hearts of Men: American Dreams and the Flight from Commitment.* New York: Anchor, 1983.

Eliot, T. S. Introduction to *Nightwood,* by Djuna Barnes. 1937. Reprint, New York: New
Directions, 1961.

Ellison, Ralph. *The Invisible Man.* 1947. Reprint, New York: Vintage, 1989.

Eloesser, Leo. "Saxton Temple Pope, M.D." *Surgery, Gynecology, and Obstetrics* 137
(November 1973): 845–850.

Eng, David. "Out Here and Over There: Queerness and Diaspora in Asian American
Studies." *Social Text* 52/53 (fall-winter 1997): 31–52.

Fausto-Sterling, Anne. *Sexing the Body: Gender Politics and the Construction of Sexuality.* New York: Basic Books, 2000.

Feigelson, Naomi. *The Underground Revolution: Hippies, Yippies, and Others.* New York:
Funk and Wagnalls, 1970.

Felix, Petal, and Jacqui Roach. "Black Looks." In *The Female Gaze: Women as Viewers of
Popular Culture,* ed. Lorraine Gammon and Margaret Marshment, 130–142. Seattle:
Real Comet, 1989.

Fellows, Dexter. *This Way to the Big Show: The Life of Dexter Fellows.* New York: Viking,
1936.

Fiedler, Leslie. "Cross the Border—Close the Gap." In *A Fiedler Reader,* 270–294. Briarcliff Manor, NY: Stein and Day, 1977.

———. *An End to Innocence: Essays on Culture and Politics.* Boston: Beacon, 1955.

———. Foreword to *Freakery: Cultural Spectacles of the Extraordinary Body,* ed. Rosemarie Garland Thomson, xiii–xvi. New York: New York University Press, 1996.

———. *Freaks: Myths and Images of the Secret Self.* 1978. Reprint, New York: Anchor,
1993.

———. *Love and Death in the American Novel.* 1960. Reprint, Normal, IL: Dalkey
Archive, 1997.

———. "The New Mutants." In *A Fiedler Reader,* 189–210. Briarcliff Manor, NY: Stein
and Day, 1977.

Fierce, Milfred. *The Pan-African Idea in the United States, 1900–1919.* New York: Garland, 1993.

Fitzgerald, F. Scott. "Crazy Sunday." In *Babylon Revisited.* New York: Scribner, 1960.

Fitzgerald, William C. "Side-Shows." *Strand Magazine* 13 (1897): 320–328, 407–416, 521–528, 696–700; 14 (1897): 91–96, 152–157.

Foreman, Joel, ed. *The Other Fifties: Interrogating Midcentury American Icons.* Urbana: University of Illinois Press, 1997.

Foss, Daniel. *Freak Culture: Lifestyle and Politics.* New York: E. P. Dutton, 1972.

Foss, Daniel, and Ralph Larkin. "Lexicon of Folk Etymology." In *The Sixties without Apology,* ed. Sohnya Sayres, Anders Stephanson, Stanley Aronowitz, and Frederick Jameson, 360–377. Minneapolis: University of Minnesota Press, 1984.

Fox, Daniel M., and Christopher Lawrence. *Photographing Medicine: Images and Power in Britain and America since 1840.* New York: Greenwood, 1988.

Fraser, Kennedy. "Seeing the Bearded Lady as Statement, Not Sideshow." *New York Times,* 20 October 1997, E2.

Freidberg, Ann. "A Denial of Difference: Theories of Cinematic Identification." *Psychoanalysis and Cinema,* ed. E. Ann Kaplan, 36–45. New York: Routledge, 1990.

Freud, Sigmund. "Analysis of a Phobia in a Five-Year-Old Boy." In *The Standard Edition of the Complete Psychological Works of Sigmund Freud,* trans. James Strachey, 10: 1–50. London: Hogarth, 1953–1966.

———. *Jokes and Their Relation to the Unconscious.* Trans. James Strachey. New York: Norton, 1960.

Fries, Kenny. "Excavation," In *Staring Back: The Disability Experience from the Inside Out,* ed. Kenny Fries, 146. New York: Plume, 1997.

Fuss, Diana. *Identification Papers.* New York: Routledge, 1995.

Gamson, Joshua. *Freaks Talk Back: Tabloid Talk Shows and Sexual Nonconformity.* Chicago: University of Chicago Press, 1998.

Garber, Marjorie. *Vested Interests: Cross Dressing and Cultural Anxiety.* New York: Routledge, 1992.

Gilman, Sander. *Difference and Pathology: Stereotypes of Sexuality, Race, and Madness.* Ithaca: Cornell University Press, 1985.

Gilman, Susan. *Dark Twins: Imposture and Identity in Mark Twain's America.* Chicago: University of Chicago Press, 1989.

Gilroy, Paul. *The Black Atlantic: Modernity and Double Consciousness.* Cambridge, MA: Harvard University Press, 1993.

Gitlin, Tod. *The Sixties: Years of Hope, Days of Rage.* New York: Bantam, 1987.

Giunti, Matthew. Review of *Geek Love,* by Katherine Dunn. *Christian Century* 106 (5–12 July 1989): 664–665.

Gleason, William A. *The Leisure Ethic: Work and Play in American Literature, 1840–1940.* Stanford, CA: Stanford University Press, 1999.

"A Goddess of Discord," n.d. Billy Rose Theater Collection, New York Public Library.

Goldbeck, Willis (with additional dialogue by Leon Gordon). *Freaks.* Screenplay type-script dated 24 October 1931, Margaret Herrick Library, Beverly Hills, CA.

Goodheart, Eugene. "Leslie Fiedler and the Mythic Life." In *Pieces of Resistance,* 30–45. New York: Cambridge University Press, 1987.

Gordon, Avery. *Ghostly Matters: Haunting and the Sociological Imagination.* Minneapolis: University of Minnesota Press, 1997.

Gossett, Thomas F. *Race: The History of an Idea in America.* Dallas: Southern Methodist University Press, 1963.

Gould, George M., and Walter L. Pyle. *Anomalies and Curiosities of Medicine.* New York: Bell Publishing, 1896.

Gould, Stephen Jay. *The Mismeasure of Man.* New York: Norton, 1981.

Graham, Peter W., and Fritz H. Oehschlaeger. *Articulating the Elephant Man: Joseph Merrick and His Interpreters.* Baltimore: Johns Hopkins University Press, 1992.

Green, Jonathan. *American Photography: A Critical History, 1945 — the Present.* New York: Harry N. Abrams, 1984.

Grosz, Elizabeth. "Intolerable Ambiguity: Freaks as/at the Limit." In *Freakery: Cultural Spectacles of the Extraordinary Body,* ed. Rosemarie Garland Thomson, 55–68. New York: New York University Press, 1996.

Gruesser, John Cullen. *Black on Black: Twentieth-Century African American Writing about Africa.* Lexington: University Press of Kentucky, 2000.

Guerrero, Ed. "Tracking 'The Look' in the Novels of Toni Morrison." In *Toni Morrison's Fiction: Contemporary Criticism,* ed. David L. Middleton, 27–44. New York: Garland, 1997.

Gunning, Tom. "An Aesthetic of Astonishment: Early Film and the (In)Credulous Spectator." In *Viewing Positions: Ways of Seeing Film,* ed. Linda Williams, 114–132. New Brunswick, NJ: Rutgers University Press, 1995.

———. "The Cinema of Attractions: Early Film, Its Spectator, and the Avant-Garde." In *Early Cinema Space, Frame, Narrative,* ed. Thomas Elsaesser, 56–62. London: BFI, 1990.

Hall, Stuart. "The Hippies: An American 'Moment.'" In *Student Power,* ed. Julian Nagel, 170–202. London: Merlin, 1969.

Haller, Jonathan. *Outcasts from Evolution: Scientific Attitudes of Racial Inferiority, 1859–1900.* Urbana: University of Illinois Press, 1971.

Halttunen, Karen. *Confidence Men and Painted Women: A Study of Middle-Class Culture in America, 1830–1870.* New Haven, CT: Yale University Press, 1982.

Hansen, Miriam. *Babel and Babylon: Spectatorship in American Silent Film.* Cambridge, MA: Harvard University Press, 1991.

Hanson, Stephen L. "Freaks." In *International Directory of Films and Filmmakers.* Detroit, MI: St. James Press, 1993.

Haraway, Donna. *Modest Witness@Second_Millenium.FemaleMan©_Meets_ OncoMouse™: Feminism and Technoscience.* New York: Routledge, 1997.

Harper, Kenn. *Give Me My Father's Body: The Life of Minik, the New York Eskimo.* South Royalton, VT: Steerfort, 2000.

Harpham, Geoffrey Galt. *On the Grotesque: Strategies of Contradiction in Art and Literature.* Princeton, NJ: Princeton University Press, 1982.

Harris, Neil. *Humbug: The Art of P. T. Barnum.* Boston: Little, Brown, 1973.

Hart, Scott. "How Circus Freaks Are Made." *Coronet,* May 1946, 49–50.

Hartman, Saidiya. *Scenes of Subjection: Terror, Slavery, and Self-Making in Nineteenth-Century America.* New York: Oxford University Press, 1997.

Hassan, Ihab. *Contemporary American Literature, 1945–1972.* New York: Frederick Ungar, 1973.

Hawkins, Joan. " 'One of Us': Tod Browning's *Freaks.* " In *Freakery: Cultural Spectacles of the Extraordinary Body,* ed. Rosemarie Garland Thomson, 265–276. New York: New York University Press, 1996.

Hayden, Robert. "The Tattooed Man." In *Collected Poems,* 160–162. New York: Liveright, 1985.

Hayles, N. Katherine. "Postmodern Parataxis: Embodied Texts, Weightless Information." *American Literary History* 2.3 (fall 1990): 394–421.

Hegi, Ursula. *Stones from the River.* New York: Simon and Schuster, 1994.

Hennessey, Rosemary. "Queer Visibility in Commodity Culture." In *Social Postmodernism: Beyond Identity Politics,* ed. Linda Nicholson and Steven Seidman, 142–183. New York: Cambridge University Press, 1995.

Hevey, David. *The Creatures That Time Forgot: Photography and Disability Imagery.* New York: Routledge, 1994.

Higham, John. *Strangers in the Land: Patterns of American Nativism, 1860–1925.* New York: Athenaeum, 1981.

Hinsley, Curtis. *Savages and Scientists: The Smithsonian Institution and the Development of American Anthropology, 1846–1910.* Washington, DC: Smithsonian Institution Press, 1981.

Hinton, Leanne. *Ishi's Tale of Lizard.* New York: Farrar, Strauss, Giroux, 1992.

Hoffman, Abbie. *The Best of Abbie Hoffman.* Ed. Abbie Hoffman and Daniel Simon. New York: Four Walls Eight Windows, 1989.

———. *Revolution for the Hell of It.* New York: Dial Press, 1968.

hooks, bell. *Black Looks: Race and Representation.* Boston: South End, 1992.

Hornaday, William. *Minds and Manners of Wild Animals.* New York: Charles Scribner's Sons, 1927.

Horowitz, Helen. "Animal and Man in the New York Zoological Park." *New York History* 56 (1975): 426–455

Huet, Marie-Helene. *Monstrous Imagination.* Cambridge, MA: Harvard University Press, 1993.

Hulick, Diana Emery. "Diane Arbus's Expressive Methods." *History of Photography* 19.2 (summer 1995): 107–116.

Hunter, Jack. *Inside Teradome: An Illustrated History of Freak Film.* London: Creation Books, 1995.

Irving, Katrina. *Immigrant Mothers: Narratives of Race and Maternity, 1890–1925.* Urbana: University of Illinois Press, 2000.

"Ishi Is Not Last of Lost Tribe: Stockmen and Ranchers of Deer Creek Country Find Traces of Aborigines." *San Francisco Weekly Chronicle,* 29 April 1914, Lowie Museum Archives, University of California, Berkeley.

"Ishi's Squaw Seen Hunting for Mate: Parties Searching Underbrush Near Oroville for Wife of Lone Survivor." *San Francisco Weekly Chronicle,* 17 September 1914 (?), Lowie Museum Archives, University of California, Berkeley.

"Ishi's Death—A Chico Commentary." *Chico Record* 1916. Reprint, in *Ishi the Last Yahi: A Documentary History,* ed. Robert F. Heizer and Theodora Kroeber, 242. Berkeley: University of California Press, 1979.

Jackson, Bruce. *"Get Your Ass in the Water and Swim Like Me": Narrative Poetry from Black Oral Tradition.* Cambridge, MA: Harvard University Press, 1974.

Jackson, Kenneth, ed. *The Encyclopedia of New York.* New Haven, CT: Yale University Press, 1995.

Jacobs, Sylvia M., ed. *Black Americans and the Missionary Movement in Africa.* Westport, CT: Greenwood, 1982.

———. "The Historical Role of Afro-Americans in American Missionary Efforts in Africa." In *Black Americans and the Missionary Movement in Africa,* ed. Sylvia M. Jacobs, 5–32. Westport, CT: Greenwood, 1982.

Jezer, Marty. *Abbie Hoffman: American Rebel.* New Brunswick, NJ: Rutgers University Press, 1992.

Johnston, Jill. *Lesbian Nation.* New York: Simon and Schuster, 1973.

Kasson, John F. *Amusing the Million: Coney Island at the Turn of the Century.* New York: Hill and Wang, 1978.

Kaveney, Roz. "Grossed Out." *Times Literary Supplement,* 8 September 1989, 968.

Katz, Jonathan. *Gay/Lesbian Almanac: A New Documentary.* New York: Harper and Row, 1983.

Kazin, Alfred. "Djuna Barnes's *Nightwood.*" *New York Times Book Review,* 7 March 1937. Excerpted in Jonathan Katz, *Gay/Lesbian Almanac: A New Documentary* (New York: Harper and Row, 1983), 529.

Kemp, Martin. "'A Perfect and Faithful Record': Mind and Body in Medical Photography before 1900." In *Beauty of Another Order: Photography in Science,* ed. Ann Thomas, 120–149. New Haven, CT: Yale University Press, 1997.

Kenschaft, Lori. "Homoerotics and Human Connections: Reading Carson McCullers 'As a Lesbian.'" In *Critical Essays on Carson McCullers,* ed. Beverly Lyon Clark and Melvin J. Friedman, 220–234. New York: G. K. Hall, 1996.

Kingston, Maxine Hong. *Tripmaster Monkey, His Fake Book.* New York: Vintage, 1990.

Kinsley, Philip H. "Untainted Life Revealed by Aborigine." *San Francisco Examiner,*

6 September 1911. Reprint, in *Ishi the Last Yahi: A Documentary History,* ed. Robert F. Heizer and Theodora Kroeber, 100–103. Berkeley: University of California Press, 1979.

Kipnis, Laura. "(Male) Desire and (Female) Disgust: Reading *Hustler.*" In *Ecstasy Unlimited: On Sex, Capital, Gender, and Aesthetics,* 219–242. Minneapolis: University of Minnesota Press, 1993.

Kirschenblatt-Gimblett, Barbara. "Objects of Ethnography." In *Exhibiting Cultures: The Poetics and Politics of Museum Display,* ed. Ivan Karp and Steven Lavine, 387–434. Washington, DC: Smithsonian Institution Press, 1991.

Kroeber, A. L. "Ishi, the Last Aborigine." *The World's Work,* July 1912. Reprint, *Ishi the Last Yahi: A Documentary History,* ed. Robert F. Heizer and Theodora Kroeber, 119–123. Berkeley: University of California Press, 1979.

———. "It's All Too Much For Ishi, Says the Scientist." *San Francisco Call,* 8 October 1911. Reprint, *Ishi the Last Yahi: A Documentary History,* ed. Robert F. Heizer and Theodora Kroeber, 111–112. Berkeley: University of California Press, 1979.

Kroeber, Karl. *Artistry in Native American Myths.* Lincoln: University of Nebraska Press, 1998.

Kroeber, Theodora. *Ishi in Two Worlds.* Berkeley: University of California Press, 1961.

———. *Ishi, the Last of his Tribe.* New York: Bantam, 1973.

Kunhardt, Jr., Philip B., Philip B. Kunhardt, III, Peter W. Kunhardt. *P. T. Barnum: America's Greatest Showman.* New York: Knopf, 1995.

Kuper, Adam. *The Invention of Primitive Society: Transformations of an Illusion.* London: Routledge, 1988.

Laskas, Kristin. "Program Notes." *Cinema Texas* 10.1 (29 January 1979): 47.

Lawrence, David. "Fleshly Ghosts and Ghostly Flesh: The Word and the Body in *Beloved.*" *Studies in American Fiction* 19.2 (fall 1991): 189–202.

Lears, T. J. Jackson. *No Place of Grace: Antimodernism and the Transformation of American Culture, 1880–1920.* New York: Pantheon, 1981.

Leitch, Vincent. *American Literary Criticism from the Thirties to the Eighties.* New York: Columbia University Press, 1988.

Lester, David. *Suicide in Creative Women.* New York: Nova Science, 1993.

Leverentz, David. *Manhood and the American Renaissance.* Ithaca: Cornell University Press, 1989.

Levine, Lawrence. *Highbrow/Lowbrow: The Emergence of Cultural Hierarchy in America.* Cambridge, MA: Harvard University Press, 1988.

Lewes, Kenneth. *The Psychoanalytic Theory of Male Homosexuality.* New York: Simon and Schuster, 1988.

Lindberg, Gary. *The Confidence Man in American Literature.* New York: Oxford University Press, 1982.

Lindfors, Bernth. "P. T. Barnum and Africa." *Studies in Popular Culture* 7 (1984): 18–25.

Linkman, Audrey. *The Victorians: Photographic Portraits.* New York: Tauris Parke, 1993.

Linton, Simi. *Claiming Disability: Knowledge and Identity.* New York: New York University Press, 1998.

Lipsitz, George. "Who'll Stop the Rain? Youth Culture, Rock 'n' Roll, and Social Crises." In *The Sixties: From Memory to History,* ed. David Farber, 206–234. Chapel Hill: University of North Carolina Press, 1994.

Liscio, Lorraine. "*Beloved's* Narrative: Writing Mother's Milk." *Tulsa Studies in Women's Literature* 11.1 (spring 1992): 31–47.

Logan, Lisa. Introduction to *Critical Essays on Carson McCullers,* ed. Beverly Lyon Clark and Melvin J. Friedman, 1–16. New York: G. K. Hall, 1996.

Logan, Lisa, and Brook Horvath. "Nobody Knows Best: Carson McCullers's Plays as Social Criticism." *Southern Quarterly* 33.2–3 (winter-spring 1995): 23–33.

Longmore, Paul K. "Uncovering the Hidden History of People with Disabilities." *Reviews in American History* 15.3 (September 1987): 355–364.

Lord, Catherine. What Becomes a Legend Most: The Short, Sad Career of Diane Arbus." In *Illuminations: Women Writing on Photography from the 1850s to the Present,* ed. Liz Heron and Val Williams, 237–250. Durham, NC: Duke University Press, 1996.

Lott, Eric. *Love and Theft: Blackface Minstrelsy and the American Working Class.* New York: Oxford University Press, 1995.

Lubbers, Klaus. "The Necessary Order." In *Carson McCullers,* ed. Harold Bloom, 33–52. New York: Chelsea House, 1986.

Luckhurst, Roger. "'Impossible Mourning' in Toni Morrison's *Beloved* and Michele Roberts's *Daughters of the House.*" *Critique* 37.4 (summer 1996): 243–261.

MacDonald, Cynthia . "The Insatiable Baby." In *Amputations,* 66. New York: George Braziller, 1972.

Magubane, Bernard Makhosezwe. *The Ties That Bind: African-American Consciousness of Africa.* Trenton, NJ: Africa World Press, 1987.

Malcolm, Janet. "Aristocrats." *New York Review of Books,* 1 February 1996, 7–8.

Maloney, Thomas. "World of Midgets Shrinks." *New York Journal American,* 9 April 1961, n.p.

Mannix, Daniel. *Freaks: We Who Are Not As Others.* San Francisco: Re/Search Publications, 1990.

Martí, José. "Two Views of Coney Island." In *Inside the Monster: Writings on the U.S. and American Imperialism,* ed. Philip Foner, 165–175. New York: Monthly Review, 1975.

May, Elaine Tyler. *Homeward Bound: American Families in the Cold War Era.* New York: Basic Books, 1988.

Mayersberg, Paul. Review of *Freaks* (Tod Browning movie). *Movie,* July-August 1963. Quoted in Toronto Film Society program, 22 March 1982.

McCarthy, Michael. *Dark Continent: Africa As Seen by Americans.* Westport, CT: Greenwood, 1983.

McCullers, Carson. *Clock without Hands.* 1961. Reprint, New York: Penguin, 1979.

———. *The Heart is a Lonely Hunter.* 1940. Reprint, New York: Bantam, 1953.

———. *Member of the Wedding.* 1946. Reprint, New York: Bantam, 1969.

Mercer, Kobena. *Welcome to the Jungle: New Positions in Black Cultural Studies.* New York: Routledge, 1994.

Meyerowitz, Joanne, ed. *Not June Cleaver: Women and Gender in Postwar America, 1945–1960.* Philadelphia: Temple University. Press, 1994.

Michaels, Walter Benn. *Our America: Nativism, Modernism, and Pluralism.* Durham, NC: Duke University Press, 1995.

———. "'You who never was there': Slavery and the New Historicism, Deconstruction and the Holocaust." *Narrative* 4.1 (January 1996): 1–16.

Miller, D. A. *The Novel and the Police.* Berkeley: University of California Press, 1988.

Miller, Mary Ashe. "Indian Enigma Is Study for Scientists." *San Francisco Call,* 6 September 1911. Reprint, in *Ishi the Last Yahi: A Documentary History,* ed. Robert F. Heizer and Theodora Kroeber, 97–100. Berkeley: University of California Press, 1979.

Miller, Stephen Paul. "Performing Quotations: Frank Zappa as *Freak Out!* Aphorist." In *The Frank Zappa Companion: Four Decades of Commentary,* ed. Richard Kostelanetz, 125–127. New York: Schirmer Books; London: Prentice Hall International, 1997.

Mitchell, David T., and Sharon L. Snyder. *Narrative Prosthesis: Disability and the Dependencies of Discourse.* Ann Arbor: University of Michigan Press, 2000.

Mitchell, Joseph. "Lady Olga." In *Up in the Old Hotel.* 1940. Reprint, New York: Vintage, 1993.

Mitchell, Michael. *Monsters of the Gilded Age: The Photographs of Charles Eisenmann.* Agincart, Ont.: Gage, 1979.

Moers, Ellen. *Literary Women.* New York: Doubleday, 1976.

Morgan, Edward P. *The Sixties Experience: Hard Lessons about Modern America.* Philadelphia: Temple University Press, 1991.

Morris, Gary, and Mark A. Viera. "*Freaks:* Production and Analysis." *Bright Lights* 11 (fall 1993): 13–14.

Morrison, Toni. *Beloved.* New York: Plume, 1987.

———. *Playing in the Dark: Whiteness and the Literary Imagination.* Cambridge, MA: Harvard University Press, 1992.

———. *Song of Solomon.* 1977. Reprint, New York: Plume, 1987.

Mowery, Edward J. "Situation Normal! Not A Circus Freak in N.Y." *World Telegram,* n.d. Billy Rose Theater Collection, New York Public Library.

Mulvey, Laura. "Visual Pleasure and Narrative Cinema." In *Film Theory and Criticism,* ed. Gerald Mast, Marshall Cohen, and Leo Braudy, 746–757. New York: Oxford University Press, 1992.

Nasaw, David. *Going Out: The Rise and Fall of Public Amusements.* New York: Basic Books, 1993.

Nelson, Dana. *National Manhood: Capitalist Citizenship and the Imagined Fraternity of White Men.* Durham, NC: Duke University Press, 1998.

Norden, Martin. *The Cinema of Isolation: A History of Physical Disability in the Movies.* New Brunswick, NJ: Rutgers University Press, 1994.

Orvell, Miles. *The Real Thing: Imitation and Authenticity in American Culture, 1880–1940.* Chapel Hill: University of North Carolina Press, 1989.

Paden, Frances Freeman. "Autistic Gestures in *The Heart is a Lonely Hunter.*" *Modern Fiction Studies* 28.3 (fall 1982): 453–463

Paul, William. *Laughing Screaming: Modern Hollywood Horror and Comedy.* New York: Columbia University Press, 1994.

Pease, Donald. "Leslie Fiedler, the Rosenberg Trial, and the Formulation of an American Canon." *boundary 2* 17.2 (1990): 155–198.

Peck, Abe. *Uncovering the Sixties: The Life and Times of the Underground Press.* New York: Citadel, 1985.

Peiss, Kathy. *Cheap Amusements: Working Women and Leisure in Turn-of-the-Century New York.* Philadelphia: Temple University Press, 1986.

Petersen, David. *Ishi, the Last of His People.* Chicago: Children's Press, 1991.

Pingree, Alison. "The 'Exceptions That Prove the Rule': Daisy and Violet Hilton, the 'New Woman,' and the Bonds of Marriage." In *Freakery: Cultural Spectacles of the Extraordinary Body,* ed. Rosemarie Garland Thomson, 173–184. New York: New York University Press, 1996.

Pope, Saxton. "The Medical History of Ishi." Reprint, as "The Characteristics of Ishi," in *Ishi the Last Yahi: A Documentary History,* ed. Robert F. Heizer and Theodora Kroeber, 225–236. Berkeley: University of California Press, 1979.

Prosser, Jay. *Second Skins: The Body Narratives of Transsexuality.* New York: Columbia University Press, 1998.

"Queer People." *Newsweek,* 10 October 1949, 52ff.

Quigley, Isabel. "Freaks with Feeling." *Spectator,* 21 June 1963, 811.

Reed, Christopher Robert. *"All the World Is Here!" The Black Presence at White City.* Bloomington: Indiana University Press, 2000.

Reising, Russell. *The Unusable Past: Theory and the Study of American Literature.* New York: Methuen, 1986.

Reiss, Benjamin. "Abolition and the Freak Show in Antebellum America," Paper presented at the annual meeting of the Modern Language Association, Toronto, December 1997.

———. "P. T. Barnum, Joice Heth, and Antebellum Spectacles of Race." *American Quarterly* 51.1 (March 1999): 78–107.

———. *The Showman and the Slave: Race, Death, and Memory in Barnum's America.* Cambridge, MA: Harvard University Press, 2001.

Robbins, Tod. "Spurs." *Munsey's Magazine,* February 1923, 24–32.

———. *The Unholy Three.* New York: John Lane, 1917.

271

Robinson, Murray. "Freaks Still Attract Curious Stragglers on Coney's Midway." *New York World,* 29 July 1947, 1.

Rogin, Michael. *Blackface, White Noise: Jewish Immigrants in the Hollywood Melting Pot.* Berkeley: University of California Press, 1996.

Roosevelt, Theodore. "Birth Reform, from the Positive, not the Negative Side." In *The Collected Works of Theodore Roosevelt,* ed. Hermann Hagedorn, 19: 152–167. New York: Charles Scribner's Sons, 1926.

———. "The Parasite Woman; the Only Indispensable Citizen." *Collected Works,* 19: 140–151. New York: Charles Scribner's Sons, 1926.

Rosaldo, Renato. *Culture and Truth: The Remaking of Social Analysis.* Boston: Beacon Press, 1989.

Rosenthal, Stuart, and Judith Kass. *The Hollywood Professionals.* Vol. 4. New York: A. S. Barnes, 1973.

Ross, Andrew. *No Respect: Intellectuals and Popular Culture.* New York: Routledge, 1989.

Rubin, Jerry. *Do It! Scenarios of the Revolution.* New York: Simon and Schuster, 1970.

Rubin, Louis D. "Carson McCullers: The Aesthetic of Pain." 1977. Reprint, in *Critical Essays on Carson McCullers,* ed. Beverly Lyon Clark and Melvin J. Friedman, 111–123. New York: G. K. Hall, 1996.

Rushdy, Ashraf. "Daughters Signifyin(g) History: The Example of Toni Morrison's *Beloved.*" *American Literature* 64.3 (September 1992): 567–580.

———. "'Rememory': Primal Scenes and Constructions in Toni Morrison's Novels." In *Toni Morrison's Fiction: Contemporary Criticism,* ed. David L. Middleton, 135–164. New York: Garland, 1997.

Russo, Mary. *The Female Grotesque: Risk, Excess, and Modernity.* New York: Routledge, 1995.

Rydell, Robert. *All the World's a Fair: Visions of Empire at the American International Expositions, 1876–1916.* Chicago: University of Chicago Press, 1984.

Sadler, Lynn Veach. "'Fixed in an Inlay of Mystery': Language and Reconciliation in Carson McCullers's *Clock without Hands.*" *Pembroke* 20 (1988): 49–53.

Savran, David. *Taking It Like a Man: White Masculinity, Masochism, and Contemporary American Culture.* Princeton, NJ: Princeton University Press, 1998.

Sayres, Sohnya, Anders Stephanson, Stanley Aronowitz, and Frederick Jameson, eds. *The Sixties without Apology.* Minneapolis: University of Minnesota Press, 1984.

Saxton, A. H. *P. T. Barnum: The Legend and the Man.* New York: New York University Press, 1989.

Schaefer, Eric. *Bold! Daring! Shocking! True! A History of Exploitation Films, 1919–1959.* Durham, NC: Duke University Press, 1999.

Schappell, Elissa. "Toni Morrison: The Art of Fiction." *Paris Review* 35.128 (1993): 82–125.

Schloss, Carol. "Off the (W)rack: Fashion and Pain in the Work of Diane Arbus." In *On Fashion,* ed. Shari Benstock and Suzanne Ferris, 111–124. New Brunswick, NJ: Rutgers University Press, 1994.

Sears, James T. *Lonely Hunters: An Oral History of Lesbian and Gay Southern Life, 1948–1968.* Boulder, CO: Westview, 1997.

———. "Race, Class, Gender, and Sexuality in Pre-Stonewall Charleston: Perspectives on the Gordon Langley Hall Affair." In *Carryin' On in the Lesbian and Gay South,* ed. John Howard, 164–200. New York: New York University Press, 1997.

Seaton, James. *Cultural Conservatism, Political Liberalism: From Criticism to Cultural Studies.* Ann Arbor: University of Michigan Press, 1996.

Sedgwick, Eve. *Between Men: English Literature and Male Homosocial Desire.* New York: Columbia University Press, 1985.

———. *Epistemology of the Closet.* Berkeley: University of California Press, 1990.

———. "Queer and Now." In *Tendencies,* 1–20. Durham, NC: Duke University Press, 1993.

Seidman, Steven. "Deconstructing Queer Theory or the Under-Theorization of the Social and the Ethical." In *Social Postmodernism: Beyond Identity Politics,* ed. Linda Nicholson and Steven Seidman, 116–141. New York: Cambridge University Press.

Sekula, Alan. "The Body and the Archive." *October* 39 (1986): 3–62.

Shell, Marc. *Children of the Earth: Literature, Politics, and Nationhood.* New York: Oxford University Press, 1993.

Schenkar, Joan. *Signs of Life.* Hanover, NH: University Press of New England, 1979.

Skal, David J. *The Monster Show: A Cultural History of Horror.* New York: Norton, 1993.

Skal, David J., and Elias Savada. *Dark Carnival: The Secret World of Tod Browning, Hollywood's Master of the Macabre.* New York: Anchor, 1995.

Slotkin, Richard. "Buffalo Bill's 'Wild West' and the Mythologization of the American Empire." In *Cultures of United States Imperialism,* ed. Amy Kaplan and Donald Pease, 164–184. Durham, NC: Duke University Press, 1993.

Smith, Dinitia. "Nature Playing." *The Nation* 248 (15 May 1989): 673–674.

———. "Step Right Up! See The Bearded Person." *New York Times,* 9 June 1995, C23.

Sommer, Doris. *Proceed with Caution, When Engaged by Minority Writing in the Americas.* Cambridge, MA: Harvard University Press, 1999.

Sone, Monica. *Nisei Daughter.* Seattle: University of Washington Press, 1953.

Sontag, Susan. *On Photography.* 1977. Reprint, New York: Anchor Books, 1990.

Spencer, Colin. *Homosexuality: A History.* London: Fourth Estate, 1996.

———. *Homosexuality in History.* New York: Harcourt, Brace, 1995.

Spivak, Gayatri. *A Critique of Postcolonial Reason: Toward a History of the Vanishing Present.* Cambridge, MA: Harvard University Press, 1999.

———. "A Feminist Reading of Carson McCullers's *Heart is a Lonely Hunter.*" 1979–1980. Reprint, in *Critical Essays on Carson McCullers,* ed. Beverly Lyon Clark and Melvin J. Friedman, 129–142. New York: G. K. Hall, 1996.

———. *In Other Worlds: Essays in Cultural Politics.* New York: Methuen, 1987.

Stallybrass, Peter, and Allon White. *The Politics and Poetics of Transgression.* Ithaca, NY: Cornell University Press, 1986.

Starr, Paul. *The Social Transformation of American Medicine: The Rise of a Sovereign Profession and the Making of a Vast Industry.* New York: Basic Books, 1982.

Steinberg, Sybil. "Geek Love." *Publishers Weekly,* 13 January 1989, 75.

Stepan, Nancy Leys. "Race and Gender: The Role of Analogy in Science." In *Anatomy of Racism,* ed. David Theo Goldberg, 38–57. Minneapolis: University of Minnesota Press, 1990.

Stephens, Julie. *Anti-Disciplinary Protest: Sixties Radicalism and Postmodernism.* Cambridge: Cambridge University Press, 1998.

Stern, Jane, and Michael Stern. *Sixties People.* New York: Knopf, 1990.

Stewart, Susan. *On Longing: Narratives of the Miniature, the Gigantic, the Souvenir, the Collection.* Durham, NC: Duke University Press, 1993.

Stiker, Henri-Jacques. *A History of Disability.* Trans. William Sayers. Ann Arbor: University of Michigan Press, 1999.

Stone, Sandy. "The *Empire* Strikes Back: A Posttranssexual Manifesto." *Camera Obscura* 29 (May 1992): 151–178.

"Stone Age Indian Hauled from Forests' Depths by Savants." *San Francisco Evening Post,* 5 September 1911, 1. Lowie Museum archives, University of California, Berkeley.

Strauss, Darin. *Chang and Eng.* New York: Dutton, 2000.

Straayer, Chris. *Deviant Eyes, Deviant Bodies: Sexual Re-Orientations in Film and Video.* New York: Columbia University Press, 1996.

Strong, George Templeton. *The Diaries.* Quoted in Philip Lopate, ed., *Writing New York* (New York: Library of America, 1998), 191–240.

Studlar, Gaylyn. *This Mad Masquerade: Stardom and Masculinity in the Jazz Age.* New York: Columbia University Press, 1996.

Sundquist, Eric. *To Wake the Nations: Race in the Making of American Literature.* Cambridge, MA: Belknap Press, 1993.

Tagg, John. *The Burden of Representation: Essays on Photographies and Histories.* Minneapolis: University of Minnesota Press, 1993.

Taussig, Michael. *Shamanism, Colonialism, and the Wild Man: A Study in Terror and Healing.* Chicago: University of Chicago Press, 1987.

Thomas, Ann. *Lisette Model.* Ottawa: National Gallery of Canada, 1990.

Thomas, David Hurst. *Skull Wars: Kennewick Man, Archaeology, and the Battle for Native American Identity.* New York: Basic Books, 2000.

Thomas, John. "Freaks." *Film Quarterly* 17.3 (spring 1964): 59–61.

Thompson, C. J. S. *The History and Lore of Freaks.* 1930. Reprint, London: Senate, 1996.

Thompson, W. C. *On the Road with a Circus.* New York: Amsterdam Book Company, 1905.

Thomson, Rosemarie Garland. *Extraordinary Bodies: Figuring Physical Disability in American Culture and Literature.* New York: Columbia University Press, 1997.

———. "Introduction: From Wonder to Error—A Genealogy of Freak Discourse in Modernity." In *Freakery: Cultural Spectacles of the Extraordinary Body,* ed. Rosemarie Garland Thomson, 1–22. New York: New York University Press, 1996.

Toll, Robert. *Blacking Up: The Minstrel Show in Nineteenth-Century America.* New York: Oxford University Press, 1974.

Trachtenberg, Alan. *Reading American Photographs: Images as History, Matthew Brady to Walker Evans.* New York: Hill and Wang, 1989

Trent, James W., Jr. *Inventing the Feeble Mind: A History of Mental Retardation in the United States.* Berkeley: University of California Press, 1994.

Trilling, Lionel. "Freud: Within and Beyond Culture." In *Beyond Culture: Essays on Literature and Learning.* New York: Viking Press, 1965.

Twain, Mark. "Personal Habits of the Siamese Twins." 1869. Reprint, in *Tales, Sketches, Speeches, and Essays, 1852–1890,* 296–299. New York: Library of America, 1992.

———. *Pudd'nhead Wilson* and *Those Extraordinary Twins.* 1884. Reprint, New York: Penguin Classics, 1986.

"Vaudeville Sweeping the Nation." *Roustabout Reporter,* winter 1999, 1.

Verner, Samuel. "Thomas F. Ryan as A Benefactor of a Carolina Boy. How the Great Financier Made the Dreams of an African Explorer Come True." Typescript courtesy of Phillips Verner Bradford.

———. *Pioneering in Central Africa.* Richmond, VA: Presbyterian Committee of Publication, 1903.

Vizenor, Gerald. *Ishi and the Wood Ducks.* In *Native American Literature: An Introduction and Anthology,* ed. Gerald Vizenor, 299–336. New York: Harper Collins, 1995.

———. *Manifest Manners: Postindian Warriors of Survivance.* Hanover, NH: University Press of New England, 1994.

———. *Trickster of Liberty: Tribal Heirs to a Wild Baronage.* Minneapolis: University of Minnesota Press, 1988.

Wallace, Grant. "Ishi, the Last Aboriginal Savage in America, Finds Enchantment in a Vaudeville Show." *San Francisco Call,* 8 October 1911. Reprint, in *Ishi the Last Yahi: A Documentary History,* ed. Robert F. Heizer and Theodora Kroeber, 107–111. Berkeley: University of California Press, 1979.

Warner, Michael, ed. *Fear of a Queer Planet: Queer Politics and Social Theory.* Minneapolis: University of Minnesota Press, 1994.

"Warning! Entertainers Everywhere Beware: Don't Believe the Hype!" *Roustabout Reporter,* winter 1999, 3.

Waterman, T. T. "The Yana Indians." Reprint, in *Ishi the Last Yahi: A Documentary History,* ed. Robert F. Heizer and Theodora Kroeber, 107–111. Berkeley: University of California Press, 1979.

Welty, Eudora. "Keela, the Outcast Indian Maiden." In *A Curtain of Green and Other Stories.* New York: Harcourt Brace, 1941.

Westling, Louise. *Sacred Groves and Ravaged Gardens: The Fiction of Eudora Welty, Carson McCullers, and Flannery O'Connor.* Athens: University of Georgia Press, 1985.

Whatling, Clare. "Carson McCullers." In *The Gay and Lesbian Literary Heritage,* ed. Claude J. Summers, 470–471. New York: Henry Holt, 1995.

What We Know about Waino and Plutano, the Wild Men of Borneo. New York: Damon and Peets, Printers, n.d. Houghton Library Theater Collection, Harvard University, Cambridge, MA.

"Where Are Freaks of Yesteryear? Not Many Left Sez Carny Exec." *Variety,* 28 October 1920, n.p. Billy Rose Theater Collection, New York Public Library.

White, Barbara A. "Loss of Self in *The Member of the Wedding.*" In *Carson McCullers,* ed. Harold Bloom, 125–142. New York: Chelsea House, 1986.

Wiegman, Robyn. *American Anatomies: Theorizing Race and Gender.* Durham, NC: Duke University Press, 1995.

Williams, Linda. *Hard Core: Power, Pleasure, and the "Frenzy of the Visible."* Berkeley: University of California Press, 1989.

———. "When the Woman Looks." In *Re-Vision: Essays in Feminist Film Criticism,* ed. Mary Ann Doane, Patricia Mellencamp, and Linda Williams, 83–99. Frederick, MD: University Publications of America, 1984.

Williams, Raymond. "Base and Superstructure in Marxist Cultural Theory." In *Rethinking Popular Culture: Contemporary Perspectives in Cultural Studies,* ed. Chandra Mukerji and Michael Schudson, 407–423. Berkeley: University of California Press, 1991.

Williams, Vernon, Jr. *Rethinking Race: Franz Boas and His Contemporaries.* Lexington: University Press of Kentucky, 1996.

Williams, Walter L. *Black Americans and the Evangelization of Africa, 1877–1900.* Madison: University of Wisconsin Press, 1982.

———. "William Henry Sheppard, Afro-American Missionary in the Congo, 1890–1910." In *Black Americans and the Missionary Movement in Africa,* ed. Sylvia M. Jacobs, 135–154. Westport, CT: Greenwood, 1982.

Wilson, Alexander. *The Culture of Nature: North American Landscape from Disney to the Exxon Valdez.* Cambridge, MA: Blackwell, 1992.

Winchell, Mark Royden. *Leslie Fiedler.* Boston: Twayne, 1985.

Witkin, Joel Peter. "Revolt against the Mystical." In *Witkin,* ed. Germano Celant, 49–63. Zurich: D.A.P., 1995.

Wolff, Cynthia Griffin. "'Margaret Garner': A Cincinnati Story." *Massachusetts Review* 32.3 (fall 1991): 417–441.

Wolff, Janet. *Feminine Sentences: Essays on Women and Culture.* Berkeley: University of California Press, 1990.

Wolfe, Tom. *The Electric Kool-Aid Acid Test.* New York: Bantam, 1969.

Wyatt, Jean. "Giving Body to the World: The Maternal Symbolic in Toni Morrison's *Beloved.*" *PMLA* 108.3 (May 1993): 474–488.

Yaeger, Patricia. *Dirt and Desire: Reconstructing Southern Women's Writing, 1930–1990.* Chicago: University of Chicago Press, 2000.

Young, Elizabeth J. "Delights of Decadence." *New Statesman,* 16 November 1990, 38.

Index

Numbers in italic refer to illustrations

Freud, 7, 8, 74, 78, 125, 148, 152, 157,
230 n. 19; and jokes, 78–79, 177; Little
Hans, 78–79
Fries, Kenny, 227
Fuss, Diana, 8

Gamson, Joshua, 2, 229 n. 4
Garber, Marjorie, 244 n. 27
Garbo, Greta, 94
gay. *See* homosexuality
gaze, 7, 28–31, 58, 83, 113, 172, 177, 181–
182, 192; "black look," 164–175; male,
75, 78; return of, 7, 8, 20, 29, 105
geek, 240 n. 37
gender, 9, 16, 17, 20, 96, 131, 144, 153,
156, 200, 207, 252 n. 20, 253 n. 26,
254 n. 34, 254 n. 38, 256 n. 24
gender ambiguity. *See* androgyny
genealogy, 187, 196, 197, 200
genetics, 189, 194, 196, 200, 205, 206–208,
251 n. 45, 256 n. 24
ghosts, 179, 55 n. 41
giants, 96, *118, 119,* 126–127, 134–135,
150, 152, 164, 243 n. 25, 247 n. 29
Gilbert, Dr., 41
Gitlin, Tod, 140, 142
Giuliani, Rudolph, 210, 217, 224, 256 n. 1
Gordon, Avery, 254 n. 41
Gordon, James H., 40
Gould, Stephen Jay, 235 n. 65
Gowdy, Barbara, 188
Great Fredini. *See* Kahl, Fred
Greenwich Village, 93
Griffith, Bill, 145, 250 n. 26
Griffith, D. W., 238 n. 14
Grosz, Elizabeth, 7, 244 n. 27
grotesque, 179, 214, 231 n. 33

Haight-Ashbury, 141, 142, 144
half man–half woman, 7, 65, 96–100, 101,
103, 125, 218. See also Albert-Alberta

Hall, Gordon Langley. See Dawn Simmons
Hall, Stuart, 141
Hansen, Miriam, 238 n. 14
Haraway, Donna, 189
Harris, Neil, 172
Hart, Scott, 166, 167–168
Hawkins, Joan, 239 n. 36
Hayden, Robert, 227–228
Hayles, N. Katherine, 187, 256 n. 13
Hearst, Phoebe Apperson, 50
Hearst Museum, 17, 25, 30, 44–45, 50
Hegi, Ursula, *Stones from the River,* 188,
193, 195, 203
Hendrix, Jimi, 138
Henry, George, 93
hermaphrodites, 75, 97, 123, 124, 126, 133,
151, 152, 157, 175, 225
heterosexuality, 18, 64, 76, 93, 95, 98, 99,
100, 102, 108, 110, 152, 153, 193, 201,
206, 212
Heth, Joice, 11, 169, 207
Hevey, David, 247 n. 33
Hilton, Daisy and Violet, 60–61, *66,* 73–
74, 212, 238 n. 11, 240 n. 39, 255 n. 10
Hine, Lewis, *"Idiot Children,"* 129, *130,*
133, 248 n. 35
Hinsley, Curtis, 50
hippies, 19, 142–145, 146, 157, 249 n. 2,
249 n. 11
Hoffman, Abbie, 19, 139, 142–145, 155;
Revolution for the Hell of It, 141
homoeroticism, 241 n. 4
homophobia, 92, 94, 100, 101, 102, 145,
243 n. 21
homosexuality, 18, 20, 92, 94, 223, 242 n.
17, 243 n. 19, 244 n. 27, 244 n. 29,
244 n. 36; connection to freaks, 93, 126;
medicalization, 93, 101, 102; "open secret," 244 n. 28
Hopper, Dennis, 141
Horatio Alger, 171

Laloo. See Jean Libbera
Larkin, Ralph, 142
Latin America, 217
laughter, 77–78, 177
Lazio, Rick, 224
Leary, Timothy, 138
Lee, Gypsy Rose, 94, 242 n. 17
leisure, 10
Leonard, Zoe, 135–136; *Pin-Up #1*, 135–
    136, *136*
lesbianism, 94, 97, 99, 126, 139, 220, 225,
    223, 242 n. 17, 244 n. 29
Levine, Lawrence, 232 n. 6
Libbera, Jean (Laloo), 122, *123*
liberalism, 91, 110, 207, 251 n. 34, 255 n. 42
Liebowitz, Annie, 220
Life's Literary Side Show, 3, *3*
Lionel the Lion-Faced Boy, 198
Lipsitz, George, 144
long hair, 4, 5, 144, 146, 154
Lopez, F. Solano, 238 n. 11
Lord, Catherine, 131
Lott, Eric, 171, 231 n. 31
Lugosi, Bella, 239 n. 35
Lynch, Jennifer and David, 238 n. 11
lynching, 106–107

MacDonald, Cynthia, "The Insatiable
    Baby," 203
Mappelthorpe, Robert, 132
marginality, 31, 113, 117, 154, 155, 226;
    and group dynamics, 20, 42, 163, 170,
    175–176, 185, 207, 228; politics of, 15,
    140, 141
Martí, José, 213, 226
masculinity, 50, 64, 74, 78, 100–103, 140,
    144–145, 221, 241 n. 55, 247 n. 33; and
    class, 80–82; and heterosexuality, 152–
    154; and male bonding, 43, 55, 235 n.
    71, 241 n. 4; and whiteness, 19, 31, 107

mass entertainment, 10–12, 21, 27–31, 211
mass media, 143
maternal imagination, 197, 199, 200
maternal impression, 186–209
McCracken, Elizabeth, 188
McCullers, Carson, 18–19, 112, 157–158,
    218; *Ballad of the Sad Café*, 97; *Clock
    without Hands*, 90, 91, 92, 94, 95, 100–
    103, 104, 105–107; disability, 89, 100;
    erotic life, 89, 94–95, 241 n. 4, 242 n.
    18, 243 n. 21, 244 n. 26; feminist schol-
    arship on, 243 n. 24, 245 n. 45; *Heart is
    a Lonely Hunter*, 97, 100, 243 n. 25;
    Member of the Wedding, 7–8, 90, 91,
    92, 94, 95, 96–100, 103, 104, 105, 107–
    111, 244 n. 30, 245 n. 44; *Reflections in
    a Golden Eye*, 97
McCullers, Reeves, 94, 243 n. 21
McDaniels, Grace, 204, *204*
meaning, collapse of, 5, 120, 174–175,
    183–185, 187, 250 n. 14
mechanical reproduction, 218–219
medicine, 9, 26, 54–55, 58, 118, 133, 146
melancholia, 254 n. 41
memoirs, 2, 162, 167–168
memory, 150, 184–185, 186, 188, 205
Merrick, Joseph (Elephant Man), 198–
    199, 207
Meyer, Larry, 57
MGM, 60–62, 64, 74
Michaels, Walter Benn, 252 n. 4
microcephaly, 123
middle class, 11, 28, 31, 33, 237 n. 2
Middleton, George, 170–171
midgets, 5, *118*, 126, 164
Miller, D. A., 28, 191
Miller, Jennifer, 135–136, *136*, 210, 216,
    219–226, 220, 224, 257 n. 15, 257 n. 18
Minik, 236 n. 79
minstrelsy, 12, 171, 231 n. 31, 253 n. 23